Pra

"Aryae Coopersmith's an̲_____ ture takes us on a wild ride through joy and tragedy towards wisdom. *Holy Beggars* reminds us of the mystery that is always hiding in the circumstances of our lives. Miracles are always happening, but it takes a special talent to see them. Reb Aryae has that talent. The stories that he weaves while filled with magic and mystery, also remind us of our humility. [. . .] *Holy Beggars* lets God's Presence shine through a story that is as deep as it is delightful."

— Rabbi Shefa Gold, author of *Torah Journeys*

"Every person, teacher or not, deserves to be seen fully as a human being, and not 'spun' to fit some fixed idea. [. . .] Aryae Coopersmith's biographical memoir of Reb Shlomo is profound, clear-sighted, and beautifully written. Most of all, it is full of courage and love."

— Murshid Wali Ali Meyer, co-author of *Physicians of the Soul*

"It has been said that when a student shares the wisdom of his or her spiritual teacher with others, it supports the flow of Divine plenty in the world. And when a student makes a bond and an inner connection with his holy teacher, it is a Divine gift and a blessing and a means for direct contact with holiness. The Sages have also taught that one's relationship with one's Torah teacher is the most heart-stirring of all human relationships. The author of *Holy Beggars* offers all of this, and more, to his readers [. . .] this important book is itself a blessing."

— Arthur Kurzweil, author of *Pebbles of Wisdom*

"What happened at the House of Love and Prayer was a critical turning point in Jewish history and marked a shift in the greater collective consciousness. It was here that ancient teachings found in a mystical branch of Judaism collided with the free spirited ways of San Francisco, California in the 1960's, and that one of those teachings was again spoken out loud: that when enough people held hands in love, those hands could reach heaven. Aryae Coopersmith takes us into this world as it was unfolding. He does so with the love and care of someone who was there, who was transformed by the experience, and who now knows he must to tell the story."

— Alan Briskin, co-author of *The Power of Collective Wisdom*

"This book is a must read for those who, like me, are passionate about the roots of genuine global social and cultural transformation. As a non Jew, in the late 60's, I met and had the privilege of being in the presence of Rabbi Shlomo Carlebach. Aryae Coopersmith has provided us a window not only into his personal relationship with one of the seminal figures of the period, but has provided us with a documentation of one of the most exciting movements of a generation.

— Craig Neal, co-author of *The Art of Convening*

ii

4/28/2011 Dave,
Thank you for your poetry, your presence
your support, as we both turn our
experience into words!
Aye

Holy Beggars

A Journey from Haight Street to Jerusalem

Aryae Coopersmith

Foreword by

Rabbi Zalman Schachter-Shalomi

Edited by

Netanel Miles-Yepez

One World Lights
El Granada, California
2011

One World Lights
P.O. Box 928
El Granada, CA 94018
www.oneworldlights.com

One World Lights is a division of Learning Synergies LLC.

Design and composition by Albion-Andalus Inc.

Cover design by Daryl McCool, D.A.M. Cool Graphics.

Photo credits: (front cover) "Meeting of the Ways" concert showing Aryae Coopersmith and Shlomo Carlebach, unknown, 1972; (back cover) photos by Moshe Yitzchak Kussoy, 1969, and Jyl Cohen, 2010.

Manufactured in the United States of America.

ISBN-10: 0615414281

EAN-13: 9780615414287

Dedicated to . . .

Reb Shlomo . . .

who saw something in me, and in each of us, that no one else did, showed us by his example how to live in God's presence every minute, and started me on my journey; 45 years later he is still travelling with me, still my *rebbe;*

Reb Zalman . . .

who coached me for four decades on how to stay awake and keep going, and as my second *rebbe,* still guides me;

Tamir . . .

who has showed me that even though our marriage fell apart, our friendship never will;

Moishe . . .

who scouted out the bridges between worlds;

Donna . . .

who, in finding her voice, also found the voice of the soul of the holy beggars;

Noe and Adam . . .

who, as they grew to be the awesomely beautiful human beings that they are, showed me how to be a father;

Wendy . . .

who joined me on the journey from Haight Street to Jerusalem, helped me in a thousand ways to keep going when I wasn't sure I could, ventured with me to places where no one else would, and has shared at every step the love, excitement, hard work, losses, heartbreak, laughter and glory along the way.

Contents

"Their end is in their beginning,
and their beginning is in their end."
— Sefer Yetzirah

Part I

The Beginning

The 1960s

The 1990s

2003

Part II

The 1960s & 1970s

Acknowledgments

Writing a book, to borrow the well-used phrase, often takes a village.

It didn't seem like that to me during the years I spent writing this, rewriting it, and rewriting it yet again. It was a lonely exercise. I was aware mostly of the daily act of sitting at the keyboard in the silent, early morning darkness, facing my blank computer screen, typing out as many pages as I could before the sun rose and it was time to begin my "daytime gig."

It's only now as the project nears its end that I can look back and see the village.

It begins with Reb Zalman who spoke to me shortly after Reb Shlomo died in 1994 and pointed out that, in order to be at peace with my own life, I had to find a way to give back some of what I had received from Reb Shlomo. In the years since then, through all my fits and starts in getting the book written, Reb Zalman was there, reading every chapter, encouraging me, offering a vision of the larger historical context of the story I was telling. And finally just before publication, resisting intense pressure from people opposed to my telling of the story, he chose, at age 86, to stand fast in his endorsement of the book and keep his preface in. His act of courage will forever be a part of this story. My gratitude also to Eve Ilsen, his wife, who also read every chapter, shared her deep insights with spunk and humor, and cheered me on.

Netanel Miles-Yepez was an absolute joy to work with as my editor, and absolutely indispensable in the final phase of turning *Holy Beggars* from manuscript into book. When we first started working together and he wanted to combine some of my short sentences into longer ones, I explained that Hemingway was an important influence with me, so please keep them short. A couple of days later he retorted by pointing to a later chapter where the sentences ran on forever. "Hemingway?" he said. "How about Faulkner?" When I alluded without explanation to obscure information about spiritual teachers and their teachings, Netanel added the footnotes and filled in the blanks. When decisions needed to be made about which passages to cut and which to leave in, I learned to rely greatly on his judgment on what was incidental and what was essential. He quickly grasped the soul of this complex story, never lost sight of it, and never let me lose sight either.

Arthur Kurzweil, publisher and author with a lifetime of experience in the book business, generously shared his valuable perspective and advice. As an added bonus Arthur, as a student of the great Talmudic scholar Rabbi Adin Steinsaltz, about whom he wrote his own book, totally understood the situation of being the student of a famous spiritual teacher and doing your best to do justice to the story. He read drafts of my early chapters, saw the possibilities, encouraged me keep going. In the intervening years at critical decision points, he was always there to offer his guidance and support.

I'm grateful to my children Noe and Adam Coopersmith for their good humor in putting up with my descriptions of them at earlier times of their lives. I'm also grateful for the same reason to their mother and my ex-wife, Lane Coopersmith. Adam read through the entire manuscript when it was twice as long as in its final version, and gave me his feedback as a fellow artist (in his case, a professional musician) and someone who was born 15 years after the end of the 1960s, so I could learn how the story looked and sounded to him.

My friends Maury and Barbara Zilber (who by the end of the 1960s were already married professionals in full career) read that same long manuscript at the same time that Adam did, giving me the benefit of their lifetime of wisdom and suggesting many needed corrections. When it turned out that just before publication I seriously needed some industrial strength legal advice, Maury, now a semi-retired former senior partner and intellectual property attorney at a major law firm, cheerfully obliged. Barbara, not to be out done, volunteered to put at my service her considerable skills as an organizer and negotiator in the early days of the feminist movement, and as a psychotherapist since then, to represent me in difficult conversations with people opposed to my book, in order to lighten the load on me.

Rabbi Victor Gross was kind enough to help me to verify and source aspects of *halakha* and Talmudic discussion in certain chapters.

Murshid Wali Ali Meyer and Abraham Sussman Ph.D., prominent leaders in the Sufi Ruhaniat International, were kind enough to share their memories of visiting the House of Love and Prayer in the 1960s when they were students of Murshid Samuel Lewis. Their perspective highlights an essential dimension of the story: how the spiritual awakening during that time transcended the boundaries of religion and was truly universal. Murshid Wali Ali has recently helped make Wendy and me aware of how, in the relationships between charismatic spiritual teachers and their students, similar complexities seem to be present in all traditions.

Regarding my fellow "holy beggars" who lived and learned and sang and danced with me at the House of Love and Prayer in that early springtime of our lives, when we believed with all our hearts in the power of love to transform the world, and were ready to follow Shlomo to the ends of the earth to make it happen—what can I say? What we shared is beyond words. Even at the very end of the journey, when some of those friendships, including two of my closest, have been seriously strained by the growing polarization of the worlds we inhabit, I believe all of us know that, no matter how divergent our lives are now—to paraphrase Humphry Bogart in *Casablanca*—we'll always have San Francisco *and* Jerusalem. I also want to acknowledge those of my friends who asked me to disguise their identities out of concern for opinions in the religious world they now inhabit—while still retaining their friendships with me. For that I am grateful.

To those of my fellow holy beggars who chose to stay connected with this story by approving the use of their real names, I am extremely grateful:

> Tamir, formerly Ruth Ochert Coopersmith, my first wife, moved into the House of Love and Prayer with me and shared the wild ride. When I contacted her years after we had been divorced, she was kind enough to share her memories of a marriage that was challenging for both of us, with good humor, forgiveness, love and blessings for the book's success.

> Moshe Yitzchak and Bernice Kussoy provided me with 35 years of generous friendship and support in so many ways, including a woodworking shop in the basement of their San Francisco house in 1969, a bedroom in their Israel house in 2003, and so much in between. Moshe Yitzchak also provided many of his wonderful photographs, some of which are in the book.

> Dr. Moshe Fohrman, of blessed memory, who died over 30 years ago when he was still young, provided all the rest of us, who were younger, with guidance on how to balance the high of transcendence ("Shabbos") with the daily discipline of being present in this world ("the week"). He still does.

> Donna Maimes has always been one of my models of courage, no less now in her 60s than when she was 18. By agreeing to tell her story in her own way, she lights a candle that illuminates the soul of this story.

Many of my friends on the journey took the time to talk with me, allowed me to record their stories, and to tell them as part of the book. These include Libby Botero, Lynne Feinerman, Rabbi Yisroel Finman, Rabbi Eliezer Garner, Reuven Goldfarb, Malka Gorman, George Gorner, Ian Grand, Ph.D., Shulamis Green, Rabbi Nadya Gross, Rabbi Victor Gross, Rabbi Burt Jacobson, Chaya Leder, Marty Potrop, Elana Schachter, Ahouva Steinhaus, and Yosepha Zarchin.

Two of these, Elana Schachter and Shulamis Green, disagreed with some of my choices in telling the story, yet chose to keep their names in the book. They have demonstrated a quality I especially admire—the ability to simultaneously hold a deeply religious view of how we should act in the world, and to also accept that others who choose to act differently can also be acting righteously.

And there are so many other people that I wanted to include in the story, but the requirements of space (getting from over 1,000 pages down to about 400) forced me to choose. Someone recently told me, "We may not remember every place we've been to in our lives, but if you ever walked into the House of Love and Prayer, you never forgot." Reb Shlomo once said: "How come I can stand next to a complete stranger and feel so much love, so much holy connection? What do we know? Maybe we were standing together at Mount Sinai." To those of us who stood next to each other at the House of Love and Prayer, we will never forget—the connection is forever.

A special group of friends became part of this story at the very end, just before publication. When I learned to my shock and sadness about the fierceness of the opposition to publishing this book as I wrote it, my wife Wendy and I felt the need to surround ourselves with people who cared about us, who deeply understood the religious, moral and legal issues involved, and whose moral compass we trusted—to advise and support us. So we invited a group of friends to form a "Wisdom Circle." As it turns out, they included seven rabbis, two attorneys, three psychotherapists, and others with useful, important skills. With their support I was able to emerge, from being stuck in a painful cycle of conflict, to firm ground with a clear, compassionate, principled course of action. Much thanks to Rabbi Tsvi Bar-David, Rita Karuna Cahn, Steve Diamond, Susan Diamond, Rabbi Diane Elliot, Marty Gross, Rabbi Nadya Gross, Rabbi Victor Gross, Rabbi Burt Jacobson, Bob Jaffe, Rabbi Daniel Lev, Rabbi Moshe

Levin, Claudia Miller, Margie Walkover, Barbara Zilber, and Maury Zilber.

Saving the best for last, there is my wife, Wendy Berk—co-conspirator, fellow traveler, conscience, proofreader of first and last resort, emotional and spiritual barometer, fiercely with me in the trenches when we had to fight, and joyfully with me dancing when we got to celebrate. Although she and I met in the 1990s, too late for her to meet Reb Shlomo in this world, she got to know him very well indeed as she accompanied me through the final chapters of my journey from Haight Street to Jerusalem. She'd get home each night, tired from a long day of seeing patients as a nurse practitioner, and make time to read every word of every chapter through the many revisions, commenting on all of them, always from her heart-centered perspective of how others would feel reading this. Although I didn't always agree with her suggestions, and in fact we often got quite emotional in our disagreements, I always benefited from her caring and her wisdom. It is to her as much as to anyone that this book owes the fact of its existence.

— A. C.

Foreword

Since the passing of my dear friend Reb Shlomo Carlebach, of blessed memory, I have seen many hagiographic accounts celebrating his life and teachings. I have also seen other not-so-complementary accounts of his life. It is usually one or the other, but not both. Until one vessel is strong enough to contain the different sides of his story, strong enough to hold the paradox of his humanity *and* his holiness, Shlomo's legacy will remain divided. But with this work, I believe Reb Aryae has begun to shape that vessel of wholeness.

Through his own humble witness, Reb Aryae takes us back into that world of the House of Love and Prayer, and allows us to relive the unique *Zeitgeist,* the spirit of the '60s that permeated it and all of us. Along the way, he gives us a glimpse into the complexities of Reb Shlomo's life—the holy ecstatic teaching, the joy-filled concerts, the humor and learning, the profound loneliness, and the conflicted feelings of many of his students after his passing. A good chronicler, he does not judge what he has heard, but simply reports the thoughts and feelings of others.

But that is not to say that it is a dispassionate book, for Reb Aryae courageously gives the reader a glimpse into his own soul, his own exaltations, his own inner struggles and exasperations occasioned by the upheaval of those times and Reb Shlomo's quirks and amazing capacity for touching people in the heart. This is *his* story as much as Shlomo's, and in some sense, the story of all the "holy beggars" who were touched by Reb Shlomo and the community they created together.

Though there are some who will be troubled by the complexity of Reb Aryae's portrait, I believe his honest reflection on those complexities, and his own deep love for Reb Shlomo, which shines from every page, raises this book to level beyond simple notions of right and wrong, black and white, to a place of simple, loving acceptance of the whole. It is this non-judgmental attitude that makes this a truly important look at a pivotal time in the renaissance of Judaism in America, one that opens a door to understanding a more ecumenical view of Judaism, and one that offers an opportunity for all of us who lived through that time to understand ourselves a little better.

It is of vital importance that we understand the difference between an *archetypal model* and an *accessible model.* Many who have heard Reb Shlomo's songs and teachings have put him on a pedestal and set him up as an archetypal model. This book, which treats him as a human being, will not serve those who insist on this view of him. Hagiographies, the biographies of saints, create big halos around the people they describe, but they also make it impossible for others to emulate them with much success. Reb Shlomo didn't ask people to call him 'Rabbi Carlebach.' He didn't even ask them to call him 'Reb Shlomo.' He was always just 'Shlomo,' and related to people in a very accessible, human way. And those who saw in him an accessible model became truly creative in the way in which they gave over the teachings and melodies that they inherited from him . . . and those that they created themselves.

Remember, all of us are concerned about his legacy, for *the legacy is not the person.* My friend Reb Shlomo left us over 16 years ago, and what remains? The stories of his bottomless kindness, the countless lives that he inspired, his profound teachings, and the thousands of songs he composed. While the person is no longer with us in body, his spirit inhabits his legacy. In that, there is still so much to nourish souls that may not be able to find what they need in more traditional sources. This is his legacy; its value is immeasurable, and it deserves to be preserved. All of us can help in this effort by contributing to the Shlomo Carlebach Legacy Trust (www.carlebachlegacy.com).

— Rabbi Zalman Schachter-Shalomi, *Boulder, Colorado, 2011*

Preface

Listen to me, my darling friends; open up your hearts. Every day, every second, God is sending us messages. The only thing is, the messages come on different levels. One level is the fact: the fact can only reach as far as the mind. Then there's the story: the story reaches past the mind to the heart. But the deepest of all is the melody: the melody reaches all the way to the soul.

— Rabbi Shlomo Carlebach, House of Love and Prayer, 1968

In human history there are times and places where the infinite intersects with the finite. I picture the finger of God poking through the fabric of the universe, causing all kinds of disruptions. There may or may not be outer events: thunder and lightning, eclipses and earthquakes, ecstatic crowds and divine revelation. But the real story is silent, invisible, a shift in the nature of reality.

For some of us living in the Haight-Ashbury neighborhood of San Francisco in the 1960s, this was one of those times. For us it wasn't about the "sex, drugs and rock and roll." It was about the spiritual teachers from all over the world, and the young people from all over the U.S., who converged here to find each other. It was about sharing a brief moment in the infinite presence of God's finger which was then breaking into in the finite world. Our lives were changed forever.

Over four decades later, as I prepare to tell you my part of that story, I feel like a kind of archaeologist, digging through the earth, searching out the fragments of an ancient text, which are often torn, blurred, faded, or missing, and trying to piece them together. I also feel like the proverbial blind man of the Indian parable, reaching out his hand to touch the elephant, and struggling to understand what it is he's touching.*

I open cardboard boxes I've carried with me for decades from place to place. Inside are old audio-cassettes, photos, and articles from magazines and newspapers, occasional journal entries, and

---

* This parable is found in Hindu, Jain, and Buddhist texts alike, and can even be found in the Persian Sufi writings of Jalaluddin Rumi.

letters—sometimes 35 years old—from fellow "holy beggars"—as Shlomo called us—who lived with me in the House of Love and Prayer and later wrote me when they had moved on. Added to these items are tapes of interviews I've conducted with some of them more recently, asking for their stories of that time. Often, their memories are different from mine, and from each other's. It's like Kurosawa's *Rashomon*, where everyone's version of the story is different, and there is no way to determine the "objective" truth.

Stories of holy beggars have long been a part of Jewish tradition. Elijah the Prophet—who has appeared to people throughout history, and will appear again to announce the arrival of the Messiah and the redemption of the world—often appears as a beggar. Our teacher, Rebbe Nachman of Breslov, in the early 19th century, told the Tale of the Seven Beggars, symbolic of our ancestors Abraham, Isaac, Jacob, Moses, Aaron, Joseph, and King David, as well as the levels of a person's soul. Shlomo once said, "A holy beggar wanders the streets of the world, begging not *to take,* but *to give.*"

After years of struggle, I've come to understand that I cannot tell this story in a linear way. I can only select from the thousands of fragments and remembrances available, occasionally enhancing them with the light of imagination. I am not writing this book as a historian recording *facts,* but to share with you a *true story* as I and others remember it.

The names of some individuals have been changed. In some cases it is to protect their privacy. In others cases they have asked not to be identified due to their disagreement with how I handle certain controversial parts of the story. Whenever there is a name change, it will be noted in the text.

I offer you this book in the hope that, as you read it, you can form your own picture of the "elephant" and will receive the *story*—from my heart to yours—and beyond the story, an echo of the *melody.*

— Aryae Coopersmith, *Half Moon Bay, 2011*

Part I

Aryae in the House of Love and Prayer.
Photo by Moshe Yitzchak Kussoy.

1

Messengers

Baden bei Wien, Austria – 1939

A knock at the door changes everything.

The prayers stop. The room is silent. Rabbi Naftali Carlebach, standing at the lectern where he has been leading the morning service, looks across the large, wood-paneled room, past the men standing in front of him with prayer books in their hands, through the front hallway of his house, until his eyes finally come to rest on the heavy oak door that leads out on to the street.

Since the Third Reich annexed Austria the year before, the Jews of Baden bei Wien (Baden near Vienna), have so far been spared the fate of Jews in other parts of Austria and Germany. But the sight of Nazi soldiers patrolling the streets of this picturesque resort city, with its healing spas and castles, is becoming increasingly common. Most of the wealthier families in the congregation have already left.

Rabbi Carlebach, the Chief Rabbi of the city, has so far chosen to stay. Direct descendents of Israel's ancient poet-musician and warrior-king, King David, the Carlebachs are one of Europe's most distinguished rabbinic families, famous for centuries for their learning and wisdom, as well as their kindness and courage. How can he abandon the people of his congregation in their time of need? On the other hand, how could he not attempt to rescue his own family— his twin sons, his daughter, and his wife—before it is too late?

Many of his congregants have been urging him to leave right away. There are rumors now that the border will be closed any day.

Today is *Shabbos*, the seventh and holiest day of the week, the day on which God rested from the work of creation. On *Shabbos* it is forbidden to work. It is forbidden to be sad, or even to concern oneself with the affairs of the world. *Shabbos* is an eternal gift from God, a gift of pure being and pure joy, a gift of remembering the creation of the Beginning.

More knocking, and more insistent this time. Everyone turns to look at the door. One of Rabbi Carlebach's twin sons stands by the door uncertainly, looking across the room at his father. The boy looks so vulnerable, standing there with only a polished oak door between him and the horrors of the world outside. He and his brother just had their *bar-mitzvah* last year, two months before the Nazis invaded. This one has a sweet demeanor and smiles at everyone. It's hard to tell by looking at him that he has been declared a genius, a child prodigy who has already learned more Torah than most men, even accomplished scholars, will learn in a lifetime. If he lives, he will have much to offer the Jewish people and the world.

The boy is still looking at his father. Their eyes meet. No words are needed; they understand each other. *It's not the door that is protecting him,* thinks Rabbi Carlebach, *his protector is so much greater.* He nods his assent to his son.

After waiting another second to make sure he understands his father's intent, the boy turns to the door and asks in German, "Who is it?"

The men in the room see the boy lean forward and say something they can't quite hear, and then watch him intently as he quickly opens the door. Framed by the dark, polished wood trim of the large doorway, rays of sunlight pour into the room. And there, in the midst of the light, looking like he has just arrived as a messenger from some distant world, stands a disheveled looking Jew, with hair, beard, and clothes sticking out in all directions, and smiling.

"My name is Moishele," he sings in Yiddish.

One of the men inside calls out: "Don't leave the door open! Bring him in!"

The boy touches the man's arm and leads him inside.

"My name is Moishele," the man sings again. "What is your name?"

The boy is taken with the sweetness of the melody, and with the sweetness he feels coming from this strange man whom he's never seen before. The boy imitates the melody perfectly and sings, "My name is Shlomo."

He smiles at the boy. "Good *Shabbos*, Shlomo!" he sings. Then he walks past the boy into the room, his arms outstretched, singing loudly now, and with joy: "Good *Shabbos, Yidden!* Good *Shabbos!* Good *Shabbos!* Good *Shabbos* to the Master of the World!"

4

Some of the men are fearful of being heard outside. Two or three of them approach Moishele to silence him; but Rabbi Carlebach holds up his hand and the men stop. The boy is still standing at the door, his eyes fixed on Moishele.

"Today is *Shabbos*," Moishele sings. "How can we be sad? How can we hold ourselves back from praising our Creator?"

"You're right," says Rabbi Carlebach. "No matter what, we must praise our Creator." He continues the service, slowing down to sing King David's psalms.

When the service is over, the men slip out of the house one by one, through the front and back doors, as unobtrusively as possible. Moishele smiles at the boy and sings to him as he leaves: "*Zei gezunt* (God bless you), Shlomo! Good *Shabbos*! Good *Shabbos*!"

The boy smiles back at him and sings, "*Zei gezunt*, Moishele! Good *Shabbos*! Good *Shabbos*!"*

The following week, the last train out of Austria is preparing to leave the central railroad station in Baden bei Wien. Moishele is on one of the last cars. The Carlebach family, with papers for passage to America, is sitting in one of the front cars.

Moishele's heart is overflowing with gratitude to God for the beauty of his beloved city, and he wants to say goodbye to it. Without warning, and before it occurs to anyone to stop him, Moishele opens the window, sticks his head out, and starts singing at the top of his lungs. He just can't hold himself back any longer; he simply *has* to sing.

Immediately, four Nazi SS officers, standing on the platform, turn to look at him. They get on the train, shove their way past the other passengers, and get off a couple of minutes later with Moishele. A moment later, the Carlebachs hear the shots.

In six months, they will arrive safely in New York.

Shlomo will never forget Moishele. Years and decades later when he is famous the world over, giving concerts to packed halls in capitals on every continent, Shlomo will tell Moishele's story and sing his melody, again and again. Even more than the story, and more than the melody, Shlomo will convey and *transmit* Moishele's simple

---

* Rabbi Moshe Heschel was a son of the Kopitzinitzer Rebbe, Rabbi Yitzhak Meir Heschel (1862-1936), and brother of Rabbi Abraham Joshua Heschel (1888-1967), the Kopitzinitzer Rebbe in New York. Both brothers were first cousins of the famous Jewish philosopher and rabbi, Abraham Joshua Heschel (1907-1972). This account is a slight elaboration on what I heard from Reb Shlomo himself.

5

love, his simple joy, and his simple glory in being a creature of God in this world. And even after everyone who was there in Baden bei Wien in 1939 is dead, Moishele's simple melody, sung on *Shabbos* by men and women in their thousands and ten thousands in synagogues all over the world, will live.

Brooklyn, New York – December 10th, 1949

Shlomo Carlebach and Zalman Schachter, young rabbis in their mid 20s, are standing in a narrow, dimly lit hallway on the second floor of 770 Eastern Parkway, the three-storey headquarters of the Lubavitcher Rebbe, waiting nervously, with their eyes fixed on the door in front of them.

Even the fact that they are here together is a miracle in itself, a blessing from God. They had first met in Baden bei Wien, before the Nazis had taken over, when Zalman, then 11 years old, showed up on the Carlebach's doorstep, holding a dead chicken. Zalman's father had sent him to ask Rabbi Carlebach if it was kosher. Rabbi Carlebach examined the chicken and declared it kosher. Then he introduced Zalman to his sons, Eliya Hayyim and Shlomo, who were 10 years old. The three boys ran off to play ping-pong.

Zalman's own family was not able to leave Austria by train as the Carlebachs had; but with the help of smugglers, the Schachters escaped on foot across the German border into Antwerp, Belgium. From there, they fled to France and wound up in an internment camp for Jewish refugees, before eventually being released to travel to Marseilles. There, Zalman met a charismatic rabbi with whom he was very taken. After his family finally arrived in New York in 1941, Zalman learned that this rabbi was Menachem Mendel Schneerson, the son-in-law of the sixth Lubavitcher Rebbe, Rabbi Yosef Yitzchak Schneersohn, head of a great Hasidic dynasty. The Rebbe had also escaped from Europe and arrived in New York just a year before Zalman, setting-up his home and headquarters in Brooklyn.

Zalman soon became a Hasid (student, follower) of the Rebbe, and when Zalman and Shlomo found each other again in New York, Zalman learned that Shlomo and his brother Eliya Hayyim had already been to see the Rebbe.

At first Shlomo was hesitant about becoming a Hasid. He was already studying at America's foremost Torah academy, Lakewood Yeshiva, the intellectual center of the Orthodox Jewish world, where he was recognized as an *illui*, a genius. It was rumored that Rabbi

Aharon Kotler, the renowned head of the *yeshiva,* was grooming Shlomo to succeed him. But over time Shlomo came to realize the life of the mind, even in a community of brilliant minds, would not satisfy him. He needed something more. What the Rebbe offered him was a path with heart. So Shlomo left Lakewood to learn with the Rebbe.

The door opens. An older Hasid, Berel Haskind, sticks his head out. In a soft voice, almost a whisper, he says in Yiddish: *Die Rebbe ruft eich,* "The Rebbe's calling you." They follow him into the Rebbe's mother's room where he held a small *farbrengen* (gathering).

The Rebbe is one of the few Hasidic masters to get out of the Holocaust alive. He is driven day and night to do what he can to rebuild in America what was decimated in Europe: the holy communities of his people. The Rebbe is a *tzaddik,* a righteous person, a fully realized being whose every waking minute is devoted to serving God. He is like a king who commands the love, respect, and loyalty of those around him. But lately he has been sick, and spends much of his time in bed.

Wearing a black silk robe, the Rebbe sits propped-up on an upholstered chair at a small table. Standing around the room are several old men with long, white beards, whom the young men recognize as the Rebbe's closest Hasidim. The Rebbe nods, and one of the old men fills three shot glasses on the small table with vodka, passing them to the Rebbe, Shlomo, and Zalman. They make a blessing and everyone says, *"L'Hayyim!"* making a toast to long life for the Rebbe.

The Rebbe looks at Shlomo and Zalman. He takes one more sip of his vodka, and hands the glass to one of the old Hasidim, who also takes the glasses from the two young men, and puts the glasses on the dresser. The Rebbe speaks softly in Yiddish. His voice is weak, but his eyes are filled with fire.

"The time has come," the Rebbe says, looking first into Shlomo's eyes, then Zalman's. *"You have been chosen. God has given you both great gifts. With great gifts come great responsibilities."*

The Rebbe coughs. Berel Haskind hands him a handkerchief, then a glass of water. After a moment, the Rebbe continues: *"I am sending you both as my personal emissaries. I want you go to college campuses, many college campuses. I want you to find the Jewish students there."*

The Rebbe takes a sip of water.

"What do you want us to say to them?" Shlomo asks.

The Rebbe looks at him. *"I am sending you to reach out to them,"* he says. *"God will show you what to say. He will put the words in your mouth."*

Shlomo looks at the Rebbe without saying anything.

The Rebbe smiles, a little sadly. *"America is a wonderful place,"* he says. *"Thank God it has provided our people with a haven of comfort and security, where we can learn Torah and live our lives without fear. But we have to remember that the Messiah — may he come soon to redeem the world — is not here yet. America is a great home for the body, but not so easy for the soul. Here they don't kill our bodies,"* he says with a sad little laugh. *"Instead, they seduce us with false gods, the gods of materialism. Many will succumb. Many will lose their way."*

The Rebbe looks down and notices that the glass of water is still in his hand. He lifts it up, and his attendant Berel takes it from him.

The Rebbe sits up straight and leans forward. He locks eyes first with Zalman, then with Shlomo. *"What happened to the six million?"* he says, in barely a whisper, *"Where are these souls?"*

The young men are silent. They look at each other, and then back at the Rebbe.

"They are being reborn," the Rebbe says. *"They are being reborn here, in a new generation. The Nazis destroyed our bodies. America,"* he says shaking his head, *"America has the power to destroy our souls. You must go and find them. You must bring them back to their Creator."**

The following week is Hanukah. Shlomo and Zalman get hold of a car, an old Plymouth, and drive up to Boston to visit their first college campus, Brandeis University. When they get there in the evening, they discover a Hanukah party in the student union, where students are dancing to 1940s swing music.

The young rabbis walk in carrying the stuff they've brought with them: a tape recorder with Hasidic music, a stack of handouts with Hasidic teachings, and a bag containing *tefillin* (ritual objects worn during prayer). The room goes silent, and all eyes are on them. Shlomo walks over to a table on one side of the room; Zalman walks over to a table on the other side.

As curious students wander over, Shlomo begins telling stories. One student says, "This sounds like Hindu mysticism." Shlomo keeps

---

* While this story is true and accurate to what I have heard from Shlomo and Zalman, most of the words of the Rebbe here are what I imagine he said at that time, and not based on any oral source.

8

going from story to story as more students gather. Zalman talks about Kabbalah and the *Upanishads* at his table, where students are also gathering. Pretty soon, everyone in the room is gathered around these two tables. The stories and discussions continue late into the night.

The following month, on January 28th, the Rebbe leaves this world.

2

Seeker

Before I leave Jerusalem, there's one more place I have to visit. Ruthie, who has lived here all her life, told me that she has a feeling about this, and that I really should do it. Now I hear the sound of my shoes slapping the stones of the street, marking the quick rhythm of my strides.

Jerusalem in 1965 is a small city with winding stone streets and open-air markets. The markets are filled with the sights and sounds and smells of people selling their wares: smoking meat on outdoor grills, falafel stands, fruit and vegetable vendors, cold drink vendors, tobacco vendors, tiny hole-in-the-wall cafes where you can sit outside and sip Turkish coffee. The narrow streets are choked with big, lumbering buses emitting billowing clouds of diesel smoke, little taxi buses constantly scooting through and around everything, and the endless cacophony of honking horns. The sidewalks are crowded with people who've come from other places: Eastern Europe, Western Europe, the Middle East, North Africa, South Africa, North America, South America, India, and Shanghai. They are mostly Jews, but also Muslims and Christians, all with the clothes, colors, faces, smells, languages, and accents of the places they've left. They mingle with the Israelis who have been here longer: the secular, athletic looking men and women with uncovered heads, arms, and legs who talk and laugh with loud bravado and always seem to be in a hurry; and the ultra-Orthodox men and women who have everything covered and move more quietly, deliberately.

The Israeli sector of Jerusalem is cut off from the Old City in Jordan, site of ancient holy places, of Mount Zion, and the most sacred holy place of all for the Jewish people, the Western Wall. The line of separation, reinforced by barbed wire with Israeli and Jordanian soldiers on either side, sometimes visible, sometimes hidden, cuts through the city like an ominous, jagged crack. It is never very far away, and the danger is always there, lurking silently.

11

Jews have been yearning for almost two thousand years to return to Mount Zion, and to the Wall, to reunite with it, to embrace its stones. Although I'm not religious and don't believe in God, I feel caught up in this longing. Sometimes I walk right up to the border, to where the barbed wire is; I fantasize about slipping through, undetected, to find my way back to the ancient Wall of the Holy Temple, still standing. I look at the hills on the other side. Everything looks peaceful. I don't see any soldiers. Maybe I could do it. Then I imagine machine gun fire.

I was born in the Bronx in December 1943, right in the middle of the War. My mother Flo told me she woke up from the anesthesia in the hospital to the sound of the radio by her bedside playing, "Oh, What a Beautiful Morning." My father Sam was able to get the day off from his job at the Brooklyn Navy Yard, where he'd been assigned by his draft board after being classified 4F due to a heart murmur. Grandpa Max, who was president of his synagogue, lived in the same building we did. He was torn between joy at the birth of his first grandson, and grief at the news that his youngest brother had died in a Nazi concentration camp the month before. Uncle Paul had already enlisted in one of the U.S. Army units preparing to invade Europe and died at the Battle of the Bulge a year later.

I remember shaking as I stood at the podium for my *bar-mitzvah* at Congregation Sons of Israel in 1956. It was a Conservative congregation whose members, like my parents, were the children of immigrants, busy assimilating into the mainstream of American life, striving to be prosperous and successful. Their relationship to the ancient tribe of Israel was paradoxical. Although not an official part of the Hebrew school curriculum, my classmates and I absorbed the key lesson: you should be "proud to be Jewish," *but you shouldn't overdo it.* Nobody talked about what had happened in the concentration camps in World War II. It wasn't healthy to dwell on the past, or think about the bad old days of Jewish life in Europe. It was better to talk about sports and business, and think about our opportunities to get ahead as Americans.

I didn't believe in God or religion, but did what was expected of me, performing my Torah and *Haftarah* readings.* I didn't understand the words, but I could chant them well. My parents and family were proud. Everyone could see that we were a successful family on the way up, and that I, Sam and Flo's oldest son, and Grandpa Max's

---

* The major ritual of the *bar-mitzvah* is a reading of that week's Torah portion and a portion from the Prophets, known as the *haftarah* (conclusion).

oldest grandson, had the potential to carry that success to new heights.

I've been in Jerusalem for a year, taking classes at the Hebrew University, living with Ruthie, a dancer, and spending late afternoons and evenings smoking hashish with her and her friends. They are an eclectic, international group of musicians, artists, and poets from places like Australia, Morocco, South Africa, Tunisia, and Romania, who like to get stoned and make music, read poetry and dance together.

I got here because Grandpa Max was worried about me.

I hadn't been to synagogue or done anything Jewish since my *bar-mitzvah*. Worse, I had left New York at age 19, after dropping out of college, to hitch-hike out to California to go see a girl who wasn't even Jewish. I was living in the Filmore, the Harlem of San Francisco, in a house I rented with three other white guys, the only white guys in the neighborhood. We grew marijuana in the back yard, smoked it, and partied at night as we strung together various odd contraptions to create light and music shows. I joined the civil rights movement that was staging big sit-ins in San Francisco and got arrested repeatedly. Convinced that the war in Vietnam was wrong, I joined the peace movement, demonstrated every Sunday in the park, and filed a Conscious Objector application with my local draft board back in New Jersey.

One day a letter came from Grandpa Max. "How would you like to go halfway around the world for an adventure?" he asked. I thought about it for a few days. I already had plenty of adventure in San Francisco, but then again, I could always come back. Three months later I was in Jerusalem, signing up for classes at the Hebrew University.

I finally see what I'm looking for: a two-story stone building with a tower on top. Each section of wall seems to have stones of a different color, different texture, and different century. I step into a kind of courtyard where two walls meet. There are large pots of plants and flowers, a single rectangular window with metal bars, and a pair of archways. I walk in through one of the archways. It is cool inside, with dim light provided by small, bare bulbs. I walk slowly to feel the mood and energy of this place. The only other person I can see is the caretaker, a small, thin Middle Eastern Jew sitting at a narrow wooden table near the entrance. He looks up at me briefly, then back down at his papers.

The sound of my shoes scraping against the stone floor echoes in the room. I approach another arched entrance, this one partially covered with metal grillwork. There is a glow coming from inside. Faintly at first and then louder, I hear an unfamiliar sound. It is like women wailing. Where is it coming from? Am I really hearing this, or is my mind creating it?

I walk up to the arch and step through. There, suddenly, raised on a platform and spread out in front of me, larger than life—framed by a partial dome of ancient stones, covered with a cloth of blue velvet and decorated with gold trim on which sit three gold, jeweled crowns, and several jeweled arks for holding Torah scrolls—is the coffin containing the remains of David, the ancient King of Israel.

On the other side of the room, where I can't see them, women are chanting the Psalms in Sephardic Hebrew in high-pitched voices filled with grief, as if they were longing for the return of a lost lover. The sound of their longing echoes off the stones and reverberates through the building. I stand there for a long time. It is not just the sight of the ancient coffin and crowns that holds me here, transfixed, nor the startling lament of the women, it is *his presence*, huge, larger than the large coffin, here for thousands of years, regal, powerful, insistent, *real*. This presence, this soul, is bigger than just one person. It is not just the king, it is also the people he led and fought for and defended and inspired for generations and centuries.

None of this makes any sense to me. My mind struggles for an explanation: *It's the power of suggestion; it's a hypnotic effect.* But the mind's struggle is abstract, passionless, isolating, unconvincing. The soul that is present here is *real*, like a mighty river pouring fourth from the vast landscape of life and time and history. Gradually I allow myself to let go, to feel it flow through me, to let it carry me along.

Images of raging battles, thousands of years ago. Countless thousands of people carrying stones for the walls of the city, for its buildings, and at the center, the magnificent and mysterious house of God on earth, with its walls and courtyards and chambers, filled with tens of thousands of people with their families coming from all corners of the ancient kingdom, bringing gifts of the firstborn sheep of their flock and the first fruits of their trees. And at the very center of all, in the Holy of Holies, the mysterious gateway where the energy of the Divine Presence, whose intensity exceeds the combined heat of all the stars in the heavens, opens into the material universe, where anyone or anything approaching without the proper preparation is instantly consumed. Radiant images appear of ancient glory, present and alive on these rocky hills for one brief, shining moment. And then the long, sad history of the Jewish people that follows: the wars,

14

the destruction of Jerusalem, the enslavement of the people, the two thousand years of exile and suffering from endless cycles of humiliation, torture, and murder. And in every cycle and every age, from countless ordinary people scattered around the world, acts of courage and faith, of humanity and love, that have kept the people and the dream alive. And here the whole time, dwelling in this stone building at the edge of Jerusalem, is the soul of King David, fierce, undefeated warrior, leader of men and lover of women, poet and singer, lover of God, steadfast, timeless, reassuring, comforting the soul with the memory of what has been, and stirring her to imagine what could be.

Later in the afternoon, when the sun is lower in the heavens and closer to the earth, the rocks are casting longer shadows, and the air is warm and still, I walk back in a stupor through the streets of Jerusalem, shaken, amazed. The cool, skeptical voice in my head, the one I am used to thinking of as *me*, has been set aside. At the center where its voice once was, there is now darkness, like the opening of an ancient cave. And drifting from the cave, like the voices of the women at King David's tomb, comes a feeling I can only identify as fierce longing, like being driven. *I long to reunite with the timeless source of being.*

Paris, France – June 1965

The woman who invited me into her hotel room introduces me to the others.

A couple of young women and a man, all French, are lounging on a bed. A Middle Eastern looking guy sitting on the floor, leaning against the wall and smoking a cigarette, looks up at me. They're all drinking wine. There's music on a portable record player, jazz.

The French guy gestures at the wine bottle and glasses on the dresser and invites me to pour myself a glass. I accept. We all exchange information about ourselves. Although their appearance fits my image of French art students going to the Sorbonne, they're actually all business majors. My French is good enough for a simple conversation; but when they talk fast, I understand very little.

I've been by myself in Paris, staying at a hotel on the Left Bank. Ruthie is coming back with me to the States, but right now she's visiting her brother in England. Her dream is to dance for the great Martha Graham in America, and she's made arrangements to take classes at the Martha Graham Dance Studio in New York. My father signed the papers she needed for a visa to the U.S., so Ruthie and I will be flying together to New York next week.

The guy sitting on the floor is from Algeria. He wants to know about my stay in Israel. What shall I tell him? There's a lot of hashish in Israel from all over the Middle East, I say. Do I have any with me, he wants to know. The others are looking at me with curiosity. Hashish is hard to get here in Paris, the Algerian says. He used to smoke it all the time at home and really misses it. He opens the leather pouch sitting on the floor next to him, pulls something out, and places it in the palm of his hand, which he extends in my direction.

"Do you know what this is?" he says.

"It looks like a sugar cube," I say, studying the clean geometry of the sparkling white object in his brown hand. The others look at each other and smile knowingly.

"Have you ever heard of Sandoz Laboratories in Switzerland?" he asks. I haven't. He tells me about LSD. He says, "It's ten times— maybe a hundred times—more powerful than the best hashish. It changes your consciousness. There are people in your country, at Harvard University, who have been studying it." Two of the French students say they've tried it and it's an amazing experience.

I look at the Algerian student. "So what are you thinking?" I ask.

He looks at the three French students on the bed, then at me, with a kind of half smile. "I'm feeling homesick," he says. "Maybe we trade a little LSD for a little hashish."

I look at the French students and the Algerian, one at a time. On the one hand, I've left Israel with a strong sense that I'm being led somewhere, and here is a new door for me to walk through. On the other hand, these are people I've never seen before and will probably never see again. I could get busted for drugs. I could get poisoned. I'm feeling like a gullible kid from the American suburbs, a easy mark. Isn't it crazy to trust your safety to people you've never seen before?

"Okay," I say. We do the trade, some of my hashish for three sugar cubes in a little box. I swallow one and put the others in my pocket.

"I don't feel anything," I say.

The French guy laughs. "Maybe you want some of this?" he says, holding out pipe with the hash that I've just traded.

"No!" says the young woman protectively, the one who introduced me to the others, "You'll be okay." She's lying on the bed and I'm sitting on the floor facing her. She touches my face with her hand. "It hasn't been 20 minutes yet. That's how long it takes before you begin to feel anything. You should prepare yourself by calming your mind and being patient."

I look at her. Something's not quite right about her face. At first I can't tell what it is. Then I see it. There are two worms, a yellow and a pink one, under her left eye. I stare at the worms, fascinated. Then I see another one, above her right eye. I pull back quickly. She smiles.

"It looks like maybe you're beginning to feel some effect," she says. "Yes?"

I try to talk. My mind is spinning. How do you say 'worms' in French? They're all looking at me with concerned looks. I'm on my hands and knees. The faded, green rug on the floor has railroad tracks that run down into the earth. Trains are running toward me. I have to get out of the way. I try to stand. It's hard, because the floor is uneven and the railroad tracks are tilting down into the earth.

The woman who touched my face gets up off the bed and comes over to me. She helps me stand. I hold onto her shoulder and her arm. Finally I'm standing, leaning over the dresser to hold myself up. If I move my eyes fast around the room, everyone looks more or less normal. If I focus on anyone's face, the worms start crawling over it. When I look in the corner across from the bed, I see a nest of snakes. The others don't notice, but the railroad trains and the snakes seem to be using up all the oxygen in the room, and it's getting hard to breathe. I have to get outside.

"I'm okay," I announce in a voice that sounds too loud, standing up on my own now. "I'm going for a walk."

The streets of Paris are filled with dangers. The people who walk past me are moving so fast. They seem like plastic puppets, moving in directions not of their own choosing, with someone else pulling the strings. They don't see the dangers, the snakes and railroad trains and machine gunners that are popping up everywhere. Every once in a while a plastic puppet turns to look at me.

As I keep walking, I am discovering the secret of getting past the dangers unharmed. I have to turn myself into a plastic puppet like the others around me. If I act like they do, walk like they walk, I can get past all the dangers, and no one will notice, no one will stop to look at me. I feel very excited at this discovery. Even though they are filled with traffic and railroad trains and deep pits leading into the earth, I can cross the streets easily. I can go wherever I want.

17

What I know with glowing certainty is that, even though other people look at me and see the plastic puppet, I am *not* the plastic puppet. I've created the plastic puppet as a mask, a disguise, a vehicle for getting around in the world. I am what is inside the plastic puppet. I am the creative force.

I am the word of God.

My steps are light now; I'm moving with ease and grace. I am one with light and truth, beauty and wisdom. I am on a mission; I am a messenger of God. Although my steps are light and I could express my joy by dancing in the streets, I am careful to keep the plastic puppet intact, to act like the others. That way I can move through the streets of Paris and no one will stop me from doing what I need to do.

I come to the Seine and turn left at the low stone wall that lines the river. There are clouds in the sky, but I am surrounded by light. Angels are gathering to join me, to walk with me. Many secrets are being revealed. The great teachers, prophets, saints throughout history have received the word of God, have come to experience the truth that they are the word of God, that we are all the word of God.

The pace of my walking is increasing on its own, effortlessly. Surrounded with light, with angels accompanying me, I cross over the river to Isle de la Cite and arrive at my destination, the Cathedral of Notre Dame. This is where I will meet with God.

The angels are surrounding me. They say that I am an angel too. I've been sent into the world to deliver God's word. The Cathedral is surrounded by angels playing harps and all the little creatures on the walls are singing.

I thought God would appear to talk to me, but that isn't how it works. The way we learned about God in Hebrew school, reading from the Bible, didn't show me, didn't give me a clue. That god, the god of Hebrew school and of the religion I grew up with, is also a plastic puppet.

Here in this moment, God is dancing.

God is radiating rainbows of being through indescribable patterns and dimensions, rainbows of joy that dissolve the mind and dissolve the self, rainbows of memory of the ancient endless changeless subtle joyful beautiful dance of universal oneness before being trapped in the crass crude finiteness of plastic puppets. There are no boundaries of self at all, no way to grasp or understand this, no way but to dissolve into the dance. The body that has housed me has let go, is sprawled out over a bench in front of the Cathedral. There are no more boundaries. There is no way to know where the body ends and the bench begins, where the bench ends and the

18

Cathedral begins, where the Cathedral ends and King David's tomb begins, where King David's tomb ends and God begins. All is one. Tears are flowing; endless rivers of tears. Tears from other times and places, flowing from the past into the future and back again. Tears of infinite longing and release, tears of recognition of coming back home, tears of gratitude, tears of joy.

Later, in the warm early evening, walking along the Seine, I watch silently as thousands of Parisian lights blink on around me, one at a time. I feel like I'm watching the lights of a carnival show, the red and blue and yellow lights on the Ferris wheel and on the other rides that spin around and around. Compared to the indescribable splendor of the world of oneness, that's what the plastic puppet world looks like now, like a carnival show. There's so much I don't understand, that I won't understand for decades, that I may never understand. What I do understand is this; now that the secret has been revealed, there's no way back.

I have to find other people I can talk to. I have to try to understand how to live simultaneously in more than one world. I have to try to understand what I've been sent here to do.

3

Shlomo

I'm on my way to a class at San Francisco State College, unprepared for the detour that will take me in a different direction.

It's one of those bright, clear December days in San Francisco, a day of sun after the rain, temperature in the mid-60s. The light has that indefinable quality it gets in the winter, as though the sun were simultaneously closer to the earth and cooler.

Students are walking in all directions, on their way to lunch, to afternoon classes and various activities. A lot of them look the way people look on Haight Street. There are guys with long hair, women with longer hair, both playfully dressed in colorful clothes and wildly colorful jewelry. There are lots of sandals. There are even some bare feet. The grass is wet from the rain of the past few days.

I hear some music coming from my left, and notice that people are wandering over toward a performance platform. I'm curious to see what's happening. I look at my watch. Class is still 10 minutes away. I follow the students.

There's a man with a guitar standing at the center of the stage, and a few people with guitars, drums, and tambourines standing nearby. The music is driving, rhythmical, in a minor key. People are dancing in several large circles. More keep wandering over and joining in, and the circles become very large and energetic. I stand there watching. The sun is shining and it's become warm. I take off my jacket and hold it in my arm with my battered leather briefcase.

The man at the center of the stage starts jumping, and the students who are already dancing begin jumping too. I walk up toward the platform to take a closer look. The man has dark hair, a small funny looking gray beard, and a *kippah* on his head.

A couple of young women are walking past. It's hard to get their attention. I tap one of them on the shoulder. "Do you know who that guy is?" I say in a voice loud enough to make myself heard. The one I tapped smiles at me. She has short brown hair with a little wave and a very cute smile.

21

"I read something in the student paper this morning about 'the singing rabbi,'" she says, a little shyly.

"The singing rabbi?" I ask. It doesn't compute. I've heard of the singing nun, but not the singing rabbi. I want to talk with her a little longer, but can't think of anything else to say. "Thanks." She smiles back, and I follow the two of them with my eyes. They walk up to one of the circles, reach out their hands, and immediately become part of it, dancing with everyone else.

I watch everyone dancing and feel left out. I walk over to a tree, set my briefcase down on the roots near the trunk so it won't get wet, fold my jacket, and place it on top. The music stops. The singing rabbi strums his guitar softly and starts to talk. His accent is European, maybe German-Jewish. It has a softness combined with intensity. I can't quite make out what he's saying. Hundreds of students crowd around the speakers' platform, and almost everyone is listening.

Abruptly, the singing rabbi jumps and starts singing again. It's a fast song, and everyone starts dancing again, as if on cue. They look like they're having such a good time, and I'm feeling left out. Someone in one of the circles reaches out a hand to me. It's the young woman I just spoke to. I reach out my hand, grab hers, and join the circle. It occurs to me that I'm going to miss my class.

I feel an enormous sense of release, of energy pouring out of me. I'm part of something larger, a celebration. My body wants to move, to jump, to rejoice in being alive. After one song ends, another begins. The music and dancing go on and on and on. At one point I slip on the wet grass. Someone reaches out a hand and pulls me up. My clothes are patched with mud. I've never seen so many people dancing together for so long. Everyone is sweaty, muddy, *and smiling*.

Later we're standing in half circles, with our arms around each other, hundreds of us pressed up close to the platform. We're breathing heavily. I feel our bodies close together, open, swaying back and forth, resting in each other's arms. It's like we're all in love with one another. To my left is a tall black man, his head tilted up, facing the sky, his eyes closed. To my right is a woman with straight blond hair, her eyes open and alert, looking straight at the singing rabbi. The rabbi has his eyes closed and is humming softly while he strums the chords on his guitar. The sun is shining strongly on all of us, while breezes blow past, rustling the trees. The world is so perfect. The moment is so beautiful. I want it to last.

I'm looking up at the singing rabbi when I notice that something is happening to me. It's a physical thing, starting with my arms, which are still holding the people next to me. The lines that separate my arms from their backs are dissolving. The boundaries that

22

separate us are *physically melting away*. There is nothing separating us. The separateness was just an illusion. The "I" is melting into a larger "We," a larger "All." A greater *Being* with lots of eyes closed, heads to one side, arms and bodies connecting, holding, feeling the rhythm of the breathing. There is so much peace, so much love.

The singing rabbi is softly strumming his guitar. He begins half speaking, half-singing: "You know my darling friends, there's a teaching from our great *rebbe*, our great spiritual master, the holy Ba'al Shem Tov. He lived a couple of hundred years ago in Poland. People would come from all over Europe to learn with him, to be in his presence. Okay now, my sweetest friends, open up your heart. What does it mean to reach out to another human being? Do we have even the tiniest clue? The holy Ba'al Shem Tov said, 'If everyone in the world would hold hands, the hands would reach to heaven.'"

I look at the singing rabbi. For a moment, he seems to be looking directly at me, speaking to me personally. I'm reaching out my hands, and my arms to the people around me. The lines that separated us have melted, and I'm back *here* again. This is what he means—"hands would reach to heaven." The truth of this jolts me like lightning, like rainbows, like a flash of eternity. "Heaven" is the Oneness! This moment transforms me. I am filled with awe and wonder, with amazement and laughter.

Later I'm standing on the platform in the middle of a group of students waiting to talk to the singing rabbi. He seems to spend a couple of minutes with each person. I feel impatient, then annoyed. Maybe I should just forget it and walk away? But I can't walk away. I would wait here a month if I had to.

"My name is Shlomo," he says, looking at me, smiling. He reaches out his hand. I take it and we shake hands. I notice his white shirt. It had once been crisp and starched and is now rumpled. Over the collar are two circles of colorful beads. On his head is a black *kippah* with silver threads in Yemenite filigree designs. He smells like patchouli oil. I try to get his image into focus.

"My name's Aryae," I say.

"Holy lion of God," he says. "That's an awesome name!"

He quickly asks me several questions about myself. I want to tell him all about myself so he can know who I am. Each time I ramble on, he cuts me off with another question. He wants to get to the point quickly. It seems like he's taking-in the essence of who I am and doesn't need the flood of words I'm trying to get out.

"Listen," Shlomo says. He puts his hand on my shoulder. "This is important. I want you to meet Efraim." He walks me over to another part of the platform where there's a guy about my age dressed like Shlomo—dark pants, sandals, a white shirt, beads, and a *kippah*. He has flaming red hair coming down in front of his ears, curled in *peyos*, like a traditional Orthodox Jew, and a sparse, scraggly beard. He is thin and hunched over a little, talking to a couple of students.

"Efraimele," Shlomo says. "I want you to meet Aryae."

Efraim stops what he's doing, looks at me for a second, smiles, leans forward, touches my shoulder very lightly, and gives me a gentle hug. I notice that he's also wearing patchouli oil. It occurs to me that he is stronger than he looks.

"Listen Aryae, you also gotta meet his wife, Leah, sweetest in the world!"* She is sitting on a chair on the platform, looking up at Shlomo, smiling. The three of us walk over to her. She gets up and gives Shlomo a hug, then me as well. When I see her and hug her, I get the amazing feeling that she is filled with happiness. She seems like she may be pregnant, but I can't tell for sure, so I don't say anything.

Shlomo quickly looks around, scanning the crowd on the platform waiting to talk to him. He reaches in his pocket, pulls out his wallet and hands me a business card. I look at it. It says, "Rabbi Shlomo Carlebach" in the center. It has a New York address and two phone numbers. "Aryae, I want you to do me the biggest favor," he says. "First, call me, okay? I'm traveling this week and next week, but I'll be back first week in January, so call me then, okay?"

I'm kind of startled that he wants me to call him, but I shake my head and say, "Okay."

"The other thing is, I want you to stay in touch with my sweetest friends here, Efraim and Leah. Efraimele, write your number on the back of my card, okay?" Efraim takes the card, pulls a pen out of his pocket and writes a number and the name of a town. I look at it. It says, "Forrest Knolls." "You gotta spend *Shabbos* with them," Shlomo says. "Efraim always knows when I'll be out here, so you can be with us the next time I'm doing a concert in the Bay Area. Okay?"

He has his hands on my shoulders, and is looking at me very intently, smiling. "Okay?" he says again.

I don't exactly know what he wants me to do, but I have to answer. "Okay."

---

* Out of respect for their privacy, I have changed their names for this book.

4
Folk Festival

The Berkeley Folk Festival is a perfect 4th of July celebration: a beautiful day, 10,000 students at the Greek Theatre, and Pete Seeger singing and urging everyone to resist the war in Vietnam. I don't believe in the war, and have filed for Conscious Objector status, but so far my draft board has denied my claim. It's scary to be resisting the might of the U.S. military all by myself, so it feels good to have a famous ally.

25

I'm here with Efraim and Leah, and our friends Donna, Moishe, and Maxine.* Shlomo is up next. Since I met Shlomo last December, he's been out to the Bay Area several times for small concerts. Donna, who is only 18, is his manager, and sets them up. The six of us, and a growing group of friends follow him everywhere he plays in California. Usually Efraim and I get to go on stage with him and play guitar. But this one's too big, too important, so we have to settle for watching him.

Finally it's Shlomo's turn. The Greek Theater is an outdoor amphitheater with the crowd up above, looking down at the performers below. The six of us, about half way up, look down silently, completely focused on Shlomo.

I recognize his style. First he sings fast music. People get up from their seats and dance. Then there's slower music, with words of love and peace. People stand and put their arms around each other.

Shlomo is standing alone on the platform at the bottom in front of two mics, a low one for his guitar, and a high one for his voice. He looks up at the thousands of young people surrounding him. He takes the energy in, the outpouring of their hearts, into his own heart. He gives it words and he gives it a melody. It's not exactly the words and the melody that they are used to in Berkeley, but they recognize what they are hearing, because it embodies their own deepest longings.

Earlier the crowd had loved Jefferson Airplane and Pete Seeger; but they go crazy for Shlomo.

He is strumming his guitar, telling everyone that *the great day of love and peace can come if we'll only reach out to each other.* Thousands of young people in the Greek Theatre are standing, swaying back and forth, with their arms around one another.

Shlomo's act is the last of the concert. For his last song he invites everyone who sang today to join him on stage. They do. Pete Seeger is there, and Jefferson Airplane too. Shlomo's words, gestures, and emotions include everyone.

I can feel the waves of love washing through the crowd. For this infinite moment we are not strangers. We are brothers and sisters who love each other, who are part of an amazing vision, an amazing *reality,* that the deepest yearnings of our soul, combined with the smallest actions of our day-to-day lives, are all part ofa plan for the redemption of the world, and together, we have the power to bring closer that great day of love and peace.

---

* Maxine is a name I have used to protect her privacy.

The emotion pouring from the crowd is overwhelming. The master of ceremonies for the Berkeley Folk Festival takes the mic and makes some comments. The crowd is still standing, arms interlaced with others. Then Shlomo takes the mic again.

"Friends, I'm staying here in Berkeley for a few days, and I want to invite you to please join me. The truth is, the world is filled with people who are fed-up with all the fighting and hatred in the world, people like you and me who are waiting for one song, for one tear, for one friend. Please join me and my friends. We'll sing the greatest harmonies together and learn the deepest secrets of the world."

Efraim and Leah and Donna have already made it down to the platform where Shlomo is standing. I follow, together with Moishe and Maxine. Hundreds of people are gathering around Shlomo, who is shaking hands, hugging people, handing out business cards.

The center of the Greek Theatre swirls with people moving in many directions, with thousands of voices raised at once, all struggling to be heard. Sound crews unplugging the equipment and gathering up the wires, carpenters starting to take apart the platforms, groupies for each of the entertainers swirling around them.

I'm in the middle of a surge of people outside the theater, flowing down Oxford Avenue to University, like a parade. A young woman who was sitting next to Moishe and Maxine in the Greek Theater is walking beside me. Her shoulders are tight. She seems shy, but eager to talk.

"Have we met?" she asks me. "I'm Cathy."

"Hi Cathy, I'm Aryae," I say. "Do you know Shlomo?"

"I met him on Haight Street a few days ago, when he was there with Efraim and Leah," she says. "I've never really had Jewish friends before. I've been in a convent, and I've just left."

I look at her. "Wow!" I say. "You were in a convent? Why did you leave?"

She looks uncomfortable. "It's hard to explain. How much do you know about Catholicism? I mean for instance, why do all the saints have to be Catholic? Don't all faiths have holy teachers, people who love God and are close to Him? Doesn't God love all His creatures? You see, I can't believe He loves some of us more than others. Can you?"

I look at her. She is smiling, but she also looks like she is imploring me, praying for understanding. I make eye contact with her. "I think I believe the same thing you do."

I walk up to where Shlomo is. Moishe and Maxine are walking together near Efraim and Leah. Maxine smiles at me. "So what do you think?" she says. "Who was the best singer?"

I smile back, turn around, and wave my arm in a theatrical gesture. "Well, I think the verdict of the crowd is pretty clear!"

We get to Shattuck and University. Shlomo, Moishe, and Maxine stop walking. "What are we doing?" I say.

"This is where Shlomo's staying," Efraim says. "It's the Shattuck Hotel." I look up at the hotel. It's a Victorian style building, several stories high. Then I look around at all the people with us.

There are hundreds of college students dressed in summer clothes, talking to each other, looking toward Shlomo, waiting to see what happens next.

"What about all these students?" I say. Leah looks around at everyone, smiles a big smile, and clasps her hands to her heart.

"Oh, it's so *beautiful*," she says.

Moishe comes up to us. "We're going inside to register Shlomo," he says. "He wants to rent some extra rooms so he can bring some of the kids with him."

"That's a lot of 'kids'!" I say. Moishe looks around with appreciation.

"You're right!" he says.

"What should we do with everyone while you're in there?" I say.

"Let's sing," Efraim says. Leah closes her eyes, holds her hands together and sighs. Moishe winks, slaps Efraim on the back, and goes inside the hotel with Maxine and Shlomo.

Efraim sets his guitar case down on the sidewalk. He bends over, opens and closes things, and emerges with his guitar. His eyes are wide open and he has a dreamy look.

Cathy is excited. "Are we going to pray and sing right here?" she asks incredulously.

"Looks like it," I say. Efraim starts to sing, and those of us standing near him quickly join in. Others in the crowd join us. People standing furthest away, who seem oblivious to the singing, are still standing around, talking to each other.

Shlomo walks quickly out of the hotel entrance onto the sidewalk. Eyes sparkling, with a big smile, he walks to where we're standing and holds up his fingers in a "V" sign. Efraim brings the song to a

28

close. Shlomo puts his hand on Efraim's shoulder and looks over the crowd of a couple of hundred students surrounding the hotel door.

Moishe follows a few steps behind. I lean over to Moishe. "What's going on?" I ask.

Moishe smiles. "He's rented the top floor of the hotel!"

Later a bunch of us are crowded into Shlomo's hotel room. Others are hanging out in the hall and the other rooms on this floor. We have the whole top floor for the rest of the week.

Shlomo is sitting on the bed in his room, with his shoes on, and his legs dangling over the edge. He has a large brown book open on his lap with Hebrew text. It has teachings from one of the great Hasidic masters, the Izhbitzer Rebbe.* Shlomo is reading the text with great concentration, swaying back and forth like he's praying, davening he would say. The rest of us are passing around refreshments that room service has just brought up: egg and tuna salad sandwiches, fruit and Cokes.

I'm sitting on the floor next to the dresser leaning against the wall. The carpet is old and worn and smells like hotel carpet. Cathy, who is sitting next to me, leans over toward me.

"Is this food kosher?" she whispers.

"This is the kind of thing that religious Jews eat when they travel," I say quietly. "Good stuff!" Cathy smiles, shrugs, and takes a bite of her sandwich. Actually I don't drink Cokes. I look around to see if I can spot a glass so I can pour myself some water.

Leah goes up to Shlomo. She hands him a glass of Coke with ice. I wonder where she's found the glass and the ice. Shlomo looks up, receives the glass in one hand, and with the other, reaches up to gently pull her head toward his, she bends over a little to accept the hug.

"Sweet like sugar, darlin!" Shlomo says. Leah smiles. Shlomo looks at the glass and pauses before drinking. It takes me a second to realize that he's making a blessing over the Coke. His lips are moving very slightly, and I can't hear him saying anything. If you didn't know about making blessings before you eat or drink something, you wouldn't realize what he was doing. He takes a sip, then hands the glass to someone sitting next to him on the bed.

---

* Rabbi Mordecai Yosef Leiner of Izhbitz (1800-1854), author of the *Mei HaShiloah,* was a master of the P'shyskha school of Hasidism, and one of Hasidism's most original thinkers. His great work, from which Shlomo loved to teach, has now been translated into English as *Living Waters* by Betsalel Philip Edwards.

"Listen my darling friends," Shlomo says. "I'm tired like a dog and have to take a little nap. But first let's learn something fast!" I look at my watch. It's almost 6 PM. It's been a long festival and a long day. We learn some teachings from the holy Izhbitzer with Shlomo. Then it's time to go.

I say goodbye to Shlomo.

"Top holy brother," he says, giving me a hug. "You gotta be with me at the concert in Oakland Saturday night. Bring your guitar and come up on stage with me. Okay?"

I smile. "Okay!" I have to get to my job as a cab driver at the Yellow Cab garage in San Francisco at 6 AM on Sunday morning, but how can I pass up the chance to sing on stage with Shlomo?

On Saturday night a few hundred young people show up at the Conservative synagogue in Oakland. The old men who run the place are uncomfortable with the unexpected crowd and aren't very friendly to us. The tension between the stiff congregation and the frenetic energy of the young people is striking, and the mood of the concert is strained.

Later Shlomo will speak of this night with bitterness. Everywhere he goes, he says, the so-called "Jewish establishment" complains that we are losing our young people. So what do they do when he brings hundreds of them into the synagogue? They chase them out! If we had a place of our own, thousands of kids would come. We could bring love and peace to the whole world.

After the concert we all go back to the Shattuck Hotel with Shlomo. We order lots of snacks from room service and learn until three in the morning from the holy Izhbitzer.

Two hours later I drag myself off the floor, splash some water on my face, comb my hair with my fingers, and head out to catch a bus back to San Francisco. When I get to the dispatch window of the Yellow Cab building, the dispatcher asks me why I'm late.

5

Be-In

David and Gene and I drift with the crowd on Haight Street toward Golden Gate Park.

People are pouring in from all over, all on their way to the Human Be-In. You can tell who's from Berkeley; they're the political contingent. They want to create a new kind of revolution to replace L.B.J.'s repressive war machine in Washington. They're wearing jeans, sweaters, jean jackets, work boots, clothes with dark, solid colors, the uniforms of modern day revolutionaries. My neighbors from the Haight are dressed more whimsically, in rainbows and pastels, lots of beads and colorful things strung on and dangling. We're the psychedelic contingent. We want to free the mind and usher in a new era of consciousness. The Human Be-In has been billed as a "Gathering of the Tribes," a coming together of both tribes in a common purpose and a common celebration.

David and Gene are my best friends from San Francisco State College. We're all majoring in English Literature and Creative Writing. We walk through Golden Gate Park, wind up at the Polo Field, and find a place to sit on the ground three rows back from the stage. I look around and behind us. There are rows of people sitting on the grass, row after row, covering the green lawns of the Polo Field, back into the trees that surround the field, endlessly, in all directions, as far as the eye can see. Thousands. Tens of thousands.

Allen Ginsberg is sitting cross-legged on a cushion on the stage, chanting in Sanskrit into a microphone, swaying back and forth, clanging the little finger cymbals in his hand. Timothy Leary and Richard Alpert, dressed in robes, sitting up straight and looking very solemn, are sitting behind him.

David and Gene and I chant with Allen Ginsberg. Everyone around us is chanting too. The sound extends in every direction, surrounding us, enveloping us, quickening us for the journey we're all about to take:

31

Om Sri Maitreya
*Om Sri Maitreya**

Guys in pirate and cowboy outfits are sitting on stage, pounding on drums. Girls dressed as Gypsies and Indians are playing tambourines and dancing. The drumbeats ripple through the tribes. People are walking back through the rows, handing something out. A plastic envelope gets passed along the row to the young woman sitting next to me. She's wearing a kind of Renaissance-style peasant blouse with no bra.

"What's in there?" I ask.

She looks up at me, her eyes wide. Her face looks so young. "It's the purple tabs from Owsley," she says.

I allow my eyes to connect with hers. She meets my gaze, smiles, and doesn't look away. Finally I look down at the plastic bag, take a tab and pass the bag to Gene. Leary had explained earlier that, as an offering to the Gathering of the Tribes, Owsley Stanley had made 50,000 of his finest purple LSD tabs for free distribution as a sacrament in celebration of this occasion. I swallow the tab and feel a thrill of nervousness and excitement as I prepare to step into the unknown with 50,000 of my fellow travelers.

Gene takes his tab, passes the bag to David, and looks at me with a kind of knowing smile. He's a few years older than David and me, probably in his late 20s. With his large 6' 2" frame, stooped posture, large head of short but unkempt hair, plaid flannel shirt, rimless glasses, and laconic expression, he looks strangely out of place here, as if the last Greenwich Village beatnik had been accidentally transported to the middle of Haight Street, and didn't quite know where he was. Holding his purple tab and looking around knowingly, he says, "Looks like we're in Acid City!"

I nod appreciatively.

David, short, muscular, wearing a tight t-shirt and a serious expression, looks like he had just stepped out of a college wrestling team practice and arrived in sociology class. He makes an earnest comment to Gene, who answers with a witty rejoinder.

David, Gene, and I spend many afternoons together, sitting on the campus lawn at San Francisco State College, smoking a joint, with Gene drinking strong coffee with plenty of sugar, David drinking a

---

* *Om,* auspicious Maitreya, the Buddha of the future. As far as I know, this is *not* a traditional Buddhist mantric formula.

32

coke, and me drinking carrot juice. We talk endlessly of Vietnam protests and acid rock concerts, visiting gurus and nude dance happenings, acid parties in the Haight and free concerts in the Panhandle—a block-wide, half-mile strip of grass and trees two blocks from Haight Street—with groups like Jefferson Airplane and the Grateful Dead. As the Sixties wash over us with gathering momentum, we try to understand it, to be part of it, and to ride the enormous wave.

We also talk about the young women all around us, everywhere, in this amazing early springtime of sexual liberation. We talk about the ones we desire, the ones who seem to desire us, the ones we would love to have sex with if only we could, the ones we do have sex with, and the frequent disappointments that follow.

The woman I would most love to have sex with, but who seems totally out of reach is Elizabeth, who sits in the row in front of me in Mark Blum's Humanities class. She is so beautiful and exotic. She seems part Chinese, part Polynesian, part French, and part other places in the world that I don't even know about. She is quiet, aloof, keeps to herself, slipping away after class so effortlessly that she almost seems to dissolve into the air. I have no idea what we could possibly have in common, or how to connect with her.

Sometimes I tell David and Gene about my experiences with Shlomo. Gene plays with the notion of a kind of Vedantic guru disguised as a Hasidic rabbi. David wants to know how he can reconcile being a mystic with the dualistic western notions of good and evil that Judaism embraces. If you operate within a system of right and wrong, guilt and expiation, how does that lead you to transcend the ego and arrive at cosmic consciousness?

Timothy Leary is at the mic now, exhorting us to detach ourselves from the web of mind-games imposed by the world around us. They serve only to imprison us, to tether us to the vast military-industrial complex and war machine, slaves to the lust for power and wealth that controls our leaders and our society. The imprisonment of millions of us in this maze of illusion is causing suffering and destruction all over the planet, and traps us in the endless karmic wheel of death and rebirth. With the tribes gathered here today to celebrate the sacrament of reconnecting on a cellular level with the source of all being, to set free the light of our true nature, we have the opportunity to shift the vibration of the entire planet, to realign the energy field around us.

The path is simple, says Leary:

TURN ON . . . to the field of cosmic consciousness in which we exist;

TUNE-IN . . . to the true nature of our being, of all beings on the planet;

DROP OUT . . . of the roles that support the destructive web of illusion around us.

Leary repeats the mantra again, and all of us join in:

TURN ON!
TUNE IN!
DROP OUT!

Then Richard Alpert comes to the mic to prepare us for the trip. His energy is different from Leary's—quiet, soothing, reassuring. Leary is the prophet, Alpert is the humble, radiant teacher. He reads from their book, *The Psychedelic Experience,* from the "instructions for use during a psychedelic session." Tens of thousands of us are quiet now, sitting in our concentric circles on the lawns of the Polo Field, serious, anticipating the reality-shift that is about to happen, listening. I am slowing my breathing, the way I've learned to do in meditation. Focusing inward, into the body, waiting for the inner trembling that is now familiar, waiting for the dissolving.

Allen Ginsberg comes to the mic to begin another chant. The pirates and cowboys, Gypsies and Indians follow with drums, tambourines and flutes. As the vast, concentric circles of the gathered tribes take up the melody and the rhythms, I hear the sound of drums and bells coming from many directions. I look around me but can't see any drummers. As I'm searching, I notice that the crowds are beginning to throb together in a huge dance. I feel the shaking and throbbing inside myself. My mind is racing to put together sense and sentences. I'm shakily searching for something. Then Alpert's words come back: "*Do not try to intellectualize it. Do not play games with it. Merge with it. Let it flow through you.*"

I let go and merge. The sweet ecstasy of oneness radiates in pulsating waves through all the bodies. Separation is dissolving. Separation is an illusion that we invented yesterday. Oneness is the natural state from the day before yesterday, the underlying reality, always here, always waiting to be embraced. Brothers and sisters in our thousands are dancing together, embracing each other, embracing the vast *Being* that we share in common. Tears of joy are pouring down Aryae's face. Yes, I remember. Yes, I remember this state. This is how we were born. This is how God put us into this world. Yes, I remember. This is why we're here. Fusing into the rainbow-light at the core of the energy dance.

Hands and knees of Aryae's body press against the ground. Body is trying to stand. Such great effort. The young woman with the sweet face and full breasts and no bra is on her feet dancing. She smiles down at Aryae. As the proportions of her face and body change, Aryae's face turns away. Everywhere the eyes look, beautiful women are dancing. Are they beckoning to him? What to do? Other instructions echo through the mind: *"Let go of desire. Release your attachment."*

Aryae's body is standing, joining the dance with the other bodies. The body-form is dissolving into energy. The cells and molecules are dancing in multidimensional cosmic flows. Gene's body is sitting, shoulders hunched, face toward the earth. David's body is not here.

Questions vibrate through Aryae's brain. Something wrong? Do something? *"Do not try to hold on to your old fears. Let your body merge with the warm flux."*

Undulating bodies all around are gatherings of energy, of cellular activity, many clusters in the flowing universe, like lumps in a huge bowl of oatmeal. Arms reaching upward. Smiling faces turned toward the sky. *"Do not fear the ecstasy. Do not resist the flow . . . Release your attachment . . . Let your heart burst in love for all life."* Aryae's body is merely an organ of a larger being, dancing with all the other bodies in a dance that is guided, not by Aryae's mind, but by the greater mind that guides us all. Letting go of the controls. Allowing the primal dancer to be in charge.

Faces are turning toward the sky. Aryae's face turns toward the sky too. Something is happening. Sounds of gasping. Someone is falling from the sky in a parachute. Thousands of faces turned upward. The sky-person is drifting down. Who is this person? Is this the Messiah?

The Messiah looks down at the multitude of upturned faces as he floats down gracefully from the sky. The Messiah, through 50,000 pairs of eyes, looks up at the descending body strapped to the open parachute. Who is the observer and who is the observed? They are one and the same.

The Hand of God is reaching through many worlds, many dimensions, into this world where our bodies are. The true oneness of *Being*, the ancient memory that we have known all along, is here revealed. We are at the portal in time where the infinite intersects with the finite, where the timeless and the time-bound have fused.

The sky-man comes to a landing on the iridescent green earth, a few hundred yards away. A vast sigh escapes from 50,000 pairs of human lungs. The single mind that embraces us all thinks a thought

35

that flashes through all our brains: something unique has happened here at this intersection. *"This is the beginning of a new age."* We may forget later, our words and our minds may distort this into something different, but now we are pure, now we remember.

The energy field is changing again. A human voice is vibrating. It is coming through the body of Allen Ginsberg, through the huge speakers on the lawn near the stage. Drums and other instruments blend in, sounds all dancing in harmony together.

Hari Om, Namo Shiva
*Hari Om, Namo Shiva**

The great Hindu god, Lord Shiva, is dancing. We are the body; Lord Shiva is the river, the energy-flow, the dancer within. Lord Shiva, god of destruction. The outer forms of the world, old, encrusted fossils, plastic puppets, masks covering and hiding the free-flowing source, are shattered, so that the boundless can emerge free and dance new creation into being.

Hari Om, Namo Shiva
Hari Om, Namo Shiva

Allen Ginsberg sings, the drummers drum, the dancers dance, over and over, endlessly. The cycle of rebirth and destruction and rebirth goes on and on and on. New creatures, new generations, new ages of history, new life-forms are born, throw themselves into the dance, experience their brief moment of embodiment, and dissolve back into the energy field, back to the infinite source.

Hari Om, Namo Shiva
Hari Om, Namo Shiva

As the millennia recycle through Lord Shiva's choreography, the sun is moving west across the sky, toward the sea. Aryae's body follows the sun, drifting through the sea of bodies, away from the stage and Leary and Alpert and Ginsberg, dancing with the dancers.

A beautiful woman dances in front of Aryae, smiling at him. Aryae's eyes open wide. His face smiles back. Waves of sunny pleasure are flowing. Is she human, or a trick of Lord Shiva? It hardly matters. His body moves with hers, carried on the tide of drum

---

* *Hari*, 'the remover,' refers to the Hindu deity, Vishnu, particularly in his manifestation as Krishna. *Namo Shiva* means, 'to honor Shiva,' the Hindu deity who, when juxtaposed with Vishnu, may be seen to represent dissolution. However, Shiva is perhaps most recognizable in his *Nataraja* form, being the lord of the Cosmic dance of all being.

rhythms, throbbing, building, intensifying, spinning, leaping, surging. A question is forming that as yet has no words. The mind is trying to say something. The body is giving itself over to the dance, the expression of overflowing pleasure whirling through the energy field. Her body moves with his.

He has let go; she has let go. The same dancer is dancing both bodies. Absorbing her image, his eyes see the embodiment of impossible, perfect grace, whirling before him and around him. As he looks at her eyes he feels her pleasure in seeing his grace, his strength, his vitality, his perfect execution of Lord Shiva's will. His heart is so full that tears of joy are pouring out of his eyes.

He sees her lips moving and hears sounds coming out. The sounds merge into the vibrations of the drums and tambourines. The thought is still struggling to form in his mind. She sees the question on his face.

"You're beautiful!" she says, laughing. More questions try to form in his mind. What does that mean? He smiles at her. The only way he has to respond is in the dance. His body jumps and spins around her, and she responds to his movements. They create an energy field as other bodies step back to give them room and other eyes participate in registering the awareness of impossible, perfect grace and beauty, a command performance at the throne of Lord Shiva.

"You're beautiful!" she says again. He laughs and leads her away from the circle of people to a patch of open, iridescent green field. A thought is gathering momentum in his mind. They are dancing on jewels, on diamonds, floating in clouds. The grass, the ground, the hills, the air, the sun, the sky, the earth, the flowers and birds, the sounds of drums and people, his body and her body, are all organs of the source, celebrating the awareness of its own dance of ever changing forms, of destruction and creation, of Lord Shiva's ecstatic being.

"You're Elizabeth!" he says. She explodes in laughter. Dancing through the field, they laugh and laugh together, endlessly. Radiance of a hundred suns exploding in his body. Running through the fields together. Dancing all over this small planet, this achingly beautiful world.

"You are so right!" she says.

"Elizabeth!" he says.

His brain is awash with pleasure. Their bodies, manifestations of one mind and one being, bountiful and boundary-less in their interpenetrating energies, sensuously attuned to each other beyond the outer edges of consciousness, beyond the power of words to describe, beyond mind, have no need yet for physical orgasm. Lying naked with her between her sheets, his face between her breasts, glorying in the smoothness of her skin, the softness of her hair, how she smells and how she breathes, drinking in her desire, her pleasure in his body and her own, in the sparks and fires they are generating, drinking it in like nectar from heaven.

Her bedroom, with its images of exotic birds looking out at them from the walls, lush tropical plants hanging from the ceiling, bamboo plants and bamboo curtains, candles and incense surrounding a statue of the Buddha, envelops them like warm tropical rain. The most delightful incense of all is the smell of her skin as he kisses her all over. She laughs, wrestles with him, bites him in places no one has ever bit him before, rolls on top of him as he lets her hold him against the bed, her arms straight, her back arched, her full, round breasts just above his lips, her head raised, moving from side to side so her hair brushes against his face and neck and shoulders.

As he wrestles her onto her back, she yields to his strength. As he goes inside her, the oneness has a new channel through the nerve endings connecting the bodies, Lord Shiva's dance, hearts pounding, pleasure throbbing ever more intensely, ever more endlessly, more pleasure then he thought he could endure in a lifetime, oceans of energy washing away everything in their wake, obliterating memory, obliterating the past, obliterating the future, obliterating sin and transgression, obliterating worry and fear and obligation, obliterating karma, hearts pounding faster, obliterating boundaries, no way to tell her heart from his, both felt equally, simultaneously. Their hearts are Lord Krishna's drummer, beating out the *raga* rhythm, escalating tempo, escalating intensity, faster and faster, further and further, more and more, until finally exploding, in crashing tidal waves from the seas, in cloudbursts from the sky, in volcanoes from the earth, releasing all that has held back, releasing the pleasure that answers all doubt and fills all voids, releasing the peace that passes all understanding.

The first thing I'm aware of the next morning is the smooth feel of Elizabeth's sheets. Then comes the stillness, the emptiness of realizing I'm alone. I look through the bamboo curtains hanging from the ceiling at the pictures of long-tailed birds on the walls.

Elizabeth and I had talked all night. She told me about her family and her ancestors, of people and tribes from Europe, from Asia, from the South Sea Islands. She told me about her quest to understand who she is in this world, and to express her identity through dance and art. I called her a child of the world. I told her about my Jewish ancestors, about Grandpa Max, about Israel, about King David, about my discovery of God's oneness, my insatiable desire to return, my experiences with Shlomo, my struggle to understand where I go from here. She called me a child of the sky. In our day and night together we had come to share not only our bodies, not only our passion; we had tasted together the longing and fulfillment, the past, present and future of our entire lives; we had experienced the interpenetration of our souls.

I remember her saying something about having to leave in the morning to model for an art class, so I could sleep-in as long as I wanted and let myself out.

By the time I'm out, it's late morning. Haight Street is strangely quiet. The sky is overcast; it looks like rain today or tomorrow. I find myself looking around everywhere. The buildings seem grey. It's like I'm here to find something but forget what it is. It seems inconceivable that, after what 50,000 of us experienced yesterday, the world can ever be the same again. Did we really all share the oneness?

I see a lone hippie walking toward me. He's a little taller than me, with a jean jacket and strings of brightly colored beads not only around his neck, but also around his wrists and ankles, bent over slightly, as though the beads are weighing him down.

There's no one else on the street. We stop to look at each other. "Hey man, were you there yesterday?" I say.

"Wow, man!" he says with a deep chuckle, shaking his head affirmatively. I don't have to tell him what I'm talking about; he knows. We make eye contact. Was he part of the oneness?

"What was it like for you?" I ask.

He laughs, shrugs, and puts his hand on my shoulder. "Dig it," he says. "I don't know how to talk about it. What is there to say? Maybe some things you can't talk about."

I continue west on Haight Street, toward where I live. The Psychedelic Shop is closed. The I/Thou Café is closed. The street looks so empty. What happened to the oneness? Where did it go? Was it just a dream?

I continue walking and have similar encounters with other people. Maybe some things you can't talk about. But that doesn't mean they're not real. Something really did happen yesterday, and it really did touch people. Beyond the grey buildings and the overcast sky, beyond the people I encounter on Haight Street, I can sense, almost see, the possibility of life beyond anything I ever imagined.

39

"Imagine a life where the reality you tasted yesterday becomes the normal experience of day-to-day living. It is so simple," a voice in my head is telling me. *"Your job is to return to the place of oneness, and to do it with other people. This is the purpose of your life."*

"But how am I supposed to do this?" I ask. "There won't be a Human Be-In every day. Do I go to more acid rock dances? Do I organize parties and drop acid with my friends? Do I chant *Hari Krishna* or *Hari Om, Namo Shiva* and find other people to chant with? Do I go to an *ashram* to do Yoga and meditate? Do I find more women to take acid and have sex with? Do I become a Hasid and go on the road with Shlomo?"

"If you dedicate your life to its true purpose," the voice answers, *"you will receive the guidance you need."*

After the semester is over I will lose track of Elizabeth and never see her again. One day when I'm in my 50s, I'll be returning to my office in Palo Alto from a meeting with Silicon Valley executives, listening, as I often do, to NPR on the radio. The interviewer is interviewing Elizabeth C___.* I pull my car over to the side of the road, try to calm my excitement, and listen. Elizabeth, who lives in New England, is a professor of cultural anthropology at an Ivy League university, and has just come out with her latest book. It is about how immigrants to the U.S. from different cultures, particularly tribal peoples, use visual arts, theater, dance, and music to come to terms with what it means to them to be here in this country, to be American. My eyes closed, my head leaning forward on the steering wheel, I will listen very, very closely to every nuance of her voice. Can I identify her? It's been so many years. Tears run from my eyes.

I reach the end of Haight Street and turn up the hill on Stanyan toward my apartment. I feel very alone, back in the world I've lived in all my life, the world of separateness. I want to be back in the oneness. I get out my typewriter, carefully insert two sheets of paper with carbon paper in between so I will have another copy, and write a poem for Elizabeth. Later in the day I take the poem, folded in an envelope, and walk back over to her apartment. She's not in, so I leave it in her mailbox.

The next day is Friday. I need to get away from Haight Street. I pack up some things, get in my VW bug, and drive to Forrest Knolls to spend *Shabbos* with Efraim and Leah.

---

* I have changed her name out of respect for her privacy.

6

Secret of Prayer

Santa Rosa, California – May 1967

"What is prayer?" Shlomo says. "Do we have any idea?" He jokes about how the synagogue is sometimes the place that is most empty of prayer. But the question is really a deep one: How does a finite being connect with the Infinite? Think about it; it's a mystery, a secret. It's one of those things where, if we think we know, *we don't know.*

It's *Shabbos,* and we've all gathered in a park. Last night Shlomo slept at the home of a local Jewish couple. The rest of us camped out here in tents.

Through my jeans, I can feel the rough picnic bench, still cold and damp from the thick night fog. A patch of mid-morning sunlight, breaking through the tall redwoods, has landed on the table and bench, warming the surfaces, steaming up water vapor from the wood. Other clouds of water vapor are steaming up all over the forest. The air is filled with the smell of wood drying, fresh and warm and earthy. The sun feels good.

Shlomo closes his eyes and starts to sing. Soon the rest of us are singing with him.

Before Shlomo came out this morning, Efraim and I were piecing together from our memories a story that he told late last night, about the secret of dying. It must have been around two in the morning, when almost everyone had left or fallen asleep. Efraim often asks me to do this with him when Shlomo has taught us something. This is how people study in a *yeshiva.* When friends go over what they learned together, it helps them remember and understand. It's called a *hevrusa*—a friendship-pair.

The point of the story is how we prepare to receive the deepest secrets. With some rebbes you have to prepare yourself for a long time before you're ready. With others, they can prepare you in a second.

People keep arriving and we squeeze together around the picnic table.

41

Jonathan is sitting next to Efraim.* He recently came from Winnipeg, Canada. His teacher there is Shlomo's friend, Rabbi Zalman Schachter. Jonathan met Efraim and Leah and spent *Shabbos* at their house. They invited him to stay, and he's been there ever since. He's wild, thin, unpredictable, and full of laughter, like an elf from the northern forests. And amazingly, as I look at him and Efraim sitting on the bench together, I think his hair is also red! They look like brothers.

I hear a car pull up in the parking lot and, a minute later, see someone walking toward us. It's Donna, with her long blond hair streaming behind her. Shlomo looks up and sees her.

"Darlin!" he says. "Greatest thing in the world!" He stands up to give her a hug. She walks over and hugs him. He gestures for her to sit down next to him. Looking a little embarrassed, she shakes her head, backs off, and sits down next to Jonathan.

Moishe and Maxine are also here with their son David. Karen and Chaya, looking like they just woke up, emerge from their tent and wander over.

Somehow a *siddur* (prayer book) has appeared in front of Shlomo, together with a couple of books in Hebrew that look like Hasidic teachings.

Shlomo's sitting at one end of the table and I'm sitting at the other, next to an awkward teenager with acne who fidgets a lot. I wish I were sitting next to someone else. Karen is sitting across the table, with the sun in her hair, looking radiant. I smile at her and she smiles back.

Shlomo talks about the two books he has in front of him. One of them is by Reb Nachman of Breslov; the other is by the Ishbitzer. It's such a privilege to learn from such holy teachers, he tells us. They're bringing down the light from such high places, we have no idea.

"What do we know about learning?" he says. "What do we know about wisdom? Without saying anything bad . . . Some of you are in college, right?" He flashes me a "V" and laughs. I smile and nod my head in acknowledgement. "You know, some teachers in college— What are they really teaching? If we're lucky, they know what's in the book. Maybe they read it the night before, right?" He laughs, and some of us laugh with him.

"But a real soul-teacher . . ." His eyes open wide, and he looks around at all of us. "Listen, let me tell you something very deep. I

---

* I have changed his name to protect his privacy.

42

heard this at Bobov. How do you know if someone is really your teacher? Imagine someone teaches me something I didn't know before. It may be very beautiful, it may be cute and sweet, but that person is not my teacher. But sometimes a person can teach you something, and when you hear it, you realize you knew it the whole time. *You knew it the whole time.* You just didn't know you knew it. But *mammash* (really), you knew it. According to the *heilge* (holy) Bobover Rebbe, this person is really your teacher."*

Shlomo closes his eyes and rocks back and forth. Everyone is silent. I can hear the wind blowing through the redwoods, and a couple of birds calling to each other.

"Remember we were learning last night about Reb Naftali Ropshitzer?"** Shlomo says. Efraim smiles and catches my eye. "Okay, listen to this. Two young Hasidim come to Ropshitz to learn with the Rebbe. So the older Hasidim ask them, 'Why are you here? What do you want to learn?'

"So one Hasid says, 'I want to learn *Gemorah* (Talmud) with the Rebbe; I want to learn Zohar; I want to learn all the holy books in the world.' And they say, 'Okay that's fine, you can learn with us.'

"Then they ask the other, 'What do you want to learn?' And he says, 'I want to learn how the Rebbe ties his shoes.'

"You know what this means, friends? This is a different level. It's not so hard to make a speech about love and peace in the world. I can get a little soap-box, put it on a corner on Market Street, round up a few shleppers who want to listen, and I'm in business, right? But to be real teachers to each other, to show each other a little bit how we tie our shoe, to remind each other of the holy secrets that God has placed deep in our hearts, this is the depth of Torah; this is where we are *mammash* (really), one with God's will."

When Shlomo's words stop, I can hear the sound of breathing, like all of us are breathing together.

We start the service with the section of the Psalms. This is where we begin, with the poetry and music from King David. He leads us in. Shlomo hands the prayer book to Efraim, who takes it in his hands, closes his eyes and rocks back and forth a little, and then begins singing the words in English: "The heavens will be glad and

---

* Rabbi Shlomo Halberstam of Bobov-New York (1907-2000), the 3rd Bobover Rebbe, and a direct descendant of the famous Hasidic Rebbe, Rabbi Hayyim Halberstam of Sanz.

** Rabbi Naftali Zvi Horowitz of Ropshitz (1760-1827), a disciple of the Seer of Lublin, and later the master of Rabbi Hayyim of Sanz.

the earth will rejoice and all the peoples will say, God has been king. The sea and its fullness will roar, the field and everything in it will exult. Then the trees of the forest will sing with joy before God."*

He sings in a soft deep voice, in a familiar melody he uses when he is singing the prayers. When he is done, he hands the book back to Shlomo. Shlomo holds the book and closes his eyes. The sun is shining, the birds are singing, and the world is at rest.

Efraim is the leader of our little group when Shlomo's not here. I'm second. I've been watching Shlomo very closely when he's with us. His way of bringing us together, of showing each of us our roles, is in how he acknowledges us during times of prayer and study. I wait for him to hand me the prayer book next.

Shlomo hands the prayer book to Karen. My face immediately freezes to mask my disappointment. I've come to accept that I'm number two. I know I'm not on Efraim's level. But what does *this* mean? Karen smiles and takes a deep breath. Her voice is strong and clear, a beautiful voice. "The heavens recount the glory of the Almighty, and the skies tell of the creation of His hands. Speech flows from day to day. Night to night expresses wisdom."** She uses a different melody from Efraim, simple, repetitive, passionate. While she's singing, I think about how I will sing when it's my turn. It's good that Shlomo chose her to go second. I would like to be as melodic and expressive as she is, but in my own way. When she's done, she passes the prayer book back to Shlomo and smiles at me. I smile back.

I wait for Shlomo to pass me the book. He passes it to Jonathan. Jonathan lights up with a big smile and sings with his high-pitched voice: "Our soul longed for God; He is our help and our shield. For in Him our hearts rejoice, for in His holy Name we have trusted."***

He sighs with obvious joy in praising God; his heart is warm as the sun.

I think Jonathan has just come from Canada and Shlomo wants to honor him. It's my turn next.

Shlomo tries passing the book to Donna, who shakes her head and holds up her hand, so he passes it instead to Maxine—then to Bill, to Leah, and others. I feel totally ignored. Is something the matter? Have I done something Shlomo doesn't like? I try to stay

---

* Psalms 96:11-12.

** Psalms 19:2-4.

*** Psalms 33:20-21.

44

positive, to smile at people, to follow King David's holy worlds, to stay with the spirit of prayer. But there's growing static in my head, and I'm increasingly distracted. I notice that my heart is pounding and the muscles in my neck are tight. I shouldn't be worrying about something as trivial as whether I get to read from the prayer book. But I feel like a jealous kid whose brothers and sisters are getting all the attention. What's the matter with me? Shlomo hands the book to someone else, a young woman who just arrived that I've never seen before.

I withdraw my attention and begin looking around for something, anything to distract me. I look at the teenager sitting to my left. He's thin, with his shoulders hunched and his black hair disheveled. His thick, black-rimmed glasses are the most regular feature on a face covered with acne. He seems very shy, and I haven't heard him say anything all morning. If a girl were to look at him, I'm sure he would look awkwardly away. Where did he come from? How did he get here?

Shlomo has the book again. I look at the teenager. He's all by himself. No one has noticed him all morning. If he got a chance to read, at least people would notice him. Maybe someone would talk to him. I want to embrace him like a brother. *Shlomo*, I think, *forget me. The least you can do is give the book to him.*

I look up. Shlomo catches my eye. I feel startled. I can't tell if he's smiling. It feels like he is looking into me. What is he seeing? I wonder. What is he thinking? Then he passes the book to the woman who just read, and nods in my direction. "Now it's brother Aryae's turn," he says.

I look at Shlomo without saying anything, and I read: "He will gather in the outcasts of Israel." I hear myself singing, using Karen's melody. "He is the Healer of the broken-hearted, and the One who binds up their sorrows, who encourages the humble."*

In the days and weeks and years that follow, I will keep going back to this moment. It will take me a while to understand what happened. Shlomo prepared me. He did it by surrounding me with stories and teachings that opened my heart to learn what I already knew. He did it by showing me how he ties his shoes. Then in one infinite moment he taught me the secret of prayer.**

---

* Psalms 147:2-3.

** Bill and Karen in this chapter are not actual names. Karen is a composite of two young women I knew from that time.

7
Choice

The sky radiates in deepening colors onto the world around us, illuminating the open, rolling hills bounded by the redwood forest. June in California has been transforming these green hillsides into golden shades of tan.

It's late Friday afternoon, almost *Shabbos*. Efraim and Jonathan and I are on the deck of Efraim and Leah's tiny one-bedroom house, watching. Twilight is softening the world's hard edges, replacing the sky's simple blueness with complex rainbow hues, carrying the sounds of crickets and birds on fragrant air. Jonathan looks in every direction with a big smile. Efraim's eyes are shining with delight. He's dressed like Shlomo, wearing a white shirt, dark pants and sandals, with *tzitzit* (ritual white fringes) hanging out of his shirt.

Leah and some of the friends who have already arrived come out to join us on the deck.

Efraim closes his eyes, concentrating intensely, rocking back and forth. In a soft, husky voice that echoes with overtones of our ancestors from distant times and places, he begins to sing. It's a Hasidic melody that has become familiar to me now, the one we sing here at sunset on Friday to bring in *Shabbos*. I join in. The melody is simple, repetitive, meditative, in a minor key. The first two melody lines stay low. The second two lines soar high. This repeats in an endless cycle. The others start singing also, entering into the orbit of the melody.

The melody becomes a mantra, affecting me like the mantras of Allen Ginsberg and Richard Alpert at the Be-In, only this one goes deeper into my soul. We all have our arms around each other, feeling the closeness, the contact, the oneness of our bodies, our hearts, our souls. Efraim is standing slightly apart, looking thin and frail, his frame a little bent, an unlikely magician unleashing vast forces whose power we cannot fathom. He seems in a trance, dancing to the rhythms of music coming from beyond this world.

We all go inside. Leah has set the *Shabbos* candles on the long table covered with a white tablecloth. She stands in front of the candles with a box of wooden kitchen matches in her hands. Karen and Shirley and Doree are standing close to her. The house is very still.

We all gather around the table with our arms around each other. Leah opens her eyes, strikes a match, lights the two tall white candles, and sets the match in a little dish nearby, where it keeps burning. Shlomo had taught her that once the candles are lit, *Shabbos* has begun. On *Shabbos* we don't light or extinguish fire, so she is letting the match burn out on its own. She circles her hands three times to gather the light, and brings the light to her face, to her eyes. The rest of us do the same. Then she leads us in the blessing (in Hebrew): "Blessed are You, God, ruler of the world, who makes us holy with your *mitzvot* (spiritual practices) and gives us the *mitzvah* of lighting the candle of *Shabbos*." No one says anything. We are all looking at the light. The room is filled with peace.

Karen, standing next to Leah, is holding Uri, who has just woken up from his nap. He's a little over a year old now, developing his own personality, curious, outgoing, very comfortable around people. His eyes are wide open, and he is looking at the people gathered around the candles. The flickering flames are making shadows dance on the walls. He looks at the shadows with great interest, then he reaches toward Leah. Karen hands him to her.

Efraim walks to a spot near the big window. The rest of us follow. The sky is spread out in all its glory with the deepening rainbow hues of late twilight settling into night.

Efraim has a *siddur*. He sings some of the prayers.

500 years ago, in the northern hills of Israel, high above the desert plains in the village of S'fat, lived a special group of kabbalists. On Fridays, in the late afternoon, they used to dance in the fields to greet the 'Shabbos Bride.' She is the feminine aspect of God, the Queen, who dwells with us here in this world. Although Her presence is mostly hidden in the Torah, the Prophets, the Psalms, and the other books of the Hebrew Bible, She is revealed in the Zohar (the Book of Splendor), the mystic text of the kabbalists. When She dwells in this world and God the King is dwelling remotely in heaven, there is a great disconnect that results in evil and pain and suffering. When the King and Queen reunite in pleasure and delight, the world is suffused with joy and light and love. Shlomo has taught that this is the level of *Shabbos*. When we dance with the Shabbos Bride, it is as though we are dancing at the wedding of the King and Queen, and are bringing about the union of all worlds. The holiest thing for a

human bride and groom on *Shabbos,* no matter how long they have been married, is to cause great joy in heaven through the joy of their love-making.

We sing Shlomo's melodies, the ones he has composed for the prayer of greeting the Bride. He has written more melodies for this than for any other prayer. Following Efraim's lead, we dance around the room in circles with great exuberance, celebrating Her arrival.

I notice that the door has opened and a young woman is standing in the doorway, looking hesitant. I pull myself out of the circle and walk over to her. She is looking at the room, filled with people dancing and singing by candlelight. Her eyes are open wide and she is looking around in amazement. I try to imagine what this would look like to someone just walking in for the first time.

"Good *Shabbos!"* I say to her. She smiles, turning her face up toward me. I give her a hug, the way Shlomo does when he greets a new person in the room. "Welcome!" She looks very happy to be here. I ask her how she found us. She tells me that she met some people on Haight Street who told her about this place. Her name is Phyllis.

It's hard to talk over the singing. I invite her in. After watching for a minute or two, she joins in the dancing.

Later we're gathered around the big table where the candles are burning. We have just blessed the wine and bread. We've passed around slices of *hallah,* which we're eating. Food is spread out on the table in front of us. Although it's late and we haven't eaten for a while, no one reaches for a plate.

Jonathan is standing in front of the table next to Efraim, his red hair shining in the candlelight. "Does anyone know the secret of heaven and hell?" he asks. His eyes open wide, dramatically. We all look at him. No one says anything.

Jonathan tells a story which he heard from Zalman in Winnipeg. A man dies and they take him first to hell, then to heaven. To his surprise, they look exactly the same. In both hell and heaven, people are gathered around a great banquet table piled high with delicious food. But they can't eat, because their arms are tied to poles and they can't bend their elbows.

Across the table, Phyllis is watching Jonathan, her eyes wide open. "Heaven and hell are the same," he says. "Their arms are tied to poles and no one can feed themselves!" He holds his arm stiff, to demonstrate. No one makes a sound.

Jonathan pauses, then reaches over to a bowl of strawberries on the table, picks one up with his stiff arm, and reaches across the table toward Phyllis.

"The only difference is, in heaven they're feeding each other!" With a big smile he feeds Phyllis the strawberry. She closes her eyes and takes it into her mouth. As if we had all been holding our breath, we let out a collective sigh. People start taking food from the table and feeding each other, and that's how we eat the entire meal. Later I see Jonathan and Phyllis sitting on the floor in the corner, talking quietly.

The next day Jonathan and I walk along a hiking trail that passes by Efraim and Leah's house and leads up the northeastern slope of Mount Tamalpais.

"How did you find this trail?" I ask.

"Well," he says, "I've been living here a couple of months now, and Efraim likes to take me to his favorite *mikveh* (ritual bath)!"

We get to a place where the stream widens and a wooden bridge crosses over it. Jonathan takes off his clothes quickly and tosses them on the bank. I follow, slowly, uncertainly, carefully folding my clothes and laying them on some ferns. Jonathan is standing knee deep in the rushing stream. I gingerly put a foot in. The water is freezing. I quickly pull it out.

I hear a splash and look up. Jonathan has gone to the center of the stream, near the bridge, and immersed himself totally in the freezing water. Soon his head emerges, but the rest of him doesn't. His hair has turned dark red, stringing down his face. He must be sitting somehow on the bottom of the stream. He's squinting up at me.

"Come on Aryae," he says. "Don't think. Just do it!"

I jump in. The pain of the intense cold slams into me like a freight train. I pop my head out of the water and breathe fast. Then numbness sets in and I'm okay. We sit there on the stones on the bottom of the stream, only our heads above the water, looking up through the tall redwoods at patches of blue sky. The wind above us is moving the upper branches of the trees back and forth. I think about the rebbes and Hasidim in Russia 100 years ago who used to go to the *mikveh* through the ice that covered the streams in the winter.

"Wow," I say, "those guys back in Russia were really on to something."

Jonathan looks at me and smiles. "You betchya," he says. We sit there listening to the stream. The world is alive and clean and beautiful.

The next morning Efraim and I are sitting on the deck in front of his house. The chairs are big old wooden outdoor chairs, the kind with armrests and long, straight backs that end on top with a kind of fan or seashell shape, with most of the white paint worn off by years of exposure, exposing the weathered, gray wood underneath.

Most of the *Shabbos* guests have gone. Efraim is telling me about Shlomo's plans to be in Mexico City this summer. He and Leah want to drive down to be with Shlomo. "How about you and Ruthie?" he says. "Why don't we all drive down together?"

Ruthie has just come out to California and moved in with me in my apartment near Haight Street. It's been a big change and we're both trying to adjust. Maybe a trip like this would be good for us. Maybe it would bring us closer together.

Efraim says something about this trip being in the year 5727. I ask him what he means. He says that's how old the world is.

"Oh you mean like on the Hebrew calendar?" I say.

"Yeah. That's how long ago God created the world."

"You don't mean that literally?"

Efraim laughs. "How else should I mean it? God tells us in the Torah that He created the world in seven days. And the rabbis in the Talmud have shown us, based on the Torah itself, when that creation was."

I look at him incredulously. "Efraim," I say, "Come on—you can't believe that! We're not living in the Middle Ages. This is 1967!"

"I know all that," he says. He smiles, strokes his beard and rocks back and forth a little. "Shlomo told us that Reb Nachman says there are two kinds of truth. There is truth on the level of the day, which is everything we know. That's the truth of science and everything that's already been written in books. And then there's truth on the level of the night, which is everything we don't know. Imagine everything we don't know, discoveries that science will make in 100 years; things that people will be talking about in 1,000 years; the things going on in other galaxies. That's the night truth," he says. "Compare that to the knowledge we've got in our heads. Which do you think is greater?"*

I watch Efraim. He's saying this so lightly and so seriously at the same time, with such simplicity and peace. I look over at the house. I can hear talking. Jonathan and Phyllis emerge. It looks like they're going for a walk. Efraim and I wave to them.

"Shlomo says that *emunah*, which is usually translated as 'faith,' is really the night truth," Efraim says. "I've got to believe something, right? The question is, where is my *emunah*? What is the truth that sustains my life? Is it the latest scientific theory? Is that what keeps me alive? Is it Karl Marx? Is it Timothy Leary?" He looks at me knowingly, laughing.

Leah has emerged from the house holding Uri. She sees that we're talking, so she stands back to give us our space. Efraim catches her eye and smiles.

"You know, it's not up to me to presume to tell someone else what to believe, where to put their *emunah*. I only know what I believe. I believe there is one God who created heaven and earth, 5,727 years ago. Shlomo says the reason why we're here is to let the world know that there's one God, and to bring *Shabbos* to the world. I believe we're here to do that."

Leah has set Uri on the ground. Uri reaches his arms out toward Efraim, takes a couple of wobbly steps, then falls. Leah claps her hands in excitement. "He's walking!" she says.

Efraim gets up out of the chair and goes over to Uri. "No-o-o!" he says with a big smile. "Are you walking?" Leah lifts Uri so he's standing up, and he takes another couple of steps toward Efraim before falling again. Efraim and Leah laugh with delight.

Efraim goes off with Leah and Uri. I stay in the big wooden chair looking out over the valley of pastureland in front of me, and the redwood forest beyond. I live in a world that is five billion years old. Efraim and Shlomo live in a world that was created in seven days and is 5,727 years old.

My world, living near Haight Street at the beginning of the Summer of Love, is rich and wonderful, but so complicated. Everything is open ended. There's school, there's the war, there's the anti-war movement, there's earning a living, and questions about the direction of my career. There's my relationship with Ruthie: is it a

---

* Rabbi Nachman of Breslov (1772-1810), great-grandson of the Ba'al Shem Tov, and the founder of the Breslov school of Hasidism.

marriage or isn't it? Nothing is settled. Then there are the events rapidly unfolding around me as Haight Street prepares for the Summer of Love. So many people arriving every day, so many new spiritual teachers 'setting up shop,' so many new musicians and rock concerts, so many psychedelic posters going up proclaiming new events, 'happenings,' truths, so many parties, so many possibilities, so many choices.

Efraim and Shlomo's world is simpler. God is one. God sent us here to proclaim His oneness through our lives. We're here to bring *Shabbos* to the world.

I see an image of two doors in front of me. The first door says, "5,000,000,000 Years." That's the world I'm already living in, busy, noisy, chaotic, the world of endless choices and possibilities. The second door says, "5,727 Years." That's the world of total commitment to a single choice. It's a mythical world, a world of miracles, where every person, every gesture, every leaf, is connected by deep secrets in the plan for redemption.

Standing in front of these doors, I feel like a magician. "*You can choose,*" says the voice in my head. By choosing which door to walk through, I can be a partner with God in creating reality. "*This is the deepest secret of all.*"

Before I leave, Leah takes me aside and tells me that Efraim's birthday is in July. Jonathan and Phyllis have fallen in love, and will become inseparable. Ruthie and I will decide to go to Mexico with Efraim and Leah. I'll write a poem for Efraim for his birthday.

8

Summer of Love: Mexico

On the Road to Mexico City — July 1967

I slow down the VW bug carrying me, Ruthie, Efraim, Leah, Uri, and all our stuff on the 3,000 mile journey to Mexico City. We've come to a little village consisting of a plaza with a cathedral on one side and low buildings on the other three. I drive around the plaza. It's raining lightly, but the wind is blowing hard.

We can't see any people. The sun has set and it's getting dark. The only sign of life is light coming from the windows of a single building across from the cathedral. I pull up in front of the building, near a couple of funky old cars. It looks like a *taqueria,* a small burrito and taco restaurant of some kind. With the engine still on, I turn around and look at my companions.

"What do you think?" I say. "Dinner?"

"*Barukh HaShem* (praise God)," says Efraim, smiling.

"*Barukh HaShem!*" echoes Leah.

I turn off the engine, and one by one, we extricate ourselves from the little car. My muscles are stiff and sore. Ruthie and Leah are both dressed in layers, wrapped in colorful and light, summery shawls. Ruthie has brightly colored clips in her hair, and large earrings with colored glass beads. Efraim and I are both wearing *kippot* on our heads, mine is made out of natural lamb's wool spun and knitted by Ruthie, and Efraim's is black with a silver filigree design from the Middle East. Efraim has *tzitzit,* ritual fringes that look like long strings hanging from his waist. We're all wearing strings of beads around our necks.

Ruthie helps Leah gather up Uri's things. I open the hood at the front of the car and Efraim gets out his guitar. After hesitating a moment, I get mine out as well. I wouldn't have the nerve to do this on my own, but Efraim is fearless and wants to sing everywhere. As long has he starts the song, I'll follow and back him up. The rain is starting to soak into us. We head for the door.

55

As we walk inside, we enter a room filled with a couple of dozen people, dimly lit by three small light bulbs, covered by paper lanterns, hanging from the ceiling. In one corner, several old men with guitars and an accordion are singing. The room is smoky with the smells of tobacco and meat, frijoles and chili. Groups of men, and some families, are sitting around small tables talking and eating, while women are walking in and out of the kitchen doorway to the rear. There are several small children standing nearby watching them. A couple of the children spot us near the front entrance. They whisper to each other and point. Soon everyone is looking at us. The music and conversation stop; the room is silent.

We stand there awkwardly, trapped by the uncomprehending stares of the brown faces around us. No one moves or says a word. I glance over at Efraim, but he too seems frozen. I notice a little girl holding on to her mother's skirt looking up at me. I smile at her. She moves closer to her mother's leg and holds on tighter.

Then suddenly, amazingly, in swift succession, as if to underscore our appearance as visitors from another world, the two small darkened windows turn white with lightning that flashes into the room, thunder explodes so loud that it rattles the dishes on the shelves and the tables, and shakes the floor we're standing on. The three light bulbs go out, leaving the room in total darkness.

For one unfathomable moment, the darkness is silent. Then I hear the sound of feet scraping against the tile floor, followed by candles emerging from the kitchen in the hands of women and girls. Suddenly people are moving in all directions, and everyone is talking at once. The room is filled with the dim glow of candlelight.

Two women and a girl come up to Leah, who is still holding Uri, and say something in Spanish. I can make out the word *"bebé."** Leah, looking at the younger of the two women with recognition and understanding, nods enthusiastically.

"Bebé," she says smiling, holding out Uri for their inspection.

"Bebé!" The younger woman—barely older than a girl, with long black hair tied together in a red bow and bare feet—smiles back at Leah knowingly, reaches out and takes the baby. Uri looks around with curiosity. The older woman bends over, touches Uri, and makes baby sounds. Several other women come over to have a look. Soon they're talking to Leah, who nods and looks over to Efraim to translate. Efraim smiles uncertainly, leans forward and tries to

---

* In my memory, the woman said, *"bambino."* But as this an Italian word, only rarely used in Spanish, I have used the more common, *bebé.*

understand what they're saying. Ruthie looks on, excited and delighted.

The older woman says something to a girl, who looks up at us shyly and leads us to a table in the corner. As we sit and everyone gets used to the candlelight, the restaurant returns to normal. A young man, the waiter, comes to take our order. We try to explain that we would like our food with no meat. He finds this incomprehensible, and goes to get one of the older women for help. Efraim goes over to the other corner to talk to the old men who were playing guitar and accordion. They come back with him.

"What's going on?" I say.

Efraim says in Spanish that these men are *"mis amigos,"* his friends, and he introduces them to us. I stand up to shake their hands. One, apparently the leader, is heavy-set, wearing a black shirt with silver embroidery and a sombrero, decorated *mariachi* style. The other men are older, thinner, with dusty looking khaki shirts. Efraim goes over to where he has set down his guitar case, and gets out his guitar. I get mine out too. The men pull up chairs and sit down. We tune our guitars to theirs. Efraim says something to them about what we'll be playing, and they talk among each other. Starting off in E minor in 3/4 time, Efraim smiles at me. This is his Spanish translation of a song that Shlomo wrote last summer—"Because of My Brothers and Friends." Like many of his songs, it comes from the Psalms.* We sing:

> Porque de mis hermanos y amigos,
> Porque de mis hermanos y amigos,
> Por favor, permítame a preguntar,
> Por favor permítame a cantar,
> Paz a ti.
>
> Esta es la casa, la casa de Dios,
> Quiero lo mejor por ti.

Once they hear it the first time, the musicians understand the song, and back us confidently. The sound is solid, like a professional Hasidic *mariachi* band. The people in the restaurant have gathered around. Someone starts playing a tambourine. Soon everyone is singing with us.

We repeat the melody and the words, over and over and over. The candle flames are dancing. Their light reflects off the faces

---

* "For the sake of my brothers and friends, I ask peace for you; for the sake of the house of the LORD, our God, I wish the best for you." (Psalms 122:8-9)

surrounding us, the children and the women and the men, eyes wide open, everyone singing together. I've never seen these people before. I know nothing about their lives, and they know nothing about mine. *But here is something we all know and feel and share.* I can see tears in the eyes of several of the women. There are tears in my eyes too.

Mexico City, Mexico – July 1967

The city is a blurred collage, like a gigantic pile of brightly colored swatches of cloth and glass beads. People of every description are mixed together in crowds on the sweltering streets: impeccably dressed, light-skinned businessmen in summer suits; smartly dressed young women who work in offices; dark skinned Indians – men, women and children in colorful clothes with burros and carts; priests and nuns; *mariachis* with *sombreros* and guitars; soldiers and policemen; and tourists from all over the world. The little street *mercados* (markets) everywhere, colorful with summer fruits and vegetables, hand made clothing, rugs, and jewelry. Crowds, traffic, heat, noise, and smog.

We find Shlomo where he's staying, at a tall, elegant luxury hotel near the center of town. He introduces us to a short, thin man in his 40s dressed in a stylish Italian suit. "This is my holy friend, Moishele," he says. "He's business manager for humble me here in Mexico." Moishele – looking very distinguished and a little mischievous in his mustache and head of tight black curls just starting to grey – smiles and bows.

Moishele has set up a week-long gig for the famous rabbi at La Taberna, the hotel's featured nightclub. The terms of the contract include rooms for Ruthie and me, as well as for Efraim, Leah, and Uri. We feel well taken care of.

We spend *Shabbos* and a long weekend with some well-to-do people Shlomo knows in one of Mexico's oldest and largest Jewish congregations. These Jews are prosperous, well educated, integrated into the cosmopolitan culture of Mexico City. They are warm and friendly to us, excited to have the famous *rabino* in their midst. Shlomo accepts invitations to meals at beautiful homes, and we go with him everywhere. He plays at a number of synagogues, with Efraim and me on-stage accompanying him, and Ruthie with us, dramatically displaying the colorful Indian clothes that she's bought at the *mercado*, playing tambourine.

Each night at La Taberna, Efraim and I get on stage with Shlomo for two sets. This sophisticated club with its darkened room and polished, elegant furnishings, crowded with well-dressed people standing at the bar and sitting at tables, is an incongruous setting for Shlomo and his message of holy beggars who bring love and peace to the world. But the famous rabbi and international folk star is a big hit. People seem genuinely moved, and Shlomo's enjoying the attention.

One night after the second set, Shlomo wanders outside the club onto the street. Efraim and I go with him. The warm night outside feels wide open after the close, smoky confines of La Taberna. The streets are almost empty, except for a storefront across the street, with bright lights and people.

"What's over there?" Shlomo asks. Efraim and I don't know. "Let's go see." Shlomo starts walking and we follow. When we get there, we walk in and discover a juice bar, like juice bars we've seen all over Mexico. It has big electric juicers and piles of apples, oranges, carrots, celery, bananas, strawberries, pineapples, all kinds of colorful fruits and vegetables, and a couple of guys with white aprons and big knives standing behind the long counter, chopping away and blending up large glasses of fresh juice on demand. What's different about this place is the clientele. There are groups of attractive young women with short skirts, well-dressed couples, businessmen, and various assorted lone night people just hanging out. The room is lit by bright florescent lights, which, together with the clientele, give it the look of a soda fountain on Broadway late at night after the theaters have emptied.

We walk up to the counter. Shlomo is fascinated by the possibilities of so many kinds of fresh juices. One of the guys in the white aprons asks what we want. Efraim goes for fresh apple juice. I choose carrot. Shlomo can't make up his mind. He has learned a few words of Spanish since he's been here, which he tries out on the guy behind the counter to ask him questions. Efraim helps translate. Shlomo wants to know if he can have more than one kind of fruit in his juice. Maybe he can mix two or three. The guy smiles and points to the sign behind him. It says *Jugo de Siete Frutas* (Seven Fruit Juice). Shlomo is thrilled. He orders a large *jugo de siete frutas*.

We sit at the counter drinking our juices, all of us wearing our *kippot*, the Singing Rabbi, single, in his early 40s, and his two Hasidim, married, in our mid-20s. Three of the young women in short skirts approach us. They are all attractive and dressed provocatively. One of them, a little taller than the others, with long, auburn hair, addresses us in halting, nervous English. Efraim smiles and answers her in Spanish, saying something like, "How are you, my sisters?" The woman seems a little disconcerted, and glances at her companions for reassurance. She wants to know if we would like to come with them to a party. Efraim translates.

59

Shlomo says, "Yeah?" He looks up at the three of them. "What's going on at the party?" Efraim and I look at each other.

"Shlomo, I think these women are prostitutes," I say.

Shlomo's eyes widen. He looks concerned. "Really?" he says. "How could they be prostitutes, God forbid? They look so young and sweet." He looks up again at the tall woman. "What's your name darling?" he says to her. "Why don't you and your friends sit here with us and join us." She sits at the counter and tells Shlomo her name. Her companions also sit. Shlomo offers to buy them *jugos di siete frutas*. Two of them accept. Soon we're all talking, in a combination of bad Spanish, bad English and lots of gestures. Shlomo wants to know where they're from and all about their families. They are curious about who we are and where we come from. One of them points to Efraim's *kippah* and the *tzitzit* that hang from his waist. She wants to know why we're all dressed like that.

"That's my religion," Efraim says in Spanish.

"Your religion?" she answers incredulously. In spite of her efforts to control herself and look sophisticated, she breaks out giggling, and her companions join her. How could strings hanging out of a man's shirt be his religion? Efraim tries to explain, but his Spanish is not up to it, and they look puzzled. He smiles and shrugs and conversation continues in good spirits. A couple of older women dressed similarly wander over and join in. They are curious about Shlomo and want to know where he's from, where he's traveled, what he does, and where he's going next. We try to explain. There are more funny moments filled with crazy misunderstandings, and we all laugh a lot.

As we're walking back to the hotel, Shlomo says, "You know, it's really sad. Why do they have to do this, *nebbukh?*"

"Maybe their families are poor and they need the money," I say. "Maybe they don't see any other way."

Shlomo quickly turns to me. "What kind of parents sell their daughter into slavery?" he says, his eyes flashing with anger. "Why do they have to settle for so little? Inside their souls are *mammash* (really) shining! These girls need someone to open the gates for them, to show them what's possible in their lives!"

For the next several evenings, after his sets at La Taberna, Shlomo regularly goes across the street for *jugo di siete frutas*. Each time he walks in, the prostitutes gather to greet him. He gets to know most of them by name. There is a lot of laughing and joking. They seem to relax in his presence. Here is a strange foreign man of God who is also an international star, who doesn't judge them, doesn't want anything from them, who genuinely likes them, who accepts them as sisters.

One night at the juice bar, sitting next to Shlomo, I glance over at him. Just for a moment he's not talking to anyone, just staring ahead. Even though we're surrounded by people, and even though Shlomo *always* seems to be surrounded by people, I get the strangest feeling that he is completely alone.

Ultimately maybe we are all alone. Shlomo seems driven to reach out to people who like him, underneath all the outside appearances, are lonely. As fellow human beings huddled together in a big city in the middle of the night, all of us here in the juice bar, free of our normal roles and social identities, with no appearances to keep up and nothing to prove, are all the same. We can share these few moments, just being together, to warm ourselves in the glow of our common humanity. This is what Shlomo does. This is what he's giving these young women. This is what he gives everyone.

One night on our way back from the juice bar, Shlomo pauses outside the entrance to the hotel lobby. No one's on the street. He strokes his beard, rocking back and forth. Something's on his mind. Efraim and I stand there with him.

"You know my manager, Moishele?" Shlomo says. Efraim and I nod. "You know, maybe he means well. I don't know, I hate to say bad things, but between you and me, he's the biggest thief in the world!" I ask him what he means. He says that Moishele isn't paying him what he promised. The thought of someone stealing from Shlomo seems incomprehensible.

"Why don't you talk to him?" I say. "You can confront him. Efraim and I can be there with you."

Shlomo shakes his head. "I already did," he says. "You know, it was the craziest thing. Moishele actually apologized to me for stealing from me. Can you believe this? He wants me to forgive him!" Moishele has a wife and children to support and has been falling behind on his bills. He has pleaded with Shlomo not to embarrass him by telling his friends that he has been stealing from Shlomo.

"Moishele the *Ganev* (thief)," Efraim says, laughing.

"This is a good manager!" Shlomo laughs too.

Shlomo is torn between feeling bad about having his money stolen, and feeling bad about Moishele's plight. Moishele promises Shlomo that he will pay him back everything he owes him as soon as he can. Shlomo decides to accept this without further protest.

61

Following Shlomo's wishes, Efraim and I don't say anything to Moishele.

On a warm Tuesday morning, Efraim, Leah, Uri, Ruthie and I check out of the hotel, pile into the VW and start our trip back to San Francisco. Shlomo, who wants to be there for the Summer of Love, is going to join us in a few weeks.

On the way north, in the mountains, we pass through the little town of San Miguel de Allende, where we stop to visit Ruthie's friend Mellie, who lives there together with her husband Martin and their young son Joshua. Mellie and Martin are followers of the Sikh *guru* Kirpal Singh, and are planning to drive up to San Francisco in a couple of weeks to spend time with his followers. Ruthie is intrigued, and invites them to stay with us. Efraim and Leah also invite them to stay with them.

We continue north. After we cross the border back into the States, I turn on the radio and we hear a new song at the top of the pop charts. The words are:

> If you're going to San Francisco
> Be sure to wear some flowers in your hair;
> If you're going to San Francisco
> You're gonna meet some gentle people there.
>
> All across the nation, such a strange vibration,
> People in motion,
> There's a whole generation, with a new explanation,
> People in motion, people in motion.*

I listen with mixed emotions. On the one hand, it's exciting that the rest of the country is catching on to the awakening that we've been living through in San Francisco. On the other hand, there's something here that I don't trust. It's too simple, too slick. I'm put off by the whole "flower children" image. Tens of thousands of young people are coming to San Francisco to be part of the Summer of Love. What are they drawn by? Is it 'sex, drugs, and rock and roll,' or is it something more? Whatever it is, I get the uneasy feeling that older people are already hovering around, observing the endless stream of young innocents, thinking about dollars and market share, looking for ways to cash-in.

---

* Scott Makenzie's 60's anthem, *San Francisco*.

Shlomo says that young people today are like holy beggars, ready, hungry like no generation before, to turn over the whole world, to bring the great day of love and peace. We can't just stand by and abandon them to every newly minted *guru* and drug dealer on the planet. We can't waste this opportunity. We have to reach out to them.

9

Summer of Love: San Francisco

San Francisco, California – August 1967

Shlomo, Efraim and Leah and Uri, Martin and Mellie and Joshua, and I are on Haight Street. So is everyone else, it seems, wearing every outfit imaginable. It feels like we're part of a great parade, an endless celebration where everyone is competing to see who can be the most "psychedelic," the most outrageous. Colors, shapes, sounds, all swirling around us like a giant kaleidoscope.

Ruthie is at a dance class. Leah, who has been working hard to unpack and trying to create some order in their new home, decided at the last minute that she would gather up Uri and his things and join Efraim for a walk with Shlomo on Haight Street. "Home" changed for Efraim and Leah as soon as we got back from Mexico, when they discovered that the landlord had sold their house in Forrest Knolls while they were away. People in town told them about another house that was available in nearby Lagunitas. Shirley and Doree, and other people who live nearby who have been spending *Shabboses* with them, helped them move. Word spread, and by the following *Shabbos,* we were all gathering at their new house. Anyone else I know would have been totally overwhelmed by all this. Leah sighed, smiled, and said it was "such a blessing to have all these holy angels" joining them for *Shabbos.* Mellie and Martin and Joshua are staying with them for a few days, helping them unpack.

Buses are lined up on the crowded, narrow street. Each time one reaches a street corner and opens its doors, kids come pouring out from the Midwest, the East Coast, the South, the Southwest, the Northwest, their faces full of excitement and curiosity and a little nervousness. They've come in tie-dyed shirts, fancy hats, bells and beads, fully clothed for the role of instant hippie.

I've never seen Shlomo so focused on meeting people. He plunges into the crowds, greeting the kids, talking to them, asking them questions, hugging them. As a bearded rabbi wearing strings of love beads, he looks right at home here, another wild and crazy

65

Haight Street character. He looks like he's having a great time. The rest of us, including Joshua who is sitting on Martin's shoulders, and Uri who is sitting on Efraim's, tag along and follow him as best we can.

Every once in a while Shlomo brings someone, or several people to meet us. Although we've never met before, we all hug like long lost brothers and sisters. He gives everyone his business card, urges them to call him, invites them to come for *Shabbos* at Efraim and Leah's.

I'm a little concerned for Efraim and Leah. "Shlomo," I say, "they've just moved into a new house; they're still unpacking, and it's really a tiny house. What are they going to do when all these people show up?"

Martin and Mellie agree. "It's a lot," Martin says with quiet seriousness.

Efraim quickly jumps in, shaking his head. "No, honestly, it's not a problem for us. Our living room is actually bigger than the Forrest Knolls house, and there's plenty of room for people to sleep out on the deck."

"Such holy angels," Leah adds. "We really want them to come. It's a blessing for us."

Shlomo puts one arm around Efraim and one arm around Leah. Uri, still sitting on Efraim's shoulder, leans forward reaches out to grab Shlomo's *kippah*. Efraim reaches up to steady him. "Holy Efraimele and Leah," Shlomo says smiling, with great affection, *"mammash*, sweetest of the sweet." Uri has pushed his *kippah* to one side. Leah reaches up to straighten it out.

Shlomo lets go of Efraim and Leah and steps back so he can see all of us. "But you know, brother Aryae is right. We can't put it all on Efraim and Leah. Simple as it is, we *mammash* need a house of our own." This is the first time I've heard him talk about a house. He calls it, the House of Love and Prayer. We're all very excited to hear him talk like this. We ask him to say more. He talks about the hundreds and thousands of young people we see swirling around us.

"How many Jewish kids are coming to Haight Street?" he says, looking around. "You know, this is *mammash* the holiest generation of young people! Their souls are so deep. They're ready to connect with God and the whole world in the strongest way."

Shlomo tells us about the time he and Zalman met with the old Lubavitcher Rebbe 18 years ago. The Rebbe believed that the souls of the six million who died in the Holocaust are coming back as the generation of young people today.

"So why are they here in San Francisco? Because they know, they *know*, something special is going on here. Something they could never find in the Jewish world of their parents. It's the saddest thing. When one of these kids walks into a synagogue, he's all alone. No one gives him a hug. No one notices; no one cares. So the kids all walk away. Then the so-called Jewish establishment complains, 'What's the matter with young people today? Why don't they come to synagogue?'

"You know, I hate to say bad things, but the synagogues today are empty. Sadly, they're not only empty when no one's there; but they're really empty when they're full!" He laughs, and Efraim and I laugh with him, knowingly. We were *bar-mitzvah*-ed in those synagogues. Shlomo says they're empty of love, empty of holiness, empty even of real prayer.

We're standing on the corner of Cole and Haight Street. The apartment where Ruthie and I live is up the hill, just a few blocks away. The crowds keep swirling around us. Sounds of excited talking everywhere, buses on the street, a Jefferson Airplane song blaring out of someone's window, conga drumming somewhere in the background. The marijuana smell from joints held only half-concealed in the cupped hands of scraggly bearded young men and bra-less young women drifting past us, mixes with the smell of grilled meat drifting our way in little white clouds of smoke from a cafe across the street. A tall thin guy with a long, ratty looking brown beard and a dark tie-dyed t-shirt saunters by, offering us free copies of the *Haight-Ashbury Oracle*. Martin accepts one; the rest of us smile, shake our heads and decline.

I ask Shlomo to say more about the House of Love and Prayer. He says it would be a place for all the holy beggars of the world, for all the young people who are hungry for a world of love and peace, who are hungry for a true friend, who are hungry for the Great *Shabbos*.

"Would it just be for Jews?" I ask.

"Can you imagine?" Shlomo says. "Let's say we put a little policeman at the front door who would say to everyone, 'Are you Jewish?' How many Jews do you think would show up?"

We all laugh. "I wouldn't!" Mellie says.

"Let's put it this way," Shlomo continues. "Do you know who stood at Mount Sinai? According to the Midrash, there were more non-Jews than Jews. Did you know that? Every holy beggar in the world, every little person who was hungry for God's presence, joined

67

us and stood with us at Mount Sinai to receive the Torah, to receive the deepest secrets of the world.

"What I say is, the House of Love and Prayer is a home for everyone who stood at Mount Sinai, whose souls are crying for God's presence, who are searching on the deepest level to find their brothers and sisters, who are ready to turn over the world."

Shlomo's face lights up, the way it does when he's just created a new song. "Here's the whole thing," he says, "simple as it is. The House of Love and Prayer is a place where, when you walk in, someone loves you, and when you walk out, someone misses you."

We all take that in. For me, these words from Shlomo will guide me in the years ahead. When things get confused, I will remember. This is what I, and all of us are here to do.

The crowds keep surging by. The boys are tired. I give Leah the key to my place, so she and Mellie can take them for a nap. Martin goes with them. Shlomo wants to stay on Haight Street. Efraim and I stay with him.

Shlomo scans the crowds. Suddenly his eyes widen in recognition. "Marsha! Rachael!"* he calls out. Two teenage girls walking toward us stop and do a 'double take.'

"Shlomo! Is that you?" says one of them. They stand there with their mouths open, amazed. They look very young, no more than 16. They are carrying back packs, and look tired. "Shlomo, how can you remember us? There were so many kids there, and you were giving so many concerts!" says the other. They both take off their backpacks and give Shlomo a hug. He hugs them back.

"Darlin' how can I not remember you?" he says. "Efraim and Aryae, I want you to meet the top holy girls in the world!" He introduces them to us. "I met Marsha and Rachael at a concert I was giving at a synagogue in New York last year for Hanukah."

Efraim smiles and gives them each a hug. I dutifully do the same.

"I hate to say bad things," Shlomo says, "but when I walked into this synagogue, it was really a bad scene. I've seen more joy at funerals than there was at this Hanukah party!" Shlomo laughs. The girls smile and roll their eyes in agreement. Shlomo asks them what they're doing here. They say they took a Greyhound bus across the country from New York. He asks them if their parents know where they are. They look at each other, and then say "No," they haven't told them. Their parents wouldn't understand. Shlomo asks them to

---

* I do not recall their actual names.

promise him that they'll call their parents and tell them they're okay. That's a hard one for them. Shlomo asks again, and they agree.

"So where are you staying tonight?" Shlomo asks them.

Marsha looks out at the crowds on Haight Street. "We'll be fine, Shlomo," she says. "There are so many beautiful people here. We'll just hang out and meet people and find a place to crash," she says, using the word "crash" a little self-consciously. Rachael smiles and nods. They both look very trusting. They believe in the Summer of Love, in the Flower Children, in the New Age of Aquarius. They are now part of it. But I also detect a little nervousness in Rachael. And I've been starting to hear stories in the neighborhood about young girls from out of town getting taken advantage of by older guys on the street, drug dealers. I look at Shlomo, wondering what he'll do.

Shlomo puts a hand on Marsha's shoulder, and on Rachael's. "Okay," he says, "I've got to tell you something very important. It says in the *Gemorah* that a Jew needs to have privacy when he sleeps." Efraim looks at him with a smile. "No seriously," Shlomo says to him, "it *mammash* says that." He turns back to the girls. "I want you to promise me that you'll find a hotel room to sleep in tonight."

"Shlomo, we don't have enough money for hotels!" says Marsha.

"Darlin'," says Shlomo, "we're not gonna let a little thing like money stand in the way of you doing a *mitzvah!*" He fumbles around in various pockets of his jacket until he finds a checkbook. He writes her a check. Looking over his shoulder, I can see that it's for $200. That's a lot of money in 1967. He gives Marsha the check. "I want you to promise me you'll stay in a comfortable place for the next couple of nights, okay?"

The girls are very excited. "Thanks Shlomo!" they both say.

"One more thing," Shlomo says. "You gotta spend *Shabbos* at Efraim and Leah's with Efraimele and Aryae and all the top holy people in San Francisco. It's the most, most special in the world." Rachael looks us over. If we looked like Orthodox Jews from New York, she wouldn't come within a mile. But it's obvious to her that we're part of the San Francisco scene, so we're okay. Efraim writes his phone number for them on the back of one of Shlomo's cards. Marsha is excited. She thanks him and says they're gonna come. They say goodbye and disappear into the crowd.

Shlomo and Efraim and I continue walking on Haight Street. Shlomo talks some more about having a house. We need it for these girls, and for all the young people like them who are coming to San Francisco. I ask him when he thinks we can do it. He says if the synagogues and the Jewish Federation and the rest of the Jewish establishment had even a clue about what is going on and could help us financially, we could start tomorrow.

I ask Shlomo if he really believes that the souls of the young people today are the souls of the six million coming back. He sighs, lifts up his hands, and looks up toward the sky. "What do we know?" he says. "What do we know?"

Suddenly he stops walking and brings his hand to his forehead. *"Oy vey! oy vey!"* he says.

"What's the matter Shlomo?" Efraim asks.

"You know the checking account I used to write the check for the girls?" he says.

"Yeah," we say.

"Nebbukh, I forgot. I gave it all away yesterday. It's empty!"

For a moment the three of us look at each other, our minds racing, worrying about the girls. Then Efraim smiles. Shlomo shrugs. We all laugh. What can you do? They're in God's hands now.

Later we walk up the hill to my apartment. Ruthie has returned, and has been showing Leah and Mellie some macrobiotic recipes. She wants everyone to stay for dinner. Efraim and Leah need to get back home, so Martin and Mellie have to leave with them. They'll come back and stay with us next week and take Ruthie to meditate with the local Kirpal Singh *satsang* group.*

Shlomo accepts Ruthie's invitation to have dinner with us. We sit on cushions on the floor the way Ruthie and I always do. For dinner we have miso soup, followed by brown rice with pickled daikon and nituke vegetables rolled up in roasted nori seaweed. This is all strange for Shlomo, who is used to eating traditional kosher meals, and is not used to sitting on the floor.

He handles the whole thing with tremendous good cheer, and keeps reassuring Ruthie that her food is "the most delicious in the world." They also talk a little Hebrew together, which makes me feel good.

The following *Shabbos,* Marsha and Rachael show up at Efraim and Leah's. They tell us how, after they had left us on Haight Street, a couple of older guys wanted them to come up to their hotel room. At first they didn't know what to say, but then they remembered Shlomo's check, so they said they were staying at a hotel downtown,

---

* Sant Kirpal Singh (1894-1974) was a Punjabi Sikh spiritual teacher. *Satsang* is Sanskrit for a "truth-gathering."

and kept walking. Later they found a group of young people their own age who were renting a large four-bedroom apartment on Clayton Street two blocks from Haight. The girls decided to move in with them.

10

House

Lagunitas, California – December 1967

"Leah and Uri and I are going to Israel," Efraim says. It's the last hour of *Shabbos* on a short afternoon in what passes for winter in the Bay Area. The sky is overcast and the air is starting to chill. We're sitting on the steps in front of his house in Lagunitas.

"Really?" I say. He looks at me with a little smile and nods. "Why?"

"HaShem (God) is calling us there," he says simply.

For a while I don't say anything. Finally I ask, "What are you going to do there?"

Efraim laughs. He talks about the longing he and Leah have been feeling to go to the Holy Land. They've been talking about it ever since we got back from Mexico. The Land is God's gift to the Jewish people. Our rabbis teach that the Jewish people, the Torah, and the Land are one. In order to be fully who we are meant to be in this world, we have to be connected to the Land.

As he talks, I have the feeling of being abandoned. "But what about everyone who's been coming to your house every week for *Shabbos?* What happens to *Shabbos?*" I ask.

Efraim laughs and puts his arm around my shoulders. "Holy brother," he says, "*Shabbos* is still *Shabbos!* Now it's your turn to lead."

"I can't lead!" I say. The thought of leading *Shabbos* services every week is terrifying.

"Yes you can." He tells me he's talked to Shirley, and that she and Doree have offered to host. Their house, in nearby Fairfax, is bigger and easier to get to, and people can stay there more comfortably. Shirley and Doree are Christian, from the Midwest. We're all amazed that they've been hanging out with us for this long. Efraim has been

73

teaching Shirley how to read the prayers in Hebrew from the prayer book, and she is learning fast.

"But what about the House of Love and Prayer?" I say. Shlomo has told us that he wants Efraim, Leah, Ruthie, and me to live in the House. As two married couples, we would be the anchor, the foundation. We would be there to run the place and welcome people.

"Shlomo has been talking about the House for half a year now." Efraim sighs and shakes his head. "Leah and I have been waiting and waiting but nothing's happening."

"Don't you believe that Shlomo is going to start the House?" I ask.

Efraim sighs again. "I don't know. It's in *HaShem*'s hands. In the meantime, I'm dreaming every night about being in Israel. So we've actually been making all the arrangements, and with *HaShem*'s help, we'll be leaving soon."

I look away from Efraim and scan the little patch of forest clearing in front of us. We sit there listening to the stream. Before I leave to go home, Efraim gives me a poem that he wrote for my birthday.

Los Angeles, California – March 1968

It's Sunday morning and I'm the only one at the pool. It's large, with curves, in a courtyard surrounded on three sides by the buildings of the hotel. I'm sitting at a round, glass table, watching the ripples in the water.

Last night there was a big concert in L.A. A group of us drove down from the Bay Area to be with Shlomo for *Shabbos* and join him at the concert. It was great. The house was full and the audience enthusiastic. Several of us were on stage with him, together with a handful of kids he had just met in L.A. Anyone who had a guitar, drum, tambourine, or even clarinet and said they could play it, Shlomo invited on stage. He especially wanted people to sing harmony with him. "Give me harmony!" he said.

I took my place with my guitar, standing just behind Shlomo, to his right. From there I can see every move he makes, and feel his energy. I've learned the chords that go with all his songs. I've been absorbing his sense of timing, the way he starts a song slowly and gradually allows it to get faster. At a certain point he will take his hands off the guitar and start clapping, and soon, everyone is dancing. I've learned to anticipate these points and when they come, I step up closer to the mic with my guitar to fill the sound gap left by his guitar dropping out. When he starts playing again, I step back.

I'm continually amazed at his ability to read and work the energy of a group of people, no matter how small or large. He's like a magician. The tools of his trade are his voice, his guitar, the vast wealth of stories and teachings that flow through him, the young people on stage that surround him, and the incredible sensitivity of his heart.

Toward the end of the concert, Shlomo talked about his dream of starting a House of Love and Prayer. "There are a lot of crazy things going on in the world right now, the war in Vietnam, the conflict in the Middle East, race riots, killing. In the meantime we hope to have a little house for the children of tomorrow, where we can *mammash* turn over the world." He hoped everyone would come to San Francisco to join us when we do.

I've heard this so many times now and still nothing is happening. It's hard to keep believing. I was on stage standing next to him, so I focused on keeping my face expressionless.

John comes over to the pool and sits down next to me. He has short blond hair, wears rimless glasses, dresses conservatively, and has a clean-cut, studious look. A divinity student at a Presbyterian seminary, John has been hanging out with us because he feels that Shlomo is truly a man of God, and he wants to learn by being with him. He's gone with us to several concerts now, and sometimes comes for *Shabbos*. It's fun to have him with us. He's very positive, and picks up the Jewish teachings quickly.

"What a great concert!" John says brightly.

"Yeah," I say, "it really was." We sit there, looking at the water. "But you know, I'm really starting to feel depressed."

"Why?" says John.

"Shlomo keeps talking about the House, but there's no House." Jonathan and Phyllis are in Winnipeg, Canada with Zalman. They're now using their Hebrew names, Yonatan and Ahouva, which Shlomo gave them. Next week they're getting married, with Zalman and Shlomo performing the wedding. Efraim and Leah are there too, and Martin and Mellie are on their way. "Everybody's leaving!" I say. "So here we are in California, with me leading *Shabbos* at Shirley and Doree's, waiting, hoping that maybe one day Shlomo will start the House."

75

John looks at me, his blue eyes wide open through his glasses. He nods sympathetically.

I'm on track to graduate in three months with my BA in Creative Writing and English Literature from San Francisco State College. What do I do then? Do I look for a job on a newspaper or magazine? Do I apply to graduate school? Will the draft catch up with me, and if they do, am I prepared to spend five years in prison? And how does the House of Love and Prayer fit in to all this?

"Maybe it's not his job," John says.

"What do you mean?"

"Shlomo travels all over the world and gives concerts. Maybe it's not his job to start the House of Love and Prayer."

I look at John, almost afraid to ask the next question. "Whose job is it?"

John looks very calm and composed, his blue eyes peering straight at me through the rimless glasses. "Maybe it's your job."

I look away from John and watch the ripples in the water. One of the hotel employees, a young Mexican guy, has come out and is wiping off tables on the other side of the pool. "How can I start a House of Love and Prayer?" I say. "I don't have any money."

John hesitates only a few seconds. "I've got some money," he says.

"What?"

"It's my life savings. It's not much, but I want to help. It's yours."

I don't know what to say. "John, you're still a student, like me. And you're not even Jewish. Why do you want to do this?"

He smiles and leans forward. "Look Aryae," he says. "The money from my scholarship and my parents is really enough to cover everything I need. What I've been learning from Shlomo, and also from you and your friends, is giving me something I can take with me my whole life. I'm really grateful to be able to help." I look at him. He smiles and nods. The young Mexican guy, still cleaning the tables, is working his way toward us.

"How much is your life savings?" I ask John.

"$350," he says. I nod silently. We both sit there in silence for a while, watching the ripples in the pool.

Later that day, in the hotel lobby, I say goodbye to Shlomo. He's on his way out to Donna's rented car, which is waiting at the curb in

76

the big, horseshoe-shaped driveway at the main entrance. She'll be taking him to the airport. I see her sitting on the front fender. Shlomo is going back to New York to spend a day with his mother before he heads back out to Winnipeg for Yonatan and Ahouva's wedding. I want to talk to him about the House. Is he planning to do anything? Is John right; is it really my job to start it?

"Holy brother Aryae," he says. "You're going to have a *Seder* (Passover ritual dinner), yeah?"

I tell him we're going to have a *Seder* next month at Shirley and Doree's. We expect about 20 people. I'll be leading it.

"Shirley and Doree, sweet like sugar!" he says. I tell him I've never led a *Seder* before and don't know what I'm doing. We look up and see Donna walking toward us. "Listen," he says, "I really gotta go. Call me, okay? We can learn on the phone a little, the way I was learning with Efraimele."

After he leaves I realize that he's only going to be in New York for one day. After that I have no way to reach him.

San Francisco, California – April 1968

When we get back to the Bay Area, John mails me a check for $350. Ruthie is unhappy about the whole idea. She likes our apartment near Haight Street. There's plenty of room, and we're up on the hill so we've got a great view of everything. She's set up the kitchen so it works well for macrobiotic cooking, and she's got a corner of the large living room to do her weaving. But most important is her privacy and quiet. She doesn't want to live with other people. Since Mellie took her to meet the people in the San Francisco *satsang* group, she's been meditating every day and going to *satsang* every Sunday. Although she likes Shlomo and Efraim and Leah, the whole thing isn't her scene. How can she live in a House of Love and Prayer when she's not a follower of Shlomo and doesn't want to be there?

As I'm writing this 40 years later, I ask myself how I could have done this to her. How would our lives have been different if I had taken her well-being, and our relationship, more seriously? Would our marriage have worked; would it have lasted? There is nothing to say in my defense. I was on fire to carry out Shlomo's dream.

On Sunday, while Ruthie's at *satsang*, I put my checkbook in my pocket and walk down toward Haight Street. The neighborhood is quiet, sleeping-off Saturday night's revelries. There's a real estate office near the corner of Stanyan and Fredrick. I don't know anything about it except that it's the closest one.

Inside a man in his 60s is sitting at a desk. The three other desks are empty. Each has a black dial telephone and stacks of papers. It strikes me that there are no psychedelic posters on the walls, only black and white photos of Victorian houses. This must be the only place in the Haight with no posters. It looks like it's from another era.

The realtor has white hair and rimless glasses. He is very polite. In an odd way, he strikes me as an older version of John. "What can I do for you?" he asks.

"I'm looking for a house to rent," I say. He asks me what kind. I haven't thought much about what I'm looking for, so I make it up as I go. I'd like a large living room suitable for many guests, a large kitchen, a large dining room, and as many bedrooms as possible. He looks at me without saying anything. Then he looks through his file. Each paper is a one-page form with checkmarks and handwriting. He stops at one and smiles.

"Here we are," he says. "This may be what you want." We drive over in his new Lincoln. He tells me the history of the house we're going to see. It was owned by two sisters who lived together in it most of their lives. They were immaculate housekeepers. The elder of the two, who outlived her sister by 18 months, recently passed away at age 93. The executor for the estate has asked the realtor to rent out the house until they decide what to do with it.

When we get there, on Arguello Boulevard, I'm stunned. This is a much fancier house than I had imagined. Although the street has four lanes and is a main thoroughfare, the neighborhood is surprisingly quiet. The house is three stories high. Its front windows curve outward in quintessential San Francisco fashion. I later learn that this particular style is correctly called not Victorian but Georgian. Temple Emmanuel, the big Reform temple whose members are said to include San Francisco's wealthiest Jewish families, is a block and a half away.

What I notice first inside are the floors: hardwood, shiny, immaculately maintained. High ceilings, surrounded by carved trim where they meet the walls, give the rooms a look of spacious elegance. When I step into the large front room, with its built-in bookshelves and large curved windows opening out onto the street, I immediately know—this is the prayer room. There are three bedrooms on the second floor, with a large attic above. There is even a large basement below the first floor and a spacious yard in the back. We go out to take a look. I can imagine many people hanging out there, having lunch on a warm *Shabbos* afternoon.

As we walk back in through the kitchen, I notice a calendar on the wall. Most of the days have entries, appointments and to-do items, in sharp pencil, with neat but slightly shaky letters. Reminders to go shopping, pay the bills, go to the doctor. The very last entry is an appointment with the hairdresser.

I'm very excited but try not to show it. I'm sure it will be too expensive. The realtor and I stand outside the front entrance, with the door still open. "What do you think?" he says.

"I like it," I say, trying not to sound too eager. "How much is it?"

"Let's see," he says, looking at the paper he has brought with him. He looks back up at me. "The rent will be $300 a month. In addition there's a $50 security deposit."

I look back at him for a moment and take a deep breath. "I'll take it," I say.

After I write out the check for John's $350, my checking account goes back to its original balance of $63. I have no idea where next month's rent is coming from, but there's a whole month to figure that out.

That night I return to the house. I tell Ruthie I want to sleep there, just to try it, and ask her if she wants to join me. She doesn't. The PG&E electricity hasn't been turned on yet, so I bring a couple of flashlights and some candles, together with my sleeping bag, pillow and guitar, toothbrush, toothpaste, a small bottle of Dr. Bronner's peppermint soap, towel and toilet paper. I lay out the sleeping bag in the large front bedroom. It slides easily along the cool, shiny floor. I light a candle and stick it on a small plate I've found. Before lying down I get out the guitar and sing some Shlomo songs. Then I fall asleep easily.

My eyes pop open in the middle of the night. Something's happening. The room is dark and silent. I have that feeling of being in a nightmare, the kind where you're trying to wake up but can't. Then I see it, a faint light in front of me, like the pale luminescence of fireflies. It takes me a few seconds to recognize its shape — a frail old woman. She seems unhappy, as if she doesn't like having an intruder on her territory. I sit up and feel myself to check if I'm awake. She hovers in front of me and doesn't back off. I close my eyes and say the *Shema*. This is our holiest prayer, which we say every morning and every night, to affirm God's oneness. A religious Jew tries to have this prayer on his or her lips at the moment of death: *Shema Yisrael, Adonai Eloheinu, Adonai Ehad*. I repeat it over and over. When I open my eyes, she's gone. I turn on my flashlight, get up, and walk out of the room into the second floor hallway. There's no one else in the house but

79

me. Maybe this was the last of the two sisters. Maybe she doesn't like me being here in her house, the house she lived in all her life.

The next morning I take my guitar, go into each room, sing, and say the *Shema*. I'm doing this to claim the territory, to sanctify the space. I also want to make peace with the old woman. I hope she will forgive me for being here and give me her permission to stay.

Later that day I manage to reach Shlomo by phone and tell him about the house. He is so excited. He'll see if Donna can arrange a concert in San Francisco after Pesah for next month. One way or another he'll be out here soon. He'll call Zalman and ask him to spend a *Shabbos* with us. He'll also invite a couple of other rabbis who are on our wavelength. Mostly, he'll let everyone at his concerts all over the world know that we're waiting to welcome them at the House of Love and Prayer in San Francisco.

"What about Efraim and Leah?" I say. "They're already in New Jersey with plane tickets to leave for Israel right after Pesah!" Shlomo says he'll talk to them. I can't imagine running the House by myself.

By early May I've persuaded Ruthie to move in with me. I say she can have the little bedroom in the back on the second floor as her private space for meditation, yoga, and weaving, and there's even a little room off the main kitchen that she can use as a separate, macrobiotic kitchen. This helps.

The following week Efraim, Leah, and Uri, with a pile of trunks and boxes filled with all their belongings, arrive at the House of Love and Prayer.

11

Jellybeans

Half Moon Bay, California – December 1991

I ask the kids to help me set up the hanukiahs, the Hanukah candle holders. Each of them has a little one and I have a big one. "Are you ready for a party?" I say.

"Let's light the candles!" they say. Noe, age 11, is jumping up and down and smiling, looking younger than her age. Her straight, long blond hair bounces as she jumps. Adam, age 6, is running around the living room. His curly brown hair is tousled and his cheeks are red.

It's Friday, December 6th, the day after my 48th birthday. I'm getting ready for a business trip to the East Coast. I have to make arrangements for where I'm going to live when I get back. I've found an apartment not far from my house, but still have to get approval from the landlord and iron-out the lease details. My plane leaves tomorrow.

Back East, in-between a week of business meetings, I'll be visiting people who know me going way back, from before I met Lane. First I'll visit my ex-wife Ruthie on Staten Island. We've stayed in touch and are still friends. Then I'll visit my cousins Judy and Joyce in New Jersey, and my childhood friend Andy in New York State. I want them to care about me. I want them to hug me and tell me that I'm still loveable, that I'm still a good person.

Most of all, what I really want, if I can find him, if he's in town, if he wants me there, is to spend *Shabbos* with Shlomo. I haven't seen him in over 10 years, and I need him now.

There was so much to do at work to get ready for my trip. On the way home I stopped off at Stanford Shopping Center, which was crowded with Christmas shoppers. It was hard to find a parking place and hard to get quickly from store to store. Everyone seemed tense and hurried. Little presents are what I always get the kids, one for each night of Hanukah. I've already given them presents for the first four nights. Somehow I got it together and found presents for the last four. My favorites, from the Nature Company, are a pair of

Laserdiscs. They are metal tops in the shape of a disc. When you spin them on a table, they make beautiful rainbow colored dancing lights.

When I got home, Lane didn't say anything to me. Until now our house has been vegetarian. She announced this week that, now that I've agreed to move out, she's going to start cooking and eating meat again. The unfamiliar smell from the kitchen makes me feel like I'm no longer home. This will be my last night sleeping here.

I'm president of the Education Foundation, and we're holding our big annual fund raising gala tonight. I have to leave for the gala at 7:30.

With some prodding Noe, with help from Adam, sets up the candles in their little metal hanukiahs and my big wooden *hanukiah*, while I rush to hide the presents and get dressed. The kids are wild and it's hard to get them to settle down. Noe has a hard time setting up the candles and gets frustrated.

We light the candles and say the blessings: then we sing "Rock of Ages" in English and Hebrew. The kids find their Laserdiscs quickly, and really like them. Noe runs to get a magic marker and writes her name on the bottom of hers. They watch the dancing rainbow lights with great excitement as they spin the Laserdiscs, over and over and over. I tell them I have to leave—it's already past 7:30. They'll have to play *dreidel* by themselves. They say, "Okay." They are concentrating on the rainbow lights.

House of Love and Prayer — December 1968

"By the big *Hasidishe* rebbes," Shlomo says, "the greatest thing in the world is to make wicks for the Hanukah lights." It's late afternoon before the first night of Hanukah. We're sitting around the big table in the dining room, across from the prayer room. A dozen of us are around the table, and another eight or ten people are on metal chairs between the table and the cabinets across the room. A few more are sitting on the floor, leaning against the cabinets.

On the table are shot glasses, dozens of them, and blue boxes of cotton, the kind you get at the drug store. At the other end are a couple of large bottles of olive oil. I watch Chaya open a box. She does it very carefully, slowly pulling out the paper roll from inside, gingerly pulling back the blue paper and removing the fluffy white cotton. She lays it on top of a little pile of cotton rolls near the shot glasses. Shlomo is also watching her. He sees me looking at him and suddenly flashes me a smile. "Chayale's the sweetest!" he says.

The late afternoon light is glowing in from the dining room windows. It makes Efraim's red beard and *peyos* look even redder. He's sitting directly across the table from Shlomo, facing the window. I'm sitting next to Shlomo, on his left, facing the room. It's starting to get dark inside but no one wants to break the mood by switching on the ceiling lights. In a couple of hours, when it's time to light the candles, other people will come to be with us, lots of them. I don't know how they'll find out. We haven't done any publicity. But when Shlomo's here, it always seems to happen. All of us sitting around the table can feel it. For now, we're enjoying the quiet, the sweetness of this special time together. No one is saying anything. I can hear people breathing. Time is moving so slowly, or maybe not at all.

Shlomo picks up one of the cotton rolls, tears off a piece of cotton, and rolls it into a wick. I'm surprised at how quick and expert his hands are at this task. Soon he has a small pile of wicks in front of him. One by one, the rest of us at the table start doing the same. I feel the soft cotton in my hands. My wick is bulging in the middle. I try to even it out, to make it straight. My hands feel clumsy. Efraim seems to have gotten the hang of it, and soon has as many wicks as Shlomo.

"By Lubavitch," Shlomo says, "the wick is the symbol of the body, and the oil is the symbol of the soul. Everybody knows that eight days is the symbol of infinity. The whole thing of Hanukah is the holiness of this one drop of oil. We each have it, one drop of pure, holy oil.

"You know, the first two Hebrew letters of Hanukah are *hes* and *nun*, which stand for *hinukh*, education. How does the world say we should educate our children? Children, what do they know, right? So in kindergarten, we give them some toys to play with, and in first grade we teach them the ABCs, and in 2nd grade, maybe we teach them the multiplication tables. Then by the time they get to graduate school, if we haven't already turned them off to everything, maybe we can start to talk about what really matters, about the meaning of life, about what they're here in this world to do, right?

"Let me ask you something else. How do you teach Einstein's theory of Relativity? Hardest thing in the world, right? I remember I sat in a class at Columbia University, where a distinguished professor gave a lecture on the theory of Relativity. It was so complicated, I hate to say it, but I couldn't understand what he was talking about." He laughs. "There was another professor sitting next to me. After the class he says to me, 'You know, once I was privileged to hear Professor Einstein himself teaching Relativity to a class of 2nd graders. And you know what? They understood it!'

"So you know, my darling friends, you know how deep this is?" He closes his eyes and rocks back and forth, like he's davening. Then he stops and looks around at us. "It means that someone who really knows, like Einstein, knows with a different kind of knowing. He sees how a child has the vessels, and he knows how to give him the whole thing."

The room is very quiet. I look across the table. Efraim has his eyes closed. Leah is on the stairs, holding Uri, looking at Efraim and Shlomo.

"After the Holy Temple was desecrated, people said, 'Why bother?' Right? There's not enough oil." Suddenly Shlomo looks up. His eyes quickly scan the room, taking in everyone. He smiles at Leah. "Okay my friends, listen with your heart. You know what our problem is? We underestimate ourselves. We underestimate our children. I look at myself, I look at them, and I say, 'How long can this drop last? How far can it go?' The miracle of Hanukah is, just light it. Just light the light, and with this one drop, you can go forever."

Half Moon Bay, California – December 1991

It's Saturday, almost 10:00, and I have to leave soon. I go over my checklist and finish packing. I include my little *hanukiah* so I can light candles on the road, and look for my box of candles. The kids offer to give me their candles. I tell them they don't have to; I'll find mine. If we all light our candles for the next four nights, the lights will connect us to each other.

Lane has gone off to buy a Christmas tree. This year, since I'm moving out of the house, she's getting one a week earlier than she usually does. On Christmas Eve she'll have some of her friends over with their kids. They'll prepare traditional Norwegian Christmas dishes while they send all the kids out to play. When the kids come back, they'll discover the presents that Santa has left for them under the tree.

Noe and Adam are waiting to play *dreidel*. I ask them if they'll help me carry my bags out to the car. Noe protests. She asks me why we can't play *dreidel* first. Then she agrees to help. Adam doesn't want to.

The next thing I know, they're fighting. Adam is sitting on top of Noe's lion. She asks him to get off and he doesn't. They yell at each other and hit each other. Noe runs off to her room screaming. I hug

Adam. "Goodbye dude," I say. "I don't think this *dreidel* game is going to work. I have to say goodbye now."

"Dad!" Adam says, "I want to play *dreidel!*

I hear Noe crying in her room. "I don't think I can do it," I say. "I have to say goodbye to you, and then to Noe."

Suddenly Noe comes running out. "Let's play *dreidel!*" she says. She is no longer crying.

"Okay," I say. The clock strikes 10:00.

We go over to the table. The kids have set up the dreidels and the jellybeans. 10 jelly beans each. Adam has won three of the last four nights. I've won once. Noe hasn't won yet.

"Let's go!" I say.

"Dad!" Noe says, "Do you know what happened to your big *hanukiah* last night?"

I look up at it. It's big and funky, fragile and beautiful. It has redwood blocks, with copper pipes that run horizontally and hold it all together. Some of the blocks are charred, black from candle flames, and most are coated with years of candle wax only partially scraped off. Many years ago, before Noe was born, I had a woodworking shop and made it. It was very special, beautiful, with clear redwood and gleaming, shining copper. Lane and I set it in the corner window of our large Victorian apartment in San Francisco, lit the candles together, and watched them shine out to the world. You could look up and see them from the street below. We had big dreams about the future. We were going to bring our family backgrounds together, with all the diverse values and traditions from each. We would create a new family that was flexible and accepting enough to encompass them both. We would raise our kids to know the traditions of both their mother and father, and empower them to make their own choices in life. They would be citizens of the world.

"Dad," Noe is saying, "the *shammas* (middle candle) caught the *hanukiah* on fire last night! It's all dry and black!" I look at it. It had caught on fire two other times this week. "Mom says we can't use it anymore!" she adds.

"She's right," I say, "I guess this is the last time."

"Let's get a new one for your new place!" she says.

"Okay," I say softly. "And when I get back, I want you guys to help me get other stuff for my new place too. Okay?"

85

"I want to help you get a new TV!" Adam says. Noe looks at me to see my response, then she looks at him and giggles.

We put in our jellybeans and spin the *dreidel*. One bean each into the kitty each time we spin. Adam loses all his jellybeans. I watch him carefully. On the first night when he lost, he went into a temper tantrum. This time he takes the whole thing very calmly. Noe doesn't notice that he's lost. I feel proud of him. Adam and I are rooting for Noe. She wins. She had promised that she would divide up the jellybeans if she won. I had promised the same and, with a little prodding from me, Adam had also.

I round up my stuff and get ready to go. "Here are your jellybeans Dad!" they both call out.

I look at the three piles of jellybeans on the table. My pile is bigger than each of theirs. "Come on guys," I say, "you gave me too much!"

"No Dad, that's okay," says Noe.

"Yeah, come on Dad, take them!" says Adam.

"How come you're giving me so many?" I say.

"There's 14," Noe says, "two for each day you're gone. Take them with you, okay?"

I get a baggie to put them in.

The kids talk about how they want to use their Hanukah money from Grandpa Sam and Grandma Flo. They debate pooling their money to buy a Super Nintendo. Adam decides he'll get some new games for his current Nintendo, and Noe decides she'll save her money for rollerblades. Then they start getting wild and silly again. They run into Adam's room, fire up Super Mario III on the Nintendo, and turn up the volume. I give them each a hug and go.

Later, when I'm on the plane, I pull out my baggie and look at the jellybeans. I think about the money that I'll be spending on this business trip during the next week. I'm very tuned into the flow of money. Lane and I are both aware of how tight our budgets will be, and how drastically our lives will change, and the kids' lives will change, starting in January. The life of our family – the only life Noe and Adam have ever known, is over. No one knows how to bring it back.

On this business trip I'll be living on an expense account, staying at expensive hotels and eating at expensive restaurants. Noe and Adam will be living in a world that is much simpler, much more circumscribed. I could buy an extra thousand jellybeans and not even notice it on my expense report. For them, those 14 jellybeans are scarce, special and precious. It's a gift so unexpected, so infinite, right from children's hearts, right from the pure drop of oil in their souls. Shlomo would understand. I feel pain in my heart and love so intense I don't know what to do except cry.

A voice inside me is saying, *"What happened?"* What happened to my family, and what happened to me? It's *Shabbos* and here I am, totally ignoring everything, traveling on a plane. Once I was Shlomo's person in charge at the House of Love and Prayer, teaching Torah, leading *Shabbos* for hundreds of people every week. My whole life was dedicated to bringing the Great Shabbos, the great day of love and peace, to the world. Then I was a successful Silicon Valley businessman, husband, father, prominent local citizen, living with my beautiful wife and wonderful children in our home near the sea. *"What happened?"* I think back to Paris, to my first acid trip 26 years ago, to the plastic puppets. I've just lost my plastic puppet, and I don't know who's inside.

I get a crazy image of walking off the plane in New York, leaving all my stuff at the airport, taking the 14 jellybeans, and walking off into the distance.

I have to find Shlomo.

12

The Trap

Broadway is a kaleidoscope of colors and lights and movement in all directions, with the chill and excitement of late Friday afternoon in December, the energy of New York. The wind gets colder as the light of the sky dims. Traffic rushes in the street and people rush on the sidewalks: Puerto Ricans, African-Americans, Chinese, Russians. Winter coats of every possible shape, size, and color. I also begin to notice some Jews. Mostly men in black felt hats and long black coats, rushing to get to their synagogues before sunset.

I'm walking north toward 79th Street, toward Shlomo's *shul*. Miraculously, I actually got him on the phone between my business meetings a couple of days ago. He said he would be here for Shabbos and really wanted to see me. Come spend Shabbos with him, he said, and we'll have time to talk. I found a small hotel just a few blocks away.

I've decided to wear my *kippah* while I'm walking, rather than put it on when I get to the *shul*. I don't know why; maybe I want to pass for Orthodox. I'm wearing the most conservative *kippah* I own. It's black felt, trimmed with a silver and gold band. Not exactly New York Orthodox. Maybe San Francisco Orthodox. Why do I want to pass for Orthodox? I don't have an answer.

The *shul* is between Amsterdam and West End Avenue, right where I remember it. I stand at the entrance and look up. It says Kehilath Jacob, "Congregation of Jacob," unchanged from when Shlomo's father was rabbi here. Now it's called the Carlebach Shul. I remember visiting Shlomo here in the late '60s, shortly after his father died. His mother had hovered around him protectively. "You hippies don't care about Shlomo," she told me in her German-Yiddish accent. "He has so much to do. He has his father's *shul* here to take care of. But you don't care about that. You just want him out there in San Francisco for yourselves. If you weren't so selfish and really loved Shlomo, you'd leave him alone."

Inside the *shul* I find myself a seat near the platform, the *bimah*, on the left side. The women's section is on the right. Although I know this *shul* is Orthodox and has a *mehitza*, separating the men and the women, I've never davened this way with Shlomo, especially in his own *shul*. It's a little jarring.

I turn around and watch people walk in. I'm amazed at the variety of costumes. Young men in black coats, obviously *yeshiva* students. Young women and men in their 20s, wearing hippie garb similar to what my friends and I wore half a lifetime ago. Middle aged New York modern Orthodox men in grey business suits, a few Hasidim with brown fur hats, older women with dark scarves over their heads, younger women with colorful scarves or stylishly tailored suits.

Everyone seems comfortable with each other. People are talking but the room is surprisingly quiet. There is a feeling of expectation, of readiness to begin *Shabbos*. Even though it is getting late, people seem patient. We'll start when we start. They obviously know Shlomo.

A change in the sounds of the room. Warmth and excitement. When I turn around, I see Shlomo standing near the entrance. He's dressed smartly in a long, dark winter coat. A couple of dozen people have walked over to talk to him. He quickly makes eye contact with each of them, one at a time, speaking with animation, flashing his smile. It's been over 10 years since I've seen him. In a dramatic contrast to his dark coat, his hair and beard are mostly white.

A man in his late 30s with reddish hair and beard puts his hand on Shlomo's shoulder, leans over and whispers something to him. Shlomo nods, whispers something back, then smiles. That must be Sammy Intrator, I think.* They start walking up the aisle toward the *bimah*. I feel an unexpected twinge of jealousy. Helping Shlomo get ready to start the service—that used to be my role at the House. They work their way toward the front, with Shlomo stopping to talk to everyone, shaking hands with the men. I watch carefully to see if he's shaking hands with any of the women. I can't tell.

As they get to where I am, I get up and walk over to the aisle. Shlomo sees me and his face lights up. "Aryae!" he says. We give each other a hug. I notice that his body is softer, rounder than it used to be. His beard still smells of scented oil.

Shlomo looks at me closely. "You're okay?" he asks.

"It's so good to be here and see you," I say.

---

* Rabbi Sammy Intrator became rabbi of the Carlebach Shul after Reb Shlomo passed away.

"Sammy," he says, "you gotta meet my top holy man Aryae from the House!"

Sammy smiles and reaches out his hand. "Good *Shabbos* Aryae," he says. "It's good to meet you after hearing so much about you. Welcome." We make eye contact. He's open, vulnerable, excited, even, it seems, a little apologetic. I like him.

"Aryae listen, you're staying for the feast-ele afterwards?" Shlomo asks me.

"I'd love to, if I'm invited."

Shlomo laughs, "Oh man!"

"I already put you on the list," Sammy says.

"Listen," says Shlomo, "stay a little bit after the feast-ele so we can talk. Okay?"

"Okay," I say, "thanks. Thanks Sammy." Shlomo smiles and flashes me a "V" sign. Sammy walks with him to the *bimah*.

Shlomo's up on the *bimah*, leaning on the table. The noise in the room quiets down, as if we were all looking up at a conductor, ready to begin a concert. Without any introduction, with his eyes closed, hands on the table, rocking gently back and forth, in a sweet slow melody, Shlomo begins the service: *L'khu n'ran'nah laShem, nariah l'tzur yisheinu.* "Come let us sing to God, let us call out to the Rock of our salvation."

In this concert everyone joins in, singing in harmony with the conductor. The melody moves slowly, without rhythm. People follow in harmony. We come to Psalm 96 and the melody changes. Fast, upbeat: *Shiru laShem shir hadash, shiru laShem kol haaretz.* "Sing to God a new song; sing to God all the earth." People are singing with him and clapping. I look around, amazed. I've experienced this kind of joy with Shlomo at the House, but not in a regular synagogue service, with prayer books and rows of seats and a *mehitza*. People are smiling.

We come to the mystic greeting of the Bride: *L'kha dodi likrat Kalah, p'nei Shabat n'kablah.* "Come my Beloved to greet the Bride; the face of *Shabbos* we will receive." We sing part way through the verses in one melody, and then switch to a second. People are standing and clapping. We all face the door to receive the Bride and bow down to greet Her. Then we're dancing, men on one side of the synagogue, women on the other. The dancing is spirited, exuberant. It goes on for about five minutes. When it's over, everyone moves back to their seats.

91

Shlomo continues to lead the service. It's traditional Orthodox davening; the difference is that many of the prayers are set to Shlomo's melodies, and people often get up to dance. For some of it, I get up too and dance with the men. I'm struck with the mix of people dancing together on both sides of the aisle; very traditional, Hasidic types dancing with New Age types.

When the davening is over, a group of women rushes back to set out food on the tables in back of the *shul*. Lots of people are gathered around Shlomo to talk to him. Sammy is standing next to him. He touches Shlomo's arm and leads him to his place. Shlomo catches my eye and motions to me to join them. Shlomo takes his seat in the middle of a very long table. I get to sit right next to him, on his right. To his left is an Orthodox rabbi, apparently an important person in the local Jewish community, whose *shul* is within walking distance. Shlomo gives him the honor of making *Kiddush*, the special Friday night blessing over the wine. We stand.

The rabbi prefaces the *Kiddush* with a teaching from this week's Torah portion. Several of the young men wearing black velvet kippahs ask questions and add their comments. When a particularly insightful comment is made, everyone nods. These are people who spend their days and their lives studying Torah, engaging in the dialectic of learning.

We bless the wine, get up to wash our hands, come back to the table and bless the bread. Then we sit down to eat. The crowd is happy, boisterous. In-between courses, the religious young men vie with each other to lead us in traditional *Shabbos* songs.

After we've finished the main course and are waiting for dessert, Shlomo raises his left hand and waves it. *"Hevra, hevra,"* he says. "There's something I want to share with you." People clink their glasses and make sounds to get everyone's attention. Finally there's silence. He puts his right hand on my shoulder. "I want you to meet my friend Aryae. He was one of the kids I met in San Francisco in the 1960s." I feel strange when he says that; I'm an ageing "kid" indeed!

"You know, something very special was going on in San Francisco," he says, "and Jewish kids from all over the United States were coming there. I used to say in those days, San Francisco is the city of tomorrow; *Yerushalayim* (Jerusalem) is the city of the day after. We would get together for *Shabbos* and hundreds of kids would show up. I knew that we had to have a house of our own, a home for everyone who was hungry for *Shabbos*. So Aryae and his friends helped me start the House of Love and Prayer." People's eyes widen. They've all heard of the House of Love and Prayer. I feel like a piece of history. They look at me curiously.

"Aryae was my top holy man in San Francisco, and a very special Torah teacher in his own right. We reached so many Jewish kids who turned their lives around. Aryae's now a psychiatrist in San Francisco, and a member of the Orthodox Jewish community there." I stop breathing. Psychiatrist? Member of the Orthodox Jewish community? *Shlomo — What are you doing?*

"So holy brother Aryae, please share with us a good teaching on this week's *parsha* (Torah portion)."

I don't know what to say. My Torah study has been very sporadic lately, and I haven't read the *parsha*. This is the first Orthodox *shul* I've been to in almost 20 years. What do I say? I look at Shlomo. *Why did you set me up like this?* He's nodding at me encouragingly.

I look around at the people looking at me. There's the Orthodox rabbi on Shlomo's left. There are the bright, feisty young *yeshiva* guys in their black velvet kippahs. There are the young men and women dressed in neo-hippie attire. There are the older members of the congregation, solid, dependable Orthodox Jews, who were here when Shlomo's father was rabbi. The only ones not looking at me are the middle-aged women with scarves on their heads who are clearing the table. Other than the clatter of the dishes they are gathering up, the room is silent.

13

27 Miles

I focus, take a couple of deep breaths, and listen to the clatter of dishes in the kitchen. I'll start off with one sentence, then see what comes next.

"In spite of Reb Shlomo's kind words, my level of learning doesn't compare to so many of you sitting around this table. I feel privileged and grateful to be here with you, sharing this beautiful *Shabbos* meal together." I lean forward and make eye contact with the Orthodox rabbi on Shlomo's left. "And Rabbi Mehlman, thank you for your inspiring words of Torah." Rabbi Mehlman smiles back at me and nods.*

"So, rather than try to add to what Rabbi Mehlman has said, I'd like to share a story with you. This is a story that happened in California in the 60s, in the days that Shlomo was talking about. Back then, my friends and I were in our late teens and early 20s, like many of you here. We were living in the Haight-Ashbury, smoking grass, going to rock concerts." I see some of the *yeshiva* kids exchanging glances. The young hippies are smiling at me.

"I was also a spiritual seeker, but I hadn't been to a *shul* in years. I 'dropped acid.' I tried chanting *Hari Krishna* with Swami Bhaktivedanta** and meditating with the Buddhists. The most important thing I learned from Shlomo is that my own people, and the holy teachings in my own tradition, contained wisdom that I didn't even know existed. And that wisdom could lead me to experience God." I look around the table. People are leaning forward.

"Shlomo never said to me and my friends, 'This is what you should do to be a Jew.' He showed us. This story is about a 27-mile

---

* I do not recall the rabbi's actual name.

** A.C. Bhaktivedanta Swami Prabhupada (1896-1977) was the founder of the International Society for Krishna Consciousness, and a teacher of the Gaudiya-Vaishnava sect of Hinduism.

walk we took in Los Angeles in 1968. It's about how Shlomo showed me, and hundreds of other people, how to keep *Shabbos.*"

Shlomo's eyes are shining with memory and anticipation. He leans to his left and whispers something to Rabbi Mehlman.

Los Angeles, California — October 1968

Squealing tires. Dozens of red brake lights. An overturned truck. White powder on the road. Traffic on the freeway has stopped.

I'm driving my VW Bug. Shlomo's sitting next to me in the front passenger seat. He looks up from his book, a Hasidic text with a thick, dark brown cover embossed with a gold crown and Hebrew letters that spell *S'fat Emet,* "Language of Truth."*

"What's going on?" He says.

"An accident," I say. "That truck up there has turned over."

"Is anybody hurt?"

"I can't tell." A couple of dozen people are standing in the freeway up ahead. It doesn't seem like there's anything we can do.

It's late Friday afternoon and we're on our way to a big Los Angeles Reform temple where Shlomo is leading a *Shabbos* weekend. We have to get there soon because, as an observant Jew, Shlomo cannot travel after sunset.

I look in the rear view mirror and see the VW van from the House behind us. We call it the Shabbos Express. Efraim is driving and Sonny is sitting next to him. Karen, Chaya, David and some of the other holy beggars are in the back. Leah and Uri are at the motel where we're all staying tonight.

Shlomo looks up at the sky. We all sit there helplessly, no one saying anything. Finally Shlomo leans over and says to me quietly: "What do you think? Can we get there?" His eyes are wide, like a curious child. I go through mental calculations, trying out different scenarios. I decide that if we can get moving in 20 minutes we'll be okay. I share that thought with the others.

---

* The *S'fat Emet* is one of the most original Torah Commentaries of Hasidism, written by Rabbi Yehudah Leib Alter of Ger (1847-1905), the second Gerer Rebbe, who was known as the *S'fat Emet.* This text has now been translated into English as *The Language of Truth* by Arthur Green.

"It's all in God's hands anyway, isn't it?" says Cathy. We sit there silently for a while. I watch a couple of police cars with sirens and flashing lights make their way to the overturned truck.

The freeway doesn't open up. By the time we can get to an exit, the sun is just about to set. We lock up the cars and start walking.

We find our way to a residential section of Sepulveda Boulevard. There are tall palm trees along the sidewalk. The sky is filled with a sunset glow slowly fading into night. The air is warm. It's clear enough to see a few stars beginning to wink in the sky. I'm feeling good. We're on a pleasant *Shabbos* stroll. Efraim starts humming one of Shlomo's melodies. Karen and Chaya join him.

"Yosepha, come here darling," Shlomo says. He's in front of our little group, walking briskly. She jogs to catch up to him and moves her legs quickly to keep up. She's shorter than most of us, seventeen years old, bright, bouncy, energetic, with springy brown hair and a huge smile.

"Shlomo!" she says. "Trust me! I've told you I know this road!"

Shlomo smiles back at her and makes the "V" sign. "Peace sister!" he says. He asks her how far she thinks it is. She doesn't really know, but thinks it may be five to ten miles. Ten miles, I think, would get us to the temple after 10:00 PM. They're expecting us to start at 7:00. This is stretching it, even for Shlomo.

An hour and half later, we're still walking, now at a slow, steady pace. The sky is dark. Through the hazy smog, we can see a few stars. A car slows down and pulls up along side us. The woman inside rolls down the window on the passenger side and leans over. "Rabbi Carlebach?"

"Yeah, who's this?" says Shlomo, walking over.

"Ellen Katz," she says with a New York accent. "I'm the secretary for the temple."*

"Darling, how did you find us?"

"Well, when you didn't show up, we were worried. Then we heard the news about the accident on the freeway."

We all crowd around the car. The motor is running and the headlights are on. Ellen Katz looks around at us, then back at Shlomo. "Rabbi," she says, "you better get into the car so I can get you to the temple."

---

* I don't recall her actual name.

97

"Darling, I wish I could, but I can't," he says.

She looks at him blankly. Then she looks at us. "Oh, don't worry about your friends. I'll get people to drive back here and pick them up too."

Shlomo puts his hand on top of her car and leans over to the open window. "That's very sweet darling, but listen," he says. "The whole thing is, you know on *Shabbos,* I'm not permitted to travel."

"Oh I know about that," she says. "But what you've got to realize is that there are over 300 people at the temple waiting to see you. We planned a long time for this." Her voice is filled with seriousness and responsibility and worry.

I lean over and make eye contact with her. "How far away is it?" I say.

"It's far," she says.

"How far?"

She leans over and looks at her odometer. The lights gleam faintly in the interior of her car. "It looks to me like 27 miles."

"Wow! That's quite a hike!" says Cathy. Everyone else is silent, digesting this information.

"Let me get you there," she says to Shlomo. "It's a *mitzvah* for you to be there for all those people."

Shlomo exhales and shakes his head. "I wish I could," he says.

"27 miles," I say to no one in particular. "At three miles an hour that's, let's see, nine hours. At four miles an hour, that would be a little under seven. So we're talking about getting there somewhere between three and five in the morning."

The black sky looks like it's starting to cloud over. Shlomo is looking down at the street. I can hear him take a deep breath. A car goes by.

"Listen darling," he says softly, "you've got to do me the greatest favor in the world. If I got in the car with you now, it would be very cute and sweet and maybe we'd have a nice time singing, but it wouldn't really be *Shabbos.*" Ellen is looking at him. We're all looking at him, and at her.

"You know, we live in a world where people want everything instant, everything easy. Instant gratification. Fast food. But you know, in their *kishkes,* people are hungry for more than fast food. We all are. And our kids aren't stupid. They know the difference. They're hungry for real soul food. Imagine, tonight the people in your temple have a chance, maybe some of them for the first time, to taste, to *mammash* taste, the sweetness of *Shabbos*."

He talks to her about asking them to wait there until four or five in the morning, or maybe go home and sleep a little and then come back. She's skeptical at first, but he gradually wins her over. She turns off the engine, gets out of the car, and joins us on the sidewalk.

We all start getting excited. Ellen gets excited. We talk about what we'll need. Plenty of wine for *Kiddush*, plenty of *hallah* to make the blessing over the bread. Lots of food. A room arranged so lots of people can gather around with us in circles. That means getting out of the sanctuary and into the rec hall. Ellen promises to get it all set up.

She tells us there's a Denny's about six or seven miles up Sepulveda, and it would make a good place for us to stop and get something to eat along the way. Shlomo explains that we can't do any commercial transactions on *Shabbos*. She offers to get us some sandwiches to take with us. I explain that we can't carry anything. She sighs and shrugs. I exchange glances with Efraim and Sonny and Yosepha. 27 miles with no food.

"But darling, there is one more favor you can do for me," Shlomo says.

Ellen is smiling. "Sure Shlomo, what do you want?"

"Maybe you can ask all the people at the temple to invite their friends to join them? We can have a *mammash* great celebration!"

Ellen laughs and says she will. Shlomo gives her a hug. Then he smiles, gives her a "V" sign, and turns to start walking. She goes to her car.

I go with her. Efraim is with me. "You know, there *is* a way to feed Shlomo and us on the way," I say.

She looks at us, curious. "How?" she says. We have to be careful about how to say this, because it's not permitted to ask a fellow Jew to violate *Shabbos*, even if they're already doing it. I explain that if the temple had already made arrangements with the Denny's before *Shabbos*, either paying them before or promising to pay them later, then Shlomo could probably sit down and have a cup of coffee, and maybe find something kosher enough to eat. I look over to Efraim for confirmation. He shrugs, smiles and looks up. Ellen smiles and nods. I don't need to say more. She hugs Efraim, then me, and gets in the car.

Two hours later we're crowded into a couple of booths at Denny's, feeling the relief of sitting on the soft benches covered in dark red plastic, drinking coffee and eating English muffins and tuna sandwiches. The rest and food revive us.

Two or three hours later, it's after 1:00 AM. We've settled into a steady walking rhythm. Shlomo's pace is surprisingly fast.

"I just felt rain," Sonny says. "Does anyone else feel rain?"

"No way!" says Yosepha.

"I felt something," says Karen. "Just a couple of drops."

"You know something?" says Cathy. "He's right! It is raining!"

The rain gets stronger. Shlomo stops walking, holds out his hands and looks up at the sky. We all stop, feel the rain, look at each other. It's raining hard and we're starting to get wet. I can feel the raindrops trickling down my face and starting to soak through my shirt.

An hour later it's still raining hard. We're soaked, walking fast, singing and laughing. Fortunately the night is warm. Everyone is in a good mood.

A car pulls up alongside us, and moves forward slowly, to keep pace with our walking. This is a big car, not Ellen Katz. Shlomo is curious and walks up to the car. The front window on the passenger side comes down. A man sticks his head out. Under the street light I can see his shock of curly black hair, tinged with grey, tied back in a little pony tail. The driver sitting next to him is looking back and forth between us and the road.

"Who's this?" Shlomo says.

"Rabbi Carlebach?" the man says. His voice is deep, forceful.

"Yes . . ."

"This is Ron McCoy, the Night Owl, from radio station KFI," he says. He's talking like he's on the air. He's host of a late-night radio show, and he's here to check us out. Shlomo keeps walking and the rest of us follow. McCoy's car moves forward smoothly, keeping pace with Shlomo.

"Tell me something," Shlomo says. "How did you know we were here?"

"The Night Owl learns from many messengers," he says, sounding like a Beatnik reading poetry. "This one was a lady from the temple."

Shlomo turns around, flashes us a "V", and smiles. "Holy Ellen!" he says.

100

"Rabbi, do you mind if I ask you some questions for our listeners?" says the Night Owl. He is holding a microphone.

"Do people really listen so late?" says Shlomo. "How many listen?"

"Rabbi, they're out there, right now, in every corner of L.A.," he says in his deep Beatnik voice, with great conviction. "They've got their radios on, they're awake, and they're listening to every word we're saying."

"Listen my friend," Shlomo says. "I'm happy to talk to you and your listeners, but can we maybe do it while we're walking?" He moves his hand over his face to wipe away the water. I wonder if he's going to wring it out of his beard.

The Night Owl agrees. We walk. Shlomo walks by the curb, fast. The car cruises at his pace. The water has formed a river in the street by the curb, almost up to the edge. The car's tires cut into the water, like a jeep in a swamp. The Night Owl leans out the window holding his microphone. "Rabbi, let me begin with the obvious question: Why are you and your friends walking 27 miles in the rain?"

Shlomo nods and thinks a moment. "Let me put it like this," he says. "We live in a world of doing. There's so much to do, right? When we're children, we're going to school. Then when we're older, we go to college, and then maybe we go to graduate school. Then we're getting married, working, having children, trying to be successful. So when we're tired and we want to rest, what do we do? We take a vacation, right? We call the travel agent, buy plane tickets to Paris, or take a cruise to Bermuda. It's all very sweet, but it's all about doing."

We come to a street corner. The traffic light is red, surrounded by red raindrops. Shlomo keeps walking. The car hesitates, then follows him. The rest of us follow too. I wonder if he even sees the red light. The streets are empty of everything except us and raindrops.

"There's such a thing as doing, and then there's such a thing as joy. So what brings us joy? Imagine I'm on a date with a beautiful girl, and I'm very taken with her, and I ask her what she wants to do. And let's say she tells me, first she wants to see a big Broadway show, then she wants to go out to a fancy restaurant, then she wants to go dancing at an expensive club. So, how does that make me feel? I better check with my wallet, right? Then I'll tell you how I feel!" He laughs. Yosepha, who's walking to his right, looks up at him and laughs. Shlomo flashes her a "V".

"Okay. But seriously, imagine if I ask her, and what she says to me is: 'It doesn't matter. It really doesn't matter, because what I really

101

want is to be with you.' Greatest thing in the world, right? That's joy." Cathy and Karen are walking on my right. Karen is squeezing water out of her hair, while looking curiously at the Night Owl, who winks at her. Cathy looks over at me, smiling. Strands of wet hair are plastered over her forehead. She looks radiant and shy, like a schoolgirl.

"You know, sadly, what kind of relationship do we have with ourselves? Honestly, what do we tell ourselves? I'll be happy later, right? When I make a million dollars. Or when I get the house clean. Or when I write a great book, or win the Nobel Prize, or win the Miss America contest.

"What kind of relationship do we have with God?" Shlomo continues. "You know, most so called religious people are relating to God on the doing level. If I do all the right things, God will be very impressed and make a list, and let me into heaven. And if I made out a big check to the synagogue, then maybe I'll get a front row seat with the angels, right?" Shlomo smiles at Sonny and flashes a 'V'.

"But you know, in our tradition, in the Torah, in the Old Testament, there's six days, so to speak, where God is doing, creating the world, and one day where God is just being. This is so deep. Our Rabbis say that when God chased Adam and Eve out of *Gan Eden,* out of paradise, that they had to live in the world of doing. But the level of *Shabbos* is that, we can go back in. We can literally go back to paradise. You know, it says in our prayers, *Yism'hu b'malkhuskha shomrey Shabbos.* Whoever is holding onto *Shabbos* is filled with joy, the joy God's world, the joy of paradise.

"Okay, listen now, open up your heart. What is God saying to us? Just be with me. Just be with the whole world. Simple as it is. Imagine if I could be on the level, just for one day, just for one *minute,* to see myself through God's eyes, to see how beautiful and perfect I already am."

Shlomo turns his head to look at us. His hair is soaked, and his *kippah* is hanging a little on one side. He smiles at Yosepha. "Imagine if I could really see how beautiful every person is. Imagine if I could feel how beautiful and perfect the *whole world* is. Just to be the way I am, for everything to be the way it already is. Just to be."

Cathy is clasping her hands together and smiling. I look up at the sky. I feel the muscles aching in my legs, the wet shirt on my back, the night air in my lungs, the rain on my face. A dozen wet people are walking in the middle of the night through the rain on an empty street in the middle of Los Angeles, with a single car following. For a moment, with his shaggy head of black and grey hair sticking out of the car window into the rain, even the Night Owl is silent. The world

102

is so vast, so infinite, so still, so open with possibility, so filled with peace.

An hour later, it's still raining and we're still walking. The water has overflowed the streets onto the sidewalks. We're walking in water up to our ankles. My socks are making squishing sounds in my shoes. Maybe L.A. isn't used to this much water and the drains aren't built to handle it.

Some headlights appear in the street behind us and a car pulls up. The window rolls down and a head sticks out. He looks like a teenage boy. He looks at us, and then sees Shlomo.

"Rabbi Carlebach?" he says.

Shlomo walks over. "Yes?" he says. "And who are you, my friend?" He smiles.

The kid sticks his head back in the car. "It's them!" he says with excitement. The car parks and three teenage boys emerge. They stand awkwardly, their shoulders hunched up against the rain, looking around them and up at the sky. "Can we walk with you?" says the first one.

"How did you know we were here?" Sonny says.

"We were listening to the Night Owl," says the kid.

Karen and Chaya are excited. "Wow," says Karen, "that's so great!" They laugh. The kids look at each other and then smile at the young women.

Shlomo walks up to them. He puts one hand on the shoulder of one of the kids and the other hand on the shoulder of another. He smiles. "This is the greatest thing in the world!" he says, "*mammash* the greatest thing! Where are you from?" They tell him.

"These are top holy brothers!" Shlomo says. "Listen, you've got to do me the biggest favor in the world." The kids are still moving around, hunching their shoulders, trying somehow to keep the rain off. I look at the rest of us. No one is moving much. We've surrendered to the rain. The kids look at Shlomo, wondering what he is going to say. "You've got to join us for our *Shabbos* celebration tonight," he says. "This is going to be the greatest thing in the world!"

The kids don't need any persuading. They're with us. We start walking again. Shlomo starts to sing one of his songs, a fast song in a major key. The rest of us sing along. I can feel a new burst of energy. We keep singing for a long time.

Soon headlights are coming at us from the other direction. The car stops when it gets to us and a woman sticks her head out of the window. "Is this the group with Shlomo Carlebach?" Chaya and Karen holler, "Yes!" The car makes a U-turn, parks, and three women and one man get out. They look college age, just a little younger than I am. They are wearing raincoats. The women have long hair and the man has a flat top. They also heard about us on the Night Owl and want to join us. Shlomo walks up to them and grasps each of their hands. He is amazed, and so delighted. They explain that they're not Jewish, but they think that what we're doing is so exciting that they want to be part of it.

"You know it says in the Midrash, in our holy teachings," Shlomo says, "that when the Jewish people stood at Mount Sinai to receive the Torah, God's teachings for the world, that people from every nationality and every religion in the world stood with us. So who knows, maybe we've been standing next to each other the whole time!" He laughs. "You better join us for *Shabbos!*"

They're ready. We all walk together. Every few minutes now, cars are pulling over. Each time someone joins us, it feels like a new celebration. People are singing, and talking and laughing. The rain is still pouring over us, and our feet are still submerged under water as we walk. But it no longer feels like we're walking in the rain; it feels more like playing in a swimming pool. Soon we form a line, three or four people wide, that stretches out the length of a block. Shlomo is walking with some teenagers who just arrived, asking them questions. Karen and Chaya are so excited. They move up and down the line, saying hello to the people they haven't seen before, laughing. I walk backwards and watch them, and try to count the number of people who are with us. Is it a hundred, two hundred? Who knows? It's a lot of people, and more keep joining. I feel all the weariness and soreness leave my body. I am filled with energy, enough to keep going forever.

Sonny comes up to me. "Aryae, this is amazing!" he says.

"It's mind blowing," I agree.

"Maybe this is really it," he says. "What do you think?"

"What do you mean?"

"You know, what Shlomo is always talking about. Maybe this is the Great Shabbos."

I look at Sonny. He looks like he's already living in that world. "Maybe it is," I say.

An hour or so later, hundreds of very wet people walk into to the temple. It's just a little past 4:00 AM. As we walk in, hundreds of people cheer. They come up to us with towels, dry clothes and hot chocolate. A guy in his 30s with black rimed glasses, a neatly starched blue dress shirt and dark, curly hair leads me around a corner, where I have the privacy to take off my wet jeans and shirt and put on a dry tee shirt and sweat pants.

I go back to the main room and see my San Francisco friends Moishe and Maxine, together with Bernice. They're all roughly ten years older than I am, and represent our small contingent of families in the inner circle of the House that actually have husbands, wives, houses, jobs and children.

"Good *Shabbos,* good *Shabbos!*" I say. "Good *Shabbos,* good *Shabbos,* good *Shabbos!*" they answer. I quickly hug all three of them.

"What are you guys doing here?" I say.

"We heard there was gonna be a party!" Moishe says.

"But nobody told us it was gonna start so late!" says Bernice, laughing.

Efraim walks over with Leah, who's holding Uri and smiling radiantly as she looks at all the people swirling around us.

Shlomo is doing what he always does, circulating through the crowd, hugging everyone he can, making intense eye contact with each person he encounters, one at a time. For a few brief seconds, each person has his complete and undivided attention. What most of them don't yet know is that the next time he sees them, he will remember their names.

I see Ellen Katz and walk over to her. With a cup of something hot in her hand, she's talking to a couple of women and looking very poised.

"Don't you think we should get started?" Ellen says when she sees me, looking around at the crowd.

"I agree," I say. "Beautiful as this is, we've only got so much energy left."

"Could you tell him it's time?" she says.

I laugh at the thought of telling Shlomo it's time for anything. "I'll do my best." I go over to Shlomo. He's talking to three women a few years younger than I am.

"Aryae, you gotta meet these top holy girls!" He introduces me. They are carefully dressed with hair carefully done. They seem very excited and a little nervous, as though they were talking to a rock star. It turns out he met them at a concert in Los Angeles last year, and he remembers their names.

I put my hand on his shoulder. "Excuse me," I say to the young women. "Ellen says it's time to get started," I say to Shlomo.

Shlomo smiles. "You're right," he says, "we better. Give me just two minutes, okay?" He flashes me a 'V.'

About a half-hour later we get started. We begin with a few circles of metal folding chairs in the center of the rec hall. There are enough seats for about 200 of us, with hundreds more standing. Shlomo is talking about *Shabbos*. Everyone is quiet, listening very respectfully, almost in awe. I'm simply grateful for the chance to sit down.

Soon we're up and singing *Lekha Dodi*, greeting the Shabbos Bride, and dancing. The dancing amazes me. I don't know where the energy is coming from. We dance for a very long time.

In a normal synagogue, on a normal *Shabbos*, people would be making *Kiddush*, the blessing over the wine, at about 7:30 in the evening. On this *Shabbos*, at this synagogue, we're making *Kiddush* at 8:00 in the morning. No one minds. The holy beggars from the House of Love and Prayer, the motley crew of 300 people who joined us on the way, and the Los Angeles Reform Jews, are all hugging each other. We are filled with awe and wonder, and love. *Shabbos* is real. God is real. The world is one.

New York, New York – December 1991

I've finished the story. The room is quiet. No one's moving, not even the *yeshiva* kids. I look over at Shlomo. "Ssss," he says. He smiles and flashes me a "V."

Rabbi Mehlman on Shlomo's left leans over and says to me, "That is a very inspiring story, and does great honor to Reb Shlomo. I want my congregation to hear it. Would you join me at my *shul* tomorrow morning? I'd like you to be my guest."

I don't know what to say. Rabbi Mehlman is giving me a great honor, but spending the day in an Orthodox *shul* with people I don't know is not exactly what I had in mind.

Shlomo looks at me and puts one hand on Rabbi Mehlman's shoulder and one hand on mine. "Brother Aryae," he says, "believe me, it would *mammash* be the greatest thing in the world! You know, Rabbi Mehlman is one of the real *menshes* on the Orthodox scene in New York, one of the top holy rabbis. Look, I'll be there to *daven* in the morning and we can sit together, okay?"

"Okay," I say. Shlomo leans over and whispers something to Rabbi Mehlman, who smiles and nods.

Somebody starts a *niggun,* one of Shlomo's melodies, and everyone joins. Then Shlomo says, *"Hevra,* let's *bentch!"* The *yeshiva* kids lead the group in a spirited, almost raucous, rendition of the traditional blessings after the meal.

Afterwards people from the Carlebach Shul crowd around Shlomo. He turns his chair around with the back to the table, so he can face the people who want to talk to him. I turn mine around too. Sammy walks over, leans down, and whispers something to him.

I am caught in a familiar dilemma. On the one hand, the reason I'm here this weekend is because my life has been torn apart, and I want so desperately to talk privately to Shlomo. I need wisdom and guidance, and he has promised we would talk tonight. On the other hand there are so many people pulling at him, as always, and it's getting late, and he looks so tired.

"Shlomo," I say, "there's a lot more people who want to talk to you. Maybe we should talk tomorrow."

"Listen, do me the biggest favor," he says. "You'll be at Rabbi Mehlman's *shul* in the morning, right?"

"Yeah."

"When you walk in the front door there's a big, like, entranceway," Shlomo says. "Meet me there at 9:00 sharp, okay?"

"Okay."

"Your story was *mammash ay gevalt!"* he says.

"Thank you."

He leans forward and looks at me intently. "Just one small thing. When you tell it tomorrow, could you maybe leave out the part about Denny's?"

I don't understand. I look at him uncomprehendingly.

"I hate to say bad things, but some people here are very *frum* (religious). They wouldn't understand about eating at Denny's."

"Okay, I understand," I say. The issue is kosher food. I don't think we ate anything that wasn't kosher. But according to strict Orthodox standards, a Jew shouldn't eat in a place like Denny's at all, where the kitchen isn't certified kosher. I don't understand why Shlomo worries so much about how he will appear to the strictest, most religious Jews. Why not stand behind his own choices?

My choice came 20 years ago when I realized that living within the strictly religious world of orthodoxy just wasn't my spiritual path. Why can't walking 27 miles in the rain, loving the people around you, and gathering hundreds of people to celebrate *Shabbos* and sing praises to God, be enough?

"Okay, Shlomo, I'll see you there at 9:00." I reach out and give him a hug. "Good *Shabbos*."

He flashes me a smile, but under the smile he looks tired. I'm glad I've decided to take some of the pressure off him. "Good *Shabbos*, holy brother Aryae. Get some rest. Sleep strong like a lion!"

Our eyes connect for one long second, cutting through the static and noise around us. One second of complete stillness. It was 26 years ago, exactly half of my lifetime, when we first met at San Francisco State College. All of those years, all of the memories and feelings, are present now between his eyes and mine. Shlomo used to say that a moment can be eternal, can be infinite. What do we know? How can we measure eternity when it pokes its finger into this world? How do we know what is possible on a God-level in one second?

One of the *yeshiva* boys, who has been waiting impatiently, inserts himself in front of me and says something to Shlomo. Shlomo and I nod to each other, and then he hugs the *yeshiva* boy.

14

Mistaken Identity

New York, New York – December 1991

I get to Rabbi Mehlman's shul a few minutes before 9:00 the next morning. Shlomo isn't there. After waiting about 20 minutes I go inside.

The *hazzan* (cantor) is going through the morning blessings, the first part of the prayers that are said in synagogue every day. I find it comforting to sit anonymously in the emptiness of this *shul*, lost in the large space, in the clean, simple lines of the familiar prayer melodies, in the traditional words of the blessings. I let myself relax, let the service carry me along.

Later I turn around and see Shlomo at the back of the *shul*, shaking hands with a few people, slowly working his way up to the front. He sees Rabbi Mehlman and walks down to greet him. The *hazzan* is now going through the Psalms with their melodies. Rabbi Mehlman stands, shakes hands with Shlomo, and nods in my direction. Shlomo looks at me, smiles, flashes me a "V." The two of them stand talking quietly for a couple of minutes; then Shlomo walks over to me.

I stand up and give him a hug. "Good *Shabbos* Shlomo," I say.

He answers in Yiddish—"A sweet, holy *Shabbos*." We sit. The *hazzan's* voice fills the air. More people are walking into the *shul* and seats are filling up. Shlomo leans over and whispers to me. He's sorry that he couldn't be here at 9:00. There are a lot of things going on right now with people in his *shul*, and everyone needs to talk to him. He can stay here and *daven* for a little while, but then he needs to leave. "Listen, I'll be here another few days. Maybe you can call me right after *Shabbos*?" I feel my breathing stop. I make eye contact with him. He looks apologetic.

"I'm not planning to be here after *Shabbos*," I say.

"Listen, you have my number, right? Do me the biggest favor. I want you to call me, okay?"

109

I feel shaking in my chest. Rage and tears. I've come so far to talk to him. I need someone to hold onto; I'm reaching out for a life raft and there isn't any. I feel abandoned.

I take a deep breath. Shlomo looks vulnerable. I can see he's juggling, trying to avoid making anyone unhappy, including me. "Okay," I say.

The congregation is standing in preparation for the *Barukh Hu,* the formal blessing that begins the next part of the service. We stand and join them. I'm having trouble concentrating on the prayers. I take some deep, slow breaths to try to center myself.

A couple of hours later I'm standing next to Rabbi Mehlman in front of a long table. A lot of people from his congregation, maybe 150, are gathered around the table, which is holding the wine, the *hallah,* and many different kinds of food. Unlike Shlomo's congregation the night before, this group is more homogeneous. Almost all the men are wearing dark suits, and the women are dressed with Orthodox modesty. This feels like a congregation of householders, settled, professional people who work hard, are financially stable, contribute time and money to the *shul,* and spend considerable effort on raising their children to be observant Jews.

Rabbi Mehlman introduces Reb Shlomo's student, the Orthodox psychiatrist from San Francisco who founded the House of Love and Prayer, and asks me to tell the story of the 27-mile walk in the rain. I can see that people are hungry and want to eat. I make it shorter and leave out the part about Denny's. After the story, people are smiling. They liked it. Rabbi Mehlman again puts his arm around my shoulder. I feel relieved.

I say *Kiddush* over the wine. Then everyone washes their hands and says *Ha'motzi* over the bread. People fill their paper plates with food and eat and talk standing up.

Rabbi Mehlman motions to me to follow him across the room, where he introduces me to a strikingly beautiful woman in her late 20s. Unlike the other women in the congregation who avert their eyes from men according to the religious custom, she looks right at me. "Aryae, I'd like you to meet Rachael," the rabbi says.* "Her parents have been members of the *shul* for many years. You know who Reb Hayyim of Sanz was?"

---

* I have changed her name to protect her privacy.

"Of course," I say. "Rabbi Shlomo told us many stories about him." He was a great Hasidic *rebbe* in the 19th century. His descendant, the Bobover Rebbe, was one of Shlomo's early teachers.*

"Rachael is a great-great granddaughter of Reb Hayyim of Sanz," Rabbi Mehlman says. I give her a look indicating that I am properly impressed. She smiles mischievously. "She is also a clinical social worker who works with children here in New York. Given your profession, I thought the two of you might have some common interests to talk about." He looks at each of us, smiles, and walks away. *What's this about,* I wonder. I watch him disappear into the crowd.

Rachael looks at me and laughs. "Well, I'm not going to bite you!" she says.

"Do I look that nervous?" I say.

"You don't exactly look like you belong here," she says.

"Well," I say, "at least I've got an excuse. You're supposed to belong here, but you don't look like you do."

"Oh no?" she says, "Why not?"

"You don't look and act like you're part of the Orthodox world," I say. "And you're a professional, single woman. I bet that's not exactly the norm around here."

"That shows how much *you* know about modern religious women!" she says with a laugh. I shrug and smile back.

We talk, the lonely middle-aged Orthodox psychiatrist and the single young Orthodox professional woman who hasn't found a man in her world who can understand and accept her for who she is.

Adults and children keep swarming past, paper plates and cups in hand, pretending not to notice us. Rabbi Mehlman's introduction has created a kind of magic circle where we can be left alone and talk. For two strangers standing in the middle of a crowd, the conversation is amazingly deep, amazingly intimate. I ask her about her work and the disadvantaged children she works with, what it's like being a member of her illustrious family, her ambitions and dreams for her life. When she asks about my life, I talk about the pain of being separated from my children, about my academic work in Humanistic Psychology in graduate school, and about how my adventures years ago with Shlomo and the House of Love and Prayer transformed me.

---

* Rabbi Hayyim Halberstam of Novy-Sanz (1797-1876), a disciple of the Seer of Lublin and Naftali of Ropshitz.

On the level of fact she really doesn't know who I am. But on the level of story and melody, I feel like she does. Standing in our magic circle, we're surrounded by a spell of enchantment. We talk a long time.

Then I look around the room. People are starting to leave.

"How much longer will you be in New York?" she asks.

I'll actually be leaving this afternoon to drive upstate to visit my friend Andy. But I don't want to tell her, especially after my story of the 27 miles that I'll be driving on *Shabbos*. "I'm driving upstate to visit my childhood friend tomorrow," I say. "Then I'm going back to California."

She looks down and asks, "Do you get to New York often?"

"Not really," I say. "I wish I could come here more." I search my mind for reasons to come here more, to stay connected. There may be one or more New York business trips for me next year, but that's hard to predict. *What did Rabbi Mehlman have in mind?* Neither of us says anything. There's no way for us to see each other casually, and I'm not exactly ready yet for another marriage. The recognition of this starts hitting me like raindrops, building momentum, becoming a cold shower washing away the enchantment.

"Rachael," I say. She looks at me. "I don't really know what to say. Meeting you has been a gift. I didn't expect this."

"You didn't expect *what*?" she says, watching me closely.

"You." I smile. "I didn't expect you. You touch me deeply."

She looks at me for a few seconds, then nods. "You touch me deeply too." She pauses another moment, her eyes wide open, looking directly into mine. Then she turns and walks away. I watch her blend back into the crowd.

I check out of my hotel at 3:30, walk with my suitcase and briefcase to the parking garage, pick up the rental car and get onto Broadway heading north.

My next stop is Andy's place, about an hour and a half north of the City. I'm in a mental dialogue with my old childhood friend, trying to tell him who I am. Former husband, home-owner, head of household, president of the local education foundation, visible and outstanding citizen in a small town in Northern California. Now a separated guy looking for an apartment, hoping to find a way keep his kids with him and put his life back together. Formerly a highly visible spiritual leader. Now, when I'm not with Shlomo, spiritually invisible, anonymous. And when I *am* with Shlomo, I'm an Orthodox

112

psychiatrist! Formerly a committed, observant Jew. Now, relationship with the Jewish people undefined.

One thing, though, hasn't changed. It's really Shlomo's doing. The most real thing in the world for me, the only thing I can count on, is God's presence. It's with me every day, every second.

Through the windshield I see a group of Orthodox Jewish couples, the men with black hats and coats, the women with their hair covered, strolling on Broadway with their children, facing me. Are these the people I was with at Rabbi Mehlman's *shul*? They seem to be looking right at me. If they see that I'm not the person that Mehlman presented, this could be embarrassing for him and for Shlomo. I quickly pull the car further from the sidewalk, over to the left lane.

Why did Shlomo invent this identity for me, and why did I go along with it? And why would Rabbi Mehlman, in whose world single men and women get introduced primarily for the purpose of possible marriage, introduce a stranger to this most special young woman in his congregation? I search my mind for clues and see images of him and Shlomo whispering and looking at me.

The answer suddenly seems blindingly obvious: *Shlomo was behind it.* He wasn't abandoning me. He was shouldering the responsibility for solving both my problems—of my shattered family and my shattered identity—in the best way he could.

I thought I was coming here to have a long talk with Shlomo about my life. I wanted him to listen to everything and help me find comfort and reassurance and guidance. I'm struck with the absurdity of it all: *We've both invented identities for each other*—two Orthodox therapists! I break out laughing. It feels good to laugh. Our real identities are far more complex. Mine, at least for now, is very much a work in progress.

What I do remember as it all comes back from so long ago, and again from last night, is that Shlomo and Aryae don't do long talks. We do infinite moments.

Ninety-Sixth Street, which will take me to the West Side Highway and out of the City, is just a block ahead. Maybe I can find a way to keep the infinite moment with me, together with Noe and Adam's jellybeans. I put on my left turn signal.

113

15
Another World

"Where are we?" Wendy says.

"I don't know," I say.

The guy in the car behind us is leaning on his horn. I'm trying to read the Hebrew street signs. There's no place to pull over so I have to keep moving.

It looks like we've wandered into Mea Shearim, the religious neighborhood near central Jerusalem. The sidewalks are thick with bearded men in long black coats and broad brimmed hats, clutching books in their hands, and walking with quick, determined steps, darting around obstacles. Women wrapped in long coats and dresses down to their ankles, their heads covered with scarves, holding plastic net shopping bags filled with groceries from the markets, walk more slowly, talking with other women. Kosher butcher shops, tiny grocery stores, bookstores, storefront shuls, outdoor stands selling fruits and vegetables, kitchenware, clothing. Piles of garbage stuffed between the buildings.

I pull out the cell phone and press re-dial. A woman's voice asks, "Where are you now?"

"I don't know," I say, "I think we're in Mea Shearim."

"Look," she says, "I have an idea. Instead of you trying to find me, let's just meet at the Wall."

"Are you sure?" I say. "That sounds complicated."

"It's easy," she says. She gives me directions, telling me how to get to the Jewish quarter of the Old City, and advising me to avoid the Arab quarter, which can be dangerous these days for Jews and Americans.

Ten minutes later we're lost in the Arab quarter.

Our shiny new rented car is conspicuous on the dusty street almost empty of other vehicles. People are walking in the street. Women in hijabs and traditional dress. Young men in jeans, cruising in packs. Older men sitting in front of shops, smoking, looking on. Compared to the bustle of Mea Shearim, there is a feeling of vacancy here, of aimlessness. People mostly avoid looking at us. I have the impulse to stop the car, get out and ask someone for directions. The last time I was in Jerusalem, 38 years ago, I spent a lot of time with Middle Easterners—Jews, Muslims and Christians—Israelis, Palestinians, Moroccans, Yemenites, communicating in whatever mix of Hebrew, English and French would work, drinking Turkish coffee, making music, smoking hashish, breathing in the exhilaration of friendship across cultures. I look at the people walking on the street. A couple of guys in jeans meet my glance, stop for a moment to look us over, then continue walking. With great sadness, I can feel in my gut that this is not a time of friendship.

We find our way back to Mea Shearim to a taxi stand on a large circle with many intersecting streets. I call Shulamis.

"Where are you?" she asks. I tell her. She's in a cab, on her way to find us. "Just stay there and don't go anywhere, okay?"

"Okay."

"Just one more thing."

"What?" I ask.

"Don't be disappointed that I can't hug you. I'm a religious woman now, and a rabbi's wife, and a grandmother. Please don't take it personally, okay?"

I laugh. "I understand."

The last time I saw Shulamis was 34 years ago, at the House of Love and Prayer. Her name was Stephanie. She was 17 years old, full of spirit, ready for anything. We all hugged each other all the time. Shlomo had given us our mission with his definition of the House, "When you walk in, someone loves you; when you walk out, someone misses you." Hugging each other was the most tangible expression of our mission.

Here it's another world, and if you live here, the rules are different. Either you're religious and follow all the laws of the Orthodox, or you're secular and avoid religion. Religious men cover their head at all times with a *kippah*. Religious women cover their hair with a scarf or hat or wig. Religious women and men cannot touch any adult of the opposite sex except their own spouse. The very religious are not supposed to look at someone of the opposite sex, and men are not permitted to hear a woman sing. If your head is uncovered it means you're secular.

I had told Wendy on the plane, I didn't know what to do about wearing a *kippah*. By the rules here, I'm neither religious nor secular. Her advice was to wear a *kippah* while we're in Israel. I'm wearing a black felt one. She's wearing a hat.

I am grateful that we have found each other at this stage of life. The wreckage of two failed marriages, particularly the second, brought me years of pain. Wendy also lived through two unhappy marriages. Amazingly, together, we've discovered the gifts of renewed hope, love, acceptance, healing — and most unexpected and most joyfully accepted — passion. As I've turned 60, I've come to feel about the pleasures of the body as I feel about life itself — fleeting gifts to be joyfully embraced for the brief moment we're here, in the poignancy of knowing that, in God's time, the moment will soon pass. Wendy and I were married just a little over a year ago. It seems like a miracle that God is giving us another chance.

I'm also grateful to her for coming to Israel with me. It's my 60th birthday. These are my friends from so many years ago. She never met Shlomo and was never at the House of Love and Prayer. She is here to share in my journey and my story — a gift of love. I want her to have a good experience too, to connect with my friends, to discover spiritual connections for herself as well as witnessing mine.

Shulamis steps out of the cab and looks up at me with a big smile. I'm surprised at her appearance. Her face is youthful and she has auburn hair, the same color it was 34 years ago. It's only later that I realize she is wearing a wig.

"Aryae!"

"Stephanie, I mean Shulamis!" I correct myself. "You haven't changed at all!" I introduce her to Wendy, and the two of them exchange a friendly hug.

We get in the car and Shulamis guides us into the Old City, to Mount Zion. Narrow crooked cobblestone streets lead up a hillside and around. Suddenly we're looking out onto stone hillsides all around us with ancient looking buildings, churches, stone houses, walls.

Shulamis tells us how, every Friday afternoon in her junior year at Berkeley High, she would pack clothes and her sleeping bag, get on a bus for San Francisco, and spend the weekend at the House. She had a spot in the attic where she would set up her things. She and a

117

couple of other girls would sit under the table while I conducted the Torah service on Saturday morning. There was so much excitement all weekend. People her age showing up from all over the country — singing and dancing until all hours of the morning. There was a feeling that the world was changing, that she and everyone around her were part of bringing a new era of love and peace.

Her parents, a doctor and his wife, kind people, Berkeley liberals who belonged to the local Reform temple, didn't understand their daughter's spiritual fervor, but they didn't try to stop her. Stephanie took the GED so she could graduate high school a year early, got on a plane for Israel, and never returned, except to visit.

The road narrows to one lane, leading under an archway into a tunnel. I feel like I'm driving back to another time.

"How do you know your way around like this?" I say.

Shulamis laughs. "We lived here for years before we moved to a different part of Jerusalem. My husband's *yeshiva* is a few streets away. I'll take you to meet him later."

We get to the Wall. I park the car. Looking down from the hill, I see it rise up in front of us, unreal in it's reality, ethereal in it's solidity, stubborn remnant of the glory of God's presence in the Holy Temple 2,100 years ago, continuing to exist against all odds, refusing to go away. It takes my breath away.

At the House Shlomo told us the story of how King Solomon (whose name in Hebrew is also Shlomo) decided to build the Holy Temple, sending officers throughout ancient Israel to collect contributions from the people. The rich people brought their gold and silver, while the poor stood aside, crying.

King Solomon's officer asked them what was the matter. "We don't have gold and silver to bring," said the poor people, "and we're ashamed to bring our pennies."

"People may not value your pennies," he said, "but do you have any idea of how much God values them?" Word got out, and people from all over the kingdom came to offer their pennies.

When they counted the gold and silver, there was enough to build three walls of the Holy Temple. When they counted the pennies there was enough for the fourth wall. The Babylonians came in 586 B.C.E., destroyed the Temple and left only one wall standing. Five hundred years later the Romans destroyed the Second Temple, and the Jewish people were scattered all over the world. But the same wall was still standing. This is the Wall built with poor people's pennies, the one that is still standing today. Our Rabbis teach us that when the Messiah comes to bring redemption to the world, the Wall will be the foundation for the Third Temple, a house for all people for all time.

We pass through the metal detectors, through the guard checkpoint, answer questions, and they wave us through. We enter the plaza that leads to the Wall, women on the right side, men on the left. Groups of men cluster together, davening. Some of them wear long black coats and black hats, like in Mea Shearim. Others wear simple black kippahs, like mine. Most of them have prayer books and are busy saying the morning or afternoon prayers, or reading the Psalms. I walk up to the Wall. I see others touching the stones; I do the same. In my pocket are a couple of dozen prayers, written on little scraps of paper. Wendy and I invited friends to write their prayers and offered to place them in the crevices and cracks in the Wall, the way Jews have done for hundreds of years. As I carefully examine the Wall, I see that every little crack and indentation, every tiny opening, is stuffed with prayers. I don't want to stuff any more into these ancient stones, but I've made a commitment to our friends, they've poured out their hearts, and these prayers are a sacred trust, so I find a way to stick them in.

I see an old man with a long white beard, a long black coat, and a prayer book in his hand, his eyes closed, resting his forehead against the Wall. He is so still amid the swirling activity around us that he almost seems part of the stones. I decide to do what he's doing. I have no prayer book, and don't want one. My heart is my prayer book.

I touch my forehead to the stones, close my eyes, and breathe the four letters of God's name, the way I do when I meditate. The molecules of the Wall and the molecules of Aryae's body align themselves so they slide through each other. Aryae's body steps partway into the Wall. Scenes from thousands of years are replayed, or rather played, since there is no time here. A flood of images and feelings, of war followed by peace, of ancient music and singing, of processions of tens of thousands gathered for the holy festivals, followed by silence and emptiness, of tears of intense, unbearable longing followed by release, laughter and tears of gratitude and joy. Whirling galaxies of light and energy without end, gathering intensity, building momentum. Aryae's body is trembling.

I step back and open my eyes. Although it's cold out, I'm sweating and breathing heavily. The world around me looks bright, unfamiliar. I look around for the old man. He's gone. My eyes search through the crowds. I can't find him. I step away from the Wall.

As I walk back across the plaza toward the entrance, two men, one young and one old, approach me and start talking at the same time. They both have beards and are wearing religious clothes. The young one says that if I give him 100 shekels to help him get married, I will be blessed in the world to come. I give him some money. The old one yells that the young one is a thief, and I should give my money to *him* instead!

Later Wendy, Shulamis and I are walking through the streets, up a hill toward the *yeshiva* where Shulamis' husband is in charge. Everything—streets, buildings, courtyards—is made of stone. There are shuls interspersed between tasteful shops and cafes.

"You were one of my rebbes back then," Shulmis says to me. "You invited me into the House and held open the door to another world. My life totally changed as a result. That's why I'm here. But I don't know anything about your life after that. I'm so curious."

Wendy and I exchange glances. We've talked about this moment.

Two weeks ago I was walking on University Avenue in Palo Alto, California, in the heart of Silicon Valley, on my way to a dinner meeting with a group of executives. It was dark and the store windows were gleaming with lights and decorations for the Christmas season, filled with high-tech gadgets, showing off the latest technology. People in the street were drawn to the store windows like moths to a flame, attracted, fascinated, mesmerized. Everyone was alone, isolated from the people around them, their eyes fixed on the gadgets. It looked like a tableau from a science fiction story where the machines had taken over.

I live and work in the capital of the Land of Stuff, I thought, *and I'm about to travel to the capital of the Land of Soul.* And the weird thing is that there are people there who look to *me* as a teacher. How do I tell them my story in a way that makes any sense to me or to them?

"Shulamis," I say. "Maybe I was a teacher for you a long time ago, but now you're really a teacher for me. You know when Shlomo died it was such a shock, for all of us. I thought he would live forever. I had so much unfinished business, so many things to talk to him about. I've struggled with this for a long time, but here's what I realize: my job then was to start the House; my job now is to find a way to tell the story. That's why Wendy and I came. It's to connect with you, with Efraim and Leah, with everyone who's here from those days. I'm here to learn *your* story."

Shulamis looks at me and nods. We're all breathing hard from the effort of walking up the hill. "Have you seen Efraim and Leah yet?" she asks.

"Not yet," I say. "We're planning to stay with them for *Shabbos.*"

We get to the *yeshiva* run by Shulamis' husband, Rav Zahavie Green. While Wendy waits with Shulamis in the women's section, Rav Zahavie gives me a tour. He has a humble manner and is very warm to me. The men sitting at the tables, from their 20s to their 70s, look briefly up at us as we walk past, smile and nod, and then go back to their books. Rav Zahavie explains that his passion, and the methodology of this *yeshiva*, is *Mussar*, based on daily introspection and practices to improve one's character. The interior of the *yeshiva* is surprisingly beautiful, with lots of glass and metal artwork of many colors that cause light to dance through the rooms. Yeshivas are notorious for concentrating only on books, he says, and neglecting the rest of their physical environment. When he and his brother started this one, they set out to create an environment whose beauty would support and inspire the spirit.

Later Wendy and Shulamis and I are sitting at a café, eating soup. It's cold out and the hot, spicy soup is just right. In the mid-afternoon we have the place mostly to ourselves. Shulamis tells us about her work as Assistant Director at Retourno, a residential treatment center for adolescents, mostly from Orthodox families, with drug and alcohol problems.

I look at Shulamis sitting across the table. She is shorter than Wendy. With the straight, auburn hair of her wig and her impish smile, she looks like a combination of matron and college freshman.

"Isn't it unusual for a woman in your world to have her own independent career?" I ask.

Shulamis laughs. "I love my husband and my kids," she says. "But they know me too well to expect me to stay at home all the time. Thank God, I'm very blessed. Zahavie is supportive, but he's still traditional. I do all the cooking and make sure they have a good meal every night."

"What happens when you're travelling?"

"When I'm gone for a few days on a business trip, I cook all the meals ahead of time and freeze them. When I go to visit my parents in Berkeley, I do the same thing."

"That's a lot of meals!" I say.

I look out at the street, at the intensity of people on their way to holy places. For religious Jews — with the Wall, the Tomb of King David, the ancient stones, and almost 3,000 years of memories of our often-stormy relationship with God — this is it, the absolute center of the world. "It must be amazing to live here," I say. "Why did you and Zahavie move away?"

Shulamis sighs. Then she laughs and shakes her head. "It can get pretty crazy here. The energy of this place attracts all kinds of people. We were surrounded by them all the time."

"Like the beggar who talked me out of my money today," I say, "or like the House!"

She nods and gestures toward the window. "There's a lot of people walking around out there, hundreds of them, who believe that they're special, that God has called them here so they can save the world."

"It reminds me of our Jewish community in Berkeley," I say. "The difference is that in Berkeley, everyone's a *rebbe*. Here, it sounds like everyone's the Messiah!" The three of us laugh together. We talk a lot that afternoon, non-stop it seems. Shulamis shares her observations about the surprising similarities between the behavior codes here and in Berkeley. Both can actually get quite rigid, and people in both places get upset when their beliefs are questioned. Wendy mentions the recent ballot measure in Berkeley that would have outlawed coffee that wasn't "fair trade." If the Berkeley police spotted us drinking coffee in this café in Jerusalem, maybe they would haul us off to jail! We laugh some more. We talk about drugs in the Orthodox world and in the Bay Area, about families, about relationships between men and women. Shulamis says that in the States women have freedom to do whatever they want, but the culture inundates them from a young age with messages about sex appeal, and pressures them to spend most of their lives worrying about whether men find them attractive. Here in the religious world the lives and roles of women are more constrained, but the cultural messages are more supportive and respectful.

No matter how much we have to say each other, there's always more. The days are chilly and short in Jerusalem in December. Talking so rapidly, we've hardly noticed the slow, silent movement of the sun, angling low on its downward path across the winter sky.

There's something I want to find in the short time we're here. Ever since Shlomo died nine years ago, I've felt driven to write the story of the House. But in spite of years of effort, dozens of interviews, hours of advice from everyone I know, days and weeks and years of sitting in front of the computer, the story hasn't come together. No matter how much I try to remember and write it down, there's always more that is blank. And everyone I talk to, it seems, has a different recollection of what happened, and who was there. The historical record exists only in our memories, which are fading fast and growing distorted with time.

122

I've been as lost trying to find my way back in time to the House as I am trying to find my way through the streets of Jerusalem. There's something in my life that I'm not seeing, something missing, that hasn't yet come into focus. Maybe I can find it here, and maybe then I can finally tell the story.

We take Shulamis home. She gives us directions on how to get back to the Moshav, which is near Tel Aviv. We can go back the way we came; that road cuts through the West Bank, and it's not recommended at night. She tells us how to get to Route 1, the Jerusalem-Tel Aviv highway that looks like a California freeway.

After night overtakes us, as Wendy and I speed along Highway 1 in our rented car, we pay very careful attention to the road signs. We don't want to get lost here in the dark.

16

Hats

Ramot Polin, Jerusalem, Israel – December 2003

Wendy and I feel self-conscious as we wander uncertainly along the paths that curve through the low condo clusters of Ramot Polin, perched on the hills high above the northwest corner of Jerusalem. People stare at us. Everything is hexagons, and there are no right angles anywhere, not even in the streets or sidewalks. There are no signs or numbers to tell us where we are.

This is a neighborhood of Haredi families—the most strictly religious segment of Israeli society. We see men in long black coats and black hats, black pants and black shoes, and boys dressed like their fathers. The women and girls, walking separately from the men, wear skirts down to their ankles and have their heads covered, either with scarves or wigs, so no hair is showing.

Wendy and I are wearing our ski jackets, mine black, hers pink. I'm wearing khaki pants, and Wendy is wearing one of the long skirts she brought for these occasions. I'm wearing a small, black *kippah* such as might be worn by Orthodox men who are more moderate, less strictly religious. Wendy is wearing her black hat, but it doesn't stop her thick, wavy, light brown hair from spilling luxuriantly out the sides.

I call Judi from my cell phone.[*] She wants to know where we are. I don't have a clue. She's wandering around with her cell phone while we wander around with ours. I haven't seen Judi in over 30 years, and I'm trying to imagine what she looks like now. The first time she came to the House, she was a thin, 14-year-old girl with a full head of black curls, dressed like a suburban high school girl's fantasy of a Haight-Ashbury hippie.

"I think I see you!" says Judi on the phone. She sounds excited. Her voice reminds me of the high school girl. I look up. At first I

---

[*] I have changed her name to protect her privacy.

don't see anything. Then I notice, on the second story walkway one building away, a grandmother holding a phone is waving at us.

Wendy and I climb the stairs up to where Judi is. She smiles and doesn't avoid eye contact with me. Although the rest of her has changed, her lively intelligence is still there in her eyes. She greets Wendy warmly by grasping her hands. Judi is very curious and very loquacious. That also hasn't changed. She asks us question after question. We all talk and laugh as she leads us to her condo. Inside, the rooms are small and filled with the family's stuff, but the unfamiliar angles create the feeling of additional space. She's apologetic about the space; they're still reorganizing since the last of her children moved out.

Judi brings us into her husband Tsvi's study. Tsvi is a thin, scholarly, frail looking man with a long, gray beard, surrounded, almost buried at his desk, by tall piles of books and papers. His quiet, almost ethereal manner makes a dramatic contrast with the solid, energetic presence of his wife. He pushes his chair away from the desk, stands up, reaches out his hand to shake mine, and nods at Wendy without making eye contact.

I ask Tsvi about his work. He smiles, then looks down, and mentions a number of medieval Hebrew manuscripts that he is restoring. I am not familiar with any of them. There are crumbling sheets of parchment and paper, some over 400 years old, where the writing is barely discernable. Using a variety of technologies and tools of interpretation, he reconstructs the actual text as it was originally written, and provides scholarly comments and references to assist in understanding it.

As their children have left home, Judi has been getting into her career as a writer. She writes inspirational stories about people who experience God in their lives, and has had them published in several religious magazines. It occurs to me with grudging admiration that, for all the limits and barriers of being a woman, mother, and grandmother in the Haredi world, she is much further along in her writing career than I am in mine.

Judi suddenly has a thought. "Are you also going to see Efraim and Leah?" she says.

"We're planning to stay with them for *Shabbos,*" I say.

"They're so close," she says. "Why not stop over and see them now?" Her question catches me totally off balance. I haven't seen them for 34 years, and don't feel emotionally prepared to casually drop-in. Before I can say anything, Judi's on the phone.

"Leah!" she says, "Aryae and Wendy are here!"

126

Before I know it, we're standing at Efraim and Leah's front door. Their condo is on the second floor near a stairwell containing a child's small, bright orange plastic tricycle. The door opens and there's Leah, smiling at us. Her face is a little fuller than I remember. She's wearing the customary type of neck-to-foot dress of Haredi women, and a scarf around her head in a traditional turban style, which covers all her hair. The expression on her face is unmistakably Leah, overcome with love and joy as she welcomes her dear friends into her home. She gives Wendy a big hug.

We step inside and there, standing in the hallway before me, dressed in a white shirt, black pants, black shoes and large black velvet *kippah,* is Efraim. He is thin as a rail, with long red *peyos* (side curls) and streaks of red still remaining in his gray beard. He is grinning with his unmistakable mischievous look, just a little softened by time. In spite of the religious attire, his appearance has changed the least of any of us. We hug each other without saying anything as the three women look on. His body feels the same as it felt to me long ago, thin, vulnerable, ethereal, as though hovering between heaven and earth.

Efraim and Leah, as well as Judi and Tsvi, are now Breslover Hasidim, followers of the holy Rebbe Reb Nachman of Breslov, the great-grandson of the holy Ba'al Shem Tov, founder of Hasidism. Toward the end of his life, Reb Nachman began to teach through stories which, on the surface, read like fairy tales, but beneath are really mystic, dream-like visions, flashes of the shining reality hidden by the veils of this world. When most rebbes pass away, their followers find a new *rebbe;* but when Reb Nachman passed away at the age of 38 in the Ukraine in 1810, he told his Hasidim that he would be their *rebbe* forever. And they have remained his devoted followers to this day. At our wedding last year, Wendy and I asked our friends to read aloud from Reb Nachman's most famous story, "The Seven Beggars" (as Breslover Hasidim do at their weddings), for the story takes place at a wedding and contains the secrets of the journey of the soul.

Efraim and Leah's condo also has a hexagonal structure. The rooms are open, clean, spacious, and filled with light. I see a wall, slanting away from us, that appears to open to the world outside. Efraim has painted it to create the illusion that we are in a beautiful garden. The placement of furniture and objects in the rooms is sparse, judicious, aesthetically aware. His paintings are surprising, dreamlike flights of soul, where gardens, birds, children, wise sages, flowing streams, Hebrew letters, people dancing, buildings and landscapes extending through thousands of years of Jerusalem's past, present and future, all swirl together in the whirlwind of imagination, in a magical present beyond the boundaries of time.

Efraim, a former Haight Street art student in the '60s, is now one of Israel's best-known, best-loved mystical artists, whose paintings hang in homes throughout the world. Several of my friends in the Bay Area, who love his work but can't afford the original paintings, have large Efraim Simcha prints on their walls.

While the women sit in the living room, Efraim takes me into his studio. I feel like I'm visiting a holy shrine. A canvas in progress is on the easel. Magical images in bright, saturated colors are splashed sporadically across the wide, white space of the canvas.

I ask him about how he works, when he paints. He has a daily routine that begins at night when he walks to the forest to meditate. Reb Nachman taught his followers to meditate in the forest, to commune with God in nature. Efraim meditates all night until sunrise.

"What do you do when it rains?"

"Years ago I found a cave." He looks at the expression on my face. "No, really! It's pretty comfortable and keeps me mostly dry."

Then he walks to Mt. Zion near the Wall, and gets together with other Bresolver Hasidim to study Torah and pray the morning prayers. Then he walks home, gets back at around 9:30 in the morning, and begins his workday as an artist.

"Efraim, when do you sleep?"

He laughs again. "Leah keeps track of that. You'll have to ask her."

On a table there is a pile of small booklets. He hands me one. It's very compact, about the size of two credit cards. On the thick, shiny front and back covers, framed in archways embedded in blue sky with white clouds, are two tiny paintings, unmistakably by Efraim. In each one, hovering above the fields and mountains, an ethereal white dove sheds giant tears that fall to the earth. In one picture there are musicians in the sky and people dancing below. In the other, there is someone praying near a barn, and children and dancing Hebrew letters in the field.

"This is beautiful!" I say. "What is it?"

"It's called a *Tikkun Klali*."

"General healing, general fixing?" I look inside. Shiny pages with Hebrew verses in black letters written over beautiful images of mountains, lakes and forests.

"It's ten Psalms," Efraim says. "Reb Nachman chose them and arranged them in this order." According to the Zohar and the Hasidic rebbes, each Psalm is like a different medicine that can bring us what we need in certain situations, like at a wedding, or when we're travelling, or when times are hard, or when we need help with *teshuvah* (returning to God), or recovering from an illness. "Reb Nachman said that the *Tikkun Klali* will open the doors of blessing and healing anytime, whenever we ask.* I keep mine with me all the time, just in case." He laughs, and pulls a booklet out of his pocket. He tells me to keep two, one for me and one for Wendy.

We go back into the living room. Judi and Wendy are sitting on the couch. Leah is standing next to them with a photo album, bent over, showing them pictures of her family. They have six children and 29 grandchildren.

Efraim appears with his guitar and sings a Shlomo melody. It seems incongruous to see this aging, mystic grandfather strumming his guitar just las he did almost 40 years ago, and hearing him sing the same way. I sing with him. The three women look on. Men are not supposed to hear the voice of a woman singing, so they won't be tempted. "You play something," Efraim says, handing me the guitar after he's done.

"Here's the *niggun* (melody) we used to sing at your house in Forrest Knolls to welcome *Shabbos*," I say, looking at both him and Leah. I strum the guitar and sing. The simple melody repeats over and over. It feels like we're back in 1967, on their front porch overlooking the redwood forest, watching the sunset. The intense feelings of longing and devotion and rejoicing, from the mystic who created this melody in Eastern Europe 200 years ago, flow across time from his heart to ours. Efraim and Leah listen with their eyes closed.

Wendy and I had a dream before we got married. We would start inviting people to our house for *Shabbos*. When people came, it would be very simple: first we would sing, then we would study Torah together, then we would eat. I've been into cooking soups lately, so I cook a different soup each time. The first time people gathered in our living room, we started off with this melody. Now people have been coming to spend *Shabbos* with us for over a year, and this is how we always begin, just as we began at Efraim and Leah's almost four decades ago. As I look at Wendy on the couch sitting next to Judi, I can see that it's hard for her not to sing with me.

---

* This is reported in his disciple, Rabbi Nathan of Breslov's *Hayyei MaHaRaN*, translated into English as *Tzaddik: A Portrait of Rabbi Nachman*, 70.

After the melody is done Leah's eyes remain closed with her hands clasped together. Efraim smiles and looks at me. "Did we really sing that?" he says.

"Yeah, really," I say.

"Where is it from?" he says.

"Well, I always thought it was from Modzhitz," I say. The Modzhitzer Rebbe* and his descendents were great musicians of the Hasidic world, known for thousands of beautiful melodies.

"I don't think so," he says. "I think it's from Rhizhin." The Rhizhiner Rebbe** was known for holding court with his Hasidim with great beauty and dignity, like a king.

"Modzhitz, Rhizhin, how will we ever figure this out?" I say. We all laugh.

Efraim suddenly gets an idea. "Let's go visit the Kever Shmuel HaNavi (tomb of Samuel the Prophet)!" he says. "It's not far from here."

"Am I allowed to do that?" I ask. I'm a *kohen* (descended from Aaron, brother of Moses, and the priests of ancient Israel), and kohens are not permitted to be in the presence of the dead.

"For special places where our holy *tzaddikim* (righteous ones) and ancestors are buried, it's permitted," he says. "You've got a car, right? Can the three women sit in the back?" As a religious man, Efraim cannot make physical contact with women.

"It's a small car, but I think so," I say. I look at Wendy and Judi and Leah. "Do you want to give it a try?"

Judi looks at Leah, then at Wendy, and smiles.

"Sure!" Leah says, nodding. "We can sit together."

It's drizzling out, and there's a surprisingly chilly wind. Wendy is cold and zips up her pink jacket. Efraim, wearing his long black coat and well-kept black hat, looks like he is going to a formal occasion. But of course, this is how he always dresses. For Hasidim, the black hat they wear outdoors is an important part of how they present themselves to the world. They try to get the best quality they can

---

* Rabbi Yisrael Taub of Modzhitz (1849-1921), a gifted composer who did not read music, but whose melodies were preserved by his Hasidim to this day.

** Rabbi Yisrael of Rhizhin (1797-1851) was the great-grandson of the Maggid of Mezritch (the successor of the Ba'al Shem Tov), and was looked upon by Hasidim almost as the King of Israel during his lifetime.

from well-known dealers, and are careful to keep their hats in good condition. I reach up on top of my head to make sure that my small *kippah* is still there. In spite of the wind, it hasn't moved. The clips are doing their job.

By the time the five of us get to the car, our clothes are all a little wet. The three women squeeze into the back seat with good humor. Efraim guides me along some back roads, which are surprisingly new and in good condition. We wind our way through the stone hills. As we pass a sign in both Hebrew and Arabic, it occurs to me that we must be in the West Bank. I'm surprised that this happens so easily, without any sign of crossing a border. Back in the States, Wendy had told me that she was frightened of going into the territories, where so much violence has occurred. I promised I'd do my best to avoid the territories, but here we are. I decide not to say anything.

We get out of the car on top of a hill, outside of a compound surrounded with sections of stone fence topped with barbed wire. A small sign at the entrance says Kever Shmuel HaNavi. As we step through the entranceway of the wall, we walk toward the doorway of the stone building that houses the remains of Samuel the Prophet. Two soldiers at a table stop us and ask us questions. I look up and see that soldiers carrying weapons are posted around the perimeter of the compound. Below us, near the building, is a large pit that looks like an excavation where crumbling walls, delineating a mosaic of large rectangular spaces of what must have been an ancient building, surround pools of water.

Inside the building, where all the walls are of stone, in the lobby, we see two more soldiers. One of them says something to Efraim. "He said that this holy place is open to Jews and Palestinians on alternate days," says Efraim. Later he will make the only remotely political comment that I hear from him while we're in Israel. "*Barukh HaShem* (thank God) that we've been restored to our holy places." He says that when this holy place was under Arab control, it was desecrated, turned into a garbage dump. Now the Jews have it back, we have cleaned it up and made it accessible to everyone, Jew and Muslim alike.

As with other holy places, there are two entranceways to the room where the sarcophagus is housed. Wendy, Leah, and Judi walk down the stairway to the right; Efraim and I take the stairs to the left. When we get downstairs, the room is dimly lit. The sarcophagus sits on a platform at eye level. Men dressed like Efraim are standing in front of it, davening. I can faintly hear sounds of the women from the room on the other side. A couple of young guys look up from their books. They look at Efraim, then at me. Efraim smiles at them, greets them by name in a soft voice, and asks them how they are. They smile

131

a little in spite of themselves, and nod without saying anything. Efraim sees them looking at me. He explains that I'm his friend from America, whom he hasn't seen in 34 years. They nod silently at me.

Efraim walks up to the sarcophagus, touches it with his right hand, bends over and kisses it. Then he pulls something out of his pocket. I see the white dove on the cover. It's his *Tikkun Klali*. With his right hand on the sarcophagus, and his left hand holding the little book. He sways back and forth and begins reciting the Psalms.

I reach into my pocket and pull out one of the two little books. Then I reach into my shirt pocket and pull out my glasses. I'm not used to reading the Psalms like this, all in Hebrew, so I go slowly and try to understand the meaning. The first one, Psalm 16, begins something like this:

> Protect me God
> For I have taken refuge in you.
> You said to God:
> "You are my Master,
> All goodness that I receive is from you."
> Through the power of
> The holy ones in the earth
> Are my desires fulfilled.

Samuel the Prophet is here in the earth, I think. This is what Efraim and the others are doing here. Our holy ancestors and teachers were pioneers, adventurers in the realm of the spirit, explorers of God-consciousness. They mapped out the territory. By connecting ourselves to them, the "holy ones in the earth," we can connect ourselves to the timelessness of God's presence, which alone fulfills our desires.

I continue reading, davening through the Psalms. I feel awkward, unpracticed, plodding through this material that Efraim knows so well. So I focus on what I learned from Shlomo, on how to open our hearts through prayer.

When we meet the women back upstairs and we all walk outside, the wind is blowing hard, driving small raindrops like little needles against our skin. Wendy is cold and wants to hurry to the car. Several soldiers with their weapons, motionless in the wind, are standing guard around the perimeter of the excavation.

Suddenly a gust of wind blows the little *kippah* off my head. It sails like a Frisbee over the excavation, hovers, moves sideways back and forth, and then begins to drift down.

"Let's go get it!" says Efraim. I look at him, a 60 year old Hasid with his long gray beard, black hat, long black coat, and shiny black dress shoes. Then I look at the excavation with its slippery, wet rocks, tall vertical walls, and soldiers standing guard.

"Efraim that's okay," I say. "I can get another *kippah*."

Efraim smiles. "I know how to get down there."

"What about the barbed wire?"

"I know the way through it."

"What about the soldiers?"

"They won't shoot somebody who looks like me!" he says laughing. He's got a point, but how can we be sure?

Wendy is shivering. Leah puts her arm around her. "While the two of you go down there, can we wait in the car?" I look at the women, and at Efraim, and realize we're going down to get my hat.

"Sure!" I say. We go to the car, and I unlock it and let them in. Then the two of us go back up to the perimeter of the excavation.

"How are you going to get through that barbed wire?"

"Follow me!" We walk part way around the perimeter, to the left. There's an opening through the barbed wire, and some stone steps leading down. Efraim leads, I follow. We walk down the steps along the side of a great wall. We get to a narrow ledge, about one-fourth the way down. The wind is still blowing hard.

"I can't see the *kippah* anymore," I say. "Do you know where it is?"

"I think I see it down there." Efraim points to the edge of a large square pool, way down at the bottom, in partial darkness. I think I can make out a tiny black dot. A gust of rain blows into our faces.

"Efraim you really don't have to do this!"

"I know," he says. "But why turn back now? We're almost there!" We make our way along the ledge. It leads to a part of the excavation where it looks like there's a way to get down further. In between there are breaks in the ledge where we have to climb up and down piles of rock. We gradually work our way down into the excavation. I look at Efraim with his shiny black dress shoes and long black coat ahead of me, amazed that he can do this dressed like that.

"You know what this reminds me of?" I say.

"What?"

"Remember Sukkos at the House?" Efraim and Leah had been there for one Sukkos, October 1968, when Shlomo was with us. Sukkos is the holiday where we build little huts or booths. We make the roofs of leaves, and decorate them with beautiful fruit. The *sukkah* commemorates the time after we left Egypt when we were wandering in the desert. We had no permanent homes, slept in little booths and, according to our Rabbis, took shelter under the wings of the Almighty. Religious Jews sleep and eat in the *sukkah* for seven days.

"Of course I remember! The *sukkah* was huge. Hundreds of people came. Shlomo slept with us in the *sukkah,* even though it was raining."

"Do you remember how we built it?" I ask.

He's leading the way over the stones. I'm following. He turns around and smiles. "No I don't. What did we do?"

"I was learning how to be a carpenter, remember?"

"Yeah."

"The way I knew how to build things is, first you draw the plans with all the measurements, then you make a materials list and get the lumber and nails and stuff, then you cut the lumber and assemble the materials according to the plan."

"Sounds pretty organized."

"Right." We've come to a steep pile of rocks. Efraim climbs up with his hands and feet and I follow. "So one afternoon," I say, "I see you in the yard in back of the House with a pile of lumber. You're nailing one end of a long 2 x 4 to the fence.

"So I said, 'What are you doing?' And you said, 'Building the *sukkah!*' And I said, 'Where are your plans?' And you said, 'What plans? I'm just building it!' And I said, 'What's the other end of that 2 x 4 going to connect to?' And you said, 'Don't worry, I can see it in my mind!' I was the carpenter, but you kept moving, and I had no choice but to follow your lead. Somehow the *sukkah* got built. It was huge, and it was sturdy."

"It was a beautiful *sukkah,*" Efraim says. "We fed so many people in there!" At night we put down ground cloths and mattresses all over the ground. We made a special corner for Shlomo with a double mattress.

We get to the top of the rock pile, and pause a moment to look around. We're about half way down to where my *kippah* is lying by the murky square pool.

134

"Do you remember? That was the whole thing!" I say. "That's the way it was back then. Whenever there was something for the House that we had to do, I wanted to talk, to think about it, to make plans, but you would just go ahead and do it! You were fearless."

Balancing myself carefully on the rock I'm standing on, I extend my arms to make a dramatic gesture that encompasses the huge excavation surrounding us. "Here we are, still doing the same thing!" I say. "Nothing has changed!"

At that instant a sharp gust of wind laced with raindrops slaps our faces. Before we know what's happened, Efraim's black hat is floating high above his head, twirling in the wind. We watch in silence as it dances above us, rising higher and higher, finally perching precariously on top of a wall, flapping a little as the wind continues to blow.

As I look at the hat and the rocks in between, I can see the way up. "I'll get it," I say and start climbing.

"You don't have to do that," Efraim says below me. "I can go get it."

I laugh and look down at him over my shoulder. "You came down here to get my hat. It looks like I get to return the favor!"

"If you're gonna do that, I'll go down then and get yours!" He starts climbing down toward the pool. I turn around, put my hands on the wet rock in front of me, and climb up. The wind is fierce and the rocks are slippery. I look down and feel a twinge of dizziness and fear. I make myself turn around and push harder. I focus on Efraim's hat.

It was wet this morning when we left the Moshav, so I decided to wear my hiking boots. I'm glad I did. They make me feel a little safer. I don't know how Efraim is doing this in his black dress shoes.

I reach the hat and hold it in my hand. Although it looks serious and well made, it feels surprisingly light. I turn around and see that Efraim is still climbing down toward my *kippah*. I feel surprisingly light also, oblivious to the wet and cold. I start climbing down.

Soon we're climbing back out of the excavation, each wearing our own hat, a gift from the other. It's as though he's giving me the gift of restoring my identity, and I'm giving him the gift of restoring his. I'm amazed that, after so many years have passed, we are still connected at this level. Until now this was hidden from me. Shlomo used to say that the whole thing of friendship is secrets. How much can I tell you my secrets, the things that no one else knows about me? Even deeper, how much can I see your secrets, which are so hidden that they're secret even from you? And what's the deepest, most hidden secret of all? It's God hiding in each of us, waiting to be found.

We reach the top of the excavation and return along the wall the way we came. As we pass the soldier who had been looking down at us, Efraim says something to him, and he laughs. Looking at him, I can see that he's just a kid, about the same age as my son Adam. As we approach the car, the backs of the heads of the three women appear in the rear window. Wendy's hat is tilted a little to the side.

17

Moshav

Moshav Meor Modi'im, near Tel Aviv, Israel
Tuesday, December 2003

"*Aryae!*" I open my eyes. The room is dark. "You can come *daven* with me if you want. I'm leaving in about 15 minutes, okay?" It's Moishe Yitzchak.

"15 minutes?" I say, my voice hoarse with sleep. "I can't get ready in 15 minutes!"

"Just get there when you can."

I kiss Wendy, pull myself out of bed, and fumble around in the dark, looking for my stuff. We're sleeping in Moishe Yitzchak's office. Our stuff is spread out among the computer, printer, digital photography equipment, other digital gadgets, tangled masses of wires and cables that connect everything, tools, stacks of paper, equipment, parts and components—the treasures of a retired space engineer who loves to stack, organize and label everything that might be of use to fix, tinker with, or build anything.

The people who first came to Israel to start the Moshav in the mid 70s had met Shlomo at the House and other places. They arrived as holy beggars dreaming of bringing Shlomo's vision of the great day of love and peace to the world. When they got here, they found harsh realities. Basics that they had taken for granted back home—things like paved roads, a local food store, and electricity—were non-existent. Getting food and other necessities was a daily struggle. Financial opportunities were severely limited. Israel, a hard enough place to make ends meet for tough-minded, career oriented Israelis, didn't have many job opportunities for idealistic hippies from the States. But somehow they hung in there, survived, and built a viable community.

By the time Moishe Yitzchak and Bernice Kussoy retired here 10 years ago, the streets were paved, everyone had electricity, and some were living in spacious, comfortable homes. The Kussoys have a

137

unique status here at the Moshav: everyone's grandparents, fixers and providers of vital household items, potential business partners, and lenders of last resort. In the short time Wendy and I have been here, we've seen a stream of people coming in and out at all hours, to borrow something, a tool, a video or CD, to use the computer, to get something fixed.

I put on my ski jacket and step out into the cold morning air. I can hear the voices of a few men on the way to the *shul*, punctuating the quiet of dawn.

I'm aware that there's something I'm hoping to find here. My life has been good and I'm immensely grateful for Wendy, my children, my business, my home on the California coast—all of it. But something's missing. There are still parallel worlds in my soul: the 5,000 year old world that I stepped out of four decades ago, and the five billion year old world that I've been mostly living in ever since. I haven't been able to connect them. For me the Moshav is the path not taken. I can't imagine myself ever choosing to live in the Haredi world with Efraim and Leah, but coming here 30 years ago to live with the other holy beggars could have been a real possibility. Maybe by experiencing a little bit of what it's like here, and by connecting with people who did take this path, I can find a clue that will help me bridge the gap.

I walk past houses along the street, and then through a field, until I come to the *shul*. This building is the center of the Moshav. It has several rooms, including the main sanctuary where the Torah is housed. There are chairs and tables, and bookshelves along the walls filled with books.

The women's section is at the rear of the sanctuary. The practice of separating men and women when they pray is called *mehitza*, and is observed in all Orthodox communities. In some old, traditional shuls, the women and girls sit in upstairs balconies, looking down at the men leading the prayers. In some modern Orthodox shuls, the men sit on one side of the room and the women sit on the other, with a barrier in-between. Here the women sit in the rear, in rows of folding chairs facing forward. The two sections are separated by a barrier that comes part way up to the ceiling, and lace curtains that are lowered during times of prayer.

For the daily morning prayers at the Moshav, only men are present. They're sitting at various tables, wearing their *tefillin*, wrapped in their *tallisim* (prayer shawls), swaying back and forth, reading through the Psalms, davening. The room is filled with sounds that are familiar and comforting to me, the sounds of traditional davening, where each person is singing the prayer on his own, in his own key, to his own rhythm. The sound of each congregation has its unique characteristics. A knowledgeable person walking past a Hasidic *shul* can listen to the davening and tell who the *rebbe* is, or which Hasidic dynasty they are part of. The davening here has the unmistakable fingerprint of Shlomo's melodies.

Wednesday

Today I visit Lois. Her house is a tiny, non-descript single-story square with a flat roof sitting on bare land. Except for a small patch of garden on the side, there is no landscaping.

A woman in her 80s, frail, bent over, with a scarf tied over her hair and a hesitant, uncertain smile, Lois opens the door and invites me in. The kitchen table, with stainless steel legs and a Formica surface, is covered with bowls, potted plants and books. Lois has cleared space for me to sit and offers me tea, which I accept.

I listen as Lois shares her memories. It was her daughter Jill, then a student at Sonoma State College, who first met Shlomo in 1968 and began coming to the house.* Lois started joining her. After Efraim and Leah left for Israel, Lois and her whole family—Jill, Lois and Lois's three younger kids, two boys and a girl—moved into the House, in the large front bedroom.

Besides taking care of her own kids, Lois became a kind of den mother to the rest of us, making sure there were meals at night and especially that there was enough food to feed the hundreds of people who came for *Shabbos*. This was on top of commuting 50 miles each way to her job as a kindergarten teacher at Travis Air Force Base.

Whenever people tell me about their memories of the House, one thing is always constant. It's Lois in the kitchen, often with young women helping her, looking tired, sorting through the available food that we were able to buy and scrounge from the local markets, cooking it all up into big pots of soups and stews so that everyone could eat.

After she left the House, Lois wound up at the Moshav with her youngest daughter, who is now married and lives nearby with her husband and children. Her oldest son also came to the Moshav, and now lives a few houses away.

After we're done I turn off the tape recorder. Lois follows me through the kitchen to the front door of her tiny house, and steps

---

* I have changed their names to protect their privacy.

139

outside with me. The ground around the house is bare, evoking the harsh desert landscape that she and the other holy beggars found when they first got here.

"Come here, I want to show you something," she says with a shy smile. I walk behind this stooped over old woman. The slow, careful way she walks does not conceal the strength and determination that move her forward. We get to the back of the house. There, in the shadow cast by the late morning sun, is a small patch of dark, moist earth that has been tilled, watered and carefully tended. Growing in the earth are tiny green vegetables.

Wednesday, Early Evening

A few hundred people wearing jackets and coats—to protect them from the cool evening breeze—are gathered for a wedding around an outdoor wooden stage. People have come, I'm told, from all over Israel. Swarms of children alternate between running around in the field surrounding the stage, and excitedly squeezing past the adults, pressing close to the stage to get a better look. Some of them find front row balcony seats in the branches of nearby trees. Everywhere there are digital cameras. People hold them above their heads, looking up at the tiny screens glowing in the gathering darkness, and point them at the people on the stage, popping off their flashes.

The musicians on the stage are playing Shlomo's melodies. The sound system is good, and people are clapping to the music. The groom, a handsome young man in his mid 20s, is dressed in a black suit. From what people say during the ceremony, Wendy and I learn that he is an American, now in Israel studying at a nearby *yeshiva*.

Rabbi Mordechai Trachtenberg is conducting the ceremony.* Moishe Yitzchak, 72 years old, the semi-official photographer for all weddings, bar-mitzvahs and other special events at the Moshav, is up in a tree, draped over a branch, his big lens pointed at the stage, snapping pictures.

The music changes. The bride, a slender, beautiful young woman with jet black hair, wrapped in a stunning white dress that seems constructed of layers of white filigree, deliberately and gracefully makes her way up the steps onto the stage. All movement among the guests, even the children, stops, and everyone is focused on her. After

---

* I have changed their names to protect their privacy.

140

glancing up at the rabbi, who nods, she proceeds to slowly walk around the groom seven times in the traditional manner.

Mordechai, facing the bride and groom, tells Hasidic stories, shares mystical teachings and gives them many blessings. Illuminated by the light bulbs and candles on the stage, and the heartfelt warmth of the rabbi's blessings, the two young people are radiant. The musicians play another Shlomo melody, and everyone sings. Joy fills the night.

After the ceremony everyone pours into the synagogue, which had been converted to a wedding reception headquarters. A band plays in one of the rooms. Compared to the quiet and orderly beauty of the wedding ceremony, the atmosphere of the reception is exuberant, raucous, chaotic. Lots of loud conversation, people recognizing each other and shouting to each other from across the room, teenagers filled with excitement at the party racing all over. People crowd around the food tables from all directions without lines, pushing to get to the food.

After the meal people get up to dance. In the room with the band, young men are dancing vigorously, wildly, kicking up their heels, flinging themselves into the air, working up a sweat. Others, mostly older men, are holding hands and moving in rapid circles around the room. One of the men gets down and squats, then jumps and squats again, while twirling a large handkerchief over his head, just like they used to do in Eastern Europe a couple of centuries ago.

The women are dancing separately, in another room, removed from the band. The music isn't as loud there. I sense that as a man I'm not supposed to be paying much attention to them, but I'm curious. Younger women and a few older women are moving very sensually. One young woman bares her midriff and does a belly dance. Other women take up the rhythm, moving their hips and swaying their bodies.

Wendy and I leave while the party is still going strong. Outside in the dark night, we can see the stars and feel the vast silence surrounding us as the music echoes like a distant dream through the cool air. Moishe Yitzchak and Bernice are also outside, and we stop to chat with them. A small group of boys and girls, young teenagers from the Moshav, walk by and Moishe Yitzchak greets them. They look at me and Wendy without saying anything.

"These are my friends Aryae and Wendy," Moishe Yitzchak says. "Aryae is the one who started the House of Love and Prayer with Shlomo." They stare blankly at the 60-year-old, partially bald man from America they see in front of them. Moishe Yitzchak looks at me

141

and then back at them. "He's also the one who wrote the Birthday Song!"

Now their expressions change and they become animated. "Really?" says one young man, "did you really write the Birthday Song?"

It takes me a moment to understand what they're talking about. Then I smile. "Yeah, I guess I did," I say. "That was, let's see, about 35 years ago!"

"Wow!" he says, "Cool!" They look at each other and giggle, and then go off in the direction they were headed.

"I didn't know you wrote a birthday song!" Wendy says. "How come you never told me?"

"You guys probably don't know this," Bernice says, "but here on the Moshav, every time a kid has a birthday, we sing the Birthday Song that Aryae wrote in the House."

"Really?" says Wendy.

"Yeah," says Bernice, "and we sang it at the House whenever anyone had a birthday. Then when people came to Israel, they brought it here with them." She gestures at the kids running around outside the synagogue. "Look at all these kids! They've been raised with it all their lives."

I watch the kids and shake my head. "I'm totally amazed," I say, "I had no idea."

Moishe Yitzchak laughs. "Nobody knows or cares that Aryae Coopersmith started the House of Love and Prayer," he says. "What counts is, he's the guy that wrote the Birthday Song!"

As Wendy and I walk through the chilly evening back to the Kussoys' house, we can feel the mood of festivity and celebration in the Moshav around us. The echoes of music keep coming from the synagogue. Groups of excited teenagers wander in the night.

I'm feeling stunned about the Birthday Song. 35 years ago at the House, I had gathered a few people together for a little surprise party for Ruthie. About 10 minutes before it was time for her to walk in the door, I decided to make up a song for her birthday. The words and melody were simple, and came to me very quickly. When she walked in we sang her the song. The melody was exuberant, playful, and lifted everyone's spirits. To my surprise we all danced and sang for a long time. Ruthie was thrilled. I left the House four years later, and less than two years after that, Ruthie and I had separated. I forgot about the Birthday Song.

Back at the Kussoy's, as Wendy and I are upstairs getting ready for bed, we hear voices below. I open the window and look out. It's a group of teenagers sitting around a campfire in an open field across the street. They're singing.

"Come here!" I say. Wendy comes to the window. We watch the firelight glow on their faces and listen to their voices. They're Israeli kids with parents from America, raised on the Moshav. They live in a strange kind of world of their own, not really Israelis, not really Americans. What will they do and who will they be when they grow up, I wonder. We can hear what they're singing. The melody echoes out into the night.

Happy birthday, happy birthday, happy birthday Eli.
Happy birthday, happy birthday, happy birthday Eli.
We wish you a good year, a very good year,
We wish you a very good year.

Wendy and I look at each other. She smiles at me. There are tears in her eyes.

18
In Our Own Image

Moshav Meor Modi'im, near Tel Aviv, Israel
The following Monday, December 2003

The house of Rabbi Mordechai and Tirtzah Trachtenberg is quiet as Wendy and I approach.

Tirtzah answers the door and welcomes us in. I see a woman with a kerchief wrapped around her head and fierce dark eyes. She hasn't changed all that much from the young woman she was at the House: spunky, feisty, with a self-confident attitude combined with a way of receiving, of going with the flow, that seems archetypically feminine. She gives us a tour of her home, and we find a lot to admire.

She tells us about her husband's latest book, which is literally coming hot off the press as we speak. Mordechai was ordained by Shlomo, heads up an institute in Israel, has written several books about Jewish mysticism, and has taught and lectured all over the world. He's on his way to the publisher to pick up the first copies of this one.

We sit down at the kitchen table. Tirtzah offers us some tea.

"The first time I ever heard about Hasidism," she says to me, "you were doing a psychodrama at the House on the *Tanya!*" The *Tanya* was written by the Alter Rebbe, literally the 'old *rebbe*,' who lived in Russia in the late 18th century.* "It was about the internal struggle of the *tzaddik* (righteous one) and the *rasha* (evil one) and the *beynoni* (in-between one) inside a person, and how we get pulled in all these directions."

I laugh. "Was one side pulling the right arm, and the other side pulling the left arm?"

"Yeah!" she says. We all laugh. I try to imagine myself back then, studying the chapter in Hebrew the night before, and then directing my fellow holy beggars to act out the drama.

---

* Rabbi Shneur Zalman of Liadi (1745-1812), the founder of Chabad school of Hasidism, and the Chabad-Lubavitcher lineage of Reb Shlomo's Rebbes.

145

Aryae conducting his class in *Tanya* at the House of Love and Prayer.
Photo by Moshe Yitzchak Kussoy.

Tirtzah tells me about how, in 1968, she had gone with her Christian friend Michael on a 'mission quest' down the California coast. "We went to all the Christian missions. I actually worked for the Holy Order of MANS, in the Mission District.* Big, giant crosses, blue robes. We would walk into the Mission District and help the junkies, help the homeless people. The first time I went to the House was one Friday night. Michael asked me if I wanted to go to a commune, and I said, 'Sure! A commune, let's go!'

"So I walk in, and Leah's lighting candles. And after being on many journeys all over California and the Southwest, looking for something, this felt like home. So whenever I needed a crash pad in San Francisco, I would come to the House. I'd stay over, catch a class in Hasidism, whatever was happening, help Leah cook for the 150 or so people who would show up every Friday night."

I ask her how she met Shlomo. "We were all hanging out in the House," she says. "I was hanging out with Leah in the foyer. And I had a tambourine. We were all standing around in a circle, and it was like, 'When is Shlomo coming? When is Shlomo coming?' And he walked in. He walks around to everybody in the circle and asks their Hebrew name. So it's the first time I introduced myself by my Hebrew name. And it stuck."

---

* The Holy Order of MANS was a Christian religious order founded by Dr. Earl Blighton, known as "Father Paul" in 1968. Its headquarters at the time were in San Francisco.

I ask her about her memories of the House.

"Candles in the bathrooms," Tirtzah says. "Candles everywhere. I walked in and it struck me. Candles we had on the mantelpiece of the big living room that we transformed into a *shul*. That was nice, but then there were candles in the kitchen, there were candles in the hallways, candles in the bathrooms . . . It was all candlelight, the whole place.

"We had lots of crazy people in the House. There were people who came in, you know, with knives, and threatening. Then we had wonderful, warm people like Lois. She used to cook us oatmeal after staying up all night, and then she would drive 70 miles to her kindergarten job."

We talk a long time and share many memories.

Then Mordechai, just back from the publishers' Tel Aviv office, comes in. He's moving quickly with great energy and a big smile on his face, looking like a combination of a Hasidic rabbi and a big elf. I get up and give him a hug. He asks Wendy and me if we'd like to have the very first copy of his new book. Wendy is excited. His book is about the seasons and cycles of the year, a subject of great interest to her. The cover shows a galaxy and stars in a dark blue and black sky.

"Would you like me to sign it?" says Mordechai.

"Yeah!" we say. He looks around for a pen. I pull one out of my shirt pocket, and he writes something in the front page.

"Let's say a *Shehehianu!*" I say. This is the blessing we say when God brings us to a special milestone in life. We say the blessing in Hebrew: "Blessed are you God of the world, who has kept us alive, and sustained us, and brought us to this time!"

I hug him again and we say *shalom* to him and Tirtzah. Later on Wendy and I open the book to see what he wrote to us. "The writings of this book go back 30 years and your friendship with Tirtzah goes back even further. May the seeds and sparks of our lives continue to intertwine."

As Wendy and I walk slowly back toward the Kussoy's—enjoying the bright light, bright colors and faint warmth of the early December afternoon—we see Hanna who, prior to the wedding last week, I hadn't seen since 1972, when she had started coming to the House on 9th Avenue just as I was leaving it. Hanna takes us on a little tour of the Moshav, showing us some of the places we haven't seen yet. I get out my camera and take pictures.

Curious about her own experiences of that time, I ask what reached her more strongly at first, Shlomo or the House?

"It was more the House," she says. "The first time I met Shlomo it was like, 'What does he want from all these young chicks?' So, you know, I kind of kept my distance. And then I got to know a little more about . . . Some of it was true. Some of that hunger was there, *and loneliness.* I saw a very lonely human being. He would go back to those hotels by himself . . .

"And some of it was just pure soul-love. It had nothing to do with the physical thing. It was also someone who loved you no matter what you did wrong, or were before; someone who could see all the good you were going to do in the future, and encouraged you to stick with that."[*]

Hanna's frankness in alluding to the controversial side of Shlomo's story, and the complexity of deciding who he was and how to relate to him, takes me by surprise. Wendy and I make eye contact. In the Jewish world in the States, and in our Jewish Renewal communities in particular, he has become a controversial figure. On the one hand there are thousands of people for whom Shlomo, with his tireless energy, wisdom, generosity and love, provided the gateway to a Jewish and a spiritual life. On the other hand, after he passed away, women started coming forward with stories about sexual misconduct. Endless heated arguments about Shlomo polarized communities and have been a source of great pain for many, including me.

Wendy and I have decided not to bring the subject up while we're here in Israel. I've learned that many people here on the Moshav don't want to talk about or even acknowledge this part of Shlomo's story. To me it seems like they're in denial. But their lives today are built on the foundation of what they received from Shlomo, so I can understand why. I have no desire to cause pain and disrupt their lives by confronting them.

Friday Evening

Bold orange and red streaks spread out across the wide desert sky on a Friday evening in December, as *Shabbos* ripples into the Moshav in waves of darkness. Wendy and I are walking with Moishe Yitzchak and Bernice to the *shul.* Everyone else is doing the same, all dressed in their best *Shabbos* clothes. The air is filled with excitement.

---

[*] I have changed her name to protect her privacy.

"You have to experience *Shabbos* on the Moshav," Moishe Yitzchak told us. "It's unbelievable! It's the only place in the world where you can feel *Shabbos* the way it was in the House." Wendy, who never experienced *Shabbos* in the House and never met Shlomo, has been looking forward to this.

The people on the Moshav are not the only ones walking to the *shul*. Visitors, mostly young people in their late teens and early 20s, have come from all over Israel to stay for *Shabbos*. In accordance with the laws and customs of hospitality among religious Jews, the families of the Moshav put them up in their homes, weekend after weekend. The young guests, who have heard all kinds of stories about *Shabbos* on the Moshav, seem to be all over the place, and are very excited.

At the *shul* we separate and Wendy goes to the women's section in the back. I go with Moshe Yitzchak to the larger men's section in the front.

Some of the men, sitting clustered around large tables, have started to sing. Other men are standing and clapping. The tempo and volume build. Soon we reach *Lekha Dodi*, the song for greeting the Shabbos Bride. One kid across the room, about 15 years old, with long *peyos* that hang by his ears, wearing a black suit and black hat, is jumping with his eyes closed and banging on his book. A middle-aged man sitting down is banging the table with both fists. A couple of older men in rainbow colored kippahs start dancing arm in arm around the *bimah*, other men follow, and soon everyone is on their feet and dancing. Most of the songs are Shlomo songs. I get up and jump in, merging with the exuberant, almost rowdy, male energy.

After a long time, the dancing finally stops and we reach *Barekhu*, the blessing where we stand and bow to God together to begin the evening service. Then we go back to our seats to continue with the prayers: "*Blessed are You, God of the world, whose word brings evenings . . . You roll light from the face of darkness, and darkness from the face of light . . .*"

Moishe Yitzchak taps me on the shoulder and points toward the back of the room. A woman is standing at the doorway, gesturing toward us. It's Wendy. She looks unhappy. She's gesturing to me to come over.

I get up and walk over to the door. She has tears in her eyes. "What's the matter?" I say. I can hear the men in the room behind me davening loudly. The women in the room in front of me are quieter and moving much less. Some look down at their books and mouth the words softly.

Wendy looks up at me darkly. "I'm out of here," she says.

"Why?" I say. "What's the matter?"

"Sitting in the women's section behind the *mehitza*," she says. I can sense her shaking inside. If we weren't here in public she would be sobbing. "I can't take it and I'm going back."

"Okay," I say. "I'm going with you."

She walks out through the doorway. I walk behind her. A guy from the Moshav in his 40s with a long beard, a long striped coat in the Hasidic style, and a rainbow colored *kippah*, is standing as a greeter outside. "Good *Shabbos!*" he says to her smiling, as she walks past him sobbing. "Have a wonderful *Shabbos!*" We get past him and walk along the path. The night air is clean and cool.

"He didn't even see me!" she says.

"I know," I say.

Her eyes meet mine. "I know this means a lot to you. You don't have to stay away. I would just like it if you would walk me back."

I put my arm around her and smile. "You mean more to me. Come on, let's go."

We walk back slowly through the night with our arms around each other and the sounds of the men davening behind us.

"What's so bad about the *mehitza?*" I say finally. "I mean, you knew they would have it, right? That's what they do here. It's their thing. It doesn't mean it's our thing. While we're here, we're just hanging out and doing their thing with them. I don't get why it's such a big deal."

She looks up at me with some anger but mostly pain. "It was *awful!*" she says. "Lots of places, the women's section and the men's section are side by side, right?"

"Yeah . . ."

"Why can't they do it that way here? This is supposed to be Shlomo's Moshav, isn't it? Sitting there in the back behind that lace curtain, trying to peek through the holes so we could see what's going on in the service . . . It felt like all the life was over *there*." She sobs. "I just can't tell you how awful that feels!"

I hold her tighter and kiss her head. "I'm so sorry," I say.

When we get back to the Kussoys', there's a big kettle of hot water on the stove. I pour us each a cup of hot tea. "The women must

150

have been doing *something*, weren't they?" I say. "There's some pretty strong women here. How could they just be doing nothing?"

Wendy sips her tea. She's calmer now. "I know," she says. "I couldn't believe it." She talks about the women's Rosh Hodesh (New Moon) celebration at the Moshav a few days ago. There was a feeling of sisterhood, a community of smart, learned Jewish women on a spiritual path, a community she could identify with.

"What happened to them?" she says. "There was no *energy*! The men were singing at the top of their lungs, and dancing, and we were just *sitting* there!" She breaks into sobs again. I reach out to touch her hand. She pulls her hands away.

After a while she's feeling better and decides to visit Judy, Bernice and Moishe Yitzchak's daughter. Judy lives with her husband Chaim and five kids downstairs in a separate living unit on the first floor of the house. I go back to the *shul* to join the men for the end of the davening.

When I get back Wendy tells me about her visit with Judy. Another woman from the Moshav about Judy's age, in her 30s, also came over to visit. The three of them sat at the table looking at the *Shabbos* candles, sipping tea and talking about their lives. Wendy felt comfortable and peaceful being with them. This felt much more like *Shabbos*, a sense of quietness, rest, and spiritual connection with other women.

"Maybe this is where women's spirituality happens here," she says. "Not in the *shul*, but in the home with each other."

Moshe Yitzchak and Bernice have invited half a dozen guests to their house for *Shabbos* dinner besides Wendy and me. The meal is awkward. The talk is mostly about the ins and outs of people's daily lives on the Moshav. Wendy is feeling too shaken to participate. I'm feeling as fragmented inside as ever. So far my experience at the Moshav isn't providing me with any answers, only more questions. I remember something that Shlomo said once: *"We can't heal the Jewish people, and we can't heal the brokenness of the world, until we heal the relationship between men and women."*

The next day Wendy will keep examining this question, both with me and with women at the Moshav: how did the women here ever agree to accept a *mehitza*, especially this one in the back of the room, and what was Shlomo's role? One of the women will talk to her about the pervasive hugging at the House and later at the Moshav, and the less mature men who did too much of it. Separating from the

151

men during prayer actually made many of the women feel safer and more comfortable.

After the meal Wendy talks with Chaya Leader. Chaya lived at the House when I was there. She's been in Israel since 1970, working for much of that time as a healer in alternative therapies. Now she works as a writer and editor. She was one of the founders of the Moshav, but left long ago. She listens to Wendy with deep understanding, and offers to do some healing energy work with her. Wendy gratefully accepts. They go to a quiet corner of the house. I follow along.

"I totally honor the Jewish tradition," Chaya says. "I've gone into it very, very deeply. But the tradition and the laws are not to be worshiped. There are laws that can cause horrible distortions, and I've seen it happen here."

She places her hands on Wendy's shoulders, closes her eyes, and breathes. Then she opens her eyes again. "I've been here 33 years. I did a lot of things in all these years. There's something I picked up by osmosis from Shlomo about healing and about life. It's that the technique is not important; it's your being and your love. That is what heals people. You're not healing them. You're being a vessel for something beyond."

"How can people here in Shlomo's Moshav do something so different from Shlomo's House of Love and Prayer?" Wendy says. "Or did Shlomo really have a different agenda than Aryae and you and everyone thought in those days? Was it all just a come-on to lure women into the Orthodox world, so they could put them behind mechitzas once they were here?"

Chaya laughs. "Everyone sees Shlomo in their own image," she says.*

---

* A Moshav leader, who wished to remain anonymous, asked me to include the following: "Both the men and women of the Moshav have worked very hard to make the women's section of the *shul* as warm and inviting as possible. On virtually every *Shabbat* the women's section is full and there is exuberant singing and dancing for *Kabbalat Shabbat,* an experience that has inspired literally tens of thousands of women over the years. What happened that particular *Shabbat* is a mystery to me. Although women dancing with the *Sefer Torah* in Orthodox shuls has spread somewhat in recent years, the Moshav was among the very first to do this. At various celebrations women speak from the women's side, and the *mehitza* was created to be as attractive and see-through as possible long before others adopted this practice. As far as the *shul* not being split down the middle, this is not based on any philosophy, but rather the physical shape of the *shul*. We did not design the *shul,* and it simply does not lend itself to this solution. Our deepest desire is that everyone should have as spiritual and joyous experience of prayer as possible."

Part II

Shlomo and Aryae in the House of Love and Prayer.
Photo by Moshe Yitzchak Kussoy.

19

Fixing the Heart

House of Love and Prayer – June 1968

I watch Shlomo's lips moving and try to understand what he's saying.

In the dancing light of a hundred candles, people are pressed together in the prayer room with arms around each other, two hundred of us, swaying like leaves on a single tree, blown gently back and forth by the winds of heaven. We seem to be dancing with the candlelight. The room is filled with the silence, punctuated only by the sounds of breathing, and an occasional creak from the floor. Young men with long hair, young women with longer hair, dancing waves of color, kippahs, shawls, panchos, serapes, beads, rainbows, and tie-died mandalas.

I can see Moishe and Maxine, and Marv and Bernice dressed more conventionally, with all of their kids, standing in the outer circle.

Efraim is on my right. His eyes are closed as he sways from side to side with great intensity, shoulders tight, slightly hunched over, dancing to a different rhythm. I touch his shoulder lightly, so I can connect with him even as my body is swaying with the rest of the circle. He smells like patchouli oil, the way Shlomo smells on *Shabbos*.

Shlomo, standing on Efraim's right, is rocking forward and back, his hands clasped in front of him, lips moving very rapidly, silently. He is wearing a freshly starched white shirt, accented with several strings of colorful beads around his neck, and dark suit pants. His eyes look out through half-closed lids, rapidly scanning the room.

I see Sarah standing in the wide doorway at the entrance to the prayer room. Ever since we met last fall there's been a spark between us. I've been trying my best to pretend that what I feel for her is the same as what I feel for the other women at the House. She smiles at me and then looks away.

155

It's only been two months since I moved in and we opened our doors, seven weeks since Ruthie joined me, and six weeks since Efraim and Leah arrived. Everything's been happening so quickly. Shlomo has added the House of Love and Prayer to his business cards. He hands them out wherever he goes and invites everyone to come for *Shabbos*.

We've just been singing and dancing *Lekha Dodi* for the holy Shabbos Bride. Her spirit is here in the room, filling us with love as we all hold each other. We don't need prayer books, because Shlomo is saying the prayers for all of us. He doesn't need a book because all of it is engraved in his memory. The prayer book, and the entire Torah, is inside Shlomo and pours forth from him effortlessly. Maybe if we stay with him and open ourselves enough, the Torah will pour into us, and will be inside of us too.

"Rabbi Carlebach!" Even more jarring than the sound, even more than the loudness breaking the silence, is the accent. Businesslike, demanding, intrusive, like the cold light of a policeman's flashlight startling a young couple in a car.

I look up toward toward the doorway in the back. There is a man in his fifties, just a little older than my father, slim, medium height, with grey hair, wearing a dark business suit, glasses, and a black knit *kippah*. The contrast between this dark figure and the rainbow of people in the room couldn't be starker. He is standing very still and straight, looking right at Shlomo. The room is quiet.

Moving himself between worlds, as though being dragged out of a dream, Shlomo stops davening and looks up. "Yeah?"

"Rabbi Carlebach, what are you doing?"

Shlomo looks at him uncomprehendingly. "What do you mean?"

The man waves his arm, gesturing at all of us in the room, as though the transgression were too obvious, and too grievous, to even be mentioned. "This! You're an Orthodox rabbi. You should know better!"

The swaying of the circles has stopped. All eyes are on Shlomo. The room is silent.

"What is your name?" he asks the man. He sounds genuinely interested, curious.

"My name is Irving Solomon," he says, "and I'm president of an Orthodox *shul* here in town. Rabbi Carlebach," he says, gesturing again at all of us, "you know that boys and girls, men and women touching each other like this—this isn't really Judaism. You know

156

that men and women have to be separated during prayer! Why aren't you showing them the real thing?"

Shlomo's eyes are open very wide. I've been learning how to lead services by watching him, and by watching Efraim. It's about working with the energy in the room so people can experience oneness with each other. It's not so hard when everyone is with you, supporting you. But how do you bring forth the spirit of love and harmony and oneness when someone is challenging you? Everyone is looking at these two men.

No one moves for what seems like a long time. Finally Shlomo steps toward the man. "Why are you standing so far away, my friend?" he says. "Why don't you come a little closer?" The people standing near him step back, and a path appears between him and Shlomo. Irving Solomon looks around a little hesitantly, and then steps forward. The two of them are standing in the middle of the room, facing each other. We're all standing still. The room is silent.

Shlomo looks at everyone around the room. "Listen to me my friends," he says. "This is very important. I want you to meet my friend Irving Solomon. And I want you to know that this is *mammash* the sweetest *Yid* in the world." Irving Solomon, alone and isolated in his dark suit, looks at the rainbow sea around him, then back at Shlomo.

"You know, you're right," Shlomo says to him. "But some things are more important than being right."

"Imagine if a patient comes into the emergency room, God forbid, with a heart attack, and the doctor says, 'His toenails are crooked; I better straighten them out.' What would you say? Stupid, right?" Shlomo's voice gets higher and louder. His eyes are bulging. "Today we're losing a whole generation of our children! Their hearts and souls are literally dying. And what does the so-called 'Jewish establishment' say? They want to straighten-out their toe nails!"

He looks around at all of us. We still have our arms around each other. The flickering lights from a hundred candles dance all over the ceiling. Shlomo's voice is softer now. "Maybe some day we'll have time to take our kids and work on their toe nails," he says. "I don't know. But right now we have something more important to do. We have to *mammash* connect with their hearts."

All eyes are now on Irving Solomon. Standing by himself in the middle of the room, he looks around uncertainly. Efraim looks over at me and smiles. The room is silent. Irving takes off his jacket. He carefully folds it over his arm, and looks around for a place to put it. Maxine steps up behind him and says something to him. He hands

157

her the jacket. He looks again at Shlomo, then around the room at all of us. No one says anything. He takes off his tie, carefully folding it and putting it in his pocket. Now he has on a white shirt with an open collar, just like Shlomo. Shlomo looks at him and smiles. As he steps back toward the circle, a young man and a young woman step sideways to make room for him. Irving Solomon puts one arm around each of them. Leah is standing toward the back of the room, her hands clasped together, her eyes looking upward, sighing.

Shlomo starts a soft melody, and we all begin singing. The melody is slow, gentle. It gradually gets more energetic and faster. Soon we're dancing again. The floor of the prayer room bounces up and down as we jump. The Queen is back in the room, shining, dancing with us all. Oneness and love radiate everywhere. Although it's very late, the room is filled with energy, enough for two hundred people to keep dancing for a long, long time. We dance; then we stop and hum softly, or just stand in silence for a while; then we dance again. Somehow, in a way where I'm only partly aware of it, Shlomo manages to slip in all the Friday night *Shabbos* prayers.

Around 1:30 in the morning Shlomo tells us it's time for *Kiddush*. He asks Irving to stand next to him. Leah makes her way through the crowd carrying a silver tray with a silver wine goblet and a square bottle of Manischewitz wine.

I look up and see Donna standing at the back of the room. How long has she been there? She is by herself, a little detached from everyone else, looking around at people, taking it all in. I wave to her. She smiles and waves back.

The door to the House suddenly opens. Entering in a swirl of color and sparkles, her shawl not quite concealing her nightclub dancer's outfit, as though making a grand entrance and suddenly discovering she's on the wrong stage, Ruthie enters the scene. Irving Solomon looks over at her, his mouth open. Ruthie has just got a job dancing at a club in North Beach. She must be out early tonight. I wave to her. As she takes in the scene and realizes that this is a quiet point in the middle of *Shabbos* prayers, she looks around sheepishly and puts a hand over her mouth to suppress a giggle.

Shlomo looks up, recognizes her and smiles. "Sweetest thing, darling," he says. "Why don't you come and joins us for *Kiddush?*" Ruthie, who seems to be half embarrassed, half enjoying herself, smiles back at Shlomo, shakes her head "No," smiles and waves at everyone in the room, and makes her exit. I can hear her lightly running up the stairs.

Later That Night

Sarah and I are walking on Lake Street, toward the ocean.[*] It's the hour before dawn, when the night is most still and mysterious. The fog has lifted, and the sky is glistening with stars. The windows from the tall, narrow houses and apartment buildings that line the street are peeping down at us. The people inside are sleeping, so the houses will keep our secret. At the cross streets, if you look to the right, you can see the short blocks that dead end at the open rolling hills of the Presidio. I can make out the shapes of tall trees against the starry sky.

We walk slowly, with the night surrounding us, and all the time in the world. The night is so quiet. As we go further west toward the ocean, the houses get wider and more upscale. There are fewer people, more space, more privacy.

Sarah puts her arm around my waist. I feel a secret, guilty pleasure. We're looking up at the stars. I like feeling the warmth of our bodies touching. Other than House of Love and Prayer hugs, this is the first time we've touched. I want her to stay close, so I put my arm around her shoulders. She leans toward me a little. We keep walking. The world is at peace and time has stopped.

Suddenly Sarah stops. I stop too. She puts her hands on my shoulders, and turns me until I'm facing her.

"Aryae!" she says.

"Sarah," I answer, smiling.

"Aryae, listen to me," she says. "This is really hard."

"What's really hard?" I say.

She looks into my eyes. "I want you so much."

I'm surprised at how excited I feel. I find myself glancing up and down the street to see if anyone is around. The headlights from a single car are slowly moving toward us, heading west. I watch the car as it passes. Then I reach out and pull her close to me. We can feel each other breathing. Her hair, which smells like a spice from the Middle East, touches my face lightly.

"Aryae, what are we going to do?" Sarah says. I hold her tight and don't say anything. We are both breathing heavily. "Let's find somewhere to be together."

---

[*] I have changed her name out of respect for her privacy.

159

I imagine us going back to the House while people are still sleeping. But there are so many people, and Ruthie's there. Then I imagine us finding a hotel room. The Seal Rock Inn is within walking distance. Maybe if we go there we can be together for a while, and then get back to the House before anyone wakes up. But it's *Shabbos* and I don't have any money with me.

"I don't know Sarah," I say. "I don't know how to do this. It's so complicated."

She pulls back and looks right into my eyes. "What's so complicated about us wanting to be together?"

I grab her and kiss her. Our hands are all over each other. My heart is beating fast. My body is flooded in intense desire. Behind her I can see the short street that leads to the Presidio. The night is chilly but not cold. We're both breathing so hard and I'm holding her so tight. Maybe we can find a grassy spot.

Without my mind thinking any thoughts or making any decision, my arms push her away.

Her hair a little mussed up, breathing fast, her eyes are open wide. "What, Aryae, what?"

I'm also breathing fast. "Let's walk," I say. I grab her hand and we walk farther west. We're getting close to Sea Cliff, where the houses are big, spaced far apart, and have manicured lawns. I turn to look at one of them and see just a hint of the dawn that is approaching from below the horizon.

"We need to talk," I say. I stop walking and she stops too.

She's silent for a moment. "Okay," she says finally.

"When I was going to school at State College, I would be having sex with more than one woman at once."

"I'm impressed," she says with a smile.

"No!" I say. "That's not what I mean. What I mean is, I wasn't being monogamous. I would be involved with more than one person at the same time."

"Aryae," she says, looking at me sideways, "I hate to break the news to you, but you're not the only person with that experience."

I look over at her, trying to read her expression. I see a faint smile. "Okay!" I say. "I understand." We don't say anything for a while. A car drives slowly past.

"Sarah," I say, "I want to try to explain my own experience. At first it was great. We were all liberated and it was a new age. Why

160

shouldn't people be giving each other the gift of such pleasure? Why should we have to narrow our world so we can love only one person? If people want to share this kind of loving and closeness with each other, what's wrong with that? It was so innocent. I had married Ruthie when I was a college student, a sophomore. I loved her and wanted to help her to stay in the States, but I wasn't ready for marriage."

Sarah looks down. Ruthie has been befriending her lately, teaching her macrobiotic cooking. I look down too. We're both silent for a while. I hear a bird call somewhere in the distance.

"It didn't work," I say.

Sarah looks up at me. "What didn't work?"

I choose my words carefully. "Having a sexual relationship with more than one person at once." She doesn't say anything. "It's not about being religious. It's just that it makes me feel fragmented. It gets so complicated and I don't know how to hold it all together. It makes me feel crazy."

She just looks at me and doesn't say anything.

"There's a part of me that says, 'I have to face the fact, I'm married to Ruthie. I care about her. And we're supposed to be running the House of Love and Prayer.'"

Sarah's looking at me, eyes wide open, serious. I put my hands on her shoulders. "At the same time," I say, "I feel so drawn to you."

"Sounds like you've got a problem," she says dryly.

"I don't know if I've told you this," I say. "When I called Shlomo to tell him I had rented a house for the House of Love and Prayer, I asked him if he wanted a *mehitza* in the prayer room. He laughed and said, 'There are enough walls in this world between people. What we're here to do is to tear them down.'"

Her eyes widen and she looks startled when I mention Shlomo.

"Maybe when we're doing what we're doing, when we're bringing love and peace to the world, and love and closeness and oneness to so many people, maybe the old rules about loving only one person at a time don't apply anymore," I say. "I don't know."

She looks like she's about to say something, and then she turns away.

There are more birds singing now, as the glow in the east moves up above the horizon.

161

I see her head shaking slowly from side to side. Then she takes a deep breath and turns back toward me. "Aryae," she says. "You've got to decide what you want." The simple truth of this hits me. I nod.

We walk back slowly on Lake Street, toward the House, holding hands, each lost in our own thoughts. The sky in front of us is filling up with light, and the sounds of many birds are coming from the Presidio on our left.

Shlomo is counting on Efraim and Leah and Ruthie and me to run the House. It's easier for Efraim and Leah because they're there as a couple. It's hard for me with Ruthie doing her own thing, only partially there. It makes me feel lonely, even while I'm constantly surrounded by people. It feels like everyone is making deep soul-connections with someone on *Shabbos* except for me. Why shouldn't I have the pleasure and comfort of someone who can deeply share these experiences with me?

But if I'm having sex with another woman at the House, how can Ruthie possibly live there? How can I possibly do my job as a leader, as someone who's supposed to be caring about everybody, if I'm secretly entangled with someone and have to keep it hidden?

Shlomo said something once about choosing. "We live in a world with so many ways to get to the *Ribbono Shel Olam*, to serve God," he said. "Maybe they're all good. What do we know? The only thing is, I don't have enough feet to walk in all directions at once. Until I choose which way I'm going, I'm going nowhere."

After Adam ate the apple in the Garden, God comes to him and says, '*Ayeka?* Where are you?' Adam doesn't know what to say. He doesn't know where he is. He has no place. So he and Eve have to leave the Garden and wander the face of the earth. When God comes to our father Abraham and calls him, Abraham says, "*Hinenei!* Here I am!" God blessed him that he and his children will have a place in this world. They will inherit a land flowing with milk and honey. The greatest blessing is to know where I am, to have a place. The way to have a place, simple as it is, is I have to choose.

"Sarah," I say. I keep walking and look over my shoulder at her.

"Aryae," she says. She's smiling now. We've left the big, upscale houses with the broad, manicured lawns behind us. The houses here are narrow, touching each other, interspersed with small apartment buildings. Fog is rising ahead of us, muting and graying the morning pink sky.

"I think I've got to be monogamous," I say. "I don't see any other way."

She's still smiling. She nods and gives my hand a little squeeze. "I know," she says.

When we get back to Arguello Boulevard, we decide that it's better for us to walk in separately. She'll go right, toward the House. I'll go left, toward the park.

Irving Solomon will persuade Shlomo and Moishe to form a Board of Directors for the House of Love and Prayer. We will print up brochures that include the following:

OFFICERS

Rabbi Shlomo Carlebach	*Spiritual Leader and Friend*
Efraim Sims	*Chairman of the Board*
Aryae Coopersmith	*President*
Donna Anderson	*Vice President*
Moishe Fohrman	*Treasurer*

SPIRITUAL ADVISORS AND HONORARY BOARD MEMBERS

Rabbi Abraham J. Heschel, PhD.
Eli Wiesel

BOARD

Ruth Coopersmith
Maxine Fohrman
Marvin Kussoy
Rabbi Zalman Schachter
Irving Solomon

Irving will be a prolific fundraiser, and a loyal and steadfast member of the House's "supervising adults."

Sarah will get married to Elishama, a quiet, serious young man who lives at the House. Shlomo will perform the ceremony at the House, with many teachings about the specialness of two holy souls like these getting together, and many blessings for them to have boundless joy in each other. It will be hard for me to watch.

The two of them will leave the House and go to the East Coast to join one of the new Orthodox communities for *ba'alei t'shuvah,* people returning to the fold. Sarah will spend many years there, living in a strictly Orthodox world, feeling like a fish out of water, wondering if she made the right choice.

163

I'll be monogamous, faithful to Ruthie until we separate five years and six months later.

I watch Sarah walk down Arguello Boulevard until she crosses California Street. Then I go left to the Presidio. The smell of eucalyptus engulfs me.

I remember the conversation I had with Efraim last year about keeping kosher. "Why don't you just keep eating vegetarian like you are now?" I had said. "Why make the sacrifice of eating kosher when there's no real reason for it?"

"So we can give up our own will and place ourselves in God's will," Efraim had answered.

It's daylight now and I have to squint to look up. The fog overhead is moving in from the Bay, a soft blanket brushing against the tops of the trees.

20
This Too Shall Pass

House of Love and Prayer – 1968

Have you ever been through a time in your life where so much is happening so fast, where the pace of it all just carries you along like a roaring river, where it seems like whole lifetimes are unfolding every month, every week? That's what it was like in the early days of the House of Love and Prayer.

It seemed like the whole world was showing up at our doorstep. Young people from all over were hearing about us from a friend who heard about us from another friend. They would show up one or two at a time, four or five or six at a time, and stay for a day, a weekend, a month, a year. Efraim and Leah and I, and others who joined us early on, were completely committed to Shlomo's vision. We welcomed everybody. We wanted them to have that experience: "When you walk in, someone loves you; when you walk out, someone misses you."

People brought their backpacks, a few changes of clothes, their sleeping bags, and moved into the basement, the attic, any nook and cranny of this large rambling house that was not already occupied by someone else.

Chaya: I felt a strange drawing to go out to the Coast, so I left college at the University of Chicago, where I was studying English Literature, and wound up living with a guy in San Francisco. One day I read in the *Berkeley Barb* that there would be a Rosh Hashanah service at the House of Love and Prayer, and for some reason it strangely moved me. I hadn't had any Jewish contact since I was a kid.

I went there and Leah came out on the steps and said, "Angel! I've been waiting for you for all eternity!"

And you know what? I didn't think it was hokey. It was like a golden key opened my heart and I knew this was it. And then I walked in. It was the afternoon of the second day of Rosh Hashanah. And I just stayed! I was footloose and fancy free in those days, no commitments. I was one of those people who just stayed in the dining room in a sleeping bag. And I helped out with cooking and cleaning, and learning and experiencing.

Something was always happening at the House, on either the main floor, the basement, the second floor, in the attic, or even up on the roof, at all hours of the day and night. For Efraim and Leah and me, it meant being always *on,* always on call, 24 hours a day, seven days a week. For Ruthie however, it was a different kind of experience:

Ruthie: What I remember is, I moved into the House because I knew that that's what you wanted to do. And yet it went against my needs, because I'm very much a loner. I don't like living with many people. I find it very difficult. It un-centers me.

It was a fight for privacy. The things I had to do . . . to have a little tiny kitchen [of my own] in a public, communal kitchen. I was casting myself in a role where I would be instantaneously judged and disliked.

Aryae: To maintain your sanity you were kind of forced to take a role that you knew would not . . .

Ruthie: Yes, unpopular with everybody, and also with you. It was like I was damned if I did, and damned if I didn't. It wasn't a relationship process. It was just—Aryae did what *he* had to do.

On the other hand I couldn't quite fault you because I was very much the same kind of person, in that I wanted to be a dancer at all costs. I was thinking of what I could do for my career. So I went off and did what *I* had to do, and didn't consult you.

Spiritual teachers heard about us and came with their followers to experience Friday night at the House when Shlomo was there, and even when Efraim and I were leading. Samuel Lewis, known to his followers as Murshid, or "guide," and to the rest of us as Sufi Sam, came and brought his Sufis with him. He and Shlomo connected instantly and seemed fond of each other.* Sam and many of his followers had been born Jewish. Shlomo seemed puzzled that Jews should wind up being Sufis, but warmly embraced every Sufi without judgment.

One Friday night Murshid Sam led us in Sufi dancing. All of us in the House were delighted. It seemed very much in the spirit of Hasidic dancing.

Wali Ali Meyer: I remember when we started in 1967 Murshid's basement with about 20 people. At that time he and Shlomo got together, I think it was probably at Sam's home. And Sam said to Shlomo, "I have to tell you, I stole something from you!"

And Shlomo said, "What?"

He said, "This idea of using dance to bring all these people together in love and peace in our age!"

And Shlomo says, "Well, I stole it from the Ba'al Shem Tov!" [laughs]

So as a force for love and peace, Shlomo deserves the credit for seeing . . . I mean he was the first one to get people up from just listening to lectures and doing various practices, to have to move their *body* and pray and make a *body-prayer* together, and sing and dance.

I remember going over to the House of Love and Prayer with Sam and some disciples. There was a tremendous joy in the atmosphere. But the memorable thing to me was when I went home that night and went to sleep, I had like a vision dream. We were all under this *huppah* [wedding canopy]; we were all under this tabernacle. It just went on, this singing and this joy, all through the night, all through my dream. It was one of those dreams where, you know it was something beyond a dream.

---

* Murshid Samuel (Sufi Ahmed Murad) Lewis (1896-1971), was a Jewish-born Sufi master in the lineage of Hazrat Inayat Khan, often called the first American Sufi saint. In his diaries, on July 28th, 1970, he writes: "Some time ago, a young man thought he would see a battle royal by introducing me to the [Hasidic] Rabbi Shlomo Carlebach. We took one look at each other and there was a love-embrace." *Sufi Vision and Initiation: Meetings with Remarkable Beings.*

The ceremony that Shlomo was doing was going on in another world as well as this one.

Catholics of various stripes were also regular visitors on Friday nights. There were people involved with the Charismatic Catholic movement, occasional Jesuit priests, and also nuns. Cathy responded to these visits by her fellow Catholics with ambiguity. On the one hand, she felt validated that people from the Church were also drawn to the community that she had now adopted as her own, and there was a natural kinship. On the other hand she seemed to keep her distance from them, as though concerned that she might get pointed questions about why a former novitiate had abandoned the Church and was living with these Jews.

Then there was Ajari Warwick, leader of a local Buddhist group that followed the practice of walking with bare feet over hot coals.* A short, stout, muscular Englishman with a fierce manner who dressed in colorful robes and walked with quick, determined movements, Warwick was a commanding presence when he entered a room. His followers, who usually walked behind him in lighter colored robes, by contrast seemed quiet, subdued, almost disappearing in their modest self-effacement.

But there were also Jewish teachers that visited us.

It's *Shabbos* morning, and we're sitting in a circle on the grass in the back yard of the House, maybe 25 or 30 of us, facing Rabbi Zalman Schachter. Shlomo told us that this is his best friend. He asked him to come to the House to spend *Shabbos* with us. In some ways he's like Shlomo, with a beard and *peyos,* telling Hasidic stories about the same rebbes that Shlomo does, and with a similar melody in his voice.

We listen to Zalman, spellbound. Like Shlomo, he has an almost magical ability to straddle worlds. He's taking the spiritual, mystic world of the old Rebbes in Europe, a world that no longer exists on the physical plane, and bringing it with him to 1960s America, speaking our language.

---

* Neville Warwick, known as Dr. Ajari claimed Dharma transmission from Suzuki Roshi, and taught an amalgamated Buddhism in the Bay area. Once he invited us to his commune in Marin to witness the fire-walking ceremony. He explained that in order to walk across the two or three yards of burning coals without getting your feet burned, you had to be on a level of complete surrender, letting go of all ego, desire and fear. Then the fire could not harm you. If you walked across the coals and ended up with blisters, it was a sign that you had not attained the necessary level of surrender. He invited all of us from the House to try. I declined, saying that I didn't think I was as advanced as his students.

But there's also something about Zalman that's very different. Being with Shlomo is about *feeling*. It's like, when I'm with Shlomo, my heart is open and I can feel the truth of love and connection, I can feel how we are all one. Being with Zalman is about *seeing*. I begin seeing the hidden connections between things, between the Catholic Mass and the Hebrew prayers and the teachings of the Hasidic Rebbes, between Bach and Suzuki Roshi and the Tanya and the Sistine Chapel and the Heisenberg uncertainty principal of physics and Alan Watts and the Tibetan Book of the Dead and the Ba'al Shem Tov.

Zalman tells us a well-known story about King Solomon, the wisest man in the kingdom of ancient Israel. He tells us how life had taught King Solomon about the illusory and transitory nature of this world, how *everything changes*. As he writes in Ecclesiastes 1:2: "Vanity of vanities, all is vanity."

This awareness causes King Solomon great suffering. So he gathers all the wisest people in the kingdom and sends them out to find one thing in this world that is constant, that *doesn't* change. But no one can find anything like this. Finally as the last of King Solomon's advisors is returning to Jerusalem, empty handed like all the others, he sees an old beggar man standing at the gate. He gives a silver coin to the beggar, who says, "I have a gift for the king."

When he approaches King Solomon, the advisor gives him the beggar's gift. It is a silver ring inscribed in elegant Hebrew letters with the words, *Gam Ze Yavor*, "This Too Shall Pass." They both praise God who, by the hand of the beggar, has answered the king's request.

Zalman tells us other stories. Then he teaches us about the mystical levels of the *Shabbos* morning prayers. In the Zohar, the Book of Splendor, and other holy texts of the Kabbalah, the sages speak of Four Worlds. These Worlds are the levels through which the Divine Light travels as it flows back and forth between the finite, material world that we inhabit, and the world of the Infinite. In each World there is a Tree of Life with Ten *Sefirot*, or spheres.

The *Shabbos* morning prayers are structured to take us through the Four Worlds, starting in the World of Action, then moving upward through the World of Formation and the World of Creation, and ending in the World of Oneness. Zalman points out how the prayers and rituals of other traditions, such as the Catholic Mass and the Sufi Zikr, are structured to do the same thing.

After the prayers, we have our *Shabbos* meal outside. Zalman shares his vision of a community of Jewish young people, *B'nai Or*, Children of Light. It would be based on crafts, the ancient crafts of our people such as making *tallisim* and mezuzas and *tefillin*. Unlike the House of Love and Prayer which relies on donations, the people of B'nai Or would sustain themselves through their crafts.*

When he's done eating, Zalman sets his plate down on the ground, and reaches for something under his chair. He sits up and holds a black velvet bag in his hand. He reaches in the bag, pulls out a silver ring, and hands it to Efraim. Leah looks excited. Efraim looks at it closely. "What's this?" he says, squinting at the ring.

Zalman reaches in the velvet bag and pulls out another ring. "Aryae, this is for you," he says. Stephanie passes it to Moishe, who passes it to Maxine, who passes it to me. The ring feels cool and heavy in the palm of my hand. I look closely at it. In elegant Hebrew letters it says, *Gam Ze Yavor*, "This Too Shall Pass."

Later I ask Zalman if he can help us explore whether the B'nai Or idea would work for us at the House. "Shlomo is your *rebbe*," he says. "You have to talk to Shlomo. Think of me as an uncle."

San Francisco, California – June 1st, 1968

It was almost 3,000 years ago when the Jewish people stood with Moses at Mount Sinai and God gave us the Ten Commandments and the entire Torah. According to our tradition it happened at dawn. So each year observant Jews prepare to celebrate this event and reenact it by staying up all night and studying Torah. Orthodox synagogues keep their doors open so anyone can come in and join the study.

This night there is a group of us sitting in the House, not quite knowing what to do. Efraim and Leah, Yonatan and Ahouva, who have come down from Canada to spend some time with us, Sonny, David and me, Chaya and Karen and Cathy, and several others. Ruthie is at a modern dance performance. Shlomo isn't with us, and we don't know what to study.

"Maybe we could find a *shul* where people are studying," Yonatan says. The rest of us nod. It doesn't seem like a bad idea. Normally most of us would never go to a "straight" *shul*, but on a special night like this, we thought it would be okay if we all went together.

---

* Reb Zalman was influenced in this by the Christian monastic communities he knew, his own experience of Hasidism, and his reading of the Dead Sea Scrolls, which speak of the "Children of Light" and similar communities of work and spiritual practice. He wrote an article describing this ideal community in the early 60s, and for many years, the first Jewish Renewal communities were called, B'nai Or.

We walk to Congregation Anshey Sfard (People of Spain), an Orthodox congregation 16 blocks away, housed in a modest, single storey building. The rabbi there is Rabbi Twerski, who is from a famous family of distinguished Hasidic rebbes.* Many of his congregants are immigrants who have been fortunate enough to achieve a measure of success in this country in business and the professions. They came here from all parts of the world, Europe, South Africa, South America, the Middle East, even Shanghai. Some are concentration camp survivors. What they have in common is that their community — under the strong leadership of Rabbi Twerski whom they greatly respect — has been a refuge and a shelter for them.

We find a well lit room with a long table piled with books, and a couple of dozen men crowded around it. Rabbi Twerski gets up to greet us.

Leah: We were studying something from the Talmud, about the laws of wandering through the desert. What stands out in my mind is this one question: What if two people are traveling through the desert and only one of them has water, and it's just enough water for one person to survive the journey? If you have the water, what should you do?

Aryae: So what's the answer?

Leah: The answer is, according to the Talmud — the way Rabbi Twerski was explaining it — you have to keep the water for yourself so you can survive.** I remember being upset with this. Most of us didn't like it. How could God want us to act so selfishly? We had come here wanting to learn something high and holy that would inspire us, and this was very jarring.

I remember talking with Efraim about this afterwards. Shlomo was so strong in those days about how we have to take care of each other. It took us a while to absorb this lesson about how we also have to take care of ourselves.

---

* This was likely Rabbi Shlomo Twerski (1923-1981), later the Hornesteipler Rebbe of Denver, who was also criticized for guiding a hippie congregation of *Ba'alei Teshuvah*. The Twerski family is one of the oldest and most distinguished families of Hasidism, descending from a disciple of the Ba'al Shem Tov, Rabbi Nachum of Chernobyl (1730-1798).

** This argument is found in the Babylonian Talmud, Bava Metzia 62A.

By the time the night is almost over we're all feeling pretty restless. Soon Rabbi Twerski and the congregation will be starting the morning services. Yonatan leans over to Efraim and me. "Let's take a walk!" he whispers, smiling mischievously.

Efraim smiles. "Yeah?" he says, "that's not such a bad idea!" We all leave as unobtrusively as we can and head toward Golden Gate Park. We wind up at Stow Lake, in the middle of the park, just as the sky in the east is beginning to glow a little at the horizon. We can see an island in the middle of the lake, connected to the shore by an arched stone bridge. We stand there in silence in the half darkness, looking at the lake. It will be dawn soon.

"Hey," says Sonny, "why don't we take a *mikveh!* We all look at each other. Hasidim always try to take a *mikveh* (ritual dip) before special times like this, and here we have a natural *mikveh* right in front of us.

"I think that's a great idea!" says Ahouvah. "And look, this is a perfect spot! The women can go on one side of the bridge and the men on the other." The stone bridge makes a complete visual barrier.

"Can we really do this?" says Cathy. "Is it legal? What if a park ranger comes along?"

Yonatan and Sonny are already headed to the water on the left side of the bridge. Efraim and I and the rest of the men follow. Leah and Karen and Chaya and the rest of the women follow Ahouvah to the right side. Cathy smiles, shrugs, and goes along.

The water is cold but not freezing. The muddy bottom of the lake feels squishy between our toes. The ritual of the *mikveh* is to totally immerse the body at least three times. We each take turns doing it. I can hear the voices and splashing of the women on the other side. I take a little swim out to the middle of the lake and back. The sky is turning lighter now, and suddenly we can see the first golden rays of the sun. On the men's side we start singing the *Shema,* over and over, to a melody that we're making up as we go. Soon I can hear the voices of the women on the other side, joining us: "Listen Israel, God is God, God is One."

Half Moon Bay, California – June 21st, 2001

Rabbi Gavriel Dror and his son are *sofrim,* scribes who practice the ancient art of writing complete Torah scrolls by hand.* He has

---

* I have changed his and his wife's name to protect their privacy.

been a Chabad Hasid for 25 years, wears traditional Hasidic clothing, has a long grey beard, bright eyes and contagious smile. He lives in a Hasidic community in Florida.

Gavriel and Efraim are cousins, but they had never met as children. He has come to my home so I can interview him.

Aryae: Where did you and Efraim meet?

Gavriel: At the House of Love and Prayer. My father sent me. We would stay in the attic.

With Efraim and me it was like instantly, we knew each other forever. It was like: 'Oh, so I finally have a cousin!' We were family. It was the same thing with Sari [his wife] and Leah. And the kids, they played and took off. It was like we started from the beginning, as if it was always going on.

So we went for *Shabbos*, and you were there too. I remember. He [Efraim] did one thing, you did another, [pointing back and forth] you, you, you . . . [laughs] But it flowed. It was beautiful. Long, long, long, long, long, long, long, long, *longest* singing of one song . . . until we were finally disconnected from everything else. So that was our entrance into *Shabbos*. So after that we always did *Shabbos*.

We didn't know what to do or how to do it. I think I even asked you. So you said we have three basic books: the *siddur* [prayer book], the *Humash* [Five Books of Moses], and the third book you told me to get was the *Tanya*. [Both of us laugh. The *Tanya* is the source book of Chabad Hasidism, which is now Gavriel's practice and community.] Which I still have! You didn't have a translation. You just had the first section, in a little brown book, and that was it.

The first time I met Shlomo, he was no longer teaching *Tanya*. He was starting a new thing, Reb Nachman. After seeing Efraim and you, when I saw Shlomo, the truth is, it was like a comedown. I was expecting the ultimate. It was great, but it was not different from what you and Efraim were doing. So both of you actually became . . . Exactly the same thing that was flowing from Shlomo was exactly happening with you and Efraim. So when Shlomo . . . I felt that I had already met him. So in that sense it was a comedown.

173

That's how you lived! You were exactly at that same place. You floated into *Shabbos* with the music and the stories. You had the whole feeling.

The only difference is when Shlomo started to teach. That part, Shlomo's learning and how he brought it down, is totally unique. After all the davening and stories and singing and dancing, Shlomo would start teaching at 3:00 or 4:00 in the morning, and he would just keep on going.

House of Love and Prayer – 1968

It's time for *Kiddush* on Friday night. Rabbi Mordecai Goldstein from Jerusalem is visiting us for *Shabbos*, sharing Hasidic teachings and stories. He is dressed in traditional Hasidic clothes, with a long black coat and *strimel* (big fur hat), long beard and long *peyos* (side curls). He and Efraim and I are standing behind the long table with our backs to the windows. I'm on his right side, Efraim is on his left. Leah is in the big kitchen, supervising young women who are still bringing food out to the table. Ruthie is in her little kitchen, putting the finishing touches on a huge bowl of vegetarian sushi made with brown rice.

Rabbi Goldstein and Efraim have asked me to make *Kiddush*.

People are milling around and talking. "Come friends," says Efraim in his gentle voice, barely audible across the room, "please join us for *Kiddush.*" Then he starts singing a song. People nearby join in, and gradually the crowd moves closer to the table.

Rabbi Goldstein, whom I remember as a solid presence, tall and somewhat heavy set, stands impassively, looking over the crowd, taking us all in. When East Jerusalem became part of Israel last year after the Six Day War, he was able to take over an ancient stone building on Mount Zion, right next to King David's tomb. He moved in and turned it into a *yeshiva* which he called the Diaspora Yeshiva. Several people from the House have already talked to him about going to Jerusalem to try it out. That's why he's here.*

Efraim brings his song to a close. Leah has come out of the kitchen, worked her way through the crowd and is standing next to him. Everyone is gathered in front of us, in front of the table, arms around each other. I look at Rabbi Goldstein, and at Efraim. Efraim

---

* Rabbi Dr. Mordecai Goldstein, a student of the renowned Rabbi Aharon Kotler, who taught Shlomo as well, is still the Rosh Yeshiva of Diaspora Yeshiva Toras Yisrael in Jerusalem.

nods. I see Ruthie in the back of the room, standing near the little kitchen. I gesture to her to come and stand with us. She gestures back that she needs to go into the little kitchen for a moment and will be right back. Everyone's waiting.

I start singing the words for the *Kiddush,* using one of Shlomo's melodies. Pretty soon everyone is joining in, eyes half closed, swaying back and forth. You can feel the energy fill the room, a spirit of sweetness, a spirit of holiness. Efraim has his eyes closed. Rabbi Goldstein closes his too.

After the prayer is done, the room is filled with the silence of anticipation. I take a sip of the wine, and pass the cup to Rabbi Goldstein. He takes a sip. I expect him to pass the cup to his left, to Efraim. Instead, he passes the cup back to me. I look at the cup, and then lean forward, so I can pass the cup in front of Rabbi Goldstein over to Efraim. I feel something heavy on my foot. It's Rabbi Goldstein's foot. He's stepping on me, hard. I look up at him.

"Your wife!" he whispers, pointing to the right. I look over and see that Ruthie has worked her way over to the table, and is standing nearby. I look back at Rabbi Goldstein, uncomprehending.

"Your wife!" he whispers again, pointing at the silver cup. It hadn't occurred to me to pass the cup to Ruthie since, due to her macrobiotic diet, she doesn't drink wine. I gesture to her to come stand next to me, and point to the cup. She doesn't understand what I'm doing.

When she gets close, I put my arm around her and whisper, "You better pretend to take a sip of this wine, or I'm not going to have a foot left!" She looks over at Rabbi Goldstein and smiles.

It wasn't only the visiting rabbis and spiritual teachers who taught us. The endless variety of visitors who were drawn to the House presented us with many opportunities for learning.

Chaya: It was *Shabbat* and we had just lit candles. Everyone was just sitting around, you know, in the peace of *Shabbat* before the prayer service started. And then Ron came in. I had never seen him before. I greeted him [in a warm voice], "Ron, welcome. *Shabbat shalom.*" And he growled or snarled or something. And he went around to everybody who was sitting in the dining room grooving on the *Shabbat* candles, and said something mean to each person.

And I said [warm voice], "Ron, that's not a spiritual thing to do." Then the prayer service started.

And someone ran in and said, "Ron's pouring the *Kiddush* wine down the drain."

I came in and said [warm voice], "Ron, don't do that. You are a brother!" And he just looked at me really crazy. And I said [warm voice], "Please stop. Come and join us. Just be quiet." And he stopped pouring the *Shabbos* wine down the drain. Then the service proceeded.

Then someone ran in and said, "Ron set fire to the bentchers [little blessing books]!"

Then I came in and said [hard voice], "You have several choices. You can get out of here. I'm calling the police. Or you can join us. If you do anything like this again, I'm calling the police right away." And he stopped.

Aryae: Good for you! Good for you! We needed *Gevurah* [boundaries]. We had only *Hesed* [unconditional love].

Chaya: Yeah, I was learning *Hesed* all the time there.

Elana was another young woman who lived at the House. Later she would marry Reb Zalman. She now lives in Israel.

Elana: Do you remember Harry?

Aryae: Hershele!

Elana: Hershele. He had maybe epilepsy or something. And whenever the energy would get strong, he was like a barometer. Whenever Shlomo would start teaching and the energy would start getting strong, he would start having fits. He would be like . . .

Aryae: Talking in tongues.

Elana: Yeah! Talking in tongues, and rolling on the floor, and doing his thing. You know, he wasn't in this world! So one day, first of all, Hershele fell in love with me. And he kept following me around and saying, "If you don't marry me, I'm going to jump off the Golden Gate Bridge."

It was too bad, because I really wanted somebody to fall in love with me, but not Hershele! One day he got really upset that I rejected him, and he pulled a knife on me. And I said, "Hershele, put that away!" And, I don't remember who it was, but somebody turned around and they said this to me, this classic line, they said, "You can't yell at him like that! This is the House of Love and Prayer!"

It's *Shabbos* early afternoon. It's been a quiet day with no visiting rabbis, and a relatively small group of us davening and studying Torah in the morning. We've finished the second meal of *Shabbos*. Most of the guests have left.

Those of us remaining, mostly those of us who live in the House, have been cleaning the dining room and kitchen and straightening up the prayer room. Efraim and Sonny and David and I are hanging out in the prayer room. Efraim is sharing some stories that he learned from Shlomo on the phone last week.

One of the special things about Shlomo as a teacher is that he never tells us what to do. If we had been studying in a conventional *yeshiva*, we would have had to learn a million laws about what is required of us and what is forbidden. Shlomo spends very little time on that. Instead we learn mystical teachings with him, teachings and stories from the great Hasidic masters. It's up us to draw our own conclusions, and each of us to begin following the laws according to the calling and timing of our own soul.

Shlomo has taught us that the Torah consists of not only the black letters but also the white spaces in between. The black letters are the laws that God gave us on Mount Sinai; the white spaces are God's light, which is coming to us every moment, every second. There are people in this world who are strictly black letter people. They're very strong on laws, on doing everything right.

Then there are the white spaces people. Maybe they haven't yet learned so much, and maybe they don't really know what to do in this world, but when you're with them, there's so much love, so much light. These are the holy beggars. Everyone else is running around, begging to take. The holy beggars are walking the streets of the world, begging to give.

The truth is, to be complete, a person really needs both black letters and white spaces, Shlomo said. But we have to start somewhere, and the place to start is with the white spaces.

In the meantime across town Rabbi Twerski is going for his regular *Shabbos* afternoon walk with some of the older and more pious men of his *shul*, Anshey Sfard.

It is a confusing world. San Francisco in the late 1960s, filled with its loud cacophony of hippies, outlandishly dressed young people, half naked half the time, anti-war protestors, civil rights activists, demonstrations, acid rock concerts, "Be Ins" in Golden Gate Park, student demonstrations at UC Berkeley — seems so bizarre, so alien, that there's no way to make any sense of it.

As this little group of Jewish men dressed in their black *Shabbos* clothes walks serenely along the quiet blocks of Lake Street past the large, well maintained houses, Rabbi Twerski makes a suggestion that startles some of them. Let's walk over to the House of Love and Prayer and see what they're up to there, he says.

The men are shocked at this suggestion. "That's Shlomo Carlebach's place for hippies," they say. "They've got to be doing all kinds of things there, taking drugs, having sex orgies, who knows what? Why would you want to go there?"

"They didn't seem so bad when they visited us for Shavuot," says Rabbi Twerski. "They were nice young people. You've got to understand what Rabbi Carlebach is trying to do. They're beyond the reach of synagogues like ours. Rabbi Carlebach is talking to them in a way that they can understand. He brings them back and teaches them to have a great love for the Torah and for *Shabbos*."

"If they have such a great love for the Torah and for *Shabbos*, why are they still hippies?" the men say. "Why don't they dress decently and go to a real *shul*?"

"Let's go and see for ourselves," says Rabbi Twerski. "Maybe we'll be pleasantly surprised. Maybe we can learn something that can help us reach our own young people."

In the mean time back at the House, Sonny brings a burning candle into the prayer room.

There are so many laws in the Torah, and by the time the Rabbis interpret them in the Talmud, they can be so complex. Since Shlomo doesn't tell us what to do and what not to do, we have to learn about the laws ourselves by observing Orthodox Jews.

Take cigarettes. From everything that any of us have observed, Orthodox Jewish men love to smoke cigarettes. The Torah does not forbid it; so it is a kosher pleasure. However on *Shabbos* and the holidays, we're not permitted to kindle fire, because that is considered a form of work. But when we visited Anshey Sfard on Shavuot, we saw men smoking during the all night studying. I asked a man how they could smoke on a holiday. He pointed to a fat candle burning on a dish on the table. You can't light fire on a holiday, he said, but you can *transfer* fire

We then saw another man bend down and light his cigarette. After that we started a custom at the House of carefully lighting a big candle each week just before *Shabbos*.

David has a pack of Camels. He gives us each a cigarette and we carefully light them from the candle. Cigarette smoke fills the prayer room and the front hallway. What a wonderful custom, I think. It feels so relaxing to have a cigarette like this on *Shabbos* afternoon. I watch Efraim. He is so much in *Shabbos* that whatever he does, he does with great pleasure, including blowing out the smoke and watching it curl up to the ceiling. I can picture Hasidim all over the world, enjoying their *Shabbos* afternoon smoke.

Stephanie and Chaya run into the prayer room chasing Uri. He runs unsteadily, laughing, then drops to a crawl. They also drop to a crawl, and pretend to be fierce animals, going after him. Uri laughs, goes past our legs to escape, and Stephanie and Chaya bump into us as they pursue him. Everyone is laughing and having a good time.

There's a sudden knock at the door. We're all curious, since when people visit the House on *Shabbos*, they usually just walk in. I walk up to the door and, holding my cigarette in one hand, open the door with the other. Efraim and Sonny and David are standing right behind me, all holding their cigarettes, curious to see who this is.

There standing in front of us on the steps to the front door we see a group of very serious looking Orthodox Jewish men from Anshey Sfard. I look back at my friends. We're all holding our cigarettes, feeling very traditional. "Good *Shabbos*!" we say to them with big smiles, as a cloud of smoke comes billowing out the door. They just stand there in silence, looking at us. Stephanie and Chaya, still running around giggling and chasing after Uri, come tearing into the hallway and crash into Sonny, who puts an arm around each woman to steady them. The women suddenly realize they're being watched. They stare at the Orthodox men, who stare back at us wide eyed, without saying a word.

Finally one of them turns away to walk down the stairs toward the street. The others follow, silently. We stand there in the doorway with our cigarettes, utterly mystified, watching the men walk up Arguello Boulevard toward Lake Street.

It won't be until several weeks later that someone will inform us that transferring fire is kosher only on holidays. On *Shabbos*, no Jew who loves the Torah and *Shabbos* would be caught dead smoking a cigarette.*

Highway 101, heading south to Los Angeles — 1968

It's Friday, and a bunch of us from the House are piled into our VW van, which we call the Shabbos Express, heading south on Highway 101 to be with Shlomo for a *Shabbos* in Los Angeles. Efraim and Leah are sitting on the back seat. Efraim is playing with Uri, who is standing up on his lap. Sonny is in the passenger seat up front. Cathy and Karen are sharing the back seat with Efraim and Leah. David and Chaya and Elana are in the back of the van. Ruthie is back in San Francisco. I'm driving.

It's a beautiful sunny day, still early afternoon. The drive goes pleasantly as Highway 101 winds its way south through pasture land, farm land, and gently rolling coastal hills. We pass Paso Robles and continue south toward San Luis Obispo. Soon we'll be at the coast, and from there it's a couple of hours into L.A.

I look down at my hands holding the steering wheel. Something's wrong. At first I don't know what it is. Then I see it. There's no ring on my right hand.

"Oh no!" I say. I reach into my pockets frantically. No ring.

"What's the matter Aryae?" Sonny says.

"My ring from Zalman!" I say. "The *Gam Ze Yavor* ring. It's gone!" I pull over to the side of the road, get out of the car and empty my pockets. Wallet, coins, some scraps of paper. No ring. People get out of the car and help me search the floor around the driver's seat. Everyone looks around and tries to help. No ring.

"I can see it so clear in my mind," I say. "It was at the gas station we stopped at. I put it on the sink in the men's room when I was washing my hands. I must have left it there." I feel like such an idiot.

"Maybe we can drive back and get it," says Leah. A few people groan. "Why not?" she says. "It's probably still there."

"Thanks Leah," I say, "that's sweet of you. But I think we have to keep going. I'll just have to let it go." I do one more search through

---

* The laws of *Shabbat* are found in the Talmud, Tractate Shabbat, and further expounded in the codes.

180

my pockets, one more search around the driver's seat, hoping that by some miracle it will turn up. It doesn't. I start up the car and we're back on the road. Soon the engine of the VW van is humming loudly, and the hills are slipping past us as we head south toward the coast.

I think about the life we're living at the House of Love and Prayer. There is no rational way to explain it. How do we pay the bills, provide meals for hundreds of people on *Shabbos*, keep it all going? The truth is, like our ancestors in the desert 3,000 years ago, and even though the Talmud says it's forbidden, we're living on miracles. Every day is filled with messages from heaven, moving our lives in directions that we can't see and can't even imagine. Every day is a miracle.

But as exciting as it is to live on miracles, I know in my heart of hearts that it can't last forever. I picture Zalman sitting with us on *Shabbos* and King Solomon sitting in his palace, pondering the transient, illusory nature of all reality. This is their message to me. Be unattached. Nothing that is here today will be here tomorrow. Let it all go. Let the stream of life flow through you. *Gam Ze Yavor*—"This too shall pass."

A couple of hours later we arrive at our destination, a large house on a cul-de-sac in an upscale Los Angeles neighborhood.

When we get inside, the house is already filled with people who keep arriving in a steady stream. There is lots of conversation, lots of movement as people wander about, lots of energy. There is a feeling of excitement, anticipation, as though a movie star were about to arrive. It's almost sunset. I look around but don't see Shlomo.

Our hosts are Carl and Rhoda.* Carl is a short guy in his 40s with a large head of hair carefully blow-dried and a gold chain around his neck. Rhoda has sparkly eyes with blue eye-liner, auburn hair piled up in a beehive that makes her taller than him and a plunging neckline on a black sequined dress. They greet us warmly. Carl shows us to some bedrooms where we can keep our things and change our clothes. Shlomo has taught us about the custom of putting on fresh, clean, special clothes to honor *Shabbos*. Everybody has brought their *Shabbos* clothes. Leah, Karen, Cathy, Chaya and Elana go to one room. Efraim, Sonny, David and I are in another.

Before I take off the jeans I've been wearing, I feel in the pockets one last time to see if the silver ring is there. It's not. I put on my *Shabbos* clothes. White shirt, white *tzitzit* undershirt, black pants, rainbow-colored wool belt that Ruthie wove for me, which I tie

---

* I do not remember their actual names.

181

around my waist, black socks, sandals, special rainbow *kippah* that Ruthie made last year. To be really dressed for *Shabbos*, you should have all your pockets empty, and especially not be carrying a wallet or any money. I feel the pockets in my *Shabbos* pants. They're empty.

I wander through the house. More people keep arriving. The house is filled with the sounds of greetings, laughter, small talk.

I find an escape: a door to the back yard. I open it and walk through. Suddenly it's quiet. The bright green of the lawn and plants surrounds me. The air is warm and pleasant. The sun is very low in the sky, which is starting to fill with sunset colors. I can hear birds singing in nearby trees, interspersed with the faint, distant hum of freeway traffic. The yard is large, landscaped with curved stone walkways and clumps of large flowering plants that punctuate the flat stretches of lawn.

50 feet away there's a man standing near a tree. I slowly walk toward him. It's Shlomo. I walk faster, until I see that his eyes are closed and he's rocking back and forth, davening. He's wearing his classic Shlomo outfit: dark suit pants, white shirt open at the neck with a few strings of colorful beads, dark socks and sandals, an Israeli *kippah* with silver Yemenite filigree. His beard looks still a little wet, and freshly rolled up and pinned to make it look short, the way he wears it. His eyes flash open and he looks at me, a little startled at first. Then he smiles, flashes me a "V" and makes that sound he makes when he pleased, something like, "Chissssssssssh!" I come up and he reaches out to give me a hug. I hug him back. He smells like patchouli oil. I feel a little uncomfortable disturbing his davening.

"Listen, Aryae! Have you davened *Minhah* yet?" he says in a whisper, looking into my eyes. I shake my head, no. "So come on and *daven* with me!" he says, still whispering. I smile and shake my head, yes. He smiles back at me, pats me affectionately on the cheek, and says, "Chissssssssssh!" Then his eyes are closed and he's davening again.

I stand next to him and close my eyes. The last few months I've been memorizing all the prayers, the evening, morning and afternoon prayers. *Minhah*, the afternoon prayer, is the shortest. The *Minhah* before *Shabbos* is special, because it is our last action of the week. The week, the level of six is doing, our actions in the world. *Shabbos*, the level of seven, is being, which we receive from heaven. God's last action on the sixth day of creation was to create us — human beings.

Shlomo once taught us, in the name of a *rebbe* whose name I can't remember, that there are three stages of entering *Shabbos*. It may have been the holy Izhbitzer.

182

The first is, because I'm entering *Shabbos*, I can look back at the week and see all the mistakes I was making, all the stupid things I was doing. Then I'm filled with regret, and longing to come back to God, to come back to myself.

The second is, I realize that that was then, and this is now. On the level of *Shabbos*, I don't have to do anything; I'm already complete and whole. Completeness and wholeness is a gift from heaven. I'm already where I need to be. What joy to be here!

The third is, with *Shabbos* eyes, I can look back at the week and see, there really were no mistakes! In order for me to be here, in this most perfect state of completion and joy, everything had to happen just the way it happened. Everything I did was perfect, just the way I did it.

My eyes closed, swaying back and forth, I start to recall the words of *Minhah* so I can say them. But it doesn't feel right. Something else is happening that is melting the words. Aryae is in the midst of a flow. Rather than *effort-ing* to recall the words, Aryae just lets himself flow. Something very powerful is carrying him, like an enormous river of light. He tries to at least hold on to the intention of the prayers, blessing God for our holy fathers Abraham, Isaac, and Jacob, blessing God for bringing the dead back to life, blessing God for holiness, healing, redemption, and salvation. The river of light keeps flowing, stronger and further.

Out of the river come the forms of our holy ancestors from different generations and different places, from Eastern Europe and Spain and North Africa and Western Asia and ancient Israel. Everyone is praying, saying *Minhah* in a rising chorus of whispers, prayers, tears. Every one of them has endured the suffering and heartbreak of this world. Every one of them is so strong, strong enough to reach beyond heartbreak to joy, to joyfully do the mission that we've been chosen and sent here to do every day, to find the holy sparks that are hidden and lost in the dark places of this world and carry them back to their source. They are calling, "Let go of all the heaviness of Aryae, let it go, let it go, dance with us, dance with us!" He lets go and dances. As he dances, new beings emerge to dance with the ancestors. They must be angels from different worlds. A flotilla of boats with bright, colorful sails move along the river. People are dancing on the boats, and lined up along the river banks, watching the boats, dancing, waving flags, jumping, clapping, making music. The vast river of light becomes a vast river of emotions, revving up to greater and greater intensity, sadness and tears beyond endurance, love so fierce that it aches, joy that explodes in firework cascades lighting up the sky with enormous flashes and descending in curlicue trails of light along the river banks. We're all

183

little drops in the river. Each drop carries its own intensity, its own life. The river travels through all intensities, all lives, all worlds, never stopping. Every drop is at once an infinitesimal part of the whole, infinitely precious in its own existence, and a temporary state always on its way to being something else. Aryae's body is swaying back and forth, shaking. The intensity is too much to contain. Fragments of the closing part of the prayer flow through the mind: "We give thanks to You for being our God and the God of our holy ancestors forever. Thank you for our lives and our souls which are in your care. Thank you for your miracles and wonders that surround us every evening, every morning, every afternoon. Thank you for the amazing gift of gratitude. Thank you for blessing us with peace."

I open my eyes. At first I don't get it. Why are the holy ancestors and angels still here, standing in silent circles holding each other, still surrounding us? The sky is darker, with narrow, bright orange and green streaks against fields of deep blue. Shlomo's still standing next to me, swaying from side to side. His hands are touching his beard and he's looking down at the ground. Then he looks up at the ancestors and angels, taking them all in.

"Good *Shabbos* sweet friends," he says. "Good *Shabbos*, good *Shabbos*!" A couple of hundred voices answer him back. "Good *Shabbos*!" Then he starts singing a song that we sometimes sing at the House to welcome *Shabbos*. Everyone joins him.

Then I recognize Efraim and Leah standing nearby, with Sonny, David, Karen, Elana, and Cathy standing near them. I look around at everyone. These are the people at Carl and Rhoda's house. They all came out silently while we were davening and surrounded us. I'm standing in the middle of the circle with Shlomo. Everyone else has their arms around each other. People are singing the melody with Shlomo, over and over, with a great outpouring of emotion, washing over us in waves.

I'm feeling awkward standing in the middle with Shlomo, and don't quite know what to do with myself. I notice there's something in my left pocket. That's strange, because my pockets were empty. I reach down, pull it out, and then look at the object sitting in the palm of my hand. It takes a moment for the mind to understand what the eyes are seeing. It's a silver ring. I squint and look at it closely. *Gam Zeh Yavor* — "This too shall pass."

I look up at the sky. Stars are beginning to come out. Then I look over at Shlomo. Still singing, he looks at me, smiles, holds up his hand and flashes a "V." Does he know?

I put the ring on my finger. Should I tell anyone? I step back out of the center and into the circle where Karen and Cathy are

184

standing. They each put an arm around me. It feels good to be touching people, friends. We're all just passing through, carried by the river, here for a moment. I'm ready to go where it takes us.

21

Fallen Leaves

House of Love and Prayer – October 1968

Leah comes out to help Efraim with the roof. Uri walks beside her, holding her hand. He is blinking and looking around wide-eyed, like he just woke up from a nap. Efraim is tying redwood branches across the top of the frame. Leah has cut pieces of string and lined them up on the table. She stands under the ladder and hands Efraim the pieces of string as he needs them.

Lois and Jill are in the kitchen. Bernice brings out a box of Indian cotton bedspreads. She says we can tack them to the frame and use them for walls. Maxine has a pile of decorations she's sorting through. The younger women are also outside with us, trying out various carpentry tools.

Ruthie comes out of the little kitchen on the side, followed by Stephanie, holding a tray of macrobiotic cookies that she's just baked. She's been teaching Stephanie macrobiotic cooking. "They're good!" says Stephanie, sounding somewhat surprised. Ruthie smiles at me triumphantly.

Marvin and Sonny show up. "Hey you guys!" Marv says, "We got something for you." We follow them to the front of the House. Laughing to himself as he opens the side door of his van, Marv pulls out an armful of freshly cut eucalyptus branches. In order for a *sukkah* to be complete and kosher, the roof has to be covered with leaves.

"Where did you get these?" I say to Marv.

He tilts his head and rolls eyes toward the north. "What are you talking about?" I say, "There aren't any eucalyptus trees on this street!" He and Sonny look at each other. I look toward the north. "Oh my God!" I say, "You didn't get these from the Presidio, did you? Did anyone see you?" The Presidio is the military base just a few blocks away. I have visions of a small squad of soldiers marching up to the House to drag me off to fight in Vietnam.

Marvin laughs and shrugs. "It's our tax dollars, right?" He grabs another armful of branches.

Donna shows up. We've all been waiting for her. Her straight hair frames her oval face, which is slightly tilted to one side. "I just picked up Shlomo at the airport took him to the Miyako Hotel," she says matter of factly.

"The Miyako Hotel," Leah says in a dreamy tone, "that must be a beautiful hotel."

Donna laughs. "It didn't look too shabby."

"Why does he need a hotel if he's sleeping in the *sukkah*?" I say.

"'A Jew needs his privacy,'" she says with a half smile, quoting Shlomo.

A few hours later when the sky has grown dark and the air chilly, there are two hundred people in the *sukkah*, standing around with paper plates in their hands, talking to each other, eating. A thick October San Francisco fog, the kind that leaves your clothes damp, has blown in, and immerses us.

I don't know where all the food has come from. I don't know where all the people have come from. After he's hugged and talked to every one of them, Shlomo stands facing us and starts singing. People standing near him immediately join in. The "A" melody is low, soft, in a minor key, like fog. The "B" melody is bright and soars up high, in the corresponding major key, like sunlight.

I watch Shlomo. His eyes are darting around the *sukkah*, taking in everything. There are two small electric lights tied to the poles, and dozens of candles everywhere. The fog diffuses the lights like the soft focus lens from an old Hollywood movie. Shlomo closes his eyes and repeats the melody, lowering the volume. People are humming so softly you can barely hear it.

Chaya: It was a very big *sukkah*. There was fog, because it was a San Francisco night. And I'd look over my shoulder. There were lots of people there, students from Berkeley, all kinds of people. But I really thought I saw thousands or millions of people stretching into the distance. I felt like I saw the whole Jewish people.

Donna brings Shlomo a chair. The rest of us sit on the straw mats that cover the ground.

"My sweetest friends," he says. "I have to tell you something very deep. Everybody knows, by us *Yidden,* among the Jewish people, Yom Kippur is the holiest time of the year, right? We're bringing our souls to God's laundry so to speak and He's washing us clean. My soul is shining from one end of the world to the other. It's the ultimate holiness, right?

"But along comes our great spiritual master and teacher, the holy Ba'al Shem Tov, more than 200 years ago, and we learn something different. We learn that, unbelievable as it sounds, Sukkos is even holier." People are sitting close, touching one another.

"Okay, listen to this. Where is God's holiness revealed in this world? What is holy space? According to the Midrash, on one level there's the world that God made, which is so sweet and so beautiful. But sadly on another level, I can walk the streets of the world all my life and never really find my place. Imagine that I would be Rothschild and build a big castle somewhere with the most beautiful paintings, and the most beautiful gardens outside.* But if I feel like a stranger there, and it's not really my place, saddest thing in the world, right? The level of Israel, the level of the Holy Land means, simple as it is, to be in this world where I am really at home, where I am really in my place. That's a higher level of holy space. Then there is the level of the Holy City, Yerushalayim, Jerusalem, where I *mammash* know that my space is also God's space. And I can keep going deeper and deeper and higher and higher. In the middle of Yerushalayim there is the Holy Temple, the *Beis HaMikdash,* and in the middle of the *Beis HaMikdash* is the *Kodesh Kodeshim,* the Holy of Holies, where the *Kohen HaGodel,* the High Priest, would go inside once a year, on Yom Kippur, and stand alone with God, and say God's Name.

"Okay now, this is the deepest and most heartbreaking thing. The *Gemorah* (Talmud) says that, since the Holy Temple was destroyed, the Jewish people are in exile, and the whole world is in exile, and there is no place for God's holiness to be revealed in this world.

"The only thing is, by the holy Ba'al Shem Tov, in our days we have to make that holy place ourselves. So how do we do this?"

The fog is making little halos around the light bulbs and the candles.

---

* The Rothschilds were a German-Jewish banking family elevated to the level of Austrian nobility. The Rothschild name is synonymous with wealth among East European Jews.

"The Zohar says there are two kinds of light. The *Or Penimi,* the Inner Light, is contained in a vessel." Shlomo closes his eyes a moment and rocks back and forth. "You know, sadly, we're living in a world of empty vessels. How many times do you see someone in the street or at the *shul* and they say, 'How are you?' but you look at their eyes and they don't really want to know. *They don't really want to know.* Maybe they're thinking, 'I wonder how much he's donated to the building fund?' " He laughs, and people around him laugh too.

"Empty vessels, right? But let's say you see someone who really loves you and they say, 'How are you?' You can see that they're shining. *Mammash, they really want to know*, they really care. Same words, right, same vessels. So what's the difference? So much Inner Light. So much holy Inner Light."

I see Ruthie standing near the entrance way to the *sukkah.* I gesture to her to come in and sit next to me. She doesn't see me at first. I put my hands over my head and wave. Then she sees me and waves back. Sitting in his chair, Shlomo notices Ruthie, smiles at her and flashes her a "V." She waves back at him. Finally she reaches me and sits down on the mat, arranging her legs in a half lotus posture. She leans toward me, puts a hand on my shoulder and says in a loud whisper, "My *goodness*, there are so many people here! Where did they all come from?" I smile and shrug.

"As beautiful as it is to have inner light," Shlomo says, "the Zohar says that there is a second kind of light that is beyond all that. It is too infinite to be contained in vessels. This is the light from *before creation*, which in the Zohar is called the *Or Mesavev,* the Surrounding Light. This light has nothing to do with our actions. It's on the level of *Shabbos,* completely beyond doing.

"The holy Ba'al Shem Tov says the most awesome thing. By definition, the Surrounding Light cannot be contained in any vessels, right? But as long as we're in this world, we need vessels to receive anything. Listen to this, friends, open up your hearts. The holy Ba'al Shem Tov says, *the only vessel big enough to contain the Surrounding Light is a broken heart.*"

Shlomo closes his eyes, then looks around at the sea of faces surrounding him, reflecting the light of the candles and the light bulbs shining in the dark night, diffused through the fog, as though in a dream. Shlomo looks around at the *sukkah,* and up overhead at the carpet of leaves and branches tied with string onto the redwood poles. Hanging from the poles are apples and gourds, flowers, clusters of cherries and berries, brightly colored plastic fruits and animals, squares of paper with abstract designs, like mandalas.

"Okay friends, listen to this" Shlomo says. "Everybody knows, everybody knows, that when we make a *sukkah*, it's gotta be beautiful. That goes without saying, right? But what makes it kosher, what makes it real? Simple as it is, the Mishnah says that it's gotta have *skhakh,* it's gotta have leaves for the roof. And it can't be attached to any plant that's still growing. It's gotta be fallen leaves. Do you know how deep this is?

"Imagine if somebody told you you've gotta make a house for, *hvayss,* I don't know, somebody very important, the President, or a great leader, you'd want to buy the finest materials, right? But by us *Yiddelakh* (Jews), what do we do when we're building a dwelling place for the King of the World? We find little fallen leaves. Maybe yesterday somebody was stepping on them. So what do we do? We take them and we lift them up above our head. Then for seven days we sit underneath them.

"On Rosh Hashanah, so to speak, we had the awesome experience of standing at the entrance to the King's palace. On Sukkos, *we invite the King to come with us* into the *sukkah,* to sit with us under the fallen leaves. Unbelievable! Can you imagine? *Mammash,* we're gathering up all the fallen leaves, and all the broken hearts of the world, and we're sitting underneath them. Why? Because, by Ba'al Shem Tov, *this is the Holy Temple for us when we're in exile.* This is the Holy Temple for everyone whose heart is broken. This is where the Surrounding Light is shining. This is where God is sitting.

"What makes us safe; what makes us secure? All year long, I would say it's a strong house, right? The bricks protect me, and the roof over my head keeps me dry. The only thing is, one time in the year, one sweet, precious week, I leave my house, and move into the little *sukkah.*

"The *mitzvah* on Sukkos is the simplest thing in the world: to eat and sleep in the *sukkah.* One week in the year, one holy week, God is revealing to us, and we have the privilege of knowing, that bricks and roofs, money and bank accounts and jobs and honor in this world, are not what make me secure." Shlomo looks around the *sukkah,* slowly, lovingly, taking in every detail. The fog is moving over our heads, drifting through the *sukkah.* It's getting chillier and some people are huddled up together against the cold.

"Sukkos we are privileged to live in the holiness of space *and* the holiness of time. This is the greatest thing in the world. When the wind blows through the walls, maybe we feel a little bit cold, and when it rains maybe we get a little wet. But living under the shelter of the wings of the Almighty, we know, we *mammash know,* what it is to be home, to be really home, in this world."

191

Later when most of the candles are out and the party is over, when the fog has grown so thick that it has turned into fine droplets, a misty light rain falling slowly to the earth, and when most of the two hundred people have gone home, the rest of us remain behind in the night, standing in the *sukkah*, feeling the water slowly soaking into our faces and hair and clothes.

Leah and Bernice and Donna are setting up a sleeping place for Shlomo in the corner of the *sukkah*. They've spread out some old Persian style carpets that look like someone got them from the Diggers Free Store on Haight Street. On top of that they put a mattress and make the bed complete with sheets, pillows, blankets and a comforter. Ruthie comes in with one of my camping ponchos and lays it carefully on top of the comforter. I catch her eye and smile. She sees me looking at her, looks startled, and laughs.

Efraim is laying down a ground cloth for himself near Shlomo's bed, and spreading out his sleeping bag on top. Leah comes up to him and they talk. She and Uri are going to sleep inside. Ruthie is sleeping inside too. Shlomo told us that when it's raining, a person is permitted to sleep in the house. Moishe and Maxine have gone home with David, and Marvin and Bernice are getting ready to do the same with their kids.

Stephanie and Chaya emerge from the House with their sleeping bags and some blankets and pillows. They set up their beds at the corner opposite from Shlomo. Sonny comes out and sets up his sleeping bag near Efraim's. I go into the House to get my sleeping bag. When I come back see Donna and Shlomo standing in the corner near Shlomo's bed, talking.

"Top holy brother Aryae," Shlomo says, reaching out to give me a hug. "So what do you think?"

"The teaching was so beautiful Shlomo," I say.

"Tsss, the holy Ba'al Shem Tov," he says shaking his head, "unbelievable."

He looks around at the *sukkah* with obvious delight. "This is the most beautiful *sukkah* in the world." The three of us are silent for a moment, just standing and looking around.

"Shlomo," I say, "it's really gonna be wet out here. Are you sure you don't want to sleep inside?" Donna has her hand on her hip, looking at him. Maybe she was asking him the same question.

He smiles at both of us. "Thank you both for being so concerned about humble me, but really, *mammash,* it is such a privilege to sleep

192

in this beautiful *sukkah*. Besides," he says, gesturing at his bed of Persian rugs, mattress, blankets, comforter and poncho, "thanks to the top holy girls and women of the House, how can I turn down a bed like this?"

Donna looks at me, smiles a half smile, rolls her eyes, and shrugs.

"Donna, where are you staying?" I say to her. Normally she doesn't sleep at the House.

"I don't know," she says. "I guess I'll drive back to Oakland."

"Why don't you sleep in the *sukkah*?"

She looks at Shlomo and looks at me, shakes her head and laughs nervously. "No way!" I try to talk her into it, and Shlomo tries too, but she is adamant. I find myself wondering why she never stays at the House. I watch her as she leaves.

Donna: I would hang out with all the Shlomo people but, as you recall, I always stood back a little bit.

Aryae: I remember you would arrive with Shlomo from the airport or the hotel, and then you would sort of be at the periphery. Then you'd pick him up afterwards and take him back to the hotel, or wherever. You were his business manager in those days. I was fascinated with that. How did you get to be the business manager of this rising star?

Donna: I've always had a clear sense that people don't arrive, and don't stay, for free. I wanted to learn with him. I got to bring him here, and this is a skill that I still have, because I am a network queen. And while other people were being blissed-out, I knew that the way to get him out here was to see how many gigs you could book for him.

And being on the outside, I was talking to people at the various organizations. Cause I wasn't in the clutch, at the front, I was busy talking to the grown ups. When he would do a gig, he'd say, you know, "Talk to Donna." And there I'd be. I'd talk to them, and it was that contact that made the other concerts happen. So we would go from one to the other. I would work with him on the phone and we would write contracts, and get him paid.

Aryae: My memory is that when you were young, your father had been abusive and your family was dysfunctional. My picture was that Shlomo, because of your relationship with him, was a pathway to rescuing you out of that.

Donna: That's absolutely the case. But it cuts both ways. It means that I was also vulnerable to the charisma and attention of an older guy. But he also, he really knew how to make somebody feel special, and that's not something that I had ever had any experience with. He did that for every single person that he touched, he made them feel special.

What happened is that he started calling me, you know? And it was flattering, and it was very seductive. It was kind of weird for me as well. People were not making those stories up. He used to call me probably once a week from the first time I met him. As you know, he had never been married and late at night he was always alone, usually in a hotel room. I remember being really conflicted, because I was interested in learning, but I was also attracted to him.

Eventually we started being lovers.

Aryae: I don't think any of us knew that you and Shlomo were lovers. I certainly didn't. We'd see you enter and leave with him, but we didn't make that connection.

Donna: Well, that was the idea. Our relationship was private. You know it wasn't just sex. I would sit and learn with him. It was fascinating. We would just sit down and go . . . I would learn so much from him. We would spend hours and hours learning. It was amazing.

Donna, inspired by Shlomo, is a convert to Judaism. Next year when she's in New York, she'll find her way to a religious Jewish bookstore in Brooklyn to pick up a Hasidic book, in Hebrew, that he's recommended. When the slender young woman with long blond hair (which, unlike the hair of all the other women who come into this store, is uncovered) carries the book through the crowded isles and brings it to the front, the heavy, middle-aged Hasidic man standing behind the counter will stare at her blankly.

Donna will set the book on the counter. The man grabs the book and spits at her. Donna doesn't flinch. Looking at him directly as she wipes the spit off the shoulder of her jacket with a Kleenex from her pocket, she quotes him a passage from the Torah, in Hebrew, from Leviticus 19:33-34: "If a stranger comes to live with you in your land .

194

.. you shall love him as yourself, for you were strangers in the land of Egypt. I am the Lord your God."*

With just a hint of a smile, Donna will continue in Hebrew with an explanation from the great Torah commentator Rashi: "Do not cause (the stranger) anguish by saying, 'Yesterday you were an idol worshiper'. . . . I am your God and I am also his God!"

For a moment the two of them will stare at each other in silence. Then, without saying a word, the man will place the book in a small paper bag and hand it to her.

Shlomo has gotten into his bed in the *sukkah*. Sonny is lying in his sleeping bag near Efraim. I look around for a place for myself. The electric lights have gone out. Someone must have put them on a timer. A lone candle is flickering and sputtering, making long shadows dance erratically along the walls of the *sukkah*. Suddenly I feel very alone. It's cold and wet here, and for a moment I wish I were sleeping inside with Ruthie. I wonder, *Am I doing the right thing? Should I move out of the House and try to have a normal life and a normal marriage with Ruthie?* I set up my sleeping bag at the far end of the wall adjacent to where Shlomo is, halfway between him and the women.

I look up at the leaves above our heads. They make a kind of mysterious carpet in the candlelight. Fallen leaves, Shlomo called them. He meant himself, he meant all of us, the holy beggars, all the people with broken hearts, all the holy beggars of the world. Gather the fallen leaves together, and we become a Holy Temple for our time, God's dwelling place in this world.

After I'm in the sleeping bag and manage to zip it up, it's warm and dry inside, and soon I stop shivering. When I close my eyes, as I'm drifting off to sleep, I'm amazed to see light all around, bright and shimmering, surrounding me, surrounding everyone, like golden wings surrounding and embracing and sheltering the world.

---

* Also see Exodus 22:20 and Deuteronomy 10:18-19.

195

22
Tzitzit

I'm standing naked in a long straight line with 200 other naked young men. We're at the Armed Forces Examining and Induction Station in Oakland. There's an orange stripe on the gunmetal gray floor, and we're all facing the stripe, with the other guys to our right and our left. Following orders, we each have our clothes folded in a bundle and placed on the floor to the left of where we're standing.

A lone doctor, together with a couple of helpers, is working his way along the line, one guy at a time. He is squatting down in front of each guy and poking him in the balls. They haven't told us the purpose of this little ritual. I assume it's to see if we have hernias.

Actually I'm not completely naked. I'm wearing my *kippah* on my head and my *tzitzit*, the fringed undergarment worn by religious Jewish men. Picture a piece of thin white cloth with a silken texture, about six feet long and two feet wide, with a slit in the middle for the head to go through. It has little stripes embroidered along its length. At each corner there is a set of white strings that are tied in a series of complex knots, which leave the ends of the strings to hang in fringes. The *tzitzit* stand for the 613 *mitzvot* (commandments) in the Torah.*

This is how Shlomo taught us about *tzitzit*. The word *mitzvah* is much deeper than commandment. The Hebrew root is *tzav*, which means to tie, to connect. Thus, a *mitzvah* is an action in this world, a right action that connects us to our deepest truth, and to God.

Shlomo said, "Why are the knots of the *tzitzit* tied to the corners? What is it about corners? The Torah says, 'Don't be led by the impulses, the lusts and fears of your heart and your eyes, which will get you lost; when you see the *tzitzit*, remember all My *mitzvot* and do

---

* The word *tzitzit* as it is spelled in the Mishnah has a numerical value 600. Each tassel has eight threads (when doubled over) and five sets of knots, totalling 13. Together, they make 613.

them.'** When we say those words in the morning prayers, we hold onto the *tzitzit*." So Shlomo says, "When do we most need something to hold onto? It's when we're backed into a corner. It's when I'm trapped and have nowhere to go; when I can't find a way out. That's when I need to let go of my own eyes and heart and mind, and hold onto God's."

Oh yeah, I almost forgot to mention, besides the *tzitzit*, I have my guitar strapped over my shoulder, and I'm holding a stack of antiwar pamphlets from the American Friends Service Committee.

The guy standing next to me is a big Hispanic dude who's been ignoring me up to this point. He looks over at me. His face has a look of total incomprehension. He turns away, looking over at where the doctor is gradually working his way down the line, poking his finger into everyone's balls. A minute later he turns to me.

He gestures at me with his hand. "Hey man, what you doin'?" he says. "Are you acting crazy so you can get out? Or are you really crazy?"

I look up at him. He looks half perturbed, half amused. "Oh, this!" I say, touching my *kippah* and my *tzitzit:* "No man, I'm not crazy. I'm wearing this stuff because I'm a Jew, and Jews wear this stuff."

He looks less amused and more perturbed. "I know some Jews," he says. "There's Jews live down the street in my neighborhood. I don't see them wear no shit like that."

"It depends," I say. "Jews that are real religious, they wear this stuff." I look up at him, straight into his eyes. He's sizing me up. I reach out my hand. "My name's Aryae," I say.

He seems to relax. Then he reaches out and we shake hands. "Miguel," he says.

"Good to meet you man," I say. He shrugs and gestures at the room we're standing naked in, at the hundreds of guys around us, at the absurdity of the whole situation.

"Yeah that's okay," he says, "but I rather meet you somewhere else, you know?" We both laugh.

Then I look down at my pamphlets. "Look," I say, "let me give you one of these."

He looks at me warily and doesn't reach out to take it.

***

** Numbers 15: 39-40.

"It's about the war," I say. "It's about how these government guys in Washington are sending guys like you and me to die in Vietnam, you know? And we don't have to go man. We don't. We have rights. We can say 'No.'"

The guy standing on the other side of me, a skinny white guy with freckles all over his body and a thick mop of red hair on his head, has been listening in. "Yeah, and get our ass in jail!" he says in a Southern accent.

I turn toward him and reach out my right hand. "My name's Aryae," I say, "what's yours?"

He looks at my hand, then at me, then reaches out to take it. "Jack," he says. We shake hands.*

"Listen Jack," I say. "You're right. Even thought we've got legal rights, and the law's supposed to protect us, they could still lock our asses in jail. But the thing is, where would you rather have your ass wind up: in jail, or under a pile of dirt somewhere in Vietnam? And for what? To go over there, 10,000 miles away, and kill people who never did anything to us, who never threatened the United States? Does that make any sense to you?"

Jack's expression has changed. He's looking straight ahead of us.

"What's going on here?!" I look across the line. An Army corporal is standing there, looking right at me. We face each other, he on his side of the orange line, I on mine. He seems to be about the same age and height as I am. His crew cut hair is blond. He's dressed in his army uniform, neatly pressed, with all the right stuff in the right places. I've got my *kippah,* my *tzitzit,* my beard, my guitar, and my anti-war literature.

I look at him and say, "I'm exercising my constitutional right of free speech by expressing . . ."

"Shut up!" he says. "Save it for outside. Here you're under the jurisdiction of the Army and will follow the rules and regulations of military conduct." He looks me over in disgust. "What's all this garbage?"

"My religion requires me to wear these garments," I say.

"And the Army requires you to take them off," he says. "Willful failure to comply is a violation of the Universal Military Training and Service Act and punishable by a fine or prison or both." He stands

---

* I do not remember Jack and Miguel's actual names.

199

there looking at me. Miguel and Jack, and the other naked young guys near us, are also looking at me.

I take a deep breath. I feel the fingers of my left hand wrap around the knots of the *tzitzit*. "The constitution of this country guarantees me freedom of religion," I say. "I'm not taking them off."

His pupils widen. He signals for two soldiers to come over, and says something to them when they arrive. Miguel and Jack stand back. One soldier stands on each side of me.

"Pick up your clothes and go with these soldiers," he says. Then he turns and walks crisply away. I look at the corporal's back. Then I look at the naked guys nearby, all staring at me, the soldiers standing next to me, and my pile of clothes on the floor. I bend down and pick up the clothes.

The soldiers take me down a narrow corridor. They stop at a door and knock. Then they open it and motion me to go in. I go in, and they close the door behind me.

It's a small, windowless room. Inside there's a middle-aged guy, partially bald, in a rumpled uniform, sitting behind a desk. He looks up at me, smiles and motions me to sit down in the chair on the other side of the desk, facing him. The chair has a gray metal frame and a green plastic leatherette seat.

"Is it okay if I put my pants on?" I say. He smiles and nods affirmatively. I set my clothes on the floor together with the anti-war literature, take off my guitar and lean it against the chair, bend over again and get my underpants and pants, put them on, and sit down. The strings of the *tzitzit* are resting on my jeans.

The guy behind the desk just sits there looking at me. I look around at the walls of his little cubicle. There are framed documents that look like medical degrees and official certifications.

"Are you a psychiatrist?" I say.

He puts his elbows on the desk and leans toward me. "Yes I am," he says. "Are you looking for a medical deferment for a psychiatric condition?"

"No, I'm not," I say.

"Then why all this?" He gestures toward me with a sweep of his hand that includes the *tzitzit*, the guitar and the anti-war literature.

I touch my *kippah* and my *tzitzit*. "These are the traditional garments worn by religious Jews."

The psychiatrist smiles. "I know," he says. "I'm Jewish myself. I don't think anyone here is saying that you shouldn't wear these garments and be a religious Jew. I believe that you're being asked to remove them only for a medical examination. Is that correct?"

I look at him and think. Then I say, "If a doctor came up to me and said to take off the *tzitzit* so he could put a stethoscope on my chest, I'd say, 'Okay. Of course.' But the deal here is, the corporal said I'm under the jurisdiction of the Army, and that overrides my religious practice, so I have to take them off while I'm standing in line. I disagree. I was just standing there, not interfering with anybody. I don't think Army rules override my religious practice."

"There are many, many Orthodox Jews serving in the Armed Forces along with other Americans. I've met some of them. These are patriotic Americans who are willing to serve their country when asked. Are you saying that you are more religious than they are?"

"No I'm not," I say. "I'm just trying to do what's right for me, based on my understanding of what God wants me to do."

"What about the guitar?" he says. "What about the literature?"

I smile. "The guitar is for singing songs of love and peace. The pamphlets are from the American Friends Service Committee in Philadelphia. The message is to consider registering as a conscious objector to war."

He looks me over and then suddenly leans forward over his desk. His eyebrows narrow. He says to me in a kind of hoarse stage whisper, "I have to tell you, you look like a freak."

I'm not sure if I heard him right. "What?" I say.

"You look like a freak."

I look back at him, not knowing what to say. Then I laugh. "Thanks," I say.

He leans back in his chair and laughs also. "I see so many guys like you come in here. You wouldn't believe the stuff they pull. Yesterday I saw a guy who had kept himself awake with methamphetamines for three days. He was a mess! He was shaking, couldn't walk straight, and could barely get out a coherent sentence. He wanted me to declare him crazy so he wouldn't have to go to Vietnam. What do you think I should do with guys like him?"

"He doesn't sound crazy to me," I say quietly. "He sounds frightened. If you're gonna send him off to die, or maybe spend the rest of his life as a cripple, for a cause he doesn't believe in, he's got good reason to be frightened."

201

The psychiatrist leans forward across the desk. "What about you? Are you frightened? Aren't you doing the same thing he is, in your own way?"

I take a deep breath. "Actually I am a little frightened. I might go to jail for my beliefs, and jail scares me. But I'm not leaving the country. And I'm not interested in a 4-F deferment. I'm interested in . . . speaking my truth, to you, to the military establishment, and to the other guys out there. I don't think that war and killing are the way. I think that peace is the way."

The psychiatrist leans back, looks at me, and nods. "I take it you've applied for CO status and been turned down?" The tone of his voice has changed.

I nod back. "Yeah."

He looks up, sighs, rubs the bald spot on his head, then looks at me. "You know, if you don't cooperate here, they'll nail you, and it's an open and shut case. If you cooperate and go through the physical, you can still appeal to have your CO application reconsidered. That way you've got a chance." His eyes almost seem to be pleading with me.

I nod again. I look down and see that my left hand is holding onto the *tzitzit*. "I don't know," I say looking at him. "I appreciate your advice, I really do. It's just that . . ." I look around the tiny room, at the framed documents on the wall, at my stuff on the floor, at the neat stacks of papers on the desk, at the guy sitting behind the desk who is now looking concerned. "I think I've got to keep doing what I'm doing, and keep speaking my truth."

Now it's his turn to nod again. He sits still for a while without saying anything, as if giving me a chance to change my mind. Then he presses a button on the row of buttons on his phone set. He makes some check marks on the form in front of him, writes a few words, and signs it. The door opens, and I see one of the two soldiers that brought me here.

I stand up. The psychiatrist stands up and extends his hand. "Good luck," he says with a half-smile.

I shake his hand. "Thanks," I say.

As they're escorting me out of the building, the same corporal who spoke to me in line comes and reads me a statement. It basically says the same stuff, that if I leave without cooperating, I have violated the law and subject to its full penalty.

Three weeks later at the House of Love and Prayer I will receive the following letter:

202

April 20, 1969

To: Lawrence J. Coopersmith:

You are hereby notified that this Local Board has declared you to be a delinquent because of [. . .] failure to cooperate in processing for Pre Induction Physical Examination [. . .]

Your willful failure to perform the foregoing duty or duties is a violation of the Universal Military Training and Service Act, as amended, which is punishable by imprisonment for as much as 5 years or a fine of as much as $10,000, or by both such fine and imprisonment.

Gloria Quinsores
Clerk of Local Board

I find the Shabbos Express in the parking lot of the Oakland Armed Forces Induction Station. I unlock the doors, put my guitar and anti-war literature on the back seat, get into the driver's seat and sit there a moment, holding the wheel and letting my mind drift. My head is spinning: images of soldiers, battlefields, and jails, mixed with images of rock concerts, peace marches, Shabboses at the House.

Then I remember. Tomorrow night is the first night of Passover. The Sosnick family, which owns a company in San Francisco that distributes kosher foods, has graciously offered to donate wine, *matzah*, horseradish and *gefilte* fish to the House for our *Seder* if we can pick it up at one of their warehouses before it closes. We're expecting over 100 people. My watch says 3:30. I start the engine.

23
Lord Get Me High

House of Love and Prayer – March 17th, 1969

As George and Pamela spend time at the House during the week before their wedding, we hover around them, drawn to them, wanting to be there with them to help them prepare. Both of them are attractive, radiant, charismatic, like a prince and princess about to become king and queen.

HOUSE OF LOVE
AND PRAYER

House of Love and Prayer brochure.
Photograph by Moshe Yitzchak Kussoy.

205

That's Efraim putting *tefillin* on George. George looks very taken with Efraim. This must be the first time he has ever worn *tefillin*. Efraim is initiating him into an ancient ritual of Jewish men, done for thousands of years. George is open, ready to receive everything.

There's no picture of Leah and Pamela in the brochure. I imagine the two of them up in Efraim and Leah's bedroom, sitting on the bed. Leah is telling Pamela about the women's rituals and mysteries, about going to immerse herself in the pure rain water of the *mikveh* before her wedding, repeating the process each month, seven days after the end of her period, renewing herself once again as a bride before having sex with her husband, and about the sexual act between husband and wife as the sacred union of the divine King and Queen.

George: I first saw you on the lawn at San Francisco State doing Tai Chi, and I was transfixed, you know? You were an unusual looking dude. You had your full Hasidic beard on, and you were unusually thin, and really, really graceful. I sat down and had a cigarette and watched you; I had never seen anything like it.

Then not more than a week or two later, Pam was at school when Shlomo came there. She told me about this guy that she had met, and he was playing at the I/Thou Coffeehouse on Haight Street that night. So we went over to see him, and *you* were there! He told us about *Shabbos.* I guess this was like on a Thursday or something. And we came to *Shabbos* with Shlomo the next day.

After that, every time Shlomo was in town he would let us know somehow. It started getting more and more important, and Shlomo would come to town, and if he was in town, then we would go to his concerts. Then there was that time down in L.A., the great trudge through the rain.

Aryae: The 27 mile walk! Yeah!

George: Yeah! Pam and I were visiting my parents in West L.A. We were driving through the storm. It was night, and it was pouring-ass-rain.

We were listening to the news on the radio, and we heard this crazy story about you guys! You had gotten bogged down, and the sun had gone down, and Shlomo had just said,

206

"We're gonna walk." We went to where the news report gave and joined you guys, and walked with you in the rain!

Aryae: Wow! That was about six months before your wedding. How did you and Pamela decide to get married and to do it that way with Shlomo?

George: One day Pamela said, the next time Shlomo's in town, will you ask him if he'll marry us? She *proposed* to me! And I said, "Sure!" Then we got Shlomo, and he said he'd do it.

Do you remember down in Santa Cruz, the engagement party? That to me was one of the most beautiful memories of all. We brought hundreds of these white taper candles. I still have one. Shlomo did some kind of prayer about our engagement, and some kind of ceremony. And there were all these hundreds of Santa Cruz college students, hippie-types, singing:

Lord get me high, get me high, get me high;
Lord get me high, get me higher.

What kind of drugs was he taking?

Aryae: He wasn't taking any drugs.

George: Shlomo never did any LSD, any mescaline, anything like that?

Aryae: No, never; he wasn't into it.

George: But he was so psychedelic! He was so much in that world!

Aryae: He was a mystic, you know? He was just *there,* naturally.

Golden Gate Park, San Francisco – March 24th, 1969

Looking at the photo from *Life* magazine taken that day, I see Donna on the left in her green blouse and green plaid skirt, looking thoughtfully down at her guitar, concentrating on getting Shlomo's chord changes right. Normally she doesn't get up on stage to play with Shlomo at his concerts (I didn't even know she played guitar) but she's trying it out at this wedding.

Photo published in *Life* magazine, September 26th, 1969.

I see Yonatan holding the poles, with his whimsical Renaissance hat and bright red hair and beard, eyes closed, heart open, face joyfully turned toward heaven. He and Ahouva have been staying with us at the House and are planning to go to Israel in a few weeks with Efraim and Leah.

There I am with sandals and my brown suede sport jacket, the only decent jacket I've got, standing in my usual spot behind Shlomo, looking serious with my eyes open, scanning Shlomo and the crowd, concentrating on allowing "Aryae" to disappear, ready to jump in and help Shlomo however I can in working with the energy.

Shlomo also has his eyes open, looking straight into the camera. His whole body and being are aligned with projecting the music that is coming through him. He takes in the feedback on how people are responding, continually tuning the level of emotional and spiritual intensity, adjusting the volume and the tempo, adjusting the words, doing whatever is needed to dance with the energy and open the heart. In this infinite moment he is completely present, for George and Pamela, for the hundreds of people at this wedding, for all the ancestors and all the as-yet-unborn descendents who, according to our tradition, are also guests at the wedding, for all the Jewish people and all the holy beggars of the world. Most of all, he is present for the mission that God and the Rebbe have sent him here to do. Shlomo is singing this song, and we're singing it with him:

Lord get me high, get me high, get me high.
Lord get me high, get me higher.

Then there's Pamela, so beautiful in her long white dress with high collar, her hair crowned with a garland of flowers, hands holding a bouquet of white and pink roses, with a single red rose in the middle, looking like a dream of a pre-Raphaelite bride, eyes half-closed, taking in the moment, expressing pleasure as she sings. As I look at her face I find myself wondering, *What is she feeling?*

There's George, barely visible, almost merged into Pamela, head turned away from us and facing only her, long brown hair with a pink flower behind his ear, dark *kippah* decorated with a pattern of woven flowers, so much in love with his bride.

Finally Efraim, with his bright red hair and beard, white shirt, *tzitzit* hanging against his dark pants, comfortably holding his guitar, eyes closed, taking in Shlomo's music and channeling it back out. It's been almost a year now since he and Leah were in New York on their way to Jerusalem and turned back at Shlomo's request. Pesah begins next week. After Pesah is over Efraim and Leah and Uri will resume their journey to Jerusalem, where they will stay for the rest of their lives. This chapter of our friendship—where he and I see each other every morning, emerging from our bedrooms across the hall from one another on the second floor of the House of Love and Prayer, rubbing the sleep from our eyes and looking around to see who's here today, what they're up to, and what we need to do to keep it all together—this chapter will be over.

George: God damn! [very emotional] That was 40 years ago and I'm still remembering this! Shlomo told us we were going through the gates of heaven. And actually it was.

San Francisco, California – April 1969

I help Efraim load suitcases and a couple of boxes, the remainder of the family's belongings they haven't already shipped to Israel, onto the Shabbos Express. He and Leah and Uri get inside, and a few others pile in. There are about 20 of us in several cars going to see them off. I bring my guitar and a couple of other people bring their guitars and tambourines.

At San Francisco International Airport's South Terminal we gather around them and sing a song. It's the one that I wrote for Joe and Shoshana last year when they left for Israel. In the years ahead we'll be singing this song many times, whenever someone leaves the House on their journey to Jerusalem. The words are from the *Shabbos* prayers, where we sing to the angels:

> *May your going be in peace,*
> *May your going be in peace,*
> *Messengers of peace,*
> *Messengers of the Most High.*

Surrounding them on the main concourse of the busy, cavernous terminal, we sing the melody over and over and over again, as waves of joy and sadness wash through all of us. Other passengers rushing past on their way to catch planes see a little band of colorfully dressed hippies standing in a circle in the middle of the crowded floor, playing guitars, hitting tambourines, swaying back and forth, singing.

When it finally comes time for them to leave, and we've all given them final hugs, we watch Efraim, Leah, and Uri make their way through the crowd to the boarding gate. This is the second time I've said goodbye to them. This time it will be 34 years—long enough for a whole generation of kids to be born, get married, and grow up to be older than we are now—before I see them again.

The 20 of us stand there unmoving, watching silently as people stream onto the plane. This little family on their way to Jerusalem is leaving a big void in San Francisco. And they're not the only ones. Sonny left three months ago to study at a *yeshiva* with Rabbi Twerski in Denver. Yonatan and Ahouva will be leaving soon to follow Efraim and Leah to Jerusalem. And others are talking about leaving soon as well.

It is up to the rest of us, and especially up to me, to try to fill the void.

Coming from a remote location that we can't see, we catch faint echoes, sounds of tambourines and voices, of another group singing at the airport:

> *Hari Krishna, Hari Krishna,*
> *Krishna Krishna, Hari Hari,*
> *Hari Rama, Hari Rama*
> *Rama Rama, Hari Hari.*

Golden Gate Park, San Francisco – May 23rd, 1969

It's dawn on Shavuos. A group of us are standing on the bridge at Stow Lake, the same spot where we jumped in for a *mikveh* at this time last year. Birds are starting to sing like a congregation of Hasidim davening the morning prayers to usher in the dawn on this holy day when God gave us the Torah at Mount Sinai. This time, although Efraim and Leah are gone, amazingly, Shlomo is with us. I got an unexpected call from Donna last week saying he was coming out for Shavuos. We didn't have time to organize any events for him. He knows about the big empty space in the House now that Efraim and Leah are gone. Maybe he's come on impulse to cheer us up and give us strength.

It's been a year since I graduated from San Francisco State College with a BA in English Literature, emphasis in Creative Writing. San Francisco State is now being run by S. I. Hayakawa, a well known linguist and political conservative brought in by Governor Ronald Reagan to wrestle control of the campus back from the unruly students and faculty, restore order and discipline, and force the educational program back to basics. When I visited earlier this year, the campus felt strange and unfamiliar, quiet, with everyone busy going to classes and no one hanging out on the lawn. I didn't see anyone I knew.

An era has ended.

The original hippies have left both San Francisco State College and Haight Street. Some have gone to the country to live in communes in the back-to-the-land movement. Others are doing what I'm doing, connecting in spiritual communities in San Francisco and elsewhere in Northern California, digging deeper to explore the revelations that came to us while living in the Haight. Others are heading back to graduate school to pursue careers.

Haight Street itself has changed. Its outward appearance is a commercial imitation of its former self, with plenty of stores that sell rock posters and drug paraphernalia and tie-dyed t-shirts. But when you walk on the Street, people are no longer smiling and offering each other hugs and flowers. The soul is gone. There is a feeling of hardship, of loneliness, of angst. And there are rumors that organized crime is moving in to take control of the drug traffic.

I've stopped smoking grass and dropping acid.

I have no career plans, no plans at all about where I'm going from here. I'm cut off from both the past and the future. I've jumped in with both feet, all the way into the world that Efraim and I talked about a couple of years ago on his front porch, the world that God created some 5,700 years ago. I have only the House of Love and Prayer, only Shlomo, only the present.

An era has also ended for George, in a way that none of us would have imagined.

Aryae: How could it be that Pamela wasn't in touch with her sexuality until after you got married?

George: I don't have a clue. I think it was probably an acid trip. She started working as a social worker and she had a boss who was gay. Ginny. And then one night she said she was going over to Ginny's and she didn't come home.

She had never had a lesbian relationship at all. And then it was suddenly, not just that she was into women. It was like, she was absorbed into the whole women's lib lesbian world. It was just weird. She didn't come home, and I'm calling her. I'm calling her at work and stuff. Then she sent me a telegram saying, "Don't try to find me," and she took off with Ginny. She was in Colorado. It's over.

I started schiz-ing out. You were gone that summer, and Efraim was gone, so I called Gavriel and Sari. I told them I was in really bad shape. Gavriel came and got me in his Volkswagen van and took me up to Santa Rosa where they were living.

I was out of my mind, literally; they were so kind.

Somehow we got into Jean Paul Sartre. Gavriel was teaching philosophy at Santa Rosa Junior College. He told me to read a certain page in *Being and Nothingness*. But I was like mentally ill at the time. [laughs] Gavriel was saying, "You'll hear the buzzing in your ears when you're enlightened."

Here in front of the stone bridge at Stow Lake, the sky is getting lighter. "Holy brothers and sisters," Shlomo says, "We gotta go to the *mikveh!*" That's why we came to this spot.

Some of us were here last year and we can do the same thing, women on one side of the bridge and men on the other. It's not a big deal, right? Still, this feels really different. I have the fantasy of another photographer from *Life* magazine lurking in the bushes, getting a big color photo of a bunch of naked San Francisco hippies cavorting with each other and the Singing Rabbi in a lake in Golden Gate Park for the cover of next week's magazine. Upon seeing us in the magazine, a group of outraged rabbis, joined by a group of incensed priests who have recognized Cathy, gather in an angry mob to run us out of town.

As the sun rises, we're all standing, damp clothes clinging to our bodies and wet hair straggling down our faces, at the center of the bridge over Stow Lake that connects the shore to the little mountain in the middle. We're all facing the rising sun, with our arms around each other. This is the moment where we are all one, where the whole world is one, receiving God's presence in our midst.

As I look at all of us, the holy beggars standing on this bridge, I realize that what we have in common is that we're each on a journey, and our lives, together with the world, are changing fast. In a couple of years none of us, *none of us,* will be where we are now.

Shlomo's eyes are closed as he rocks back and forth, davening. His lips are moving very quickly. Thinking about this later, I realize that he is praying all the morning prayers for this holy day, as well as reciting the Torah portion that describes this moment 3,000 years ago. It's all there, precisely inscribed in his memory, in his mind, in his heart, in his soul. His whole being is a cosmic transceiver, transmitting these signals from other times and other dimensions into our portion of the time-space continuum so that the rest of us can receive them. Time has stopped. The exquisiteness of the moment is indescribable.

We're all standing on the bridge between worlds. The story of how we got here and where we go next is an endless story, one that will be told as long as there are stories to tell. For now, we're not going anywhere, because there is nowhere else to go.

24

Israel

Gavriel: Sari and I were pretty well situated in Santa Rosa, in terms of all the ego things of the world: income, nice house, teaching career, lots of students . . . Sari was pregnant then with our son Bahir.

Aryae: So how did you decide to pick up and go to Israel? That's a pretty radical move.

Gavriel: The question was—Where would our son be born? It was easy. It was like a vision. My wife said—We just gotta go!

Aryae: So you went to Israel in order to be there for his birth? Was that Sari's vision?

Gavriel: Yeah! It was very, very important. In the end, it was just so strong, so . . . Okay, here we go! It's like you follow the Cloud [in the Torah which led the Jews through the desert].

Aryae: Going to Israel was like following the Cloud?

Gavriel: No question. So if it sat, you stayed. If it went, you go.

Ahouva: It was around March in 1969 when Yonatan and I drove down from Vancouver to the House in San Francisco and Efraim and Leah took us to meet Sari and Gavriel in Santa Rosa. On our way home to Vancouver I told Yonatan, "I had a dream last night." The dream was, I saw Sari on the streets of Jerusalem, and I was greeting her. Yonatan and I looked at each other and said, "I think that means we need to go to Israel!"

We packed everything up very quickly, came back to the House for Passover, and then went to Israel. It was strange because, even though Sari and Gavriel actually drew us there spiritually, they didn't physically arrive until later.

Letter from Efraim and Leah
Jerusalem, Israel – July 28th, 1969

The message that we must allow ourselves to have delivered through us: *Asaper lakhem eikh [tihiyu] s'meihim* [I will tell you how to be joyous]. Oh, what hard work is this business of being joyous [. . .]

How appropriate that Shlomo, our most beloved friend and *rebbe,* will be arriving [. . .] on the 15th of Av, the day, when the Holy Temple was standing, that all the young maidens who were ready to be married would dance in the field near the Temple. [. . .] A branch from the Tree of the boy and from the Tree of the girl would be twined together and they would be One.

We miss you with a great longing, we speak of you, to you, at every place that a tear has been shed and a baby has smiled. This morning I/we prayed at the Wall that we should be together with you again so when I/we came to Joe's house and there were your letters so gently folded inside of each other, we cried and we sang. The whole world is waiting to sing the song of *Shabbos.* May the Great Peace of the Land fill you with Eternal Bliss.

[Unsigned from Efraim.]

I love you both so much. *Shabbos* dreams of [being] together again.

Leah.

Ahouva: When we first went to Israel we stayed with Joe and Shoshana. Efraim and Leah had been there first. Then we came. They were the first parking place for many people who came from the House to Israel.

Then Efraim and Leah got an apartment and we stayed with them. It was a one bedroom place for all of us: Efraim and Leah and Uri and their new baby, Yonatan and I, and Eliezer [Sonny] who lived in the hall leading to the kitchen.

A Breslover guy named Moshe Klevrinatzer would come teach us late at night. We would do Rebbe Nachman stories. That was just after we got there, so it was very magical. We could . . . you know, there wasn't a sex discrimination thing going on. We didn't have to have a *mehitza* or anything. We just studied.

Letter from Efraim and Leah
Jerusalem, Israel – probably January 1970

Dearest Aryae and Ruthie,

Just read your holy Hanukah message of Shlomo last year. Thank you so very much for the great holy work [. . .]

A million things are happening—each day a triple somersault into the endless sea of time and every moment so precious and holy. Uri is a beautiful child, delight full *[sic]* and joyous. He spends his days singing Shlomo songs very loud as he rides his tricycle from one end of this House to the other, and it is a very big House. Nosson is divine glee: Holy, Holy, Holy. My life is very full—mostly joy permeated.

We miss you very much. We long to be reunited to strengthen again the eternal bond our souls have with each other. Eliezer [Sonny], sweet and sensitive heart and soul, is staying here.

We are so very blessed but we miss you so very deeply. *Shabbos* walks into the forest remind us so much of you.

Yonatan, Ahouva, Karen, Barbara, and dear Anna are all on various *kibbutzim* learning Hebrew and picking oranges.

Please give our love to everyone—body at and of the House. We miss and kiss each gentle-dream-person-man-woman-child. And please write soon again. Your letter gets passed all over and brings you closer to all of us—almost touching. Thank you, thank you, thank you.

Leah.

Dear Aryae and Ruthie,

The Land waits patiently for Her People to return to Her. She is a Land working up to Her Divine Mission. Every day is filled with new joys and depths. We long for the day when all the peoples will be gathered together and the great Dance shall begin.

Efraim.

Tirtzah: So after our wedding Menachem and I went up to Seattle to start a House of Love and Prayer for Shlomo, and I bolted and went back to Berkeley. Then around March, it was after Purim, we decided to go to Israel. Give it another chance. Maybe we'd have better luck there.

So we were going to stay with Menachem's brother in Jerusalem. We tried to find his apartment for the longest time. We were exhausted out of our brains. Coming from San Francisco, the jet lag was intense. And we couldn't find his place, so we sort of just lay down in the park.

Aryae: To go to sleep?

Tirtzah: Yeah! [laughs] 'Cause we were so tired. And while we were resting there, some people noticed us and helped us out and showed us where the streets were, and we found him.

Then we went over to the Jerusalem House of Love and Prayer, in this upscale neighborhood. Leah and Efraim were living there, and a few others. Eliezer [Sonny] gave up his room for us.

We got so sick. Coming to *Eretz Yisrael,* you used to get this thing called the "purification." Like the water in Israel was not of the best quality in those days, and everybody had to go through this transition. For Passover I was literally under the table, on the floor, on a mattress, the night of the *Seder* [. . .]

Later we went to live on Kibbutz Shalom Bayit. I loved it. I loved getting up before dawn and going out to the broccoli fields, laying on the ground so that you could look up to the underside of the leaves, and making sure that there were no aphids. I watched the sun rise up out of the earth, and that started my love affair with Israel.

Letter from Efraim and Leah
Jerusalem, Israel – January 26th, 1970

Dear Aryae,

Each day by day I think at least a few minutes each hour by hour of you, and when the light begins to spark and *HaShem* opens the gates of prayer we are again together. I have been hearing such wondrous reports of the House and of your and Shlomo's work there, that I am truly jealous [. . .]

One day when I was learning at the Breslov *yeshiva* [. . .] a twinkling Hasid came and sat with me and spoke to me for an hour about a certain Reb Eliezer Berland* who he believed to be a great hidden *tzaddik* [spiritual master] a real joyful follower of the Rebbe [Rebbe Nachman] who he thought that I must come to, explaining that there was something about our souls that we must meet.

Two days later I met Reb Eliezer. Everything the Hasid said of him is even more true, and we have been meeting more and more, until this past *Shabbos* he spent with us at our house. He is married and has four wonderful children, yet he is young and really one of us. When he dances he jumps so high that he flies, and everywhere he goes he makes people happy, yet he is serious and his learning is deep and wide. He says that when a person is truly glad and happy he can learn more of the true Torah in one night than the greatest student can learn in 100 years.

We are speaking of traveling together in the next month or so to Uman, Ukraine to go to the grave of Rebbe Nachman if it is the will of *HaShem*. Rebbe Nachman promised that anyone who goes to his burial place and recites the *Tikkun Klali*, 10 Psalms which the Rebbe ordered in a specific way [. . .] he will personally lift up that person's soul from the depths of hell to the very highest of rungs. May it be so, *Amen!*

---

* Rabbi Eliezer Berland (b.1937) is a leader among Breslover Hasidim and Rosh Yeshiva of Yeshivat Shuvu Bonim in Jerusalem.

Yet of course we have no money for the trip, besides there being many dangers involved, yet we are forbidden to think of such things, only to have faith [. . .]

Love to All, Good *Shabbos!!*

Efraim, Leah, Uri, Nosson.

Ruthie,

How are you? I am beyond belief happy here. Our children are beautiful. Uri remembers you. We love you so much.

Leah.

25
Rabbi

House of Love and Prayer – November 1969

Shlomo wants me to go to Miami next week to lead a special weekend for an Orthodox youth group at a big kosher hotel. He's too sick to go himself.

I'm standing in the closet under the front stairs that go up to the second floor. We can't have a regular phone, because we'd have no way to stop people from making long distance calls. So we have a pay phone in the closet, bolted to the wall. A girl named Shelley has been living here, sharing the space with the phone.

"Shlomo, I can't do that!" I say, trying to avoid stepping on Shelly's stuff. "These kids have spent all their lives in Orthodox schools! They know way more Torah than I do! What happens when they figure that out?"

"That's outside learning," Shlomo says. "They've already had their *kishkes* stuffed with outside learning. That's not why they're there. What you can show them is *mammash* real inside learning."

I try talking him out of sending me, but after five minutes, I realize there's no point: I'm going to Miami. I ask him if Ruthie can come with me.

"*Mammash,* that's a great idea!" he says.

"What do you mean?" I say.

"It would be very sweet in Miami," he says. "She can be your *rebbetzin* (rabbi's wife)."

"Why do I need a *rebbetzin?*"

"Well, I already talked to the youth group leader about you," he says. Then he coughs.

"Yeah?" I say. "So?"

"Look, it's a long story, but they think you're an Orthodox rabbi."

221

"They think I'm a *what*?"

"Look, Aryae, it's the greatest thing. The truth is you can reach more of these kids than a whole *shul* full of Orthodox rabbis. Trust me. The only thing is, they don't want me to send anyone else who's not an Orthodox rabbi."

"You told them I'm an Orthodox rabbi?"

"I know, I know; but it's not so crazy. You've been learning so fast. Another two years, I can give you *smikhah* (ordination)."

"I'm supposed to pretend to be an Orthodox rabbi, for a whole weekend, with an Orthodox youth group, at a hotel in Miami?"

"So what else are we supposed to do? We have a chance to bring a real *Shabbos* to 250 kids!" His voice is high pitched. He sounds upset.

I don't say anything. Now it's my turn to cough.

Miami Beach, Florida – November 1969

Ruthie and I get out of the car in the hotel parking lot. Ruthie laughs. "Aryae, I can't believe we're actually doing this!" she says.

I laugh and roll my eyes. "I know," I say. "Okay. But we can't embarrass Shlomo and ourselves, right? So, please, let's do what we've gotta do." I walk around and open the trunk.

"Do I look like an Orthodox *rebbetzin?*" She's wearing a black embroidered scarf over her head, a bright green blouse with long sleeves and a high neck, with embroidery around the sleeves and neck, a jade green sash tied around her waist, dark purple slacks made out of a silk-like material, and lots of Yemenite jewelry dangling from her wrists and neck. She's also brought her belly dance outfits, in case she has the chance to do some belly dancing. She has friends here who know people in the belly dance scene.

I glance nervously around the parking lot. "Maybe if you take off the thing around your waist and some of the jewelry…"

"What's wrong with the jewelry?" she says, looking at me wide-eyed with a kind of mock innocence. "Women in the Middle East wear it when they come to the door to greet their husbands! Isn't it a *mitzvah* in the Torah for women to make themselves beautiful for their husbands?" She looks mischievous.

We bring our luggage to the main entrance. A doorman holds open the front door for us, and two bellhops take the luggage to the front desk. The lobby has high ceilings, chandeliers, Greek columns, marble floors, plenty of big, overstuffed chairs, a few guests, and lots of staff in uniforms scurrying about. We walk up to the front desk and check in.

"Rabbi, is that you?" It's a loud woman's voice, high pitched, with a thick East Coast accent. I look up and see a heavy woman in her 40s approaching me, wearing a dark dress that goes from her neck to her mid calves, layered with ruffles and punctuated by pink tropical flowers, and lots of large costume jewelry. She moves toward me with the determination of a tank. I find myself quickly glancing around the lobby, furtively looking for an escape route.

"Yes?" I say, holding my ground.

"I'm Zelda Steinberg," she announces, "youth director of the synagogue."[*]

"It's very nice to meet you Zelda," I say, being careful to not offer to shake hands. "I'm Aryae Coopersmith and this is my wife, Ruthie."

Zelda grabs Ruthie's right hand and holds it with both of hers. "We've been so looking forward to the both of you conducting *Shabbos* for our young people," she says. "Rabbi Carlebach spoke so highly of you." She looks at Ruthie, then at me, carefully checking us out. Ruthie looks at me nervously. "And you're so young, both of you. You must be very accomplished!"

"Well thank you," I say, "that's very kind."

"All I ask is that you do a good job with our boys and girls. They've been so excited about spending *Shabbos* with Rabbi Carlebach, and I don't want to disappoint them" she says, giving me a meaningful look.

I glance sideways at Ruthie. "I understand." I say to Zelda, "You know, we've held beautiful Shabboses for thousands of young people at our House in San Francisco, and Rabbi Carlebach has asked me to bring, with God's help, some of this spirit and energy to the kids in your youth group."

"Well if Rabbi Carlebach sent you, I'm sure you'll do fine. I'd like to show you the hotel. Here, let me take you to inspect the kitchen."

"The kitchen?" I say. "Why?"

Zelda looks at me in surprise. "Rabbi!" she says. "Don't you want to inspect the kitchen to make sure of the *kashrut* (make sure it's kosher)?"

---

[*] I have changed her name, as well as that of the chief chef, to protect their reputations.

I look at her, at Ruthie, and at the bellhops standing near the luggage, waiting for instructions, and the desk clerk who is watching us. They're all looking at me.

"Zelda," I say, "I have no concerns at all about this hotel. I'm sure they do an excellent job with *kashrut* in their kitchen." I can see she is looking a little disappointed. "But that's okay," I add quickly, "let's go anyway and have a look." Zelda nods with a little smile and starts walking toward the kitchen.

Ruthie and the bellhops are still looking at me. "Ruthie," I say, "why don't you go up to the room and settle in and get comfortable, and I'll join you in a few minutes."

Ruthie nods and smiles. Then she turns to the bellhops and points to two pieces of her luggage, the ones with the belly dance outfits and Middle Eastern jewelry. "Please put these on top," she says to them. They load her luggage onto a big cart. I take her aside and give her a couple of dollars for tips.

"Okay," I say to Zelda, "Let's go."

The kitchen is big, gleaming, modern, spotlessly clean. It is divided into two parts so it is really two kitchens joined in the middle, each side with its own stainless steel refrigerators, stoves, sinks, dishwashers: one side for meat and meat meals, the other for dairy. The kitchen staff consists mostly of blacks and Puerto Ricans. The chief chef is a Russian Jew, a large man used to giving orders, with a thick accent.

I have no idea of how an Orthodox rabbi would go about inspecting such a place. I ask the chef to show me around and let me take a look at the inside of the ovens and the refrigerators. He shows me everything, and tells me the details about how everything is cleaned, and where they buy the food, and how they prepare it, with a great deal of pride. Zelda walks behind us, paying close attention.

Finally I shake the chef's hand and look up at him. He looks down at me. "This is a great kitchen!" I say. "I'm very impressed. It looks to me like you've met the highest standards. You guys, I mean you and your staff, are doing a great job here, and I'm looking forward to some delicious meals for *Shabbos*."

What I don't say is that, since Ruthie and I are vegetarians, we won't be able to eat much of what they're serving. Especially Ruthie, who is strictly macrobiotic and vegan. She probably won't be able to eat anything. It occurs to me that I've forgotten to talk to her about food. She gets emotional and disapproving about food that doesn't meet her standards. We better talk before dinner, I think.

The chef is smiling broadly, beaming actually. He makes a little bow toward me. "Thank you Rabbi," he says, "we work hard and do our best."

I glance over at Zelda. She is smiling too. "Thank you Boris," she says to the chef. "Rabbi," she says, turning to me, "why don't you come out with me to inspect the swimming pool."

"The swimming pool?" I say. I try to imagine what she wants me to inspect.

"The *eruv*," she says, walking out the back door of the kitchen in front of me. Her tone is playful, suggesting something like — *Come on, Rabbi, don't play silly games with me; you know exactly what I mean!*

I follow her through the long, narrow hallway toward the pool. *Eruv, eruv,* I say to myself. That sounds familiar. I wonder what that is? I wrack my brain and try to remember.

We emerge from the dark hallway out to a glaring burst of sunlight. The pool is a large elongated rectangle, with buoy ropes across in two places. It is surrounded by alternating areas of smooth white concrete and colorful Spanish tiles. There are a few teenagers splashing around in the pool, and adults sitting on the sides around tables with beach umbrellas, sipping drinks, smoking cigarettes, and playing cards. As we're walking, Zelda waves and says hi to some of the teenagers and adults.

We stop at a strip of shrubbery that borders the pool area. "Here it is!" she says. I look in front of me, trying to discern what she wants me to notice. There are two kinds of leaves. One kind is dark green and large and flat; the other kind is small and sort of curled and light green. There are also small white flowers. Then there's a horizontal strand of black wire. *That's it!* I think. *Eruv* . . . fence. I reach out and touch the black metal strand, then look over at her.

"Where does this start?" I say.

"Let me show you Rabbi." As we walk, I'm thinking. *Eruv* must have something to do with *Shabbos*. It must mean that if an area is fenced-off, you can carry stuff within the boundaries without violating *Shabbos*. It would make sense then to have it around the pool for *Shabbos*, so you can carry your towels and stuff. Probably the most important thing would be to make sure the *eruv* is complete and unbroken.

We look at the place where the end of the *eruv* is connected to the wall of the hotel. Then we go find the place where the other end is connected, and check out a few points in-between. "Looks good to me," I say. "Zelda, you've really paid attention to the details."

Zelda smiles and nods. "Thank you. Our reputation as a kosher community for their children is really important to our parents," she says. So far so good, I think. Maybe now we can all relax, and I can start getting myself ready for *Shabbos*.

We go back to the lobby. Somewhere in the buzz of chatter, I hear a familiar voice. "I'm looking for Larry Coopersmith, my grandson." I look up. *It's Grandpa Max!* I do a double take. He's standing at the registration desk, talking to a desk clerk. My breath stops. Yikes!! *What's he doing here?* Zelda looks up also.

"We have a Rabbi Aryae Coopersmith and his wife registered here," says the desk clerk.

"No, I think this is a mistake," says Grandpa Max. "I'm looking for my grandson, not a rabbi." Zelda and I are now a few feet away from the desk. I know that Grandpa Max spends winters in Florida, but I didn't know he would be so close. How did he find out I was here? Seeing him in this situation, I feel like we're all in a time warp. He's short, with thick, curly white hair and glasses, in his early 70s. His hands are shaking slightly. He looks frailer than I remember.

"Grandpa, what are you doing here?" I say.

He turns around and peers at me through his thick glasses. "Your mother and father told me," he says. "They said you would be staying at this hotel and leading *Shabbat* services for a big youth group."

"Grandpa, this is Zelda Steinberg, who is in charge of the youth group. Zelda, this is my grandfather, Max Klein."

"It's a pleasure to meet you Mr. Klein," says Zelda. "You must be very proud of your grandson."

Grandpa Max looks at me sideways. He's not used to seeing me wearing a *kippah* and *tzitzit*. As a Conservative Jew, he wears a *kippah* only in synagogue and for religious occasions, and I've never seen him wear *tzitzit*. "I paid for him to study in Israel a few years ago to try to make a Jew out of him," he says, smiling ironically. "It looks like I succeeded more than I thought."

"Well, he must be very brilliant to become a rabbi so quickly," Zelda says.

"Rabbi?" says Grandpa Max, "this is the first I've heard of it!" He looks at me. "Since when did you become a rabbi?"

Both Zelda and the desk clerk are looking with me with curiosity. No one says anything. "I've been doing this for a couple of years

Grandpa," I say. I touch him on the shoulder with my right hand, and gesture toward the front door with my left. "Let's take a walk."

He looks at Zelda and the desk clerk, uncertain of whether he's going to let me off the hook without getting a straight answer to his question.

"We start the *Shabbos* services with candle lighting at 5:15 in the Dolphin Room, right?" I say to Zelda.

"That's right," she says quietly.

"Come on Grandpa," I say, hoping he'll follow me toward the door. He does.

As we're walking, I turn around and look over my shoulder at Zelda and the desk clerk, who are watching us silently. I tap my head a couple of times, roll my eyes toward the ceiling, and shrug. Suddenly, Zelda's blank face lights up with a smile of recognition. She and the desk clerk look at each other and nod knowingly — *Poor old guy; he's been losing his memory.* Then she smiles at me sympathetically and waves.

The bright light and heat of late afternoon Miami Beach hit us as we leave the air-conditioned lobby. We walk along the hotel's big curved entrance walkway until we get to Collins Avenue, then we turn left and head south. Neither of us says anything. I watch people walking in and out of the hotels. When we get to a cross street I can see the beach, filled with the bright colors of beach umbrellas and swim suits.

Grandpa Max takes a cigarette from the pack of Kents in his shirt pocket. Then he pulls a lighter from his pants pocket, stops walking a moment, and lights the cigarette. He blows a cloud of smoke at me and looks me in the eye.

"Did you tell those people that you're a rabbi?" he says.

Friday night goes well. I've asked Boris for vegetable plates for Ruthie and me, and they are served unobtrusively. The kids are enthusiastic about singing Shlomo's songs. They're primed like wound-up springs, and ready to jump up and dance on the fast ones. The boys dance with the boys, and the girls dance with the girls, in two lines that snake all over the dining room. Once they get started, they don't want to stop, so we just keep going. Dinner, which was supposed to be done at 8:30, isn't over until close to 10:00. Zelda is pleased.

Saturday morning also goes well. We study the Torah portion of the week. What I've figured out is, these kids spend lots of time listening, absorbing religious lessons from adults, and not much time having others listen seriously to their views. So I've asked a few of the kids to start us off by standing up and giving us their thoughts on the Torah portion. I follow with Hasidic commentaries and stories from Shlomo. Then I invite them all to say what they think. Everyone's excited, everyone's got an opinion, everyone wants to talk at once. They're having a great time, and so am I.

I'm struck by how bright, motivated and enthusiastic these kids are. It dawns on me that, in spite of all the reservations I feel about the Orthodox world, this congregation truly deserves my respect. Clearly they are doing something right.

By Saturday afternoon I'm feeling home free. This is all turning out well. There's a break in the program and I'm hanging out in the main lobby, talking with some of the kids. One of them says she is coming out to San Francisco with her parents next summer and wants to know if she can come to the House.

That's when I see Ruthie on the other side of the lobby. She's leaving the hotel through the main entrance in plain view of everyone, carrying an overnight bag out to the street, an action that on *Shabbos* is strictly forbidden. The kids are facing away from the entrance and don't notice. I keep talking with them about the House, hoping that my face doesn't show the alarm I'm feeling. Finally they go off to the pool.

I find Ruthie outside. "What are you *doing?*" I say. "If anyone saw you, walking outside carrying something on *Shabbos* . . ."

"Aryae, I can't *stand* this any more!" she says, her eyes wide. "I'm going crazy! Practically the only thing I've had to eat all day has been the rice cakes and seaweed crackers I've brought . . ."

"I'm sorry."

"It's not your fault. But that's not the worse part. It's the constant, constant scrutiny from everybody, and I can't be myself. It makes me want to scream."

"I'm sorry about that too . . ."

"Look, here's my cab," Ruthie says. The doorman walks up to open the door for her. I watch him closely. She looks at me and then at the doorman. She holds up her hand and nods, signaling him to wait a minute. "I'm going to see some of my friends I told you about. There are some great, great musicians, and they've asked me to belly dance!"

I try not to roll my eyes. "When do you think you'll be back?"

"Don't worry Aryae. It'll be late tonight, way after sunset." She puts her hand on my shoulder and kisses me on the cheek. Then she gets into the cab. The doorman closes the door. As it pulls out, she rolls down the window and waves. I have another nervous look around, but no one except the doorman is here to see.

The next morning I call Shlomo early from the hotel room. My stuff is all packed, ready to go. Ruthie, who woke up later than I did, is in the shower. Grandpa Max and Aunt Sadie are expecting us soon for brunch.

Shlomo asks me how everything went, and is very pleased with what I tell him.

"Greatest thing in the whole world!" he says. "*Mammash* the greatest thing! You should get out and do this more."

"Shlomo, really, this is too crazy. The next time you tell someone I'm an Orthodox rabbi, please make sure and give me *smikhah* first, okay?" I say laughing.

"You know, Aryae, that's not such a bad idea. You and Efraim are both like rebbes in your own right."

"Shlomo . . ."

"No, I mean it! I could give you *smikhah* faster than you think."

We're both silent for a moment. "I don't know," I say. "I don't know if being a rabbi is really my thing."

"Don't give me an answer now," he says. "But do me a favor. Think about it, okay?"

"Thank you Shlomo," I say. "Okay, I'll think about it."

From the first second we met, Shlomo saw things in me that no one else saw, things I didn't see in myself. Am I the person I thought I was, or am I the spark, the possibilities that Shlomo has seen and encouraged? Rabbi Nachman of Breslov says that if we want to be connected with God, we have to be able to negate the ego, so that the innermost point of our being can be filled with light from the Most High. Who am I, and who is anyone, really? Who is the real Aryae, and who is the impersonator? I'm starting to lose track.

26
Covenant

After Efraim and Leah were gone, holding the House of Love and Prayer together was up to me, and the relentless rush of people, events, and life showed no signs of slowing down. It took the rest of 1969 and all of 1970 for me to gradually accept that I couldn't do it—at least, not the way it was. My picture of that time is a collage of fragments pieced together from my own memories and the accounts of others.

Letter from David Deen
Washington, D.C. – April 28ᵗʰ, 1969

My Dear Aria! [sic]

I received a letter from Don and Barbara telling me—among other things—that Efraim and Leah were splitting with [Yonatan and Ahouva] right after Pesah to Israel. In their plan, according to Don, there was only the problem of someone to come and help you in keeping that beautiful scene together—obviously too much for one person's head. [. . .]

I want to come because my own head has been very, very hassled here, keeping together a scene very much like the House of Love and Prayer, and having to do most of it myself, with no real help, mostly because people are so often indifferent. Little by little the beautiful, beautiful people who were together with me have ebbed away, and I have been left alone in a kind of deafening voice [. . .] Perhaps there are things I can help with—things I can do: I seek only to find myself in helping others find each other in joy and love. [. . .]

Love,

Ahavah v'Simhah [love and joy],

David.

I had never heard of David Deen before receiving this letter. The timing was amazing. Ruthie and I were planning to be on the East Coast for a couple of months in the summer, and I needed to find someone to stay at the House, look after things and lead services while we were gone. I wrote him back and said, "Please come on out!"

Gavriel: That summer we drove across country, Sari and I and our kids, and you and Ruthie, from San Francisco to the East Coast, the whole way. We had a giant van, a Dodge Ram. We had a front seat, two seats, and we had a back three-seater, and then we had a full size bed for the three children [laughs]. We were singing. We were learning. We always traveled with Shlomo's tapes. We had taped all of his records that we had then; it was very beautiful.

We dropped you off in New Jersey. You weren't far from my sister, where I was staying. You didn't stay that long.

Aryae: Yeah, we went up to Vermont. Ruthie wanted to go to the Kirpal Singh Ashram there. She really needed to get away from the House, and to tell the truth, I needed a break too. David Deen had come out from the East Coast, and was staying at the House and leading services.

George: That summer they brought this other guy into the House of Love and Prayer, who was this really strict, like Hasid guy. He was like remonstrating the women for showing their wrists and stuff. It got really gloomy there.

Aryae: Are you talking about David Deen?

George: Yes. He was very thin, and dressed all in black. It was like — all the love and joy — the joy was gone. I remember, after Pam had split, he was there. I went over for *Shabbos*. There was no singing and no dancing, it was just gloomy.

I kind of felt deserted. Nobody was there. Shlomo wasn't there. Everybody was in Israel. If I was smart, maybe *I* should have gone to Israel. But I didn't have any means. I was down and out. It was the heaviest time of my life. Everybody had bailed. The one guy who was there, who I'd keep seeing, and who was driving me crazy, was this guy named Hershele.

Aryae: Oh no! Hershele? [laughs] Amazing!

George: You remember he would go into talking in tongues?

Aryae: Yeah!

George: And I would go like, "Oh my God, Pam's gone, Shlomo's gone, Aryae's gone, Ruthie's gone, Efraim is gone, Leah's gone, and here I am with this really strict rabbi, and Hershele!"

House of Love and Prayer – October 1969

Ruthie and I are no longer living at the House, but I still get my mail here. I look at the letters sitting in front of me on the dining room table.

Ruthie just couldn't handle it any more, and I realized we had to move out to save our marriage. So after we got back from Vermont, we found an apartment on 44th Avenue near the ocean, about three miles from the House.

In order to pay the rent, I got a job, working in a cabinet factory in Redwood City. On Friday afternoons I punch out at 4:30, get in the VW bug, fight the traffic, drive back as quickly as I can to San Francisco, and take a shower. It's important to Ruthie for us to eat together, so I rush through a macrobiotic meal with her. Then, with a full stomach, I walk the three miles to the House and try to get myself into the spirit of *Shabbos* so I can lead inspiring services for people who have come and are waiting to sing and dance. I'm exhausted. David Deen and others who have been living at the House all week, seem much more energetic, much more connected with the House and the people there. The House has become a different place.

Ruthie: One day you came home [from the House] Friday night, sopping wet.

"Aryae, what happened, what happened?!"

You were walking through the park, and you fell asleep. And you walked right into the lake! [laughs]

Aryae: I walked into the lake?!

233

Ruthie: [still laughing] Yes! And the water woke you up! You'd always walk, because you didn't want to violate *Shabbos.*

One of the letters says "Selective Service — Official Business." I'm surprised to see that my hands are shaking as I pick it up. Late afternoon light, grey with fog, seeps in through the dining room windows of the House. I take a breath and open the letter.

What I see is weird. It's completely identical to letters I've been getting every year for the past five years, stating that my request to be classified as a Conscious Objector has been denied, and that I need to report for induction into the armed forces. It occurs to me that in two months I'll be 26. At that point I'm no longer eligible for the draft.

There's no one around to say goodbye to, so I just leave with my mail.

When I get to our apartment, I think back over the advice I've received from the American Friends Service Committee in Philadelphia: *"You have the right to an appeal. If they don't schedule you for an appeal, you can send a copy of the request that you previously sent."* I take two pieces of white paper and a piece of carbon paper from the drawer, carefully line them up and insert them into my old Underwood manual typewriter.

Yisroel Finman: So I got to San Francisco. I went there to go to San Francisco State.

My friend Steve, who wound up at the Sutter Street Commune said, "We've got these crazy Jews living by us, and they're connected with a rabbi, Shlomo Carlebach."

So I went down for a *Shabbos* at Sutter Street. It was a full moon. I didn't know about the House of Love and Prayer because Steve never mentioned it. By "crazy Jews" he meant David Deen, who later became Dovid Din, and one or two of his friends. So I came down to spend *Shabbos* with them, and was just totally blown away that Judaism was that deep, that spiritual.

I became very taken with Dovid. He had just been thrown out of the House. There was a steadfast rule in the House of Love and Prayer: no drugs. Everybody respected that. There was no drug use in the House of Love and Prayer, so if you wanted to get high, you took a walk outside. The story that I

234

heard was that Dovid was thrown out by the board of directors for dealing drugs in the House of Love and Prayer.

When I asked Dovid about it, he said, "Well, not exactly." He was living in the House, and he was dealing drugs. But the drugs were in the garage roof of the neighbor [laughs]. Whenever he needed it, he would hop over the fence, reach into the roof rafters, and sell it, but not on the House property.

I never pursued it further than that. But when I got to the House of Love and Prayer, I looked at the garage.

Aryae: [laughing] To see if there was any left over?

Yisroel: [laughs] No! Just to authenticate the story!

———————————————————

Aryae: Dovid Din [then David Deen] seemed to have so many contradictions. I couldn't figure out who he was.

Rivka Yaffe: Dovid was very complicated. We became good friends and I got to witness the drama of his inner struggles. And when Dovid left the House, he went to the Sutter Street Commune and I went with him. Then he went to Winnipeg, Canada to study with Zalman, who gave him a job being his secretary. He studied with Zalman for quite a while.

So I went to stay with Dovid in Winnipeg. I remember it was snowing. I went on the train with [my son] Asher and stayed there for a number of months. Dovid wanted to get married, but he was becoming more and more *frum*. And I said, "Whoa! You know you're my friend, you're my brother, but I can never go down that road as far as you're going." [laughs]

Anyhow, we were always very close, even after that.

House of Love and Prayer – December 1969

My 26th birthday comes and goes and I receive no response from the Selective Service Board. I hadn't realized the enormous weight of anxiety and uncertainty I was carrying until it was finally lifted. I never hear from them again. I laugh and cry and say prayers of thanksgiving to God. We have a little celebration at the House. In the coming years the war in Vietnam will wind to a close without me.

Abraham Sussman: One day Murshid [Samuel Lewis] came up to me. I spent a lot of time with him, and was very connected to the community, but he didn't talk personally to me a lot. This time he came up to me and stood in my face and said, "You! You're the one! I want you to do a favor for me."

I said, "What is it Murshid?"

He said, "On Friday night there is a gathering at the House of Love and Prayer with my very dear friend Shlomo Carlebach. I can't go; I have another commitment. I want you to go as my emissary." A few days later, in December 1970, Murshid took a fall and he was in a hospital. He had hit his head and he was kind of in-and-out of a coma state. Our community went into very deep prayer and vigil.

On that Friday night I was torn because there was a prayer gathering for Murshid, but I decided to fulfill his mission, so I went to see Shlomo. I went to the House of Love and Prayer, and I remember having the opportunity of telling Shlomo the story of Murshid falling. He was very moved by it. We went upstairs and he took out the Zohar and he just started reading from a passage. He said, "This is very deep; come sit with me." And he read a passage that had to do with the Exodus. I was in a very open state and everything had multiple meanings.

I was very moved by his depth of being. In my eyes he was clearly a mystic, one who was living on many planes at the same time, you know? I mean, he was embodied, and he was in the here and now, but he had a very great link to the Eternal, to the Source of Wisdom that is beyond time and space. And I was very moved by his taking the time to include Murshid in his prayers.

Murshid Samuel Lewis died a few weeks later on January 15th, 1971.

Aryae: Yisroel, what was it like the very first time you came to the House?

Yisroel: I called up the House and said I need to come for *Shabbos*, that I was involved with Dovid Din, and they said, "Oh, welcome! Please come by! Come for *Shabbos!*"

So I got to the House of Love and Prayer, and it was for sure after sunset. I was having a lot of trepidations, feeling embarrassed about getting there so late. Lois Bennet opens the door. And I say, "I'd like to come in for *Shabbos.*"

And she says, "Welcome, welcome, welcome, welcome! We were waiting so long for you." So I come in. And the thing that blew me away, just totally: somewhere between 10 and 20 women are in the middle of candle lighting. They're lighting candles on the window sills around the prayer room, doing it one at a time. Each woman is doing a deep meditation and lighting her candles, and her sisters are behind her, and they're singing softly.

So I became a regular at the House of Love and Prayer. One day two young women, Barrie and Joanie, two friends from Queens, young hippie girls with their backpacks come in. And they knock on the door one Friday evening, around candle lighting time, and they said they're looking for a place for *Shabbos*. And I said, "Ah, we were waiting so long for you! Come on in!" Bracha Din [Barrie's name when she became Dovid Din's wife] tells the story over and over again to this day.

Aryae: When did you move in?

Yisroel: April of 1970. I realized I needed a place to eat. I was keeping kosher at college as best I could on my meal tickets. But at Pesah I realized I couldn't be there at all; so I asked to come to the House and stay for Pesah.

I moved into the basement "dungeon." [laughs] The boiler room was the men's dormitory. What a nightmare! It was a boiler room, for crying out loud! One big old boiler over there, and bunk beds made out of wood all over the place. If there wasn't bunk bed space, you're on the stone floor in a sleeping bag. That was the boys' dorm. The girls' dorm was in the attic. *Koved* (respect) to the women! [laughs]

Day in and day out, the House was very high. *Shabbos*, and week-to-week, it was an extremely special place. But when Shlomo came out, he just blew it out of the water. When Shlomo was there, I got a sense of what it must have been like with the Ba'al Shem Tov — completely beyond time and space.

237

With Shlomo we would *daven,* and the davening would go on forever, and the meal would go on. Sometimes we wouldn't be sitting down to eat until 11–12 o'clock at night. Just the singing and dancing was two hours. Then we'd *bentsh* [say the blessing after the meal] at 3 or 4 in the morning.

On Saturday, more often than not, we'd walk out to the Presidio. There was this big old tree. Shlomo loved to sit by this tree and teach. It's hard to describe what he was doing; but it was absolutely incredible just watching him be himself! Being in *Shabbos,* being there for people.

Letter to the Editor, Midstream – May 1970

Several months earlier, a freelance writer named Leo Skir had written an article about Shlomo and the House of Love and Prayer for *Midstream: A Quarterly Jewish Review.* In it he expressed admiration for Shlomo and what he was trying to do, but was very critical of the House—it was messy, dirty, chaotic, disorganized, hypocritical—a far cry from Shlomo's expressed ideals.

Reading this, Shlomo was moved to respond. He said that, although everything has a body and a soul, "I missed the soul in Skir's description of the House and in his description of all the very beautiful people like Aryeh *[sic]* and Gedalya *[sic]* who are shining lights in Israel. I guess he didn't get the message. Some people are experts on bathrooms, some on living rooms, some on people and some on angels."

Shlomo said that there was something special going on in the world; the "people of tomorrow" were moving in and preparing to inherit the world. But the "people of yesterday" were trying to prevent it. "The House of Love and Prayer," he said, "is for the people of tomorrow. For the people who are waiting for the *Shabbos,* for the people who celebrate *Shabbos* as it was never celebrated before."

In his eyes, San Francisco was becoming a beacon of light for young people all over the world, including the Jewish youth. In his travels, he said, he had never met any young person who was not hungry for God's word, who was not "desperate for a true loving friend. It is only that the synagogue turns them off, that the Hebrew school has driven them away." This generation, he declared, "has holier souls than any previous generation—maybe they are the six million who came back."

He complained that the synagogue was "empty not only when nobody's there; it is empty when it's full. It is empty of holiness, empty of love, empty of soul-stirring prayer." And nobody seemed to be doing anything about it. We should be ashamed of not reaching out a hand to help our children, to bridge the generation gap.

But in this little House of Love and Prayer, it was happening. A few hundred people, "who want to tell the world there really *is* One God" that unites us all, were bringing "heaven down to earth." This "little house" could reach thousands if people would only look up to see the light shining in the darkness, if they would only remember how they were once together at Sinai, how they built the holy Temple together, and how they have been in exile since its destruction. Finally he said: "Let's rebuild the holy Temple again, here, everywhere, on every street, in the hearts of our young people who are waiting, ready, and who know, as nobody before ever knew, how much G-d is waiting for them."

My Response to Leo Skir

Mr. Skir [. . .] is obviously fond of Rabbi Carlebach, but he does him a great disservice. [. . .] Shlomo Carlebach is the greatest teacher I have ever known. He teaches not just from the head, but also from the heart and the hands. Anyone who spends just a few hours with him is not the same when he leaves. There are many teachers in the world who can teach you how to read words of Torah from a book. A great teacher can teach you how to read the Torah that is written in your heart. And when you learn *that*, it's not just for the minute. It's also for tomorrow, and for the day after.

We who have come to the House do not always live up to our ideals. I wish we could. One of our greatest Hasidic masters, the Kotzker Rebbe, who had tens of thousands of followers, said that if he had ten people who were with him all the way, he could bring peace to the whole world. He couldn't find ten people, and there is still no peace in the world. But one thing I can promise. Anyone who is searching for his way, anyone who is ready to open his eyes and his heart, anyone who is fed-up with all the hatred and killing in the world, anyone who can't wait for the great day of love and peace, and is ready to begin now, can come to our House, and find his brothers and sisters waiting. [. . .]

Aryae Coopersmith.

Leo Skir's Response to Shlomo and Me

[. . .] The Society of non-residents formed by Shlomo
(called "greatest teacher" by Aryeh) *[sic]* and Aryeh (called
"shining light" by Shlomo) is a Mutual Admiration Society. It
has not given rise to a House of Love and Prayer. It has
perpetrated those evils it castigates and which it claims it came
to alleviate: i.e. the dominating Parent (replaced by Shlomo
who decides who is to head the House although he is not a
resident member. Daddy has been replaced by Big Daddy)
and *Complete immediate Dependence on the Establishment for
financial support* (while denouncing the Establishment).

There are limits to self-deception and I hope Shlomo and
Aryeh will reach them and draw back [. . .]

Leo Skir.*

Rivka: Everybody was davening and the kids were playing
around. Asher had a dirty diaper and was playing in the dirt,
and I remember Bernice coming over to me and saying — in the
sweetest way that was not judgmental, but was also like
[laughs] — *You need to pay attention to this, your baby needs to
have his diaper changed!*

I don't think I ever thanked her for that, because it just
kind of brought me right back to earth. I was just spacing-out
for a while. That was a really nice thing that Bernice did for
me.

In some ways Marv and Bernice were like the mom and
pop. I appreciated that about her. Her concern about, *Okay,
you guys are all out here in . . . Reb Nachman world; but the baby
still needs his diaper changed!* That's all it took. I think from then
on I was a little more attentive.

Bernice: We used to take a camper and park it in front of the
House. I remember doing that several times . . .

---

* Reb Shlomo's letter, my own, and Leo Skir's response can be found in *Midstream: A
Quarterly Jewish Review*, Vol. 16, No. 5, May 1970: 66-67, 67-68, 68-69.

Moshe Yitzchak (then Marvin): Yeah, just living in the House. Cause the House was crazy so we'd live in the camper, in the truck outside the House.

Bernice: One time in the old House everyone went off and left us in charge . . .

Moshe Yitzchak: No, no, no! That was *meant* to be . . .

Bernice: Yeah, yeah! It was *meant* to be, and left us in charge. I got German measles. [laughs]

Moshe Yitzchak: You didn't get German measles. You got a rash.

Bernice: That was German measles.

Moshe Yitzchak: [To me] What we had decided was to take a load off you, I think . . . You were doing every *Shabbos.*

Bernice: Yeah.

Moshe Yitzchak: So the married couples, Moishe Fohrman and Maxine would take it maybe once, one *Shabbos* every month, or one *Shabbos* every two months. And we would take it . . . responsible people would take it.

Aryae: [laughs]

Moshe Yitzchak: And that would let you off the hook to decompress. Okay, so we had it. And that was . . . *scary.* . . . 'Cause I had never done that before, and I didn't *know* anything. It was quite a responsibility, you know? You try to remember the Shlomo songs, and try to tell a few stories. *I can't tell stories!* [laughs] It was really scary. It was like stage fright. The thing is, what drove me nuts — not drove me nuts, but that was amazing — several years later, after the old House of Love and Prayer had moved across the park, people remembered us doing that more than we did. They came up to us and said, "Hey, I remember when you were in charge of the House for that one *Shabbos"* — *blah, blah, blah* — "and it was really nice." And I thought, *Wow! I didn't think it was nice at all, but* . . .

Bernice: I couldn't get out of bed! I was so sick.

241

Moshe Yitzchak: Yeah, it was . . .

Bernice: High fever . . .

Moshe Yitzchak: Just amazing that we survived that *Shabbos.*

Washington Street, San Francisco, California February 1971

Sunday afternoon. I'm in Marvin and Bernice Kussoy's basement, in my woodworking shop, cutting smooth finished redwood 2 x2s on my table saw into four-inch blocks. Then I drill a large hole part way through the length of each block and carefully run it at various angles through the table saw. This creates a kind of redwood diamond with a unique shape that reveals the grain pattern of the wood. When I've sanded it and put a large cork in the hole, it becomes a spice box. Each spice box is one-of-a-kind, different from every other. We use one filled with cloves for *Havdalah* (the ritual for ending *Shabbos)* at the House.

Last year I learned the hard way that running the House of Love and Prayer and working full-time in a factory didn't go together; I just couldn't do both. Marv and Bernice have a four-unit building on Sacramento Street that needs renovation, and other properties as well. They offered to pay me to do this work and give me space in their basement to set-up a wood-working shop. So I quit the factory job and turned in my union card.

I hear clatter and commotion upstairs. Marv and Bernice together with the girls — Missey, Charey, and Judy — are back from the lumber yard. This is how the Kussoys spend their Sundays, on construction and remodeling projects. I go up and help them unload the van.

Later, after everything is unloaded — the conversation about lumber, plumbing, hinges and cabinets is done, the girls are fed, and things have calmed down — we're ready for the call to Shlomo. They have three phones, one on each floor of the house. We each go to our floor and take a phone. The phone rings on the other end, and amazingly, Shlomo answers. We all say hello.

Shlomo: Brother Aryae, and holy Marv and Bernice! So what's going on in San Francisco?

Bernice: Oh, the usual craziness.

242

Marv: Between the *House* house, and *our* houses, we can't keep track of everything!

Bernice: I have a hard time shooing him out the door in the morning so I can get some work done around here!

Shlomo: So Aryae, what do you think?

Aryae: I think we need to talk about the House, Shlomo.

Shlomo: (sighs) *Oy vey!* When I was there in December, it was *mammash* (really) a bad scene, you know? This is not the House of Love and Prayer! This is not what our kids are waiting for; it's not what the world is waiting for!

Bernice: Shlomo, they want to tear the House down soon anyway.

Shlomo: Yeah? Why?

Bernice: They want to build some kind of home for old people.

Shlomo: They want to throw out the young people and build a place for old people? *Nebbukh!*

Aryae: So Shlomo, listen; I think we gotta do two things: the first is, you've gotta let everyone know, we've *all* gotta let everyone know, that the House on Arguello Boulevard is officially closed.

Shlomo: Yeah? So what else?

This is what I've been waiting to talk to him about. I want to share my dream, the one I've been obsessing about since December: the House of Love and Prayer Yeshiva.

In the 60s it was simple. It was enough to get people turned on, inspired, by Shlomo's message. In the 70s that's no longer enough. We need the next step — a more sustainable community where we can go deeper, embody our dreams in how we live our lives, grow families, and grow old together — where not just our concerts and celebrations, but also our learning and our lives, can be a light to the world.

God has given me an unexpected and unasked for blessing: I know how to be a carpenter — I know how to build — not only with wood, but also with people. I can't do what Shlomo does. But I know, I *know* that with leadership from Shlomo, and with the hands and

243

hearts and minds of our friends, I can build a stronger, more durable, more functional House where he can do it. We can build on *his* energy, learning, passion, vision, and love, to bring together great rabbis, great teachers, great students, great people with all kinds of resources and skills, to build a sustainable community—a great center of Torah learning—that will embody and carry forward his dream. This would be the culmination of everything I've been learning, a cause I can devote my life to.

When I'm done, Shlomo says quickly, "Aryae, this is *mammash ay gevalt!* Marv and Bernice, what do you say?"

Marv: Shlomo, you're traveling all around the world! You're in Russia! You're in Israel! You're in New York! You're in Mexico City! You're in London! You're in Buenos Aires . . ."

Bernice: I don't see where you're going to get the time to be here.

Shlomo: Why not? Who says I can't set aside time each year to be in San Francisco?

No one says anything. Shlomo's quick response takes us by surprise.

Shlomo: So what do Moishe and Maxine have to say?

Aryae: They like it.

Bernice: But they have the same concern we do; it all depends on you making the time for this in your life.

Shlomo: Okay, listen holy friends; do me the biggest favor and don't say anything about this yet, but there are people on the East Coast, wealthy people, who are *mammash* ready to help—Orthodox Jews who *mammash* want to do something for our kids.

We all digest this. I tell Shlomo I want to talk to him alone. Marv and Bernice are fine with that and hang up.

"Shlomo," I say, almost in a whisper, like a conspirator. "Are you really serious about saying you're ready to spend part of your year here?"

"Why not?" he says. "To have hundreds of kids in San Francisco, *mammash* learning all the time? You know what I'm telling people all around the world? San Francisco is the city of tomorrow. Yerushalayim is the city of the day after tomorrow. If we start tomorrow with San Francisco, with you and all the kids there, the next day we can turn over the whole world."

"How much time do you think you could be here each year?" I say.

"Three or four months," Shlomo says.

"Really?" I'm stunned. Most of the Torah I've studied with Shlomo has been in tiny, random pieces—a couple of hours at the House on *Shabbos*, forty-five minutes in a motel room late at night after a concert, twenty minutes on the way to the airport.

"How would you do it?"

Shlomo laughs. "That's my *gesheft* (work-thing)! You do your *gesheft* and I'll do mine!"

I laugh too. "Okay Shlomo, so here's my *gesheft*," I say. "If you promise me that you'll spend three or four months a year here, and learn with us, here's what I'll I promise you. I'll spend *all* my time, all year round, doing whatever it takes to make it happen—fundraising, recruiting teachers, recruiting students—whatever it takes."

Now it's Shlomo's turn to think. "Aryae, that's *ay gevalt.*" He's silent a moment.

"So have we got a deal?" I say.

"Okay," he says, "*mammash*, we do. But Aryae, one more thing."

"What's that?"

"If you're doing this full-time, you should have a salary."

I haven't thought about how I can do all this and support myself at the same time. I'm grateful that he has. "Thank you Shlomo," I say. "But how can I have a salary? We don't have any money."

"Maybe we can do something," he says. "I'll talk to Moishe and Marvin about it."

It's late afternoon on a short, chilly February day when I leave the Kussoys. On the way home I pull up in front of the House and shut off the engine. No one's living in it now.

I walk up the steps to the front door, unlock it, and walk in. The House is cold and dark and empty. I walk into the prayer room. The shelves are still filled with books. We'll have to move them out. I open one of the glass doors that guard the shelves near the fireplace. I reach to the top shelf, searching with my fingers until I feel a familiar object. The redwood box is comforting in my hand.

Havdalah is the ceremony we use to transition between the holy space of *Shabbos* and the ordinary space of the rest of our lives. I pull down the *Havdalah* spice box and hold it in front of me. The grain of the redwood changes in each of the different angles. Sometimes the lines are far apart and wavy. Sometimes they're close and straight. I pull off the cork and whisper the blessing in Hebrew, "Blessed are you God, Lord of the world, who creates the varieties of spices." The dark, sharp smell of the cloves is smoothed-out by the smell and presence of the redwood.

I stand for a moment in the darkening prayer room, listening to the silence. Shlomo talks about how everything we do in this world has an echo in heaven. I try to hear the echoes of all the Shabboses we've had here, of all the songs we've sung, of the tears and prayers and laughter of everyone who has been in this room.

With the key in one hand and my spice box in the other, I lock the door carefully and leave the House. I have been privileged to inhale and bless the smell, the soul, of heaven. Now it's time to carry it with me out into the world.

27
Different Shoes

San Francisco Jewish Bulletin – February 1971

Shlomo Carlebach, the 41-year-old singing rabbi who founded San Francisco's House of Love and Prayer, has told the Bulletin the need to establish a *yeshiva* and house for prayer here, for those who have left organized religion, is greater than ever before [. . .]

In recent weeks, the building at 347 Arguello Blvd. used to house the organization since May, 1967 *[sic]* closed because "it no longer was adequate for our needs," said the bearded Carlebach. It had become the meeting place for hundreds of youngsters during the past three years.

The small two-story structure with dormitory was down the block from Temple Emanu-El. The House became famous for its 24-hour *Shabbos* "happenings," and a meeting place for "turned-off" young followers of the mystical Carlebach. Two families lived there full-time [. . .]

[Carlebach says,] "To build a *yeshiva* here where Jews from all over the world can come to study and pray, presents a need for a full-time spiritual guide [. . .] I would very much like to stay here and give concerts only on weekends, if financially possible.

"My theory is that six million Jews who died in the Holocaust have come back as today's young people. Let's not lose them again."

House of Love and Prayer Yeshiva Brochure
April 1971*

Yeshiva means *sitting.* *Yeshiva* is a place I come to on my journey and stay for a while. *Yeshiva* is a place to sit and study the Torah (the Teaching, the Way)...

---

* I wrote the original text for this brochure. Here some of the spellings have been changed to make them consistent with the rest of the book.

This *yeshiva* is a place where you learn to study the holy books. Rabbi Zalman Schachter calls this "breaking the *sefer* (book) barrier." It means developing the necessary language skill to be able to pick up any of our holy books in its original language and learn from it. It means getting our Teaching in its purest form, before it got translated, filtered, and predigested. It means getting the Teaching at its source, with all of its light, in all if its mystery. We will learn basic Hebrew, *Humash, Mishnah, Gemorah,* and *Hasidut* (Hasidism).

This *yeshiva* is a place where you learn to open the doors to your heart and your mind and your soul.

In this *yeshiva* we learn with women as well as men. Because what a man can learn is only half the story. What a woman can learn is the other half. In Hebrew there is no such thing as a word with one letter. Every word must have at least two letters. We want a Torah where every letter is strong, where every word is shining [. . .]

This *yeshiva* is different from any *yeshiva* you've seen or heard about. You will fail the course if you learn only what is in the book. According to our tradition any word which is truly holy speaks on three levels: the fact, the story, and the melody. The fact reaches only as far as the mind. The story reaches as far as the heart. And the melody reaches all the way to the soul. In this *yeshiva* you pass only when you learn the melody [. . .]

San Francisco, California – September 1971

Ne'eman, Pesah, and I pull up in the Shabbos Express to the new House at 1456 9th Avenue. The back of the van is filled with my carpentry tools: metal tool boxes, Skill saw and saw blades, hammers, carpenter's square, power drill and drill bits, jig saw and jig saw blades, router and router bits, hand saws, steel measuring tapes, boxes of nails and screws, boxes of sandpaper, planes, belt sander and orbital finish sander, clamps, chisels, glue, pry bars, orange and yellow 25 foot extension cords, all sprinkled with plenty of sawdust.

Riding in the van together like this early in the morning, heading off to our next carpentry job, has become a familiar routine for the three of us. Ne'eman and Pesah have been working with me in my carpentry business.

Today is our most important job yet: finishing the work of getting the new House of Love and Prayer ready to open its doors. The event:

the start of Rosh Hashanah, the Jewish New Year, 1 Tishri 5732 on the calendar of creation. Number of people expected: unknown, could be hundreds. Head service leader: me. Additional service leaders: any of the holy beggars who knows something about the High Holiday services. Amount of time required to finish all the carpentry work: unknown. Showtime: 18 minutes before sunset today.

I get out of the van and look up at the building, still amazed that we could own something like this. Shlomo came through with a down payment from three donors on the east coast: Moses Feuerstein in Boston, former president of the Orthodox Union, and Michael Steinhardt and Stanley Stern, two wealthy businessmen in New York. Henry Klein, our realtor, did his job brilliantly and found the perfect house for us. The bank accepted Moishe and Marvin's signatures on the mortgage, and *voila* — we own a house!

It stands in front of us, three stories high, painted dark red. On the upper floors are apartments where people can live. On the ground floor, at exactly ground level, originally a basement, is a large room that sweeps all the way under the building through to the back yard. This is the room that we are transforming into the prayer room. The back yard has lots of potential and will be great for a *sukkah*. And the neighborhood, busy, eclectic, diverse, near UC San Francisco, the New Age Natural Foods store, and Golden Gate Park, with lots of young people and college students, is a perfect setting for the House of Love and Prayer Yeshiva.

Pesah and Ne'eman help me unload tools and pile them outside the door to the prayer room. I pull out my keys, open the door, and we bring the tools in. Hopefully we can finish by sunset. On the floor are piles of rough redwood boards, which we're using for the walls. When we're done, the walls will look, feel, and smell like a redwood forest.

As the day unfolds, the prayer room, filled with the sound of the Skill saw, clattering boards, hammers hitting nails, and our voices, gradually transforms its look and feel from plaster to redwood. In the afternoon, people wander in to join us. First comes Bernice, with sandwiches and cookies, as well as some old furniture from one of her buildings, which we help her unload from the van. Then come some of the people who will be in the Yeshiva—Elana and Donna who have just found an apartment nearby, Joe who has come out all the way from Massachusetts, Yankele, who lived in the first House and wants to be part of the second one, Yosepha, Rivka, and others. Later Marv arrives, and Moishe and Maxine.

As the sun slides inexorably toward the Pacific, I stop for a moment and look up from my Skill saw to check out the scene. There

249

is so much movement, so much noise, so many things happening, that for a moment I'm lost, disconnected, and I can't make sense of it all. This is amazing! Shlomo says that when the gates between heaven and earth are open and it's time for something great to happen in the world, it doesn't happen step by step according to logic. It happens suddenly, beyond logic, all at once.

A half-hour later Pesah nails the final board onto the prayer room wall. The rest of us applaud and cheer. Moishe leads us in a *Shehehianu*, the prayer we say for special occasions and joyful events. "Blessed are You, God, Master of the World, who has kept us in life, and sustained us, and brought us to this time."

I look around. Sawdust, pieces of boards, nails, screws, and tools are everywhere. "Come on you guys," I say to everyone, "we've got to get this place cleaned up!" The response is a mad flurry of activity, with everyone running around bumping into each other, tools clattering into boxes, boards rushed out the back door to be stacked against the house, brooms and sawdust and loud excited voices with competing plans on what to do. At a certain point I manage to catch Ne'eman and Pesah's attention, and point up. We slip unnoticed out the front door, get our clothes from the van, and bring them upstairs into the apartment levels of the house. We each manage to find a shower and wash.

Just at sunset, a half hour later, feeling clean and serene, like the Hasidim of old who prepared for the High Holidays by jumping into the *mikveh* of a freezing river, hair and beard still a little wet, eyes clear, body relaxed, heart pounding, hands trembling just a little, I walk into the prayer room of the House of Love and Prayer Yeshiva.

Moishe walks up and puts his arm around my shoulder—"Are you okay?" I nod.

"Can you do *Musaf* tomorrow?" I say. *Musaf* is the special prayer for the day, which corresponds to the special sacrifices for the day that were made in the Holy Temple.

Moishe laughs. "I'm not the world's greatest singer," he says.

"That's okay," I say. "At least you know the *Musaf*. I don't."

Moishe agrees to do the *Musaf* tomorrow. We look at the people in the prayer room. We are full. "I think it's time to get started," Moishe says.

I begin with a song. This is the last Rosh Hashanah service that I will lead in the House of Love and Prayer.

There's a long table in the middle of the *sukkah* that we built in back of the new House. We put it together with three smaller tables. Shlomo is sitting at the head, at one end. A large volume of the Talmud is spread open on the table in front of him. He looks down at it, his eyes darting through the text intently, nods his head, rocks back and forth, closes his eyes, then looks up, sighs, and looks back down at the text again.

The rest of us sit and wait. Volumes of the Talmud are large and expensive. The Yeshiva has only one set. So the rest of us are learning mostly by listening. Occasionally someone wanders in back of Shlomo and stands there for a few minutes, looking over his shoulder at the text. A couple of us have cassette tape recorders on the table, which we turn on when Shlomo speaks. Others have notepads and are busy writing. Others close their eyes and rock back and forth as they listen.

Shlomo arrived in the middle of the eight days of Sukkot. He will be leaving for the holiday of Simhat Torah, and then back again for another week. It's like a miracle. None of us has ever had the experience of being with him this long at one stretch. He's keeping his end of the bargain. The House of Love and Prayer Yeshiva is for real. Every day I walk in, I am amazed and grateful.

Ian Grand: Shlomo could take you to the heart of a *mitzvah*. I thought about this event at the second House. It was Sukkos, October 1971, and we were going to do *lulav* and *etrog* [a palm branch and lemon like fruit that we shake, together with myrtle and willow leaves, in a sacred ceremony of unity]. *Lulav* for me is one of the most amazing things that there is, because it's totally primitive. You're going to take these four things and shake them in different directions, and what's going to happen? Crazy stuff from a modernist perspective.

So there we were in the back yard. We've got the *lulav* and the *etrog* and everything. Shlomo does it, and then hands it to me. And I start shaking. I was *shaking*. There was this charge that was running through me. There was this amazing connection with something that was quite beyond me. I understood in that moment something about *lulav* and why we would do it.

Learning Talmud with Shlomo is very different from learning Hasidic stories or mystical teachings with him. This is left brain stuff, the record of the conversations of generations of rabbis almost 2,000 years ago, about every conceivable topic of human behavior from prayer to property law to sexual conduct, reasoning and disputing with each other for the sake of heaven, producing an endless stream of dialectic logic that teases out interpretations of the Law and the lessons to be drawn, so we can understand the details of how God wants us to act.

In the 1940s when Shlomo was a brilliant young *yeshiva* student totally immersed in the life of the mind, studying at Lakewood Yeshiva with Rabbi Aharon Kotler, it was said that Rav Kotler believed that his young prodigy had the potential to become the greatest Talmud scholar of his generation, and the leader of the ultra-Orthodox world. Sitting here at the table as Shlomo explains passages from the Talmud, we get to experience this side of his brilliance in ways we hadn't before.

That afternoon, after the class has ended, I'm sitting out in the *sukkah* with Elana. It smells fresh and green like cut leaves. Everyone else has wandered off to one place or another, and it's just the two of us there. She and Donna have just moved into their apartment together nearby. I'm excited about this, and hopeful that others will find ways to live close to the Yeshiva as well. I haven't seen Donna today. Shlomo has left for the afternoon, probably taking a nap at the hotel where he is staying.

It's a classic San Francisco afternoon in October: the air is warm, the sky is blue, and the sun is hanging low with brilliant autumn intensity. An occasional breeze twirls the decorations that are hanging from the roof of the *sukkah*. Elana tells me how she's been transcribing some of Shlomo's tapes. There are so many of them now. Whenever he teaches at the House, usually two or three of us have our tape recorders. And she's been in contact with people on the East Coast and Southern California who are also making tapes of Shlomo's teachings when he's there.

"What's going to happen with these treasures?" she asks me. "Are they just going to stay in people's closets? How can we get some of these amazing teachings out to the world?"

"How much have you transcribed?" I ask. She tells me what she's done so far, typing up scores of pages, including some great teachings and stories. "You're right," I say. "This should be reaching the whole world. We really need to do something."

We sit there silently for a while, under the leaves of the *sukkah*, listening to the muffled sounds of the city streets surrounding us.

"I wonder if there's a way we could start publishing this stuff," she says.

We talk about that, brainstorming all kinds of ideas. We could make it a quarterly journal and sell subscriptions. We could start very simple. The longer we talk, the more excited we get. Maybe we can actually do it!

"What can we call it?" she says. We try out all kinds of names.

"How about 'The Holy Beggars' Gazette?'" I say.

She looks at me and smiles.

House of Love and Prayer Yeshiva – February 1972

Shlomo was here for two days in January for his birthday. His guitar had been looking pretty beat up lately, so we all chipped in and bought him a new guitar, a really nice one. Ruthie and I presented it to him. He was very moved, and immediately used it to play a song that we all sang together. It was a magical moment.

But that was the only time we've seen him since October. The House of Love and Prayer Yeshiva has been feeling empty, chaotic, directionless. Something's gone terribly wrong.

Last week Moishe, who is a master facilitator, organized a meeting of all of us at the Yeshiva. The idea was to speak honestly and take stock of where we are. I was surprised at the intensity of negative feelings that people expressed: hurt, disappointment, even anger. People like Joe, who came a long way to learn with Shlomo and paid their tuition fees, are feeling that they aren't getting what they were promised. Others, the holy beggars who were at the old House, all have their own ideas of what the new House should be about. Most people don't buy into my vision. They disagree with me, disagree with each other, are angry at me, want to do things differently, but can't agree on how.

I feel traumatized. I've been living an illusion, in a bubble, disconnected from everyone else. I have to face an unpleasant truth: the House of Love and Prayer Yeshiva isn't working.

I feel isolated, alone, depressed.

Shlomo is planning to be here for one day next week, for the Meeting of the Ways Concert. I've been planning this event together with my counterparts in other spiritual groups in San Francisco: Sufis, Buddhists, Hindus, Yogis, followers of Kirpal Singh, Christians. There is a very special energy in San Francisco right now, and a feeling of great affection among those of us in the various spiritual communities. The idea has been to get our teachers together for a big concert, a common celebration of the spiritual path. I've been asked to write the theme song.

I'm excited about the concert, but have no idea of what happens to the House of Love and Prayer Yeshiva after it's over.

Decades later, when my business will be to arrange leadership programs for corporate executives—where they learn about how effective leaders get people to follow them—I will understand more about why my efforts to build a *yeshiva* failed. And after getting a graduate degree in psychology, undergoing psychotherapy, and two years on antidepressants, I will come to understand more about isolation and depression, about my coping mechanism of running away from life when I felt overwhelmed, and about how I might have asked for help and made different choices than I did, if only I had known how.

I reach Shlomo by phone the day after the meeting with Moishe and try to explain what's going on with the House and what's going on with me. He listens. *"Oy vey!"* he says. "This is a bad scene!" He tells me that his plane doesn't leave until a few hours after the Meeting of the Ways concert. Why don't I drive him to the airport? We can stop for coffee on the way and have plenty of time to talk. He'll bring his calendar so we can schedule some more times for him to come out and learn with us at the Yeshiva.

Holy Beggars' Gazette
Vol. 1, No. 1, Purim 5732/ February 1972

Welcome to the Holy Beggars' Gazette! The [. . .] purpose of our publication is to respond to requests from our friends all over the world for transcriptions of the teachings of Rabbi Shlomo Carlebach. Shlomo is a true poet of the soul. In his travels around the world he leaves behind him words of Torah of shining wisdom and beauty which inspire thousands. We feel strongly the need to gather these words together and share them, so they will not be lost. [. . .] We invite you to send us a copy and help in this work. We extend this invitation with a strong sense that *the historical importance of this work might well be greater than any of us visualize.* [. . .]

We wish a time of peace and revelation to all our friends, when we will all merit that G-d should shower His blessings on us, and send great lights into the world to lead us on the way. *Shalom*.

Elana and Aryae.

This first issue of the Holy Beggars' Gazette consists of two 8½" x 11" pages, mimeographed on both sides, folded and stapled in the middle to form a little booklet. The text inside is a beautiful story and teachings about Purim that Elana has transcribed from tapes of Shlomo. Above the mailing window is a little ad that says, "Please order your Judaic books from Steven Maimes" with his contact info.

This is the last issue that I will work on. By the time the second one comes out, I will have left the House.

The Holy Beggars' Gazette will continue publishing for about four years. Elana and Steve will be the editors, and Steve will be the publisher. Future issues will be more sophisticated and look more like a professionally published journal, with a nice cover, interesting graphics and layout, photographs of Shlomo and Zalman, and over 50 pages. A lot of the work on the Gazette will get done at Elana and Donna's apartment.

Shlomo will show up at the House with Neila, a beautiful, strong and accomplished woman who lives in Toronto, and announce their engagement. Donna and Steve will also get engaged. They will be traveling in India at the time of Shlomo and Neila's wedding. They will return, get married and have two children, a daughter and a son. Steve will sell Jewish books through his business, the Judaic Book Service. After they get divorced, Donna and her two kids will move to the East Coast, where she will come out as a lesbian, and become a corporate executive with a company that manufactures maternity wear.

Elana will marry Zalman. Shlomo will perform the wedding. They will have three children, a daughter and two sons, before they get divorced. Elana and her daughter will move to Jerusalem.

Shlomo and Neila will be married at the World's Fair Pavillion in Flushing Meadows, New York. Over two thousand people will be there, including Efraim and Leah and others who will travel from Israel, and friends from all over the world. I won't be there. Shlomo and Neila will live in Toronto. They will have two daughters before they get divorced.

Ruthie and I will get divorced just after I turn 30. We won't have any children.

Donna: Before the Meeting of the Ways concert there was a smaller concert in Marin that Shlomo did with [Swami] Satchidananda.

The following day there was a gathering of the masters where I took Shlomo, which was held at Yogi Bhajan's place. It was at lunch. Pir Vilayat Khan was there, Yogi Bhajan, Satchidanada, and others I can't remember.* It was magic to listen to them talk to each other, rather than to their disciples. They talked casually and respectfully, mostly by telling stories. But in the end what was really clear is that they were all telling the same story. It was just an amazing time.

I had my red sports car then. At a certain point Shlomo needed to be somewhere else, and I was supposed to get him there, but he wouldn't leave. I was getting really frustrated, so I decided to walk back to the car with the guitars, and then go back and try to snag him. On the back of my car I had a bumper sticker in Hebrew that said, *Shomer Ahi Anokhi* [I am my brother's keeper].

Satchidananda came walking out. He stopped at my car, pointed, and said, "Me too!"

And I said, "What?"

And he said, "Me too. I am my brother's keeper."

Masonic Auditorium, San Francisco, California February 1972

Shlomo, standing alone onstage in the huge, darkened hall, is the last act of the Meeting of the Ways concert.

Masonic Auditorium has a large round stage that juts out into the audience and is surrounded by 3,165 seats arranged in concentric semicircles. The hall is filled with row after row, wave after wave of

---

* Swami Satchidananda (1914-2002) was a well-known Hindu spiritual teacher and founder of Integral Yoga; Harbhajan Singh Khalsa Yogiji (1929-2004) was a Sikh spiritual teacher who taught *kundalini yoga;* Pir Vilayat Inayat Khan (1916-2004) was a teacher of Sufism in the lineage of his father, Hazrat Inayat Khan.

people wearing the outfits of their various spiritual tribes, some in orange robes, some in turbans, some with large gold crosses, some in hippie kippahs, all in different varieties of colorful attire.

Those of us who help run the spiritual communities in San Francisco, who have been inspired to bring our teachers together for this concert, have worked hard to convey what we so passionately believe with all the hope and idealism of the early 1970s—that though our paths may seem different, they are all leading to the same place. The concert began with the song I wrote. We all sang the final two lines with great feeling:

> *Nothing can stop us when we are together.*
> *Peace in the world when we are together.*

There have been so many traditions represented here today, Buddhists, Sufis, Hindus, Christians, Jews. I stand below the stage, holding my guitar, looking up at Shlomo, wondering how he will pull it all together.

He grabs the mic and speaks softly. *"Shalom, shalom,* my darling friends," he says. "The highest, sweetest peace to you, to me, to all of us here in this room, to all of our brothers and sisters all over the world.

"You know my sweetest friends, it's such a privilege to be here on this same stage with so many holy teachers." He turns to the front row to nod to some of his colleagues, Yogi Bhajan, Swami Satchidananda, and others.

Shlomo begins strumming his guitar, and singing his words, passionately, in tune with the chords. "Everybody knows, everybody knows, everybody knows," he sings, "that when the great day is coming, the day of love and peace, when the great day is at hand, that heaven is sending us holy teachers and messengers to show us the way."

He stops strumming and looks out over the audience. The whole room is silent. "But what are you and I supposed to do?" he says softly into the mic, in a near whisper that all 3,000 of us can hear. "How can ordinary people fulfill the words of our holy teachers and bring the great day. This is an awesome responsibility, right?"

He strums his guitar again. "My sweetest friends, my sweetest friends, my sweetest friends," he sings, "please listen from the depths of your heart. In ancient days a long time ago, a long time ago, in Jerusalem the Holy City, we would come to the Holy Temple and we would bring gifts, the best produce of our land, the best of our fields, the best of our olive trees, the best of our vineyards, the best of our herds, we would bring gifts as an offering to God. Everyone would bring gifts according to the abundance that God had blessed them with on their own land.

"But one time of the year, one special, one sweet and holy time, we brought something different. On the holiday of Sukkos, the time of the harvests from our land, strange as it seems, we would bring water. We brought pure water from the deepest well in Jerusalem, and we would carry the buckets up to the altar of the Holy Temple, turn over the buckets, and pour the water over the holy stones."

He stops strumming and talks again. "You see my darling friends, every field is different. Maybe you grow grapes and I grow olives, right? So we each bring what we can, according to our tribe, our land, and the fruits of our labors.

"But water is a gift from heaven. It has nothing to do with the land where I live, or what my tribe is, or who I am, or what I do. It falls the same for the rich and the poor, the same for every Christian and every Jew, for every Hindu and every Buddhist and every Muslim, for every person in this world.

"So what does this mean? There are times for coming to God's house with the gifts from my land. And there are other times where God wants us to reach beyond all that, to reach all the way for the gift that heaven is sending straight to all of us, the gift of pure water."

I look out at the audience. People are leaning forward, all eyes on Shlomo. Some are smiling and nodding.

Shlomo starts strumming intensely, and his voice goes high. "Can you imagine the Holy Temple on Sukkos? Can you imagine every person with their bucket in their hands, the greatest landowner together with the humblest little beggar, waiting to pour their water over the holy stones? Can you imagine the joy? Can you imagine the joy? Can you imagine the joy?

"So how did the people express their joy? It is written in the Talmud, according to our Rabbis and teachers almost 2000 years ago, that while the *Levi'im,* the holy musicians, were playing on their harps and trumpets and drums and flutes and singing, while the Levi'im were making such beautiful music, the people got up and danced."

Shlomo's strumming gets more quiet now, and his voice softer. "Do you know how deep this is my darling friends? Please open your hearts, open your hearts, open your hearts. Because everyone knows, everyone knows, that what we do with our hands, what we can do in this world by serving God, by serving another person, is very holy and beautiful, but that is only half the story. Because if we want to lift

258

ourselves up to heaven, if we want to lift the whole world up to heaven, we can only get there by dancing on our feet."

Suddenly, before anyone knows where he's taking us, Shlomo shifts to a fast song. This is our cue. Those of us standing by with our instruments rush up to join Shlomo on stage. He starts jumping up and down as he sings. "Please join me my friends," he says over the chords of his song. "Let's lift the whole world up to heaven!"

Within seconds three thousand people are on their feet, dancing in the isles. The thunder of their feet striking the floor echoes with the notes of the music through Masonic Auditorium. The energy of the crowd, of all of us, seems endless. People jump up onto stage, dance there for a while, then jump back down again to make room for other people to jump up. The singing and the dancing go on and on and on. As I'm standing on the stage behind Shlomo, strumming my guitar, keeping up with his chords and his rhythm, looking at the waves of people dancing in front of us, my chest is shaking, and tears are pouring out of my eyes. This must be what it is like, this is what it is really like on the Great Shabbos, when the whole world is together.

When it's finally time to bring the show to a close, Shlomo asks everyone in the room to please come close, "Please come close as you can, because to bring the great day of love and peace to the world, we have to start by being close to each other." He especially invites Yogi Bhajan, Swami Satchidananda, and the other teachers in the front row to walk up onto the stage and stand close to him. Soon Shlomo is surrounded by the other teachers, and they are surrounded on the round stage by circles of people holding each other, and the round stage is surrounded by countless circles of more people holding each other.

Meeting of the Ways concert at the Masonic Auditorium in 1972. Shlomo is in the center and Aryae (in white) is on his right, facing him. The photographer is unknown.

As I write these words many years later, the world will be a very different place. But in February of 1972 in Masonic Auditorium, how can we not believe that we are at the dawn of a New Age? Intolerance and hatred among peoples will become a thing of the past. The idea that people would fight and kill each other over religion will be unthinkable to our grandchildren. All of us here are the messengers. It is up to us to bring the message back to our tribes, and through our tribes, to reach out to people all over the world, to practice love, compassion, understanding, and acceptance toward all.

This is the highlight of all my memories of this time in my life. It is also the last concert that I will ever play with Shlomo.

Shlomo is strumming softly on his guitar now, and singing. A guy from one of the ashrams is standing next to him, accompanying him on his flute. I'm standing a few feet away, accompanying him on my guitar. A few other people are gently shaking tambourines.

"I want to share something personal with you," Shlomo says into the microphone, while his hands are still strumming, and the rest of us are still accompanying him. "Here's what occurred to me while I was listening to the inspired words of my friends and teachers with me here on stage." He looks around him and nods at the teachers wearing the turbans. "Some of you said that while we may be on different paths, the paths are all going to the same place." He stops playing.

He says, "I respectfully disagree." Then he says nothing. Everyone is silent, people still with their arms around each other, swaying. Then he sings: "If I may be so bold to say so, in my humble opinion, *we are all on the same path, we're all on the same path, we're all on the same path.*" I can see the arms of the people around us pulling each other closer, eyes closing, savoring the closeness, as we sway back and forth.

"The only thing is," he sings, "that for now, while we are walking, for a little while longer, *we're just wearing different shoes.*" As the 3,000 of us in that room stand there with our arms around each other, this infinite moment stretches all the way to the end of time.

After the concert, chaos. The teachers are mobbed by students and well-wishers from the audience. People are running around, everyone with an important message for someone, or with something urgent to do. The biggest clump of people is pressing around Shlomo.

I watch him put his hand behind the curly head of a 12-year-old boy, and bend down and kiss his head. I see a pretty young woman with long, straight black hair step up and speak very earnestly to him. He talks to her for a while, then writes something on the business card and gives her the card. Then he writes something on another business card, probably her phone number, and puts it in his pocket. I watch him talk to other people, dozens of them. I look at my watch. Almost an hour has gone by. There are still people waiting to talk to him.

I push my way to where Shlomo is. He's talking to a young woman with blond hair and blue eyes, wrapped in a sari. I point to my watch. "We gotta get going," I say.

"Holy brother Aryae," he says. He introduces me to the young woman in the sari. I look at her and nod. Then he puts his hand on her shoulder and kisses her on the head. "Call me tomorrow, okay?" he says to her softly. She smiles and says she will. She's holding his business card with a phone number written on it.

While the people who are still waiting to talk to him stand there, Shlomo turns toward me and leans forward. He looks right into my eyes, like he's looking for something. "Aryae I'm sorry, promise me you won't be mad at me, okay?" he says.

I just look at him.

"It's a bad scene," he says. He looks apologetic. "To make a long story short, when we talked last week, I forgot that I already promised somebody else they could take me to the airport, and they've been waiting the whole time."

I feel my jaw tighten. I don't say anything.

Shlomo is still looking into my eyes, searching. "Look, do me the greatest favor. Call me at my hotel room in Los Angeles at 9:00 sharp tomorrow morning, okay?" He pulls out a business card, and writes the number of his hotel, and gives it to me, just like he has for the others. "I have my concert schedule with me, so we can talk and go through all the dates, okay?"

I look down and nod. My chest is tight and my breath is shallow. Shlomo puts his hand behind my head, and holds it close to his, so my forehead touches his forehead. Then he lets go. My hand comes up and pats him on the shoulder.

Then, without thinking about it, before I know what I'm doing, I turn and walk away. Through the noise of many voices, I think I hear Shlomo behind me, calling my name. I don't turn around; I just keep walking.

Journal Entries – 1972

April 25th, 1972

We had the House meeting to elect new officers. I am officially relieved of my responsibilities to the House. Whatever happens to it from this point on is no longer my concern.

Sarah almost got raped on Haight Street. [. . .] Moishe wanted to go on a weekend retreat. It all floated around in my head as I dozed off during the meeting[. . .]

Yankele is filled with words and feelings of great inspiration. Moishe said he's the right man for president. I'm a little jealous, because that's my old role, but not too jealous [. . .]

I'm saying the *Shema*, over and over. It's so good. To love [God] and to always cleave to His presence and even if just for a few seconds here and there, to step out of the ego, with all its whirling little trips, into the place of eternity and peace.

May 4th, 1972

They are about to tear down the old House on Arguello and everything in the house is up for grabs [. . .]

May 27th, 1972

Shabbos with Zalman. I really like Zalman. I feel closer to his approach now than I did a year ago.

The choice is with the individual on how he will relate to God. It won't work for me and people like me to say that the Rabbis laid down everything [. . .] and all we have to do is learn their teachings, understand them properly, and follow them. We can tell ourselves that for a time, but after a while, when someone from [the Orthodox world] asks, "Why don't you follow all the halakhas [laws]?" we really don't have any good answer. [This is] because we are choosing to operate within a framework which says, you *should* follow all the halakhas, but in actual fact we are not doing it [. . .]

Zalman is saying, we have always used root metaphors as a model for our relationship to God [. . .] "Father" and "King" no longer work as they used to. He suggests "Friend."

May 29th, 1972

Took Zalman to the airport and had a chance to talk, which satisfied my need to make some kind of contact with him [. . .]

He was suggesting to me in various ways that it may just be that there isn't a *rebbe* for me right now. Rather than look for someone to assume the burden of bringing me close to God, I should assume it myself and strike out on my own, taking all the risks and burdens and delights inherent in this.

He said that the need for a Jewish place where seekers can come is very great, and suggests that there is a tremendous resource in the Bay Area in the form of many talented, together, aware people who would be eager to come together and share what they know. He suggested a spiritual community growing out of people such as Moishe, Ian, Stanley Keleman, Claudio [Naranjo] Sufis, coming together, in a way where each gives and receives. A leaderless community.

Use of the root metaphor "Father, King" for our relationship to God implies a *rebbe* who directs one's spiritual efforts and guides one on the way. The root metaphor of "Friend" for a relationship to God implies, perhaps, a community of friends, equals, without one central figure, where each is responsible for his own spiritual direction and all learn in the process.

Could this be the reason [. . .] that God isn't giving me a *rebbe?*

28
Rebuke

There's a knock at my door. I get up to answer it. Standing in front of me is a guy I've never seen before. He's a little older than I am, a little shorter, with a head full of curly dark brown hair, dark eyes, and a serious and steady gaze. I ask him who he is.

"Burt Jacobson," he says. "I was at the House of Love and Prayer, and they told me to look you up."

"Great," I say, "come on in!" We shake hands.

I make us some tea and offer him some macrobiotic cookies that Ruthie baked yesterday. We sit down at the kitchen table and talk.

Burt tells me about how he was ordained as a Conservative rabbi in the '60s after finishing his studies at the Jewish Theological Seminary in New York. After years of wrestling with doubts about that path, he pulled away from the Conservative movement, and from Judaism generally. He had spent the past month studying Jungian psychology at the Jung Center in Houston. He's come to the Bay Area to teach at an alternative high school, and he wants to see if there's anything in the area in alternative Judaism that might work for him.

"Wow," I say, "that's amazing!"

"Why?" he says.

"It seems like God brought us together at this crossing point in our lives."

Burt laughs. "In Jungian terms this is called synchronicity."

I've been reading books by Carl Jung, and starting to learn about Jungian psychology. It seems to address a yearning I'm feeling for a more universal way to relate to the human soul, beyond the confines of any particular religion, yet learning from all of them.

265

Burt stays with me and Ruthie for a couple of days. I share with him some letters I've been receiving from my friends in Jerusalem. We talk about the kinds of choices that are confronting people on their spiritual journeys. After he leaves, I fantasize about being a Jungian psychologist.

―――――――――

Ahouva: I was very frustrated the whole time I was in Israel. I had read about the *kibbutz,* and I had this idea about women's egalitarianism in Israel, which turned out not to be the case. The *kibbutz* that we stayed at for a few months divided the tasks by sex. The women were all in the laundry and taking care of the kids. There were men and women in the kitchen, but I ended up being in the laundry, and there were all women there. So, you know, it was very disillusioning.

At one point we lived in Migdal, and we each had our own little house. Efraim and Leah were down the street, and Sari and Gavriel were down the street, and there were other Shlomo people too. Leah and Sari, and most of the other women who were part of our group, became Orthodox and didn't have a problem with it.

But for me, trying to relate to the larger religious world that we were part of, it felt like women were really afterthoughts or something. You were supposed to be in the kitchen looking after the kids. You were supposed to have more babies. When Pella was a year old, everybody was asking me when I was going to have the next baby and stuff. It didn't give you an awful lot of room to think about . . . anything! About what life you wanted, or how you wanted to express yourself, or how you wanted to learn, you know?

I had this very specific incident of hanging out Pella's diapers on the laundry line and feeling like, I was 25 years old and my life was over.

―――――――――

Abraham Sussman: When I went to Jerusalem, Shlomo himself was not there, but I knew many of his students. I had a sense that, as a community, there were ways in which his teaching was really powerful, and there were also some gaps. Men and women were not getting guidance about their relationships. I didn't feel that the deep, natural wisdom of women was adequately recognized and appreciated.

My sense is that there are historical issues in the relationship of men and women in Judaism that are very intense. That's what I was perceiving. There were couples who were not talking to each other honestly about the nature of their relationship, and not getting guidance about how to resolve conflict, but instead were translating things through — I don't know — theological terminology. Women should do this, or men should do this . . . There was a lack of directness. There were couples that were suffering, and many of them broke down.

It was not any different with the Sufis in Murshid's community. Some of it was the time. There was energy passing through that made everybody radiant and beautiful without any training about how to build and grow a relationship. Most of the relationships that were around Murshid Sam had the same issues, and many of them did not survive.

I once went to Shlomo and kind of boldly said, "Shlomo, you're a great teacher, but your students need to learn more about relationship."

House of Love and Prayer — February 1973

It's Friday night. From where Ruthie and I are now living at 29th Street and Mission, it takes over an hour to walk to the House on 9th Avenue. When I get there it feels strange, since this is no longer my House and I am simply a guest like other guests. Shlomo is here for *Shabbos* and the prayer room is full. People are sitting on the benches, on the floor, and on a few folding chairs along the sides and back of the room. Shlomo is sitting in a chair at the front, looking into a big book.

I look around at the room, at the redwood walls and benches, at the fixtures, at the holy ark that houses the Torah. I feel a flash of pride. This place is still the embodiment of my dream. I see people I know and exchange smiles and hugs and quiet greetings of "Good *Shabbos*." I also see a lot of people I don't know.

I don't want to draw attention to myself. I'd rather just melt into the crowd and find a comfortable spot to sit near the back of the room. I don't really know who to be here, or what my new identity is, now that I'm no longer Shlomo's "top man" at the House. It feels too complicated, too painful. I just want to take in the energy of Shlomo leading *Shabbos*.

Shlomo spots me. "Holy brother Aryae!" he says, "You better come in fast!" He stands up, puts down his book on the chair and gestures to me, waving his arms. I wish I could disappear, but everyone is watching. I have no choice but to walk up to him. We put our arms around each other. He is wearing a fresh white shirt and smells like patchouli oil, just like in the old days. My feeling of stiffness melts. I feel a flash of love for him.

"Good *Shabbos*, Shlomo," I say quietly. "It's really good to see you."

"Good *Shabbos*, Aryae," he says, stroking my beard affectionately. "This is the greatest thing! Listen, you gotta say a few words of Torah, okay?"

I feel panic. I'm not prepared. I realize that Shlomo is honoring me and reaching out to me. I just don't know what to say.

"Thanks Shlomo," I say. "I really would rather hear what you're teaching right now. Maybe I can say something later."

Shlomo tries asking me again, and I decline again. He looks at me a second, then puts his arm around me and holds my head to his. I reciprocate, holding the back of his head with my right hand, and touching his elbow with my left. He looks at me a moment as I walk to the back of the room, then resumes his teaching.

The thing about Shlomo is, he never rebukes anyone, never judges anyone, never tells you what to do. "If you're my greatest friend in the world," he says, "do you think I'm worrying about how kosher you are? The only thing that matters is that we're friends. Being friends, loving another person, is the deepest thing there is."

In a way, it would be easier for me if Shlomo would judge me, if he would get angry with me for not staying with him and running the House the way I used to. Then I could get angry at him. I could push back. That would feel better. This way I'm left with only my own conflicts to push against, my own jumbled feelings.

I leave early, before *Kiddush*.

Westerbeke Ranch, Sonoma County, California
September 1973

Westerbeke Ranch is a retreat center nestled in the rolling hills of the Sonoma wine country north of San Francisco.

There are 24 of us hovering around the *hors d'oevres* table near a large swimming pool, surrounded by beautiful landscape with fragrant gardens and tiled walkways, sipping chilled chardonnay out of wine glasses, talking and getting to know each other. Four people are in their 40s and 50s, the three men and one woman who make up the faculty advisors of the graduate program in Humanistic Psychology at Sonoma State College. The rest of us, mostly in our 20s, about half men and half women, are the graduate students who make up the incoming class. I'm three months away from turning 30.

It's been over five years since I've been a college student. During my time with Shlomo and the House, I was pretty removed from the ordinary secular world. I've lost touch with things I used to take for granted, like the latest pop music, political developments, movies, TV shows. And apart from showing up on college campuses for Shlomo concerts, I've have had no contact with the academic world. It's like I've got a five-year memory gap, a kind of mini Rip Van Winkle effect, and am now just emerging back into the "normal" world, blinking, looking around, trying to make sense of it all. I've been different people at different times of my life: high school nerd, radical political activist, Haight Street hippie, House of Love and Prayer Hasid. I haven't yet figured out who I am now.

So far I'm still an observant Jew.

The faculty has put together a curriculum that is richly influenced by Jung, what they are calling Depth Psychology or Archetypal Psychology, and oriented toward inner exploration. That's what made me decide to come here for my master's degree. There will be groups for dream work, co-counseling with partners, work with fantasy images and active imagination. There will also be more interactive experiences such as Gestalt, group process and family therapy. I feel like a kid in a candy store of the psyche, excited and hopeful that all this stuff can be an exploration of the new direction in which my soul is taking me.

My fellow graduate students are wearing shorts, t-shirts or tank tops, sandals or bare feet. I can't help noticing how attractive some of the women look in their casually revealing outfits. Wearing my long black chino pants, buttoned down short sleeve Ivy League shirt, leather shoes, together with my *kippah* and my *tzitzit,* I look out of place. I try to make up for that by the one-on-one conversations I'm having with people, asking what brought them to the program, what's most inspiring about their work, where they hope to go from here. I notice that I'm good at engaging people.

The chair of the department, Gordon, who is also my faculty advisor, a tanned, athletic looking man in his 50s with a large shock of white hair, a playful smile, and piercing blue eyes, welcomes us to the orientation for the graduate program in Humanistic Psychology. The September sun is warm, and most of us have had at least a couple of glasses of chardonnay. A couple of guys sit and lean against a post in the shade. A smiling young woman sits at the edge of the pool and dangles her feet in the water.

After we've each had a chance to introduce ourselves, and after some discussion about the program, Gordon looks at all of us mischievously. "Well, I think that's enough, don't you?" he says. "Enough talk. I think it's time to get in touch with our bodies." And before any of us know what's happened, he has stripped off his clothes and is standing in front of us stark naked. I have to admit, with a touch of jealousy, that he looks good. Then he walks up to the pool, and without hesitation dives in. When his head pops up, he has a big smile, and he looks like a wet sheep dog as he shakes the water from his white hair.

"Well, what are you waiting for?" he says to all of us. "The water's great!" We all look at each other in silence. Then a couple of the women laugh and clap. The other faculty members take off their clothes and join Gordon in the pool. The two men, David and Victor, who are both younger than Gordon, get into a kind of rough house exuberance, and cannon-ball into the pool, making big splashes. The woman, Norma, who is about Gordon's age, walks in from the shallow end.

The young woman sitting at the edge of the pool stands up, slips off her clothes, and laughs. I watch her in fascination. Then she dives in. A couple of the guys do the same.

I feel panic. Six or seven years ago when I was living near Haight Street, doing something like this would have seemed pretty natural. But today, still living more or less as an Orthodox Jew even after leaving the House, what do I do now?

Pretty soon everyone else is in the pool, swimming around, splashing, talking to each other, laughing. I'm still standing there with my clothes on, watching. At one point Gordon looks up at me. "Aryae why don't you come on in?" he says. He knows my situation. When he sees that I'm not about to move, he smiles, nods and turns away to swim alongside one of the women nearby.

At first a few people call up to me, encouraging me to jump in. "Come on Aryae," says Gene, splashing me. He's a burly looking guy about my age with thick black hair, long sideburns and a mustache. "It's okay! You can get wet now and still be religious later, okay?" I smile and nod. But after a while people stop paying attention to me.

The swirl of laughter, motion and energy of 23 naked people inside the pool becomes self-contained.

I feel so left out, jealous and tense and sad. Why don't I join my classmates? Why am I separating myself like this? Am I really coming from a place of religious commitment? My most honest answer is, *No, I'm not.*

I'm really coming from a place of fear.

There was a time when the purpose of my life was clear to me — it was to help Shlomo bring the Great *Shabbos* to the world. But now I've already made a different choice. I've chosen to stop depending on miracles from heaven and to take responsibility for my life here on earth. I've chosen to prepare myself for a career and a profession where I can earn a decent living and support a family. What I'm most afraid of is to admit this choice to myself that I've already made.

I've left the world that's 5,000 years old and am back in the one that's five billion years old. I've chosen not to be a holy beggar anymore.

Keeping my eyes on the 23 people in the pool, I slowly unbutton my Ivy League shirt. I remove the shirt, fold it, set it carefully on the ground. Then I take off my *tzitzit*, fold it, and carefully set it on top of the shirt. I take off my *kippah* and set it on top of the *tzitzit*. When everything else is off, I dive into the pool. After the initial cold shock, my body adjusts quickly to the water and soon feels comfortable.

Ahouva: I found out about Goddard College's adult degree program where you could go there every six months. And I thought, *This will work! I can keep living in Israel, and I'll finish my degree.* When I got to Goddard, there was a woman from the Boston Women's Health Collective doing a consciousness-raising thing. And suddenly I understood what it was that had been happening for me, in terms of having a feminist context for understanding my dilemma. It was really life-altering for me. I understood at that point that I *wasn't* going to go back to Israel, that I couldn't live that life.

Aryae: Was that what broke up your marriage?

Ahouva: More than anything, yes. We were really moving in different directions. Yonatan was becoming more religious, and I was definitely wanting to move in a different way.

271

Berkeley, California – February 1978

Lane and I emerge from my new Honda CVCC in the parking lot of the Berkeley Marriot Hotel. We met four years ago after Ruthie and I got divorced, when I was 30 and Lane was 26. She is a slender, attractive, blue-eyed California girl who grew up living and surfing on the beaches in Orange County, south of Los Angeles.

Lane is not a holy beggar, and not particularly involved in any religion or spiritual practice. Her father is Jewish; her mother is from a Lutheran Norwegian family. Both are atheists. Her experience of God growing up came from going to church on Sunday mornings with her Norwegian grandmother.

When we first met she found my Hebrew name, the way I looked, and the Hasidic stories I told, exotic and intriguing. I found her "California-ness," her lack of strong identification with any particular religious or ethnic group, and her openness to learn from different peoples and traditions, refreshing. We've been living together for a couple of years in San Francisco.

We're planning to get married. I want a Jewish wedding and Lane's willing. The problem is, no rabbi I know will perform one unless both the bride and groom are Jewish. Since her mother isn't Jewish, Lane is not considered Jewish. We're here to see Shlomo, who's in the Bay Area for a few days, to ask him if he would perform the wedding. I'm hoping that, with his vast knowledge of Jewish law, he'll find a way to do it.

Lane frowns. "Are you sure he'll accept me?" she says. "Won't he think I'm some kind of evil witch stealing you away from the Jewish world?"

I smile at her. She looks very sweet. "I don't think so; I think he'll give you a big hug and say, 'Sweetest thing in the world, darlin'!" She looks at me skeptically.

The hotel is right on the waterfront at the Berkeley Marina. The sky is overcast and it's drizzling. Swarms of sea gulls are swooping in high, slow arcs over the boats docked at the marina, and out to the Bay. The waters are choppy, blue-grey, extending out to vast bright emptiness in all directions, and finally merging into the fog.

In the hotel lobby the colors are warm, and a fire is burning in a fireplace. The desk clerk rings up Shlomo and tells us how to get to his room. The hallway is long and narrow and dark.

I knock on the door. "One minute!" says a muffled voice inside. The door opens. Shlomo looks a little heavier than I remember, a little greyer, a little more tired. In his left hand he's holding, still open, a large hardbound book that looks like a Hasidic text, which he's probably just been studying.

"Shlomo!" I say.

His face lights up. "Aryae!" he says. "Greatest thing in the world! You better come in, fast!" With his right hand he closes the door behind us. He kisses the book, closes it, sets it on the dresser, gives me a quick hug, tugs my beard, and then turns his attention to Lane.

He takes her hands and looks at her. "Darlin', it's so good to see you!" he says. "I can see that Aryae's been holding out on me; you're even more beautiful than he said!" She smiles, blushes a little, and looks over at me.

"So how are you? What's going on?" Shlomo says.

She looks a little uncomfortable. He's still holding both her hands. "I've been nervous about meeting you," she says. "I didn't know what to expect."

He gives her a hug. "Sweetest thing in the world, darlin'!" he says. She catches my eye and we both smile.

"Are you hungry?" he says to both of us.

I look over at Lane. "No thanks Shlomo," I say, "we just ate."

There are two queen size beds in the room. One has two suitcases and a guitar case on it. The other, the one he was sleeping in, has the covers spread over it but still looks a little rumpled. He walks over to the bed with the suitcases and opens one of them. It is filled with food: two boxes of matzos, jars of *gefilte* fish, a can of coconut macaroons, a bottle of wine and a couple of bottles of kosher grape juice, as well as other stuff.

"My holy mother," he says, lifting up his arms and shrugging, "she's still taking care of me."

I laugh and shake my head.

"You gotta help me eat some of this so I don't have to *shlep* it back with me!" he says, laughing. We find some paper cups and Lane and I each have a cup of grape juice. Lane starts drinking hers. I look over at Shlomo and quickly say the blessing for wine and grape juice, ". . . *borei pri hagafen.*" Lane, realizing she may have done the wrong thing, looks a little startled. Shlomo is going through the contents of the second suitcase, which is filled with holy books. He pulls one of them

273

out. I take a few macaroons. It hits me that he's fulfilling the *mitzvah* of feeding his guests.

"This is *mammash* the greatest," he says. "Reb Levi Yitzhak Berdichever." He holds up the book and waves it back and forth. "Tsssss," he says, rolling up his eyes, "highest in the world." He holds the book out to me. It's been years since I've studied holy books in Hebrew. I read the title, in gold Hebrew letters embossed on the black cover. *Kedushat Levi* (Holiness of the Levi). "Have you learned from this?" he says.*

"No I haven't," I say.

"It's *mammash* so sweet, so holy," he says. "Keep this one. I have another copy at home."

"Thank you Shlomo, but I can't do that. It will get much more use with you." I give it back to him. He looks at me a moment and sets the book back in the suitcase.

The hotel room is large and there are enough chairs for all of us to sit down. Shlomo moves his chair so he's facing Lane. I'm sitting off to the side. He asks her about herself, her childhood, her family, her interests. She opens up and tells him a lot. She talks about her parents, about her relationship with her grandmother, about her experiences in the Lutheran church, about her curiosity about the Jewish side of her family.

He listens with great interest to what she is saying. I'm not used to seeing him spend this much time patiently discussing the details of a person's life. I try a couple of times to steer the conversation to the subject of our wedding, but he doesn't seem interested.

Then he talks to her. He tells her about the sweetness of living a life of holiness and love as a Jew, about how this enhances all of our lives.

Lane looks down at her hands which are folded in her lap. Then she looks up at him. "I understanding what you're saying Shlomo," she says. "I'm sure you're right, that living a Jewish life is very beautiful and everything." She takes a deep breath. "It's just that only *half* of me is Jewish." She looks over at me. I nod. "The other half is Norwegian. That's the part that's connected to my grandmother and grandfather, and that's so much of who I am Shlomo! If I converted,

---

* Rabbi Levi Yitzhak of Berditchev (1740-1809) is one of the most beloved Hasidic masters. Portions of his *Kedushat Levi* have been translated in Reb Zalman's book, *A Merciful God: Stories and Teachings of the Holy Rebbe, Levi Yitzhak of Berditchev.*

I'd be denying so much of me." Shlomo hasn't used the word "convert," but Lane sees where he's going.

I feel myself stop breathing. I look over at Shlomo.

Shlomo shakes his head back and forth. "God forbid, God forbid darling!" he says. "Being a Jew doesn't mean denying any part of yourself. God forbid, it's not about taking something away from you, it's about *adding*, becoming more."

I glance outside the window at the bay. A couple of seagulls are flying into the grey sky. He looks at both of us now. "Do you light candles on *Shabbos*?" he says to her.

Lane looks at me then at him. "We do Shlomo," she says. "Most of the time we do."

"Do you know what the two candles stand for, darling?" he asks her.

She looks at me and shakes her head.

"The reason we light two candles and not just one," he says, "is that on *Shabbos* we believe that every person receives a second soul. The soul we have during the week doesn't go away. The second soul is from the world of the Surrounding Light, and connects us to the highest, sweetest, most infinite places. We're still who we are, but we're also so much more.

"A Jewish wedding is *mammash* on the level of *Shabbos*. We believe that the holy, infinite Light surrounds the bride and groom, and that God himself so to speak is standing under the *huppah* with them."

Lane smiles and nods. Shlomo talks some more and she listens. I begin to see that her mind is made up, and he's not going to persuade her to change. For her the issue is about her identity, of being true to who she is. I sense that, and Shlomo must sense it too. What I also sense is that, without actually addressing it, Shlomo has already answered my question. There are no loopholes on this.

When Shlomo and Lane are done talking, we all stand up. I ask him if he has any additional concerts in the Bay Area. The folk music scene is no longer what it was in the '60s, so his concerts are now all at synagogues. He says he wants to walk Lane to the lobby and asks me to wait for him in the room. They go.

After I get over the disappointment that Shlomo won't be doing our wedding, Lane and I will find three friends to officiate at a creative ceremony that we'll put together. The wedding will be in May.

Burt Jacobson will conduct part of the ceremony and say the traditional Seven Blessings. Burt has reentered the Jewish world, initially as part of the Aquarian Minyan, a Berkeley community of Zalman's followers. Although he too says our wedding won't be recognized as a Jewish wedding, there's no reason why we can't use Jewish prayers and practices as part of a more universal ceremony. Lane will make a *huppah* with a dyeing process of using actual leaves to create leaf images on the cloth. When we hold up the *huppah* on four poles, it will look so beautiful, as if we are under the leaves of a *sukkah*. Two other friends will conduct other parts of the ceremony that will be spiritual but not Jewish. The wedding will take place in the Shakespeare Garden in Golden Gate Park. The invitations will have a verse from Shakespeare, as well as a verse from the Seven Blessings.

In the years that follow, Burt will make an important contribution to Jewish liturgy with new translations of the traditional Hebrew prayers which make them more accessible to people from all backgrounds. He'll start a community in Berkeley, Kehilla, which will become the largest Jewish Renewal congregation. And he'll become a leading scholar of the Ba'al Shem Tov, founder of Hasidism.

Once we're married Lane and I will discover that the differences between us are greater than we had imagined. The birth of Noe and Adam, and the experience of raising them, will only amplify our differences and intensify the conflict. We'll try for years to "work on our relationship," including six months in family therapy, but nothing will reverse the increasing stress of being together. The marriage will finally fall apart in October of 1991.

The door opens and Shlomo comes back into the room and closes the door behind him.

"*Oy vey! Oy vey!*" he says. "I wish we could do something." I watch him pace back and forth. "Aryae, as much as I'd like to, and believe me I would, I can't do it. Simple as it is, for a Jewish wedding, you *mammash* need two Jews."

"I understand Shlomo," I say.

We both stand there for a while without saying anything, without looking at each other. Then he comes up to me and puts his hands on my shoulders. As I think back now about all the years I knew him, this is the only time that he every rebuked me for anything.

With his hands still on my shoulders, he sighs. Then he looks right at me. His eyes are dark, intense. He speaks softly. "You never showed her what it is to be a Jew."

29

Valentine's Day

Palo Alto, California – February 14th, 1992

It's Friday afternoon at the Tom Peters Group and most of my colleagues have already left for the day. I'm sitting in my cubicle staring at the phone and computer in front of me. Today is Valentine's Day and of course tonight starts *Shabbos*. I have no plans for the weekend.

My title here is Principal. The firm offers leadership training programs to executives and managers in companies throughout the U.S., including some of America's largest and most respected companies. Tom Peters is the most famous of all America's business gurus. The best-selling books he's written, and all the hundreds of speeches he gives each year, boil down to two things: customers and employees. Give them your genuine attention and interest, understand them, treat them with respect, set up great experiences for them, do the right thing by them, and you will thrive.

This job is perfect for me at this point in my career, the embodiment of the direction that began to crystallize for me in the late '70s. It's about soul in the workplace. That's what motivates me to do this work.

Working with Tom and his colleagues reminds me of working with Shlomo at the House. I'm mostly behind the scenes, supporting a famous person in his mission to make a big difference in the world. It's a role that I'm comfortable with; but there's one big difference. Here the bottom-line is business. With Shlomo it was love.

Normally I enjoy calling customers and talking with them, but today I'm not into it.

My eyes move away from the phone and computer to a framed drawing from my daughter Noe. It's a brightly colored Japanese vase precariously perched on the edge of a colorless table, in front of a colorless window opening to the outside world. Falling near the vase are two delicate purple objects, either flower petals or tear drops. On the vase is a small, delicate world, a curved bridge over a curved stream with two tiny Japanese figures, a woman and a man, meeting at the center, and a red and yellow sun smiling down on them. The intensity of the effect, of a small, colorful world of the imagination perched precariously in a larger, colorless world of straight lines and teardrops, is extraordinary.

I pick up the phone and dial. After five or six rings on the other end, a high-pitched, 11-year-old girl's voice answers. "Hello?" She sounds uncertain.

"Hi Noe," I say. "It's Dad. Happy Valentine's Day!"

"Oh hi Dad," she says. "Happy Valentine's Day. I got the card and the chocolates. Thank you so much!"

I feel a surge of happiness and relief. The challenge for me of getting stuff to the kids during the weeks they are with Lane can be daunting.

"You're welcome sweetheart," I say. "I love you so much." There's a long silence. "Noe," I say, "are you still there?"

More silence. Then, "Yeah, I'm here." I listen hard into the silence, to try to hear if she's crying.

"Noe, are you okay?"

"Of course I'm okay Dad! What do you think?" she snaps back at me. I proceed carefully, asking about her day. It turns out that she didn't get many valentine cards compared to the other girls in her class. We put her into her current school, a small, alternative school in the redwoods, last year. She doesn't make friends easily.

I tell her how pretty I think she is, how smart and nice and funny, about how it's hard to be in a class where everybody knows each other and you're the new kid. When she goes in to the large middle school next year, where *everybody* is new, I bet she'll get lots of cards. She's silent. This is hard. I wish we could be together right now so I could give her a hug.

"I wish this was your week with me," I say. "You and Adam and I could light candles together and have *Shabbos* and watch a movie and eat lots of chocolate hearts."

"I'm glad I'm with Mom," she says. "She's sad today. I made her a big valentine, and I'm keeping her company."

I tell her what a wonderful daughter she is. I ask her if Adam is around and she says, "No, he's at soccer." I tell her I miss her and look forward to seeing her on Sunday night. She sounds noncommittal. I hear Lane's voice in the background, calling something to her. Noe and I say goodbye and hang up.

I take a couple of deep breaths. I don't have any Valentine cards either. The thought of driving home on Valentine's Day to my apartment in Half Moon Bay, where the whole town consists of families and almost no one is single, cooking dinner for myself, lighting *Shabbos* candles by myself, and eating by myself, is pretty depressing.

Ellen, who handles our graphic design, database administration, and various other computer things, comes up to my cubicle. She's got her coat and her purse.

"Aryae, I'm going home now. I think Eddie and the kids are making me a surprise dinner. So it's up to you to lock up for the weekend, okay?"

"Okay, thanks Ellen. Have a nice evening with your family, and a nice weekend."

Okay, there's nothing more to do here, I think. Time to go. I grab my briefcase and then stop to look at the phone. No that's silly, I just picked up my messages. I find myself dialing one more time anyway. To my surprise, there's a new message:

> "Aryae, this is so amazing to hear your voice on your machine. Hi, it's me, Sarah! It's been so many years and I'm sure it's crazy for me to be calling you like this, so if you want to hang up, I understand. But I just heard about you from a friend. 'Aryae!' I said. 'Is that the same Aryae I knew from the House of Love and Prayer!?' So hearing your voice, I know it's you! Anyway, I'd love to hear your voice in person. I don't know anything about you at this point, about your life or what you're up to or anything, but maybe we could get together sometime for coffee or a drink and catch-up."

I play the message again and write down her phone number. I sit there for a minute. Then I call her. She's home. We talk. Her voice sounds just like it did 20 years ago. She's been divorced for some time. She's living in San Francisco, and is not doing anything tonight. I tell her that I'm not either. She asks if I'd like to drive up to the City and get together for dinner. I say that sounds great. She suggests a restaurant. I know the neighborhood.

After we hang up I'm flooded with memories from the days of the House of Love and Prayer. Memories of a young man and a young woman so attracted to each other, of desire that was never consummated.

The restaurant is on Castro Street in San Francisco. The mood here is festive. Sarah and I sit at a table in the corner. The room is dark, filled with conversations of couples at all the tables. About half of them are gay men, a few are lesbians, and a few are straight couples like us. Each table has a candle and bright red paper hearts. The waiters are being especially attentive to all the guests here tonight. One is walking around with a tray with little bowls of candy hearts, pink and white and yellow and powder blue. He approaches each couple, smiles at them, and carefully sets a bowl near the candle on their table. Another waiter walks around with roses, and gives each person one. There is a jukebox playing in the background, mostly sentimental love songs from half a century ago.

Sarah and I are both dressed in our business clothes. She looks great—confident, successful and still very attractive. If you were watching us from another table and didn't know us, you wouldn't have a clue about our hippie, holy beggar past; what you'd see is a professional, fit, middle-aged couple, perhaps here to celebrate our 20th anniversary.

I don't get to San Francisco very often these days. It feels incongruous for me—a straight guy living in the suburbs, working with business executives, just coming out of a 14-year marriage and worrying about my kids—to be here on Castro Street. I look around at everyone, the gay couples in business suits, drag queens in flowing dresses, a lesbian couple who look like two sweet little old grandmothers, butch dykes in short hair and overalls, people in leather and spikes, young college age men and women looking not all that different from the way I and my friends looked a quarter century ago, all of us sitting in this dark room with candles and hearts and roses. It hits me how much we're really all so amazingly the same. As Shlomo used to say, "What do we know?" What do we really know about the human heart, about why we love the way we do, about why and how we screw it up, about how God wants us to love another person?

On the jukebox Dooley Wilson is singing straight out of Rick's saloon in *Casablanca:*

You must remember this,
A kiss is just a kiss,
A sigh is just a sigh;
The fundamental things apply
As time goes by.

Sarah doesn't live too far away, so after the meal I walk her back to her apartment. We talk to each other about our lives.

Soon after she and Elishama settled into the ultra-Orthodox *ba'al teshuvah* community on the East Coast, where they went after they left the House, Sarah got pregnant and gave birth to their first and only child, a son, Raphael, whom they called Rafi. Life was okay for a while. Elishama discovered that he had a real talent and passion for learning Torah, and did well in the *yeshiva*. They paid him a stipend to support his learning, which, together with occasional help from family, was enough to cover their basic expenses. As a new mother, she got plenty of support from the women in the community.

Although they tried, Sarah and Elishama were unable to have more kids. Over time this began to isolate her from the families around her, where the typical number of kids was five to ten. The other women, gathering together, surrounded by thick, noisy clouds of kids, always seemed to be looking at her with judgment or pity, or both. She wanted to go back to college, to have a profession and a life of her own. She felt that Elishama, who was increasingly absorbing the strict, traditional views about the roles of men and women, was not supportive. She had none of her own money and had come to him like a child whenever she needed to buy or do anything. She increasingly felt trapped, held hostage against her will.

When she was finally able to leave with help from friends in California, Sarah's freedom came at a terrible price. With full moral, financial, and legal support from the community, Elishama was able to gain complete custody of Rafi, and a court order strictly limiting her contact with him. Rafi was too young to understand why his mother was abandoning him and not coming back. The indescribable pain that this left in her heart, and his, has never fully healed.

When she got back to San Francisco, Sarah took a series of waitress jobs and put herself through law school. While she was still in school, she filed a motion in a New York court to get her custody situation reviewed and modified. After years of struggle, she was able to gain a little more access to Rafi, who would spend a few weeks with her in the summer. He has recently turned 18, and she is looking forward to seeing him soon. Their relationship has been difficult, but is on the mend. She now works as an attorney for the San Francisco Public Defender's office, defending people caught up in the legal system who are too poor to defend themselves.

I tell her how hard it's been for me the past couple of months, trying to cope with the pain and anger and disorientation that have taken over Noe and Adam's lives, and mine.

We get to the stairs leading from the street to her apartment and stand there in the night, looking at each other, sharing a moment of deep understanding. We have both experienced the terrible pain that happens when our relationships with those we love most get damaged.

Sarah looks concerned. "Aryae, you look awfully tired," she says. "Are you sure you can drive back okay?"

"Thanks Sarah, I'll be okay."

"Why don't you come up for a few minutes. We can light *Shabbos* candles, I'll make you a cup of coffee, and then I'll send you on your way, okay?"

I smile. "Okay, that sounds good. Thanks."

Her apartment is neat, cozy, comfortable, filled with interesting pictures and books.

She sets out a couple of candlesticks with fresh candles on the table in the kitchen area. She puts a white lace kerchief over her head, lights the candles, circles her hands around the candles three times in the traditional way to bring the light of *Shabbos* into her eyes and heart, and says the blessing. Then she brings some grape juice out of the refrigerator and pours us each a small glass. We say *Kiddush* and drink the grape juice. We both lead pretty secular lives at this point, but the soul-connections that Shlomo led us to make, and the light of *Shabbos,* will be with each of us forever, no matter what.

We sit on her living room couch and talk. She is very animated and her face goes through a whole range of emotions. It feels amazing to me that we are connecting like this after so many years. On one level we have each changed and experienced so much. On another level nothing has changed at all. We make a lot of eye contact. Her eyes are so intense, and I feel the electricity as we look at each other. I'm aware of our knees touching ever so slightly, and the smell of her hair and her perfume.

I glance at my watch and realize how late it is.

"Aryae, you can sleep here tonight if you like," she says. I must look pretty startled, because she laughs. "No it's not what you think! This couch folds out into a pretty comfortable bed. It's where friends stay when they visit." She smiles at me mischievously. "A couple of decades is a long time. Just because we're both living alone doesn't mean I'm going to jump into bed with you."

I look at her and laugh. "Yeah, we're grown ups now! We're more mature and responsible." We hold each other's gaze for a moment, the smiles and laughter gone, just looking at each other. Behind the eyes of the confident attorney, I can see the eyes of the passionate young woman at the House looking at me with such intensity. The young man in me wants to hold her and kiss her right now. I'm aware of the rhythm of her breathing, and of mine.

She breaks eye contact and stands up. "I'll get the sheets and help you make this bed," she says. I take a deep breath and nod. We rearrange the furniture in the living room, and pull out the sofa bed. She goes into her bedroom to get the sheets and blanket and pillow.

"Have you got an extra toothbrush?" I call out to her.

She laughs. "I'm sure we can arrange something." She comes back out with the sheets and we make the bed. I don't know exactly how it happens, but somehow that sofa bed never gets used.

Lying in her bed with her, holding her naked body against mine, feels unreal. It's like this is happening in another world, or in a dream that has suddenly become reality. It's as if, together with our clothes, we've also removed our current bodies and our current lives, unloading all the baggage with which those lives have burdened us. We're back to being those young 20-somethings, the passionate young man and woman who have been holding back their desire for each other for so long, now finally free to throw away the restraint, to completely let go and come together at last.

Later we're both sitting up as our breathing gradually slows to normal, heads and shoulders resting on the pillows propped up against the headboard, legs and feet touching under the blankets. We've brought the *Shabbos* candles into her bedroom with us, and shadows are dancing on the walls and ceiling.

Something doesn't feel quite right.

I can't quite put my finger on it; something still isn't complete. It's like our bodies in the present haven't quite satisfied our longing and passion from the past. I feel confused, unsettled.

For a while we just sit there without saying anything, watching the candle flames, each lost in our own thoughts. Then she looks at me and smiles: "I remember when I first saw you after coming back from my year in Israel. It was at Jonathan and Phyllis' engagement party. Do you remember?"

"Yeah I do," I say.

"I looked at you and I realized how attracted I was to you," she says.

I look at her and smile. "I wasn't aware of that; I was attracted to you, too. But there was something else I saw in you then that I didn't understand."

283

"Really?" she says. "What was that?"

"It's hard to say. It's like there was some kind of barrier, some kind of darkness in you."

Her eyes widen. She looks at the candles and nods to herself, as if remembering something she had forgotten. "I had just come back from Israel with Shlomo."

"With Shlomo!" I say. "I didn't know that!"

"Yeah," she looks over at me and smiles. "I was in Israel for six months at an *ulpan,* learning Hebrew. I met Shlomo one day when I wandered into an outdoor concert he was giving for soldiers." She looks away again.

"Wow, that must have been very special."

She looks back at me. Her eyes seem to be pleading with me to understand. "Aryae, do you have any idea of how lonely he was in those days?"

I shrug. "Well, I don't know. I guess so. I mean, I certainly used to think about it."

"You have no idea. He was a passionate man in the prime of his life. He had always lived alone. Wherever he went he was always surrounded by people, always the center of attention." Her eyes are still pleading with me. "I could see how lonely he was, Aryae. He was all alone in the world." She puts her hand over her mouth, looks down, and shakes her head. Neither of us says anything. Then she looks back up at me.

"I was lonely too," she says.

I notice that my breathing has stopped. I just look at her.

"I had just turned 21, I was in Israel by myself, and didn't really know why I was there. Shlomo and I became friends. For a few weeks I traveled around Israel with him and we were together everywhere."

I pull back from her so we're not touching anymore. I see the profile of her face as she looks at the candles. My chest is feeling tight. I try to control my voice, so as not to sound dramatic.

"Were you lovers?"

She shakes her head back and forth, not like she's answering my question, but like she's dismissing it. Then she turns over on her side so that she's facing me. She looks so beautiful, so frail, and so vulnerable, like she's 21 again. I don't know what to do with the swarm of feelings buzzing through me.

284

"He said he wanted to marry me," she says.

"What did you say?"

"I didn't know what to say; it felt like, I don't know . . ."

For a moment we're just lying there next to each other on our sides, so close, facing each other, breathing. Her eyes lock into mine. "Aryae, I had never felt anything like it. It was like the universe was bringing us together, like we had known each other in other lives. It was like we had been soul-mates since the beginning of time, and the energy pulling us together was so strong that neither of us could resist it, even if we wanted to."

She stops a moment, without moving her eyes away from me, and says, with just the hint of a smile, "The only thing I've ever experienced that even comes close was with you at the House."

I close my eyes and nod.

She turns toward the candles, which are now very low and flickering. "But even then at age 21, somehow I had enough of my wits about me that I knew I couldn't be married to him, that it just wouldn't work. He said he was disappointed, but I think he secretly agreed with me. We flew back to San Francisco together and then stopped seeing each other."

There doesn't seem to be anything else to say. First one of the candles goes out, then the other. I turn away from her, lie flat on the bed, and close my eyes. I can feel my arms against my sides, as if I'm hugging myself.

I suddenly have this image from many years ago. I'm in the *sukkah* at the first House, sitting on the ground with that big crowd of people, listening to Shlomo talk. He's saying, *"The only vessel big enough to contain the Surrounding Light is a broken heart."*

Saturday morning Sarah has a tai chi class and I go home. Over the next five months we'll get together for walks through San Francisco parks and neighborhoods, hikes along the coast in Marin and on the Peninsula, for dinners and shows and nights at her place and mine. Gradually and reluctantly, we'll both reach the same conclusion: the fire between us from so long ago is not enough to sustain a relationship now. We'll disappear again from each other's lives.

Late afternoon on Sunday when I pick up Noe and Adam at Lane's, they're all wound-up and fighting with each other. I try without much success to get them to stop. We pick up a couple of videos, comedies, and bring home an extra large pizza.

285

We sit on the couch in my apartment, eat the pizza and watch the movies. Eventually the kids settle down, and so do I. I find a blanket big enough to spread over us. It's like we're fending off the emptiness that's lurking, waiting to grab us in the night that surrounds us, by forming a little patch of warmth where we are safe together.

I wake up at three in the morning and see that we've fallen asleep on the couch.

30
Last of the Mohicans

Berkeley, California – Saturday Night,
March 19ᵗʰ, 1994

The Aquarian Minyan of Berkeley, which Zalman started 20 years ago – now one of the world's oldest and largest Jewish Renewal communities – is co-hosting a *farbrengen* (a Hasidic gathering) for Reb Shlomo and Reb Zalman, celebrating the 20ᵗʰ anniversary of when they were both here for a *farbrengen* in 1974.

Reb Shlomo and Reb Zalman at the original Berkeley *farbrengen* in 1974.
Photos by Steven Maimes from *The Holy Beggars' Gazette.* Used with permission.

This is the first time I'll be seeing Shlomo since my visit to his *shul* in New York over two years ago. What I don't know is that it will also be the last time I see him.

287

The meeting room at Berkeley Hillel House is packed with people. There are folding chairs set up in rows of semicircles. Like most events that involve Shlomo, this one is starting late. Everyone seems to understand and accept being on "Shlomo time." People have reserved their seats by setting their coats and other belongings on them, and are now mostly standing up, wandering around and talking to each other.

I find a seat near the back. My place in the Aquarian Minyan has been very much in the background. In the 22 years since I left the House, I haven't yet found either a new role for myself in the Jewish world, or a consistent spiritual identity. So when I do come to Jewish events, I mostly sit in the back and observe.

Reuven Goldfarb, tonight's master of ceremonies, decides it's time to get started. We'll begin by hearing from Reb Zalman, and Reb Shlomo can join-in when he arrives. Reb Zalman, wearing a beret and smiling impishly, sits behind the mic in the seat prepared for him in front of the room, and begins to talk about how the Lubavitcher Rebbe sent him and Shlomo out to college campuses in December of 1949. He describes their first visit to Brandeis University:

Reb Zalman: So I had an accordion with me, and we had some literature and *tefillin* I had collected from the shuls in New Bedford and Fall River and repaired, and we come in the middle of Hanukah to the Brandeis campus, to the cafeteria. They're playing some music and people are dancing and there was a guy with a spotlight, who was shining it on different couples. So we come in with our material, the *peklakh* [packages] and everything else—the *tefillin*, the tape recorder, and the accordion, and so on [laughs]. And it's almost as if the jukebox stopped for a moment—"Who are those people?" They hit us with that spotlight in the face, you know?

And we just set up our wares at one of the cafeteria tables, and Shlomo begins to talk and tell stories. There's one guy saying to me, "It sounds like what he's saying is like Hindu mysticism." [audience laughs] So I say, "Come here."

So Shlomo's in this corner telling stories and I'm in the other corner talking about the *Upanishads* and the *Sefer*

Yetzirah.[*] And so it happened, we set up shop at that time, and it's been going like this for a long, long time.[**]

Reb Zalman reminisces some more, gives teachings, sings *niggunim* and tells beautiful stories about Shlomo. After about a half-hour, there's a commotion in the back of the room. It soon becomes clear that Shlomo has arrived. He is greeting people, hugging and kissing them. Zalman stands up, claps his hands, and sings *Shalom Aleikhem* and a melody that is traditionally sung on Saturday night:

> *Dovid, Melekh Yisrael*
> *Hai, hai, vekaiyam.*

"David, King of Israel lives, lives and endures." Everyone in the room follows Reb Zalman's lead, standing and singing to give this honor to Reb Shlomo. Then Zalman changes one of the words:

> *Shlomo, Melekh Yisrael*
> *Hai, hai, vekaiyam.*

The mood is joyful and playful. After trying to hug everybody in the room, Shlomo finally makes his way to the front. He and Zalman hug each other and exchange a few words. Then Shlomo sits next to Zalman.

Reb Shlomo: Zalman told me that he was sharing with you the beginning of our humble careers. We're coming to Brandeis University. Did you tell them that the director of Brandeis said that he'll arrest us next time if we come? No? [laughter]

Listen to me, if he would not have told us he'll arrest us, most probably we wouldn't have gone there twice! But ah, he wants to arrest us, that means we're doing so much good. You know, if you ever want to do something and nobody's against it, don't bother doing it. [laughter and applause]

---

[*] The *Upanishads* are a collection of Hindu mystical-philosophical scriptures. The *Sefer Yitzirah*, the 'book of formation,' is one of the earliest kabbalistic texts.

[**] This and the selections that follow are edited transcriptions of Reb Zalman and Reb Shlomo's dialogue (used with Zalman's permission), recorded and distributed by the Aquarian Minyan. My edits were for the purpose of clarity and concision.

Anyway, I don't know the way Zalman told it to you, but here's the way I remember it.

Okay, we are walking in there and there's this Hanukah dance. Because what is Hanukah? Let me tell you: Hanukah is latkes and having fun. At Brandeis University, that was all there is to Hanukah, right? [laughter]

So Zalman and I, we come like great generals and divide this big dining room. Zalman says, 'I take left,' [laughs] and I take right. Okay, I want you to know, it really took a lot of *kishkes* out of us because, now we are a little bit professional, right? [laughs] But then we were just like, beginning. And suddenly, slowly, slowly, the whole dancing stopped. Half of the *hevra* were sitting at Zalman's table; Zalman was talking to them, and the other half was talking to me. Because the young people were really hungry; they wanted to know what Hanukah was all about. It was going on for a long time.

Finally it was time for the dining room to close, and we were just about to leave. And there was this young pre-med student who took a liking to us, actually more to Zalman. So [to Zalman] if you remember, at Brandeis University from the dining room down to the parking lot there were two thousand steps. [laughter] They were absolutely ice. So he says to us, "Aren't you afraid to go down? It's ice!"

So Zalman told him this unbelievable Premishlaner story.* It's a story we heard from the old Lubavitcher Rebbe. This is approximately 200 years ago. The *heilege* [holy] Premishlaner would go every midnight to immerse himself in the *mikveh*. But the *mikveh* was not as simple as it sounds. It was a river. And in order to go down to the river, you had to go down a very steep hill. Okay, maybe you make it down, but it was ice! How do you make it up? He made it down, he made it up! [For the Hasidim who saw him do it, this was considered a miracle.]

The next *Shabbos,* the Hasidim say to the Rebbe, "How did you do it?"

This is a good line to remember forever. He says, "If you hold on to above, you don't fall below." If you hold on to *above . . . ssss . . .* you don't fall below.

---

* Rabbi Menachem Mendel of Premishlan (1728-1771) was a disciple of the Ba'al Shem Tov who eventually emigrated to the Holy Land and is buried in Tiberias.

So Zalman told him this story. Then we went down [and somehow we made it]. Obviously we were holding on to above! [laughter]

The next time we come, this boy is [totally different] . . . Fire, fire, fire! So we asked him what happened. So he says, "Do you know? I went down, but I [slipped and] rolled down. I couldn't make it. When I got down there, completely broken and bruised all over, I realized that I am not holding on to above." Ssss . . . .

So I want you to know something friends . . . you gotta hold on.

Now I want to share with you one more thing, which is, saying a little *Toirah-le* (teaching) in honor of my holy Rebbe Zalman.

You know, when I go to the synagogue, when I go to learn, when I open the page in the holy book, I'm not interested in more information. Sure, the Torah's *gevalt*, I want to learn every word of the Torah; but what we need the most—we need something to hold on to. When I go to the synagogue, I want someone to tell me one word to hold onto.

You know what is a true friend? You know, 20,000 people can walk up to me and tell me, "Hey, we love you." But it's not strong enough for me to hold onto it. [whispers] And then I meet one person who says, "I *really* love you." [silence] Oh, and I can hold onto that . . . for a long time. So I want you to know, Zalman and humble me, we realized: the *Yiddishkeit* [Judaism] the way [it was when we started]—I'm not knocking it, it's holy and beautiful—but it wasn't strong enough to hold onto.

You know today, a lot of people invite people for *Shabbos,* and it's maybe like, getting better. Well I would say most probably Zalman was the first to *mammash* [really] realize that *Shabbos* is something to hold onto. . . . [whispers] I need a *Shabbos* to hold onto. . . . So *borukh Hashem,* we have a teacher like Zalman.

You know what the Torah is? *"Eitz hayyim hee l'mahzikim bah."* [She is a Tree of Life for those who hold onto her.]* Do you know the difference between the Tree of Knowledge and the Tree of Life? It's very simple. The Tree of Knowledge has

---

* Proverbs 3:18.

nothing to hold onto; it's good information. The Tree of Life . . . [you can hold on to forever.] When you teach Torah, [you're not just giving information]. It's *mammash* from my heart to your heart.

I want you to give the biggest *yasher koah* to Zalman for all the teachings you're doing, for all the *Shabboses,* for all the weddings, for everything. I can only tell you Zalman, you have to live another hundred years, because we need you, *mammash.* [cheers and applause]

Reb Zalman: Shloima, I don't like to be lonely. I don't mind another hundred years, but without you, *toive nisht* [it's no good]. [cheers and applause]

Reuven, who has been sitting in the background, watching and listening closely, steps in at this point. He says, "Can you talk a little bit about the differences that exist between you and how you manage to bridge that?"

Reb Zalman: People used to say, "I'm more of a Shlomo Hasid than a Zalman Hasid," or the other way around. [Sings the familiar melody for the Four Questions on Passover] *Ma nishtana* . . . What's the difference between Shlomo and Zalman? [laughter]

I used to say it like this: I'm the most Piscean Aquarian, and he's the most Aquarian Piscean, and this is how we make our link together. I think the wonderful thing about Reb Shlomo is, the way in which he is permeable toward the right; they don't have access to come to me.

Reb Shlomo: Has v'shalom (God forbid) why not?

Reb Zalman: Because that's the situation: it's not that I'm stopping them, you know? If you want to know what's the difference, the difference is that Shlomo manages to keep people from prior to the paradigm shift [in evolutionary consciousness] connected to his vision. That's the wonderful, wonderful thing; that they find a common language and a common experience with Reb Shlomo, and he midwifes them to experiences that otherwise they wouldn't have, and which they can share with you. It's a lot easier when you begin from the heart than when you begin from the mind.

Way back then at Brandeis it was sort of clear, you know? He was in the corner telling the *mai'ses* [stories] and teaching about Hanukah, and I was talking about the *Upanishads* and evolution to some guys on the other side. And if you want to know a difference, that's a difference.

Reb Shloima, how would you characterize it?

Reb Shlomo and Reb Zalman at the Berkley *farbrengen* on March 19th, 1994. Photo by Laurel Cline, used with the permission of Zalman Schachter-Shalomi.

Reb Shlomo: If you think that we are less good friends because we are not the same — *thank God we are not the same* — 'cause God doesn't need two Shlomos, and he doesn't need two Zalmans, right? He needs one Zalman, and he needs one Shlomo. [laughter]

But, let me tell you the difference, and Zalman correct me if I'm right. [laughter]

I'll tell you something very deep. When Zalman and I began, there was something in the world to become more universal. There was something in the world, and it was good. Zalman is *awesomely* universal; and I am *awesomely* Jewish.

293

Zalman first takes you for a trip around the world. Then he says, "Come to my Simhas Torah [holy day of rejoicing with the Torah], and you have it all right there." I say, "If you want to go to India, *mazel tov* . . . it's holy to be there; but . . . for me, I say, 'It can't be that it's not in *Yiddishkeit* [Judaism], *it can't be!* So I drown myself in the old, holy books. It has to be [there].

And you know something, both approaches are very holy. Some people need Zalman's way, and some people need my way. Obviously God needs both ways, you know? Otherwise we wouldn't be here.

Zalman has to leave, because he has some days of travel ahead, and he needs his rest. Shlomo will stay to do some singing with his daughter Neshama who is traveling with him. She is a beautiful young woman, a talented musician, very devoted to her father and his music, but obviously with the creativity and drive to be a voice in her own right.

Reb Zalman and Reb Shlomo get up to say goodbye to each other. I look at these two old men, standing together in front of us. They go back to the Jewish world of Europe before the Holocaust. They knew the Hasidic rebbes of that era. They are carriers of the seed-stock of spiritual wisdom of a generation that was destroyed. They brought it to America and planted it in the souls of a new generation.

Zalman stands with his arm around Shlomo, smiling. "We're the last of the Mohicans," he says.*

The next day, Sunday, Shlomo is at the Sunday school of Berkeley's Orthodox synagogue, Beth Israel. Passover will be the following week, so Shlomo is conducting a kind of practice *Seder* for all the children. I want to take Noe and Adam to see him. They've heard me talk a lot about Shlomo. Whenever we have a *Seder,* or light candles for Hanukah, or spend *Shabbos* together, I try to tell at least one Shlomo story.

Noe, who turned 13 last year and decided not to have a *bat-mitzvah,* says she doesn't want to see him because it would be too embarrassing. I try to talk her into it, but I can't. Adam, who is nine, is curious and wants to come with me.

---

* A reference to the James Fenimore Cooper novel of the same name, in which the Mohican warrior, Chingachgook speaks of the end of his family line.

When we get to the synagogue and go into the room where Shlomo is, we see him sitting at a low table with lots of little children. We've arrived a little late and there is no more room to sit, so I stand behind him and Adam stands next to me. Shlomo is telling stories to the children, and they are listening with eyes wide open.

After the practice *Seder* is over, children and their parents are milling around, waiting to talk to Shlomo, who is still sitting in his chair. Shlomo looks a little tired, a little unfocused. I walk up to him, bend over, give him a hug, and introduce him to Adam. Shlomo's face lights up and he says a few words to Adam. Adam doesn't say anything, looking a little shy and smiling. I look at the two of them. I want to remember this moment.

The president of the *shul* walks up and says the adults are waiting for Shlomo in the next room. He's promised to spend an hour with them. Looking tired, he laughs weakly, flashes him a "V" and says, "Peace, brother, I'll be right there." I help him get up out of the chair.

Once he's standing, Shlomo's eyes focus on mine. "So when will I see you again?" he says. After he's done at the *shul*, he has to rush off to the airport. I've got to get Noe and Adam back to Half Moon Bay.

I look at him, take a breath and shake my head. "I don't know," I say.

31

Kaddish

The New York Times – October 22ⁿᵈ, 1994

Rabbi Shlomo Carlebach, the foremost songwriter in contemporary Judaism, who used his music to inspire and unite Jews around the world, died on Thursday at Western Queens Community Hospital.* He was 69 and lived in Manhattan, Toronto and Moshav Or Modiin, Israel.

The cause of death was a heart attack [. . .]

Jerusalem, Israel – October 24ᵗʰ, 1994

Rabbi Yisrael Meir Lau, Chief Rabbi of Israel, spoke at Shlomo's funeral:

> I believe that it would be a grave neglect of one's duty not to speak on behalf of many people who should beg Rabbi Shlomo Carlebach's pardon and forgiveness. We did not show him sufficient respect, nor did we have sufficient appreciation of his qualities, and we did not exert ourselves sufficiently in defense of his honor — something that he never asked for but which he thoroughly deserved. So I beg his pardon and forgiveness in the name of everyone gathered here and in the name of the many, many people who ought to have been here and who never came. But come they will, and they will learn to appreciate that great soul wandering in our midst. [. . .]

> Though connected with every Jewish world, he sometimes appeared detached from them because of his loneliness and isolation. Occasionally, when we met on a plane, it struck me that his guitar was the one loyal

---

* Reb Shlomo died on October 20ᵗʰ, 1994.

companion that he had. Yet he had belonged to the scholarly world of Rabbi [Aharon] Kotler in Lakewood, to the Lubavitcher Rebbe's circle in Brooklyn, and to the [Breslover] followers of Rav Nachman. All three of them must have welcomed his great soul to the realm above.

On one occasion, more than twenty years ago, he stayed at my home in Tel Aviv until four o'clock in the morning. "Rabbi Yisrael," he said, "you are a child of the *Shoah* (Holocaust) and I'd like to sing you a song." There and then he wrote a melody that has never been published, a setting to the verse which has now accompanied him to his resting place: "Though I walk through the valley of the shadow of death, I will fear no evil, for You are with me." Those words, "You are with me," gave him strength on his journeys throughout the world, East and West, on the campuses of America, England, France, Austria, Germany, South Africa, and Australia [. . .]

You were a great soul, Shlomo, a truly great soul. Only once in each generation does that kind of soul emerge, from a rock in the heavenly world perhaps [. . .] Alas for those who have gone and who cannot be replaced!*

Half Moon Bay, California – October 30th, 1994

I've phoned some of my old friends from the House of Love and Prayer and invited them to a memorial gathering for Shlomo at my place. The apartment, which I moved into when my second marriage ended three years ago, is small but has a large deck with a vast, unobstructed view of the Pacific Ocean. The day is sunny and mild.

Donna has flown in from Boston; Jill has driven in from Idaho; everyone else has come from their homes in the Bay Area. There are about 20 of us sitting on the deck. We introduce ourselves and begin to reminisce:

Aryae: When I heard the news about Shlomo, I was numb with shock, so I sent an e-mail to Zalman to ask him for guidance.

---

* As recorded in M. Brandwein, trans. Gabriel A. Sivan, *Reb Shlomele*, Jerusalem, 1997.

There is so much I've been wanting to say to Shlomo, but I kept putting it off; he was always surrounded by so many other people who wanted to talk to him, and I always had the next thing on my schedule to rush off to. Besides, he would always be here, right? So there would always be time later. Now it's hit me: I missed my chance. [silence]

I've been hiding-out for a long time. But before I started hiding-out, I was given a great gift. What I learned when I was with Shlomo is, I learned how to live in the presence of somebody who lives in God's presence all the time, and it changed my life.

I need help getting out of the closet and figuring out who I am today in relation to what I learned from Shlomo, and what my work is in passing it on.

I feel that all of us who are his students, we have the great privilege and the great responsibility to pass it on. So I hope that those of us here today can give each other strength and courage to do that.

Donna: My name's Donna Maimes. I get the award for coming the furthest. I flew in from Boston last night — *da-da!!* [applause]

You know, my whole life is different. I met Shlomo in 1963 — I'm 45 years old now — I was 14. I met him on Pesah in New York, and really met him when he came here for the folk festival in 1965, and I can't imagine what my life would be like . . . [she stops, overcome with emotion]

Jill: My name is Jill Bennet [voice filled with emotion], and I'm still in shock. Rivka called me last Friday, and it's sort of unbelievable to me. I also thought he would always be there.

I met Shlomo early in 1969, and dropped out of college and moved to the House of Love and Prayer. [laughs] I was really more part of the first House. I ended up going to New York in '73 and marrying a guy in 1974 from a nice *frum* family, and spent many, many years in New York City.

You know, my whole life changed. I would have been going to college, and being some kind of . . . I was gonna be a politician! That was my goal. I was gonna go to law school. It was all set up. And I just dropped out of everything and went to live at the House of Love and Prayer! [laughs] It's been a long, strange trip. [laughter] I'm not quite sure where one

299

goes now, you know? [tearfully] It's gonna be a real different world.

Aryae: Jill, to you and Donna, I just want to say that both of you being here is the most incredible gift I could imagine. [To Donna] I would not have had the *hutzpah* [nerve] to ask you to fly out from Boston. By the time I learned that you might actually want to do that, it was Friday afternoon.

Donna: I got the message at 5:15.

Aryae: 5:15 Friday afternoon; it was quintessential Donna. I just don't have the words to thank you.

Jill: She calls me up and she says, "Darlin! I'll meet you for lunch in San Francisco tomorrow!" [laughter]

Donna: Did you mention what time of day that was? [laughter]

Aryae: Jill, you got into a car and drove out from Idaho?

Jill: Donna called. I was walking out the door to go to dinner, and I said, "I'll have to come over there for dinner!" [laughter]

Donna: I was at Shlomo's funeral in New York last Sunday. I took my son Natan. Rabbi Moshe Tendler [professor of Biology and Jewish Medical Ethics at Yeshiva College] spoke. He said—and I think that he was quoted in the New York Times—that Shlomo Carlebach touched more Jews than any other person in contemporary history.

On Sunday there were, the police estimated between five and seven thousand people standing in front of the [Carlebach] *shul* on 79th Street. They blocked off the entire street. And there were so many kinds of people, black-hatters [Hasidic types], reform types, young hippie types, all kinds of people. I haven't stood in a group of people that diverse, that could have been fighting with each other, where everybody was . . . there! It was an amazing, amazing thing.

There was something about the way that Shlomo connected people that was about forgiveness, and humility, and accepting people as they are. There were people who wouldn't have spoken to each other 20 years ago, who could

300

stand next to each other and remember Shlomo, and cry. It was an amazing thing.

So I needed to come *here* to stand next to people that maybe it didn't seem so *weird* to stand next to! [laughter] And to also remember what it is to live from the inside, compared to how very much on the outside I used to be. It's different. Being grown up is hard.

Jill: Donna suggested that we say a word about people that haven't made it this far. She told me she was gonna talk about Moshe Fohrman.

Donna: [On the verge of tears] *Maybe* Donna's gonna talk about Moshe! [warm laughter] It just kind of occurred to me that there are a lot of people that we've lost along the way. And I know some of 'em. I guess being at Shlomo's funeral reminded me of a lot of these people. Actually, there's a story of Moshe Fohrman and Shlomo, and somebody else we lost along the way, which was my daughter [voice breaks].

We traveled a lot of ground. We dealt with all kinds of really simple stuff, and fun stuff, and really up stuff.

And then people started to get sick, and people started to die. I had a daughter whose name was Divia Chaya who died when she was two weeks old. And it was really the first time that the House was touched by death.

Shlomo . . . I was on the phone with him a lot, and he came later. I had a conference call with Shlomo and Moshe Fohrman [who died of cancer shortly thereafter]. Moshe had been very sick before this, and was in remission when Divia died. There was *no way* that I could go to the burial. I just couldn't do it. So Shlomo and Moshe and I came up with an agreement. We decided, it was actually Shlomo's idea, that if Moshe would bury Divia, I would be in the front row to bury Moshe. And of course Moshe was never supposed to die either.

The thing that I remember really clearly is Shlomo and Moshe both saying that we all need connections to the other side. What Shlomo said about Divia was that she was a "messenger. " She was going to check it out to make sure it was okay for everybody. And Moshe—*ah!* [voice breaks] Shlomo said that what his job was going to be was to deliver the messenger. And . . . hopefully Moshe checked it out for Shlomo.

301

For me it was really critical that I be in New York last Sunday. I still don't do burials much but, it really did feel like another conference call. It's like, you gotta be there. *You gotta be there.*

And Moishe Fohrman gets remembered. My son Natan Moshe Bahir is now 16 years old, and his *bris* was in Moishe's home. And he is named for Moishe Fohrman. So it just keeps on going and going. It just seems really important to remember that we didn't all get this far. We've been left behind by other kinds of folks.

The last conversation that I had with Shlomo was two weeks ago. He said that the thing that amazed him most about the way that I've changed is that somehow I managed to find a voice. Cause he would always say [at events, concerts, etc.], "Donna! Darlin! Say something!" And it's like, don't even *look* over here! [laughter] Don't even look at me. Don't ask me to read anything. Don't ask me to say anything.

And at my son's *bar-mitzvah* he said to me, "You know, the thing that you haven't found yet, you haven't found a voice." So at my son's *bar-mitzvah* he said, "I've blessed you with this before, my blessings are not that strong [laughter], but sometime soon, you're gonna find a voice."

It's an awful way to try it out. So two weeks ago he asked me if I'd found it yet. Maybe a little. [cries]

Reuven Goldfarb: I was really in a broken condition in '69; I had nowhere to go. And I needed to put myself together; but I didn't know how to do it by myself. I was fortunate to meet a lot of strong spiritual teachers in those days. The area was flooded with them.

One of them was Stephen Gaskin. A lot of people from the House used to go in convoys to Steven's Monday Night Class.* One time I was there and someone told me about the House of Love and Prayer.

So the next *Shabbos* I walked over to the House. And someone named Richard, he kind of glided down the stairs and put his arm around me and said, "Welcome brother!" And I felt a real heart-connection. I had felt spiritual connections with teachers and groups before that, but I

---

* Stephen Gaskin (b. 1935) was an influential teacher in San Francisco in the 1960s and founder of the intentional community called "The Farm."

hadn't felt a heart-connection, that feeling of homecoming that I felt from this greeting.

So I started coming regularly Friday nights. And after that I learned with Aryae, and with everyone else who was singing Shlomo's tune.

But I hadn't met Shlomo yet. A couple of months later I heard from somebody: "Shlomo is doing a concert in Berkeley." I hitchhiked over, and I walked in late, later than him! And there was a lot of music and dancing in big circles. So I joined one of the circles, and I saw people were kind of very friendly, and didn't have a lot of barriers, and it felt nice and sweet, but I hadn't checked out the main man yet.

So I walked over to Shlomo, who was standing in the middle playing his guitar, and he looked at me coming over toward him, and he strummed some more chords, and in the middle of the song he said, "Street people are building bridges for all of us to walk on."

Wow! [laughs] I didn't even have to ask him anything, you know; he just gave me an appropriate teaching for that moment. So that was enough for me. I went back and I continued dancing.

Yosepha Zarchin: When I met Shlomo I was really young. [laughter] No, really! Maybe 14, maybe even earlier, 13, 'cause it was in Los Angeles. It was before the House of Love and Prayer.

Several people: Your name was Janey!

Yosepha: Janey—right! Shlomo gave me my name. I mean, I found my name at the House of Love and Prayer, which in and of itself . . . I think lots of us found our names and that part of ourselves there.

I was really young and I think it was in Los Angeles in a big temple that was in, like, on the way out towards the Valley, up the canyon . . . this big temple, Leo Baeck [Temple], I think. And Aryae, and Leah was there, and Efraim. I remember that the room was big.

And then we started dancing and singing. And we danced and we sang, and we danced and we sang. And it just went round and around and around. And eventually, at some point, we stopped. We had been dancing kind of in a circle in the middle of this big room, and there was blood all over the floor. We stopped and I went, "Oh my gosh! What happened? Did somebody hurt themselves?" And everyone had no sensation of having hurt themselves. Finally I looked at my feet, and I had danced through the calluses on my toes. My feet were just bleeding; but it didn't hurt. [laughter] I didn't know they were my feet that were bleeding on the floor.

And I think it's an incredible privilege to have had that. That's what everybody here is talking about, is having that experience where you don't know where your arm stops and the next person's arm begins. You don't know whose blood is on the floor because nobody's feet hurt. I mean they're not "your" feet. You're so wrapped up in the transcendence of it. To experience that, through a person, through each other, is a rare gift. And I'm here because you are the people that I experienced that with. It transformed my life. I mean, that gave me my *name*, that gave lots of us our names and our identities. We all have layers on top of what happened 25 years ago, but the level of experience that came through us back then, that's the core.

Aryae: Yosepha I'm remembering those times when you and Stephanie [now Shulamis in Jerusalem], you were what, 15 maybe? *Shabbos* morning at the House we'd be reading the Torah . . .

Yosepha: And we were sleeping! [lots of laughter]

Aryae: Yosepha and Stephanie were under the table while we were reading the Torah. And somehow the fact that the two of you were there, *added*. I mean you were *there*, your spiritual presence was there, as you slept under the Torah.

Jill: I sit here and I think of so many different things. I don't have clear pieces of memories. I have all these little vignettes in my head.

I remember when I met Shlomo. He came to Sonoma State. There were signs up that said, "The Singing Rabbi." I thought, I'll check this out. I went over, and he was playing in this open-air thing, and they had, like, concrete with the little stones in it, you know? I remember dancing for so long that I had blisters. I danced barefoot and I had blisters on the bottoms of my feet. But I didn't notice it either. [To Yosefa] This must be something that happens! [laughs]

He said, "You've gotta come *Shabbos* to the House of Love and Prayer!" And I did, and the rest is history; not only for me, but for much of my family. [laughter] My mother [Lois, now at the Moshav] came along. And now my older brother, who was in Vietnam when I was at the House of Love and Prayer, he's now on the Moshav.

Shlomo impacted my life so tremendously. He was always in my life. I didn't see him so much, every blue moon or two, you know? But it was like, I knew he was out there, and he knew who I was.

I went to his wedding, and we went to *Sheva Brakhas* [Seven Blessings] at his brother's house. And I started to give him a blessing, and he responded, and he started telling a story of the girl that he met at Sonoma State University. I could not believe that he actually remembered where he had met me; I mean, I was nobody. It was just incredible to me. Anytime anybody ever said to me anything about Shlomo's memory . . . He was *unbelievable*. He could remember things . . . it was incredible.

Donna and I were talking. I remember doing mikvehs, was it Stow Lake?

Lots of people: Stow Lake! [laughter]

Jill: In this dark, freezing cold . . . [lots of voices and laughter] Here we are, we're supposed to soak every bit of our bodies in water . . . [continuing voices and laughter] We were up to our knees in mud anyway; I mean, it was *hysterical* . . .

Aryae: It was on Shavuos.

Others: Yeah, it was Shavuos!

Jill: We learned all night and then we went in!

Those are the kinds of memories I have. And I would see Shlomo off and on, mostly when I would go to the Moshav to see Mama. He was a father to me. I know he probably hated that [laughs]; but he was that person in my life that took care of some things that needed to be taken care of for me emotionally in that way. Like when I left my first husband, and he was getting really abusive and drinking really heavy, and it was really, really ugly, and I was afraid to be in a room with him. I went to all the rabbis and asked about a *get*

305

[Jewish divorce], and they wouldn't give me a *get*. They said I had to go to counseling and try to forgive him.

So I went to Shlomo, and Shlomo said that he would fix it. And within days he had it set up for me to go to Los Angeles. He had the rabbis there; he had everything there. He said, "You should just walk in the door; you take the piece of paper; you walk out again. That's all you do. Everything is set up for you. And you go, you're going to stay at the Chabad House.* People know you're coming, and it's going to be okay."

It was just amazing! It was like, if he really had to take care of something and it was really, really urgent, it really did happen. Because he did that for me. [pause] I miss him.

Aryae: [To Ian Grand] I feel as honored by you being here across the gulf of time, as I feel by Donna coming, and Jill coming across the gulf of time and space both. So I'm really, really happy you're here. We haven't seen each other for a long, long time.

Ian: I wanted to be here personally because, when I heard about Shlomo's death, what I realized was that, I actually wanted to be around people who had the experience, where we shared in the thing together, you know?

I had the great privilege of knowing Shlomo when I was 15. Before Shlomo was running around doing stuff, he came to St. Louis for a year, as the youth rabbi [laughter] of a local synagogue, right?

He was just out of Lubavitch. So the thing was, is that a friend of mine sent me over to his place, you know? And then for that year, I would spend day after day at Shlomo's apartment. He was just composing his tunes, he hadn't put them out . . .

Unidentified Speaker: He was *there*, like most of the time?

Ian: He was *there*! He was just actually *there*! [laughter] He was actually there for a year, you know? It was a *job*. He had

---

* Chabad Houses are run by *shulhim* (emissaries) of the Chabad-Lubavitch organization. It was Reb Zalman who first proposed the idea of such Chabad "outposts" to the seventh Lubavitcher Rebbe.

a *job*! [laughter] He didn't *keep* the job more than a year, but he had a job. [laughter]

It was extraordinary. So he was just composing his first tunes. The album hadn't come out yet, the first album. It came out during that time. He would tell me stories; story after story after story.

One of the themes for me too is the song and the dance and the joy that we all know, right? It's informed my whole life. Everything that I do, in teaching, came from that place. The second is the stories. And everything that I do comes from that place too; 'cause I learned how to tell stories.

Shlomo came out to the Berkeley Folk Festival, and my friend Efraim and I, who were living in the same house at this time . . . I said, "Efraim, man!"

Aryae: You and Efraim were living in the same house?

Ian: Yeah! So I said, "Efraim, man! We gotta go see this guy! It's my old friend Shloim!" So we go to see Shlomo. You should also know I was raised Reform, right? [laughter]

The next thing we know is Efraim, who's a hippie art student going to the Art Institute, and Ian, start putting on *tefillin* and davening, and going up and down the coast doing concerts. We eventually go to some high school in San Francisco where Moishe Fohrman comes along. One thing leads to another, and then comes the House.

Reuven: I noticed a lot of changes in the House from the time it was on Arguello to the time it was on 9th Avenue. No one's talked about that yet, so I'll try to briefly describe my feelings.

I had gone to Sonoma County and lived on Wheeler's Ranch for a year and a half. And in the interval, the House had moved from Arguello to 9th Avenue. I didn't know where it was, but thankfully, I was able to locate it again.

I think the *mehitza* [ritual barrier between men and women] was in place at that time. I remember meeting Meyer, and Meyer looking at this *mehitza* and saying, "What? What happened?" [laughs]

To me, like, when Aryae was running things, I understood sort of what was going on; but I really didn't understand who was running things on 9th Avenue. It was a

307

little bit anarchic. It felt like, whoever had *ko'ah* [strength] that Friday night would lead the service.

Toward the end of things I tried to become a member of the House. You could become an official member, actually. [laughter] And there was a little board, and there were officers, and they had meetings. I went to this one meeting, and I have to say, this was one of the more terrible meetings I've ever been to. People were so up and out nasty. Someone called it the House of Hate and Spite. [laughter]

What was the reason for this? [silence] I don't know.

About that time people started going to the East Bay, where Zalman was coming and leading services for High Holidays. So one year I was at the House for Rosh Hashanah, and at the Aquarian Minyan for Yom Kippur. I noticed a number of people I knew from both places kind of having to choose, in a way, where to be for a particular holiday, or a particular occasion.

The House was on its way out, and whatever kicking and screaming it did in its dying throes, it was inevitable. There were economic reasons and other reasons, but the real reason it seemed to me was that the spirit was gone. Whatever had kept it going had gone somewhere else. The *Shekhinah* [Divine Presence] had flown the coop.

When I checked out the [Aquarian] Minyan, one of the things I wanted to find out was—Is there a place in this group where you can, like, express yourself, and your feelings will be honored, and your views will be honored, and you can help determine the direction of things, and you don't just have to go along with the party line? And I was assured, "Yes, definitely, that's what we're about." So when I heard that, I felt, okay, then I can be there for awhile. And that's what I've done ever since.

Ian: One other story—Shlomo's wedding. Shlomo's wedding was this incredible event. It was held in the World's Fair building, as some of you know, anybody who was there. It was like this place was kind of rocking the whole time. [laughter] It was very weird.

So before the wedding, Saturday night after *Shabbos,* we went to the Bobover Rebbe. It's this extraordinary thing; because here's our guys, long hair, right? And here's their guys, very traditional. So the basement is someplace in Boro Park. They're sitting there doing their thing. Their

308

adolescents are looking like Talmudic adolescents. We're looking weird.

So here's the Bobover Rebbe, sitting there. They haven't finished *Shabbos* yet. It's the last meal of *Shabbos;* everybody's sitting around together. And the Rebbe is holding up his glass of schnapps, and all the Hasidim are holding up their glasses, and he's saying to them, and they're answering him back: *L'hayyim!* Good *Shabbos!* And at one point, the Rebbe says, he wants to do a toast to Shlomo's Hasidim—us! You could hear the gasp! [Makes gasping sounds, which are followed by laughter] It was this amazing thing.

Jill: I just want to say, not being disrespectful, but I remember Shlomo's mother, *aleyha haShalom* [peace unto her], calling him at the House of Love and Prayer, many, many times. She was a wonderful woman, *but* . . . [laughter]

When my son was born, she sent me this blanket for the baby, addressed to "the hippie grandson." [laughter] But with all the stuff Shlomo had with her, he never spoke badly about her. He came close so many times. [laughter] And we knew what he *wasn't* saying! But never, *never* . . . He always was respectful.

Ian: I was in jail in Saint Louis for civil rights stuff, you know? My wife at the time and I went to New York. We saw Shlomo at his house. So he was in the other room. His mother was there. She said, "So, you're the freedom fighters?"

We were kind of proud of ourselves. We said, "Yeah, yeah."

She said, "I'm not impressed." [long laughter] Then Shlomo came in. It was awful, you know; it's like, what do you say after that? [laughter]

Donna: I always got the soft side of her for some reason, I have no idea why . . .

Jill: Once she showed me her soft side, and I was terrified! She was soft, and I was almost horizontal! [laughter]

Aryae: It's amazing how she really did have these two sides.

One time in the late '60s, I visited Shlomo in New York, and his mother was there. She told me how selfish I was to take Shlomo away from New York, which is where he really belonged. She said, "If you and the hippies really cared about Shlomo, you'd never see him again!" [laughter]

Then in 1973, a year after I left the House, I got this book in the mail. [I hold up the book, *The Carlebach Tradition.*] Have any of you guys ever seen it? It's writings about the Carlebach family by Shlomo's father. Anyway, when I opened the cover, I saw a note to me. But what blew my mind was, it wasn't from Shlomo, it was from his mother!

"To: Mr. Aryae Coopersmith

A good friend of Shlomo and me with my best wishes.

Paula Carlebach"

Like Shlomo used to say, you never know.

Donna: Two years ago Shlomo came to Massachusetts to do my son's *bar-mitzvah.* I have pictures of my son Natan—from the time he was *this* big [holds her hand low], til he was *this* big [holds her hand higher], 'til he was taller than Shlomo— all underneath Shlomo's *tallis* [prayer shawl].

I think that what Shlomo gave me was the same thing that he gave to my son. He made me believe that I was all right, that there was something of value in me. When *I* couldn't see it at all, *he* could. *Pay attention, there's something here; there's something here.* He is truly the only person in my life who consistently—from the time I was 14 or 15 years old—only saw the good in me.

I have one little, tiny story about how flexible this man was. There was a period of a year and a half when Shlomo and I did not speak. I thought he was very, very angry with me because of this lesbian thing. I called him, and he wouldn't call me back. You know, who knows what it was about?

I called him the day before Rosh Hashanah, and I said, "Look, I don't know what's going on here, but you have been the most important person in my life, and I'm not prepared to lose you. This is a big thing for you to adjust to; I understand that." And I said, "But what I demand of you is that before Yom Kippur, you call me, and you tell me that you don't love me anymore."

This happened six years ago. I said to him, that's the least ... You know, I don't ask him for things. I said, "That's what

I *demand* of you. You call me before Yom Kippur, and you tell me that you don't love me anymore."

And he says, "Darlin'! That's not what it is; that's not what it is!"

And I said, "I don't want to talk to you anymore. Sit with it. I've been sitting with it for a long time. This is really, really hard."

He called me Erev Yom Kippur. He said, "Darlin'!"

I said, "What?"

He said, "This is really a hard thing for me to adjust to," and he said it without an accent, and without sounding like the *rebbe* of the black Jews in Harlem, which was one of his shticks that he would do [laughter]. He was talking to me straight, like he used to when I spent time with him long ago and he wasn't in his, you know, his *meshugunah* [crazy] *rebbe* mode. [laughter]

He said, "This is really a hard thing, and I don't know if I can adjust to this or not. But there's one thing you need to know: there is no way that I can stop loving you." And he said, "You should forgive yourself for letting that enter your mind. I've done something wrong in the way that I've loved you if I haven't communicated that clearly."

We talked about it on a number of occasions past that. And at my son Natan's *bar-mitzvah,* which was two years ago, Shlomo came to a modern Orthodox congregation in North Hampton, Mass., that my lover and I had evaded. Now they're very different in the way that they approach gay people, but then . . . Shlomo came, and he took Natan under his *tallis,* and he said . . . [long silence] He turned to my son, and he said, "You have holy people in your life. And you are fortunate enough to know that your mother and Ellen have parented you well. And you have a family that doesn't look like some other families, but this is the family that you came from."

He put his *tallis* over him and he said, "You have been special since the day you were born." And that's all he needed to hear.

And he had a way of telling people that, in a way that's real, even though it's completely impossible to believe that there's anything special about *me*, you know, what could it be? He had a way of saying it that resonated somewhere,

311

where it got into your neurons. It's like—*There really is something special about me.* And that's all that *any* of us needs to hear.

The next day after the gathering at my apartment, I get an e-mail back from Zalman. He's upset that Shlomo has died penniless, with no estate for his daughters. He's also upset that, for all of us who knew Shlomo, and to whom Shlomo gave so much, we've not responded in kind, either with financial support for his family, or by giving him the honor that he deserved while he was here with us.

Zalman tells me I need to pray for guidance about two things: a way to give back what I received from Shlomo, and a way to find my place in the world spiritually, as a Jew. Immediately a thought hits me—maybe I should try to write a book and tell the story.

32
Shomer

Half Moon Bay, California – December 2007

The book is finished except for this chapter, which I've been putting off for years because it's too painful. But I know, and I've known all along, that without this chapter the story isn't complete.

After years of wrestling with this, I've come to understand that I cannot edit-out the dark side of Shlomo's story, or my own – to airbrush the photo to remove the shadows – without turning it two-dimensional and bleaching out the humanity. Shlomo taught us in the name of Reb Nachman of Breslov that the brightest sparks are hidden in the darkest places, and that it's our job as human beings to go there and find them.

In the years immediately following Reb Shlomo's death, stories began circulating about women who claimed to have had disturbing encounters with him. Some of these women confided in Rabbi Lynn Gottlieb, a Jewish Renewal rabbi.

This part of the story begins in September of 1997. I was then on the Council, the governing board of the Aquarian Minyan of Berkeley, when Rabbi Gottlieb, who is also a storyteller and performance artist, visited the Bay Area to do a one-night show at Chochmat HaLev, a Jewish meditation center in Berkeley. Later she wrote that she did this performance out of a sense of responsibility to the women who had confided in her.

Although I've interviewed people separately, I have decided to present their voices as they sound in my mind, in a kind of chorus:

Reuven Goldfarb (co-founder and leader of the Aquarian Minyan): I was at Rabbi Lynn Gottlieb's talk at Chochmat HaLev. Lynn, whom I have known for many years, is a very gifted and charismatic storyteller. So I had no issue with her *per se.* On

313

the contrary, I admire her very much and I enjoyed her telling that night.

The last story that she told was kind of like a fictionalized account of an encounter that a young woman had had with a visiting rabbi. And we all knew that it was a stand-in for Shlomo, and a person that Lynn knew personally.

Wendy Berk: (my wife, and a witness to Gottlieb's performance): [Speaking to me] This all happened before you and I got together. Lynn Gottlieb was being a very engaging storyteller. She told beautiful stories using gestures and body movements. It was very pleasant and very dramatic.

Then what I remember is, all of a sudden, something switched. She was talking, she was telling this story that happened many years ago to a woman she knew. A rabbi who was a musician came to a summer camp and this woman was very enamored of him, and he behaved inappropriately with her.

I remember being shocked. We all knew who it was; but if anyone didn't know during the story, with everybody getting together and talking afterwards, the word very quickly got out. So it was very clear it was Shlomo.

Reuven: I walked backstage. I just wanted to greet her. I touched her hand. We both knew that she had blown some cover, and I guess we both felt that it was a healthy thing. But it hit hard, and I think it hit some people harder than others.

Later I found out that Lynn had also written something, I believe an article for publication. And in this article, she made very explicit what was only indirectly hinted at in her story. It's one thing to tell a story, and you kind of know who it's about, and it's profoundly moving, and you see that there's a problem here, and you hope it never happens to anyone else, and you should be on your guard, etc. But it's another thing to label [and condemn] someone, and basically implicate anyone who ever had anything to do with him.

Lynn Feinerman: (a member of the Aquarian Minyan) I was aware at that time that there were women in the community who were not happy with Shlomo in terms of how he had behaved with women. But there was nothing personal with me. I had met Shlomo in 1989 or '90 when I was writing a script about Crown Heights [in Brooklyn], about the relationships there between blacks and Jews. And Shlomo

314

took me very seriously, so my experience with him was quite positive.

The talk by Rabbi Gottlieb was reported to me. This happened during the days of *Slihot* [prayers for forgiveness] just before the High Holydays. I was in a high dudgeon over it, and I got involved in the committee that was going to do all the healing work, the Healing Committee.

Aryae: When did you arrive in Berkeley to start your new job as rabbis of the Aquarian Minyan?

Rabbi Nadya Gross: Halloween! I actually remember this 'cause we arrived in the middle of the night.

Rabbi Victor Gross: During our preparation for moving, we received a phone call from Reuven and [his wife] Yehudit, apprising us for the first time that there was a community split over this issue . . .

Nadya: The storytelling.

Victor: Yeah, over the storytelling of Lynn Gottlieb, and how it had split the community. And they recommended that this wouldn't be the best time for the new rabbis to show up, and counseled us that we give serious consideration to holding off our move until springtime. We responded to them by saying that *davka* [especially] this type of situation in a community calls for the presence of spiritual leadership, and that we weren't going to shy away from entering into the fray, and our intention was to keep according to our schedule and arrive when we had planned to arrive.

Half Moon Bay, California – October 1997

When the phone rings I feel annoyed at the interruption of my dinner. I'm still living in my "temporary" apartment near the beach. This week the kids are with Lane, so I'm eating by myself, sitting at the little round table near the sliding glass door, looking out at the sunset over the ocean.

I listen as the answering machine takes the call. It's Marty Potrop. I get up quickly and go to the phone.

After Shlomo passed away three years ago, and after following Reb Zalman's recommendation to pray for guidance, I decided to join the Aquarian Minyan's board, which we call the Council. I like the feeling of being connected in this way to the community. Marty chairs the Council. He holds the title of Shomer. In Hebrew, *shomer* means guardian, keeper, protector. One of God's names is *Shomer Yisrael*, Guardian of Israel.

I pick up the phone. "Marty, what's up?"

"Aryae, I'm glad you're there," he says. "Listen, there's some stuff I really need to talk to you about."

"I think I can guess," I say.

Marty laughs a gallows humor kind of laugh. "Look, we've got Victor and Nadya Gross coming to be our new rabbis, right? Reuven couldn't persuade them to delay coming here, so they're on their way!"

I take a deep breath. "It's crazy—at this point we can't agree on anything!" I say. "How are we going to get it together to welcome them?"

"Aryae, I swear to you, I'm getting a dozen Minyan calls a day, at least! I've been spending *hours* on the phone listening to anger, shouting, sadness, tears, outrage—you name it!

"I'm also getting calls from people who say that this whole conversation is destructive and unfair. Shlomo's dead, he's not here to defend himself, all these stories are 2nd or 3rd party hearsay—the whole thing is *lashon ha'ra*." *Lashon ha'ra*—literally "language of evil"—refers to a body of Jewish law which prohibits injuring people or destroying their reputations by making derogatory statements about them. *Lashon ha'ra* is taken especially seriously when applied to people who are dead and can't defend themselves.

We're both silent for a while. Finally Marty speaks. "Aryae, can I ask you something?" he says, a little tentatively.

"Sure," I say, "What?"

"You were close to Shlomo. During those years, just between you and me, did you know about any of this stuff that people are talking about? Did you ever witness any of it?"

I think for a moment. "Okay Marty, here's the truth: when I was at the House, what I knew was what everyone else knew, about the stories of Shlomo calling women late at night. That's it."

"Aryae, between you and me, what about those phone calls?" Marty says. "I mean, this was a guy in his 40s, a rabbi, making

316

suggestive, late night phone calls to women. How did you deal with that? How did you put that behavior together with someone who was your spiritual teacher?"

I sigh. "That's a fair question." I close my eyes and try to go back to my feelings about Shlomo 30 years ago. "Look, if I could travel back in time as the guy I am today with what I know now, it would all be a lot clearer, right? It would be easier. I could say, 'Shlomo! What are you doing calling up women late at night like that?! Are you crazy? What's going on with you?' Looking back at it now, I wish I could have said that to him.

"But, you know, as a 24-year-old in the 1960s in San Francisco, it was a different world. Our gatherings at the House, like other spiritual communities in San Francisco, were filled with love energy, and that love energy was laced with sexual energy. As young people we were all swimming in it ourselves.

"We all knew that Shlomo had his quirks; the thing is, *we* all had quirks too, and Shlomo never judged us for *our* quirks. He loved each of us, saw the best in us, and accepted us for who we were. He was our teacher and this is what we were learning from him. How could we judge *him*?"

We talk about Victor and Nadya. How will the community come together to welcome our new rabbis when they arrive? It's only two weeks away. With all the animosity and distrust that people are feeling, neither of us can figure out how to do it.

Rabbi Victor Gross: So when we arrived, on Halloween, we received several phone calls that day we were unpacking, informing us about our first *Shabbat* which was going to be the following week, the first *Shabbat* where we were going to be the new rabbis of the community. Because of the controversy and the split in the community, there were going to be *two* Friday night services, one for those that identified with Reb Shlomo, and one for those that didn't. And it would be our baptism by fire to choose which one we were going to lead!

Lynn Feinerman: Now this is where I began to have some feelings, some strong feelings.

It wasn't so much a personal thing with Shlomo at all that I felt. It was a much deeper issue. It was about really all of the millennia of placing women in certain subordinate positions,

317

positions that required them to behave in certain ways, to cover for men in certain ways, to implicitly accept certain kinds of behaviors from men.

Reuven Goldfarb: Things got very polarized. The Council, I felt, was intimidated by people who were issuing threats. Finally there was a decision to hold a series of meetings designed to address the issue that had been raised, and raise our consciousness and sensitize us more to the problem.

I felt helpless to influence the course of events.

Victor: For the next 10 months, this by and large consumed the community.

There was a gathering that took place at different people's houses. The purpose of it was to find some ground for reconciliation of the two sides, for exploration of the issues . . .

Rabbi Nadya Gross: It was the Healing Committee.

Victor: Yeah, it was the *Healing* Committee! I remember the tenseness of those meetings.

Lynn: There was a great deal of agitation. I mean a *lot* of agitation, a lot of anger. It was very, very disheartening and upsetting for me to see how *passionately* people held their ground with regard to the issues that Rabbi Gottlieb had brought up, and how incapable they were of looking at the seriousness of the allegations, looking at the seriousness of the issues and, you know, compassionately listening to each other without blame.

Reuven: All of these Healing Committee meetings tended to reveal something emotionally profound and disturbing at the heart of this whole thing. On the one side there were people who felt a sense of outrage and protest because they felt they, and women's voices generally, had been stifled. On the other side there were people who felt that there was something unfair and something one sided about all this. We were trying to find the balance, so that we could resume our normal, previous congenial relationship with one another. And I don't think it ever quite got restored.

Lynn: My relationship with people who had been some of my closest friends has never been the same. People whom I really

318

held dear were permanently alienated from me, and I from them.

Reuven: I had a lot of reasons to defend Reb Shlomo. One of them was that none of these accusations had ever been presented in a court of law. They were all allegations, and they were posthumous. He couldn't defend himself. Most of these accusations were made by second and third parties, not by the supposed victims themselves. Understand? People were like . . . they were self-appointed champions. So it was very hard to argue with that. I mean, there was no evidence! It was only hearsay. And I felt therefore, there was a problem here!

There were even people who were my adversaries who said, the laws of *lashon ha'ra* should not apply, because they are just tools to protect men from the accusations of the women whom they have victimized.

Lynn: There's a very fine line for me between following a *rebbe* — or *guru* or *imam* or *sheikh* or *roshi* or whatever — and committing idolatry. Not that we don't want teachers. Not that we don't want to admire people. Not that we don't want to emulate people or learn from them, but there's a certain point at which your whole survival instinct gets kicked in, and there's an incapacity to face what's really in front of you.

Let me define what I think idolatry is: I think it's *survival attachment* to any mind-set. If you are pressured to change that mind-set, it's as if you are dying.

Victor: A certain member of the Minyan came to us at our house and said that she strongly objected to the invoking of any aspect of the laws of *lashon ha'ra*. Her grounds were that so much of it revolved around gossip, which was seen primarily as a women's activity, and that these laws existed in order to silence women. Nadya and I discussed this at great length, and we made a decision to suspend the application of the laws of *lashon ha'ra* for the duration of the Healing Committee's work.

At the end I felt that I had made a grievous mistake. This was extremely painful for me. Because the power of the word is so strong, and what was said was all over the place, both truth and fiction, that I think that our decision to rescind those laws allowed for too much speech that went far beyond

319

Jewish law and, quite frankly, beyond American law about what is libelous and what is slanderous.

[. . .] I'm still disturbed by the inability of the accused to defend himself. Shlomo could not answer for himself.

Lynn: For me the two feelings personally that I had were a kind of bewilderment and a desire to clarify the issues, and disappointment and pain in the way that the men in the community kind of put up a wall against looking at it.

Victor: Maybe this is just personal to me, but I think it also affected other men in that process. I felt that I was suspect for the first time in my life, simply because of my genitalia. [laughs] So Victor being Victor, I walked up, sat down in a chair, and said, "I want to make it very clear that I have no apologies whatsoever to offer to anyone, for having a penis!"

Nadya: An awful lot of our time and energy went into those Healing Committee meetings. I believed that the reason we were meeting was in order to create a healing for the greater community. But every time we were getting close to making some progress, something would come up within the committee that would set us back.

In the smaller setting we weren't able to heal. How were we going to create healing for the larger community?

Reuven: The final Healing Committee meeting ended in an uproar.

Nadya: I remember producing a final gathering, a "tent of healing." It came way too late, way after many people no longer remembered what precipitated the trouble in the first place. Some people had become so polarized, and in some cases re-traumatized — because it brought up their own personal traumas, and ways they been taken advantage of, or sexually abused, or whatever — so that by the time we got to this tent of healing, there was no way to do something that could be both inclusive and productive. I still don't feel to this day that we actually accomplished much of anything.

Half Moon Bay, California – December 1997

Hanukah is late this year, falling on the last week in December, between Christmas and New Year's. Noe and Adam and I are in my living room, sitting on the floor at the low table, playing *dreidel* while we watch the flames on the candles in the big wooden *hanukiah.* Through the window right in back of the candles, we can see the black night sky filled with stars. Around us, where we're sitting, the floor is strewn with paper, torn wrappings of Hanukah presents.

The phone rings and I answer it.

"Aryae?"

"Hi Marty. Listen, I'm with my kids and we're doing Hanukah. Could we talk another time, maybe tomorrow?"

"Aryae, I know. I'm sorry about the timing, but I really need to talk to you. This will just take five minutes, I promise. If there's more to say, we can finish tomorrow."

Marty's not normally this insistent. Something's wrong. I tell Noe and Adam I need to take this call for five minutes. Noe looks at me knowingly, then rolls her eyes and shrugs. "Whatever," she says.

I go into my bedroom, close the door, put on the reading light and sit on the bed. "Marty what's up?" I say.

"Between you and me," he says, "I'm really not doing so good."

"Why? What's the matter?"

"I'm quitting as Shomer," he says. "I'm going to announce it at the Council meeting in January."

"Quitting? Why?"

He laughs. "Do I need to spell it out?" he says. "Between the demands of my graduate school program, my work, and *this,* I just can't handle it anymore!" Marty is in the midst of a masters degree program in organizational development at Cal State Sonoma, which is about an hour's drive from Berkeley. He goes into the latest details from the Minyan, about who's shouted at him, who's pleaded with him, who's tried to manipulate him. He needs to get away from it all.

"Marty, I totally understand," I say, "but we're still in the middle of this thing, and the community needs you. You're the steadiest and sanest one around. Without someone strong to hold the center, the Minyan will fall apart."

"Thank you," he says, "I appreciate that vote of confidence, I really do. And believe me, if I felt that I could do any good at this point, I'd try to hang in there longer. But I know of one other person who's strong enough, and has the respect and trust of everyone, who could handle it."

A couple of seconds of silence. "Marty, no way!" I say. "Besides, what about Reuven? He's much more of a pillar of the Minyan. He can do it!"

"Aryae, you're forgetting one little thing, and that is, he decided to take a hiatus from the Council and isn't a member this year."

I tell Marty there are two reasons I don't want to be Shomer. The first is it's hard enough to juggle being a single parent with all my other responsibilities. I hate leaving Noe and Adam alone in the evening to drive to Berkeley, and being Shomer would make it worse. The second is that I'm not neutral when it comes to Shlomo.

"Look Aryae," he responds, "Reb Zalman started this holy community over 20 years ago and—you're the one who said it!—without a strong Shomer now, it just won't hold together. You know it, and I know it. I gave it my best shot, and I just can't do it. It's that simple. Now it's your moment to step up."

"Okay, Marty, thank you for *your* vote of confidence in me." I laugh. "I'll think about it, pray about it, and get back to you tomorrow, okay?"

Noe and Adam have turned on the TV set in the living room and are laughing at some kind of comedy show. I struggle to get their attention and it takes a while, but eventually the TV is off and we're back to the game of *dreidel*.

Later that night, when Noe and Adam are both asleep, I sit on my bed, close my eyes, and talk to Shlomo. I still do that. When I have an important decision to make and need help, I talk to Shlomo, just like when he was alive. And he doesn't answer me in words; he shares an infinite moment. His presence is filled with love. Tonight he feels tremendously sad, filled with sorrow at the pain he has caused.

What should I do? I ask him. Until now I've been sort of standing on the sidelines, keeping myself out of the fray. Should I jump in and vigorously defend your memory? Do you want me to do that? Should I try to find women who feel you've hurt them and try to talk to them? What does God want me to do?

In response, I see images of him when he was here in this world, doing what he did in situations where people were upset. I see him loving people on both sides of the argument, not taking sides, trying to forgive everyone, trying to get them to forgive each other, trying to make peace between them.

322

It's too late now for Shlomo to undo whatever damage he has done, too late for *him* to ask for forgiveness. I get another image in my mind, of sitting by that swimming pool with John Seaman 30 years ago, talking about the House of Love and Prayer. *Maybe it's not Shlomo's job,* John had said. *Maybe it's yours.*

I call Marty the next morning. I'll do it, I tell him. If the Council wants me to be Shomer, I'll do the best I can.

Aryae: So after all the drama and pain of that year in Berkeley, what did you learn? What are the lessons? And from your perspective today, who was Shlomo?

Lynn: There's a wonderful Sufi saying. I think Rumi said it. *You have no idea of how many tigers are running between the legs of your teacher.* Is that great or what? You know spiritual teachers can be really wonderful and they can offer tremendous things to communities and to other human beings and so forth, but they still have to grapple with their own tigers all the time.

Nadya: I had lived a pretty sheltered life until then! [. . .] This experience burst my protective bubble. It really prepared me to work with my eyes wide open and with much more awareness and consciousness around the varieties of wounding that people, particularly those who are drawn to Jewish Renewal and other spiritual communities, bring with them. I would not have been able to serve as a rabbi in the Renewal world without those lessons. It was a really hard way to get those lessons, but it was sure a quick immersion. [laughs] It made me aware that I had to get educated.

It was *painful* to try to hold all of those things in balance. The pain of people we were coming to love so deeply, and the real pain of other people who had been re-traumatized, who had nothing to do with Reb Shlomo, but that their own abuse stories had been reactivated. Then there were those who just liked to jump on the bandwagon and pretend, or also get attention. We had to learn to discern amongst those.

Reuven: I was 100% a Reb Shlomo partisan, because I felt he was being unfairly attacked. And I'm still 100% a Reb Shlomo partisan.

I never had an exaggerated idea of Shlomo as a demigod or a big *[tzaddik] gamor* [completed, perfected human being], and neither did he, you know? I didn't have to be disillusioned about Shlomo 'cause I never had any illusions in the first place. Okay? [laughs] But I think a lot of people did. And a lot of people couldn't handle the fact that he was a rabbi. You know? A *rabbi*? He was a *man!*

Haven't all of us done things that we're ashamed of, or embarrassed about, including in the sexual realm? Have we all been such perfect saints? We've all done stuff like this. I think in a way it's like, putting the finger on Reb Shlomo and excusing ourselves for things we don't want others to know about and it's like *"He* did it, *he* did it!" You know?

I don't think the argument about what Reb Shlomo did or didn't do has ever been resolved, and maybe it never will be, but one thing is clear. Such behavior is looked down upon in the Jewish world, and in the Jewish Renewal world in particular, and is now generally penalized, often severely. Since Shlomo was outed after he was dead, people who are alive and do these kinds of things today have less camouflage to protect them.

So maybe something good actually did come out of all this.

Lynn: Some of the main people who had issues with him, I think they were responding maybe not so much to Shlomo in particular as a leader, as a *rebbe,* but to the whole question of the position of women in Judaism.

He was a fine musician who gave a lot of very beautiful songs to Israel and to the Jewish people. He was a person who was deeply a Jew, and very steeped in Jewish tradition, whose mind went back before the Holocaust. And he adapted in a very beautiful way to having lost all of that and to living in a new era in America. A very, very high person in a lot of ways, and a person who could teach and who could *transmit.*

You know they talk about *shaktipat* a lot in Hindu tradition.* Well I felt that kind of thing from Shlomo. I felt him when he was performing in particular, but also when he

---

* *Shaktipat* is the transferal of spiritual energy, most often discussed in the Kashmiri Shaiva tradition of Hinduism. Its recent usage owes much to the founder of Siddha Yoga, Swami Muktananda (1908-1982).

was just with people; he had a certain kind of energy flowing through him that was, for want of a better word, holy-energy.

I think that he was fairly young and unmarried when he had most of these incidents that people brought up, and he may have been able to understand himself better as a sexual person once he was married. So here was a person who was not able completely to handle the tigers between his legs that had to do with sexuality. That was my personal look at him.

But my personal viewpoint was also affected by the fact that my community did not seem to want to really look at and acknowledge women's positions, in all these millennia, what women had had to put up with. [sighs] *Most guys on the planet* are not able to take a look at what's happening with women, and what women are going through, and what women put up with. One has to understand that women like me feel the pain of those women. Their lack of safety is also our insecurity. Their pain and torture and torment are also ours.

I can understand people's survival attachment to Shlomo. I really, really can. It's just that we need to keep an eye on that for ourselves.

Wendy: As someone who never met Shlomo, I feel a great deal of sadness about missing such a great teacher. My image of him is of somebody who channeled such great light, and who had so much love for others, and who really tried to reach others, and who did so much good. [Speaking to me] Not only did he bring so many people back to Judaism but also, from what I've learned from you about your years with him, he also had a very *universal* message.

He also slipped up and caused hurt. It's sad that there wasn't a way to make amends . . . That's the sad thing.

He *also* was hurt. You can see that in his teachings, you know, his Torah of the broken heart. He preached to the *wounded*, to the holy beggars. His message reaches all of us who have been wounded and who are hurt. We feel that we still matter in this world, that there's still goodness. It's a teaching for all of us. We're all wounded. We can also reach out to others with love and with joy, and can do good in this world.

Victor: I grew up in the 1950s in a congregation that was morose, depressed, Holocaust survivors for the most part.

Being a Jew meant, *stick it to Hitler!* There wasn't a hell of a lot of positive stuff. The first person that I ever encountered that expressed the opposite side of the coin of that morose Judaism was Reb Shlomo.

In Ecclesiastes it says that there's not a righteous person who sins not. He wasn't a *tzaddik*. He was a *beynoni* [in-between person, like most of us] who strove to achieve righteousness. He erred. He sinned.

And his accomplishments . . . he was, like in the words of Reb Zalman, a *tzinor,* a pipe, between God's desire and the people that he encountered. He raised our consciousness. He opened up avenues to experience Judaism in a very, very different way. He was one of the book ends of Reb Zalman and Reb Shlomo, for the renewal, the rejuvenation, the revitalization of Judaism in our day. *And* he was a man who worked in the 60s, coming from a background that was repressed. He needed help, as all of us need help, to get over the confrontations with things we don't understand and don't know how to deal with.

I'm so, so grateful that there was a Reb Shlomo in our time who offered his music, his teachings, his passion, and his love for *everyone*, particularly the downtrodden. Particularly teaching us that the *beggar* is the *holy beggar*, and not to be denied.

His wrong offended me. It's probably why I didn't become a Hasid of his. Does it consign him in the *Olam HaBa* [World to Come] to a lower level when you measure somebody in the scale of merit and wrongdoing? If it hadn't been for this, the scales would be tipped *so far*. But they're more balanced now, because of the errors of his humaneness, and of the time he lived in, and of his own personality. *Vezehu* — that's all I can say.

Wendy: What is it when you feel that your teacher has no flaws? You're denying your teacher his or her humanity as well. If it's just Shlomo the *tzaddik,* or just Shlomo the bad guy, then you're not giving him his wholeness.

None of us likes to think of our spiritual teachers as making mistakes or not walking their walk. How do we hold appreciation and compassion for Shlomo, and also for the women who have come forward with their stories of being hurt by him? I'm learning a lot, just by going through this with you. I'm becoming more compassionate and accepting, more of a whole person.

What we're all looking for is wholeness.

Nadya: One of the things that became so, so clear to me in that period of time through you and others, is this: his greatest gift was the thing he tripped over, and that was his enormous capacity for love. When it was channeled in its best possible way, his heart cracked open to God, and he invited people to take a ride on that love and know God the way he knew God.

But when he turned to his small self, when he found himself trapped in the *katnut* [smallness] of his humanness, that incredible capacity for love, and the need to express it, got [distorted].

I remember a personal experience, a retreat I was on one time without Victor. After every session I would run out and call Victor. I did it to ground myself; because the love that was flowing there, the energy, the vibration was so *huge* there was nothing I could do. Victor got more phone calls from me! [laughs]

So I identify. Maybe I'm projecting onto Shlomo, but that's what I'm projecting. He had such an incredible, an enormous capacity to feel that love and that longing, and he used it for so much good. And when he didn't have that vehicle for the good, he unfortunately didn't know how to *ground*. He went to ground himself in inappropriate ways.

It was painful coming to terms with all of that during those years, and during that year particularly at the Minyan, but today here's what's left for me. I firmly believe that he suffered, in the process of his *aliyat neshama* [ascent of the soul], that he had to go through the process of being and living and experiencing the embarrassment, the pain, the discomfort that he may have caused to anyone else in his lifetime. I believe that that's part of our process. I know that he suffered. And I know that, as a result of that, his soul has integrated the lessons, and he's that much bigger even than before, *because* of the harshness of those lessons.

And today all I want to do is take a ride on his capacity to love.

327

Accord, New York – July 2000

Wendy and I are standing outside of a little cabin at the Elat Chayyim retreat center in New York State, waiting to see Reb Zalman. It's very warm on this summer afternoon, quiet except for the sound of insects buzzing, some leaves rustling, and an occasional muffled human voice somewhere in the distance.

Two years ago at this time Adam had his *bar-mitzvah*. Victor and Nadya officiated. Reuven and Yehudit were on the platform with them, co-officiating as elders of the community. Wendy was also onstage with her guitar, singing during the service as part of a local Jewish music ensemble. It was at a funky but well-known jazz joint at the beach near where we live. Lynn Feinerman, who was making a documentary about the history of Jewish Renewal, filmed an extended interview of my father Sammy, me, and Adam each describing our own bar-mitzvahs over three generations in our family.

In his *bar-mitzvah* speech Adam talked about his great-great-great grandfather, Aaron the *Kohen* [priest], brother of Moses. Aaron's role, and the role of his children who came after him, was to bless the people. Adam felt that, like his great-great-great grandfather, he was here to bless people, to make people happy, and his way was through music. So after the ceremony he brought his band of 13-year-old musicians onto the stage. The music was great, and everyone—from his friends to his grandparents—danced for a long time.

Noe has made it through two years of college at University of California at Santa Cruz. She's like a kid in a candy store, exploring all kinds of knowledge. I love driving down there to visit her, to take in the creative counter-culture atmosphere of this campus in the redwoods, to hear her speculate about the many exciting possibilities in her life. There's a state park nearby on the coast that's a nesting ground for thousands and thousands of butterflies. We love to walk through the tall trees, watch the butterflies, and engage in long philosophical conversations about meaning and truth.

Wendy's turning 50. When I asked her what she wanted for her birthday, she said, "A blessing from Reb Zalman." So I signed us up to spend the week here at the time of her birthday so she could get his blessing.

When she and I met at the Aquarian Minyan, we were initially drawn together as friends. Her second marriage was ending. Mine had ended years ago. We were both hesitant to open our hearts and try yet again. She volunteered to be on a Minyan committee that I was leading. The drama and conflict generated by the stories of Reb

328

Shlomo never entirely healed and soon the attention shifted to Victor and Nadya, to whether the Minyan would invite them and fund them to stay permanently as rabbis. The community became polarized around *this* question, just as it had around the other. Wendy and I had become close friends with Victor and Nadya and wanted them to stay. We got to feeling like we were war buddies, battling together in the trenches.

When the level of turmoil and instability became unsustainable, Victor and Nadya accepted a job offer to move themselves and their kids to be rabbis in Boulder, Colorado. They're moving this month. In response to a situation where I felt I could no longer have a positive influence, I resigned last month as Shomer and left the Minyan. Half the Council and much of the community followed.

Wendy and I, war buddies and now lovers as well, still feel traumatized. She's shared a dream with me. It seems so simple. "Wouldn't it be amazing," she said, "to be in a spiritual community that was all about people loving and caring for each other?"

"Imagine that!" I said. "What a concept!" *V'ahavta L'reyakha Kamokha* — Love Your Neighbor as Yourself — is the central commandment of the Torah, literally written right in the middle of the Scroll.

"This is the entire Torah," Rabbi Hillel said a couple of thousand years ago. "All the rest is commentary." When Victor and Nadya were with us at the Minyan, they were always talking about "holy community" and trying to lead us in this direction.

A community where "love your neighbor" would be the shared focus, to practice conscious relationship with each other as a path to becoming more aware, compassionate, loving, God centered human beings — this is a dream that has grabbed us.

Somebody once asked Shlomo, who is this "neighbor" that we're supposed to love? Shlomo said, "It's the person who's standing closest to you right now."

Suddenly the door opens and there's Reb Zalman looking at us, beaming. "So what are you waiting for?" he says. "Come in!" In his mid 70s now, he looks like a grandfather delighted with his grandchildren.

Inside the little cabin there's a fan blowing, and a table with three chairs. Reb Zalman offers us some cold juice and we accept. He wants to know about the Aquarian Minyan. We talk for a while about our experiences over the past few years, about the heartbreaking controversy over Shlomo, and the traumatic exit of Victor and Nadya, followed by the splitting of the community. I feel like I've let Zalman

329

down. As Shomer, it was my responsibility to guard the Minyan, to look after its well-being. I've failed terribly, and feel awful.

Reb Zalman looks at both of us with great love and great sadness, and sighs. "Reb Aryae," he says, "many years ago when I came to Berkeley, I couldn't get things with the Minyan to turn out the way I wanted either! These things aren't in our hands." We sit in silence for a while.

Then Zalman stands up and motions us to join him. He opens the door of the cabin. The three of us walk out and stand there, looking at the trees.

He puts a hand on each of our shoulders. "So when are you getting married?" he says suddenly. We're both startled. Wendy's divorce hasn't come through yet; there's a lot that's still unsettled in both our lives, and we haven't made any decision about getting married. We try to explain all this to him.

Reb Zalman waives his hand impatiently and interrupts us. "I want to be at your wedding to give you a blessing," he says, "and I don't have forever!" He puts an arm around each of us and holds us tight.

"*Nu?*" he says, looking first at her, and then at me. "So what are you waiting for?"

33

A Place to Pray

Ramot Polin, Jerusalem, Israel – Friday Afternoon, December 2003

It's a little after 3:00 PM. In December it gets dark early in Jerusalem and *Shabbos* starts by 4:00. Wendy and I park our rented car in one of Ramot Polin's two parking lots. We take out our overnight stuff, changes of clothes, wash kits, books, etc., and lock-up the car.

Besides being *Shabbos,* tonight is also the first night of Hanukah. In Israel, people put their *hanukiot* (eight-branched Hanukah candle holders) in glass cases, which they place outside their doors. We see lots of people rushing around with their glass-cased *hanukiot,* making their final preparations for *Shabbos* and the holiday.

We find our way to Efraim and Leah's. Leah, wearing a colorful neck-to-ankle-length dress, opens the door. She smiles warmly at us, holds her hands together and closes her eyes. Then she gives Wendy a hug, and tells us that Efraim has gone to *daven* and then to the *mikvah,* and should be back soon.

There's Shlomo music playing from what sounds like a small tape recorder in the living room. The striking look of their condo hits me all over again: the beehive architecture with wall and ceiling surfaces that tilt toward each other at various angles, the dome-like feeling of the space, the walls alive with Efraim's mural paintings that make it seem like we're in the midst of a garden that opens onto other gardens.

Sitting on the couch in the living room, bouncing up and down to the music, is Yehoshua. He's 11 years old, a Down Syndrome child that they adopted several years ago. He needs continual supervision and lots of attention. He has become Leah's responsibility; she now spends most of her time with him. He looks at us with curiosity. Then he looks at Leah, then at us again. The tape recorder is sitting on the little table in front of him. He makes some sounds and points to the tape recorder and then to us.

Leah laughs. "Yehoshua, that's Aryae and Wendy! I'm sure they like the Shlomo music too!" I smile and clap my hands to the music. Yehoshua gets up, bobs up and down, and steps sideways around the living room. Leah claps. "That's wonderful dancing Yehoshua!" she says. I move around and dance with Yehoshua. Wendy joins Leah in laughing and cheering us on.

"He's such a holy angel," Leah says. "He brings joy to everyone. A pure, holy angel!"

Time passes and Efraim still hasn't returned. Wendy goes into the kitchen with Leah. I sit on the couch with Yehoshua.

In the ultra-Orthodox world, if you're waiting for someone and have some time on your hands, you don't read the paper or surf the Internet or watch TV; you study Torah.

I've brought a book with me from Moishe Yitzchak and Bernice's: the S'fat Emet on Hanukah. The S'fat Emet, who died in 1905, was the second Gerer Rebbe, one of the last of the great Polish Hasidic spiritual masters. I pick a passage in Hebrew and start to read.

My understanding of the text is that the word Hanukah can be separated into *hanu kah*, "thus we camped," meaning in the spiritual reality hidden within the material one. Because the essence of the miracle of Hanukah is the battle we won in the material kingdom, or illusory reality, within which we were dwelling in those days. Therefore the Sages wanted to reveal to us that the essence of joy is the liberation from our servitude in the kingdom of flesh and blood, in order that we will be able to enter into the congregation of those who (instead of serving their oppressors) are serving God. This is also a consolation in our own generations. For even when we think that we have fallen so low and things seem to keep getting worse and worse, why are we filled with such great hope? It is that God is also liberating us, right here and now. With God's help we can return to wholeness in one minute.

Efraim comes in, breathless, light as an angel, his eyes shining, his beard still wet from the *mikveh*. He smiles at me. "You're here?"

"Yeah, I guess I am!" I say.

"*Barukh HaShem* [praise God]!" Leah says from the kitchen.

I get up and Efraim and I hug each other. He takes off his coat and hat, then goes into the kitchen to greet Leah. I follow him. In the middle of the kitchen is a large table where she has laid out the meal she has been preparing, which is remarkable. Besides the obligatory meat dish, there are a variety of vegetarian dishes laid out in a colorful, attractive way that looks more like California cuisine than Jerusalem *frum.*

"What's this?" Efraim says, gesturing at the food on the table. "It must be take-out food they sent down from heaven!"

Efraim and Leah aren't touching each other, but the warmth between them is palpable. Wendy and I exchange a smile.

It's time to light the Hanukah lights. Efraim and Leah and Yehoshua each have a *hanukiah,* with little oil lamps. They've also set up one for Wendy and me. We say the blessings together and each light our lights. Yehoshua is very excited. Efraim holds his hand and helps him light his oil lamp. We sing *Ma Oz Tzur* (Rock of Ages).

After we've lit the Hanukah lights and the *Shabbos* candles, it's time for Efraim and me to go to *shul* and *daven.* Leah and Wendy stay at home.

Efraim is wearing a *kappote,* a garment worn on *Shabbos* and holidays that looks like a long silk jacket or robe. It is white with thin brown stripes. Over his *kappote* he wears his long black outer coat. On his head he is wearing his *strimel,* the traditional fur hat that Hasidic men wear on *Shabbos* and holidays. He looks like a king from Poland 300 years ago. I'm wearing my black ski jacket and my simple black *kippah,* the one that Efraim rescued earlier in the week.

It's dark out and drizzling. We walk quickly through the streets of Ramot Polin. Everywhere, men dressed similarly to Efraim with strimels, and boys wearing fedora hats, the kind that used to be worn by men in the U.S. in the 1930s and 40s, are rushing quickly in all directions, on their way to *shul.* There are no women in the street.

"Where are we going?" I ask Efraim.

"To one of the Breslover shuls," he says. "There are two here. This one's a little further away." He says there are 36 shuls all together in Ramot Polin.

The Breslov *shul* is a large room with high ceilings and many small electric lights, filled with men and boys wearing their strimels and fedoras, milling around and talking. The room is arranged with long wooden tables, each with chairs on one side, all facing toward the front of the room, toward the ark that houses the Torah scrolls.

As we walk through the room, men and boys turn to look at us. Efraim smiles and greets everyone. *"Gut Shabbos, gut Shabbos!"* Most of them smile back at him and return his greeting. The men and boys look at me with curiosity. "Good *Shabbos,"* I say. Some then nod to me in response, others look away and continue talking to each other.

It looks like everyone has a table where they are accustomed to sitting. Efraim walks me to a table to the side near the back. "This is a good place to *daven*," he says. I sit down. He remains standing. "I usually *daven* by myself near the front." He's going to leave me there to my own devices. I feel a sudden flash of panic. "Is that okay?"

"Sure," I say. "No problem."

In the middle of the room is the *bimah*, a raised platform with a large lectern called a *shtender* that faces forward. From here the *shaliah tzibur*, the representative of the community before God, leads the davening.

The *shaliah tzibur* is tall, in his early 30s, with a long black beard. His voice is an intense, piercing tenor. His eyes are closed, his hands are on the *shtender*, and he is rocking back and forth. The way the davening works is, the *shaliah tzibur* chants a sentence or two at the beginning of a section. Then the congregation davens. This starts loud, as everyone begins together, and then the volume tapers off, as everyone davens on his own. It's like a wave crashing, where it starts forceful and then spreads out. Sometimes the *shaliah tzibur* will chant something else out loud in the middle of the passage and some people will follow him, like the crashing of a smaller wave.

I realize that the trick in following along is to pick up on the rhythm of these waves. Since I've never prayed in a place like this, it takes me a while. My instinct, based on my experience in Orthodox shuls in the States, is to rush through the words as fast as I can for fear of being left behind. When I try davening like that here, I quickly get lost. As I look around and listen, it gradually dawns on me that no one here is rushing. People are pouring out their hearts to God, not just as a ritual, but for real. To find the rhythm I need to slow down.

It is *Shabbos and* the beginning of Hanukah, a time of double joy. These men are followers of Rebbe Nachman, who emphasized serving God with joy. I can feel the Hasidim around me reaching deep into themselves to the place of joy, and giving it a voice with passionate intensity. The room is filled with joy.

Even the young boys are making passionate gestures in their prayers. I can see that some of them are trying on these gestures self-consciously, like trying on clothes, imitating the men, seeing what fits. The oldest men, the ones with long white beards, seem the most graceful, with joy radiating from them softly, naturally, unself-consciously, the sweet fruit of long lives of spiritual work.

I gradually find the rhythm and let the waves carry me together with everyone else, connecting with the joy within *me*, dancing like a small wave with the other waves in this harbor.

At the end of the prayer service the Hasidim make a big circle around the room and dance. I join in. As we dance we sing *Shabbos* songs to Hasidic melodies. The men on either side of me sing loudly, with enthusiasm.

After the dancing is over, the Hasidim shake hands with each other and wish each other *"Gut Shabbos"* as they button up their coats and prepare to leave. They come up to me as well, and I return the greetings. It's like I've been initiated and can now be accepted, if not as part of the community, at least as a recognized guest.

I'm feeling tired and hungry, and looking forward to our *Shabbos* meal. Efraim's talking to a couple of men, one of whom has a couple of boys with him. I walk up to them. Efraim's the grandfather, the old sage of this group. He introduces me to the others and we shake hands. Efraim explains to me that, as is their custom, this little group is going to spend a few minutes studying Torah before going home to their *Shabbos* meals. I mentally roll my eyes, wondering how long this "few minutes" will last.

An hour later as we're walking home in the light drizzling rain of a chilly Friday night, Efraim and I are the last two people out on the streets in Ramot Polin. We can see Hanukah candles still burning in glass cases in people's doorways.

I ask Efraim to tell me more about his teacher, the Rav. He reminds me of the letter he wrote me from Israel over 30 years ago, in 1970, about how he and Reb Eliezer Berland first met. They were both young men then. Efraim never calls him by his name anymore, always referring to him as the Rav.

The Rav persuaded Efraim to accompany him to the village of Uman, which is near Kiev in the Ukraine, on Rosh Hashanah, to make the pilgrimage to Reb Nachman's grave. In 1970 during the heyday of the Soviet Union it was almost impossible for an outsider to travel in and out at will, and travel was especially dangerous for Jews who looked like Jews. But somehow these two managed to get to Uman and return in safety.* They went back every year, taking more and more people with them. Today thousands of Breslover Hasidim from all over the world make the pilgrimage to Uman each year. I have

---

* For nearly 50 years, this most important Breslover pilgrimage was impossible, due to Soviet control of the region. However, the Rosh Hashanah pilgrimage was re-established in 1965, after an intrepid Breslover Hasid, Rabbi Gedaliah Fleer, made secret journey to the grave in 1963 a great personal risk.

read that the business from housing and feeding them has become Uman's largest source of income.

Efraim and Leah, and the Rav and his wife, the Rabbanit, became close friends, often spending *Shabbos* at each other's apartments. But as the years passed and the Rav gained more and more followers, and the demands on his time kept increasing, it was no longer possible for these friends to spend much time together. The Rav is now the spiritual leader for thousands of Breslover Hasidim in Israel and around the world. He seems to serve a function that is similar to a *rebbe* but is more hidden, more in the background, more like a kind of vice president than a president. Efraim now gets to have private conversations with him only once or twice a year.

Back at home, Leah and Wendy and Yehoshua are waiting for us. Wendy later tells me that, in a strange way, she feels more comfortable as a woman here than at the Moshav. Here the men and women each have their own world. The men's world is the *shul* where they are in charge; the women's is the home where they are in charge. Here women at home, totally separate from the men, are free to create a holy space of their own.

We sit around the *Shabbos* table, which Leah and Wendy have set with great love and care. Efraim holds up the silver *kiddush* cup and says *Kiddush* to a Breslover melody: "Blessed are You, God, our power, ruler of the world, who has made us holy with your *mitzvot* and taken delight in us, and your holy *Shabbos*. With love and favor you have granted us, memory of the creation of the beginning of all things." When he's done, we all say "Amen!" Then, rather than taking a sip and passing the wine around to the rest of us, the way I expect him to, he slowly drinks the whole cup, with great relish. Then he passes the silver cup and the wine bottle to me.

"What's this for?" I say.

Efraim laughs. "For you to make *Kiddush!*"

"But you just made *Kiddush!*" I say.

"You make it too!" he says.

I look over at Leah. She smiles and nods. I pour the glass full to the top, the way Efraim had done, the way we used to do at the House, and make *Kiddush* to the "Good *Shabbos*" melody that Shlomo taught us 35 years ago, the one that he had learned in 1939 in Baden bei Wien, Austria from Moishele. Leah closes her eyes and nods her head. Efraim closes his eyes, goes "tsssss!" and lifts his hands toward heaven. Wendy looks at me and smiles.

After the meal is done, and the blessings and singing are done, and the table has been cleared, we're all tired and it's time to go to sleep.

"What's the plan for tomorrow?" I ask Efraim.

He smiles and lifts up his hands toward heaven. "The plan is *Shabbos!*" he says. *"Shabbos Kodesh* (Holy *Shabbos)!"* He does a little dance.

I laugh. "Where are we going to *daven?"* I say.

"On *Shabbos* I *daven* at Mea Shearim where the Rav is," Efraim says. "After davening we go to a place near the *Kotel* (Wall). The Rav gives a *shiur* (lesson) and we learn Torah. Would you like to come with me?"

"Why not?" I say. "I don't have other plans!"

"It's a long walk," Efraim says. "It's about an hour and a half to go to Mea Shearim, and then another half hour to the *Kotel.* On the way there it's almost all uphill. Can you handle it?"

"I think I can handle it. What's the *shiur* like?"

Efraim closes his eyes and waves his right hand. "Tssss!"

"Is it all in Hebrew?"

"Hebrew and Yiddish."

"How long does it last?"

Efraim laughs. "I don't know; I don't have a watch! I'd say, maybe two or three hours."

I consider the situation. I can see myself sitting for three hours, in the middle of a large group of Hasidim who are carrying on a lively Torah discussion, me not having a clue about what anyone's saying, tired, hungry, and stuck there without a way to leave until Efraim is ready to leave. It's a sobering image.

"Do you think it's going to rain tomorrow?" I say.

Efraim shrugs. "It's raining tonight."

"Do you walk there if it's raining?"

"Why not," he says, imitating me. "I don't have other plans!"

Wendy and I are sleeping in the bedroom where the children slept when they were young. We each have a child's bed, separated with a little dresser in between. We kiss each other goodnight and then lie in our beds, talking in a whisper for a while.

Saturday Morning

It seems like I've just managed to fall asleep when there's a knock at the bedroom door. My eyes reluctantly pop open. "Yeah?" Everything is dark.

The door opens a little. "Are you awake?" says Efraim softly. I can't see him.

"I don't know." I say. "Is it morning?"

"Yeah, it's quarter to five. I just went out and it's raining a little. Do you want to come with me or stay?"

I'm feeling disoriented. "I don't know."

Efraim laughs softly. "Well if you're coming, we have to leave in 10 minutes. You better dress warmly because you'll probably get wet."

"Maybe I should stay."

Efraim laughs. "Maybe that's a good idea." He says he'll be back in the afternoon, wishes me "Good *Shabbos,*" and the door closes.

When my eyes open again, everything's still dark. We can't turn on any lights because it's *Shabbos*. I manage to find my clothes and get them on. Wendy wakes up. "What are you doing?" she says.

"I don't know." Here in Ramot Polin the only people in the house on *Shabbos* morning are women and girls. My presence would probably make everyone uncomfortable.

"Wendy, what should I do with myself?" I say in a whisper. "I can't stay here. And it really feels kind of intimidating to just show up at a strange *shul*, looking like I'm from a different planet, not knowing anyone, not speaking Yiddish. I wouldn't know what their customs are or what they expect from people or how they *daven*. I couldn't even explain who I am or why I'm there. I'd feel like an idiot."

"Why don't you ask Leah for advice?" she says.

Leah's in the kitchen. The clock on the wall says a quarter to seven.

"Good *Shabbos* Leah," I say.

She looks up at me and smiles. "Oh, good *Shabbos,* good *Shabbos!*"

338

She asks how Wendy and I slept and I assure her that we were very comfortable, and that it was special for us to sleep in her children's bedroom. I ask her advice on where to *daven*.

She looks thoughtful. "Oh, I don't know," she says with a little bit of a frown, "there are so many places. I honestly don't know them so well, but I'm sure they're all wonderful." We both stand there for a moment, not saying anything.

Then she looks at me again, and we make the briefest of eye contact. "Aryae," she says.

"Yeah?"

"Just ask *HaShem* for guidance."

"How do you mean?"

"Just ask *HaShem* to take you where He wants you to be."

I take a breath and consider that. "Okay," I say, "okay, I can do that. Thank you." I smile at her. Then I go back into our bedroom and say goodbye to Wendy.

It's cold out even with my ski jacket on. A few men and boys are walking quickly in various directions. It seems like the *Shabbos* morning rush hour is probably drawing to a close, and most of the men and boys are already in *shul*. "God please show me where you want me to *daven*," I say to myself. I wander around slowly, trying to figure out where the shuls are.

A man in a *strimel* and a long black coat spots me wandering, so he comes up and asks me in Hebrew where I'm going.

I'm feeling a little tongue-tied but express myself as best I can. *"Ani tzrikh makom l'hitpalel,"* I say. I need a place to pray.

"Nusah Ashkenaz ou Nusah Sfard?" he says. Do you want to pray according to the rational Litvaks or the mystical Hasidim?

"Nusah Sfard," I say. The way the Hasidim pray.

He looks at me. Perhaps he's a little surprised. He points to a nearby hilltop and says there are shuls there. I thank him and wish him "Good *Shabbos*." He turns and hurries in the opposite direction.

There are three shuls at the top of the hill. Each one has a different style of architecture. At the first, three teenage boys with fedoras look at me curiously as they hurry past. At the second, there is no front door. An old man standing at the side door looks up at me. At the third, the sign says something about Karlin and the Karliner

Rebbe.* I remember Shlomo telling us about the Karliner Rebbe. From inside this *shul,* I hear voices, really loud, that sound as if as if they're yelling and screaming out to God. *This is the one,* I think.

Inside it looks like part Hasidic revival meeting, part madhouse. Everyone is in motion. The cacophony of voices is all encompassing. Some Hasidim are pacing back and forth, mumbling prayers in their own melodies. Some are holding up their hands to heaven and yelling. A couple of men are pounding on the walls. One old Hasid is leaning against the wall and crying. Another is slouched over his table with his head in his hands.

Everyone is so absorbed in his praying that no one even bothers to look at me. It hits me immediately: *I feel safe, completely at home. This is my place to pray.*

I find my way to an empty seat at a table near the middle, take off my ski jacket and wrap myself in Efraim's black and white *tallis.* A Hasid standing nearby notices me and shows me where we are in the prayer book. I listen and watch to catch the rhythm of the waves in this part of the Ocean. After five or ten minutes, I've got it, and for the next three and a half hours, I'm riding with the rest of them. The passion and intensity are overwhelming. I give myself over to it, allowing the waves to sweep me up and carry me along.

At one point, during the Torah reading, a couple of Hasidim come over to me. One of them asks my name. "Aryeh ben Shmuel HaKohen," I say. Aryae, son of Samuel the Priest.

They look at each other. *"Kohen?"* he says to me. I nod. They exchange a few words, then smile at me and shrug. At first I don't understand. Then I get it. They wanted to call me up to bless the Torah. Being called up to bless the Torah is the greatest honor that a congregation can bestow on anyone. It is usually reserved for their distinguished members. But because I'm a *kohen,* and a *kohen* has already been called, they can't call me up, because it would dishonor me, or rather the *kohen* in me. I whisper that I understand, and thank them for wanting to call me up. They smile and step back.

I'm amazed. Even though no one seemed to notice me when I walked in, I obviously was noticed, and someone wanted to give me the honor of including me. It seems like a miracle that I found my way here, a stranger praying with these Hasidim whose world is so different from mine, merging with them in pouring out my heart to God.

---

* Rabbi Aharon the Great of Karlin (1736-1772), the first Rebbe of Karlin, was a senior disciple of the Maggid of Mezritch, known for the great intensity of his prayers.

After the service is over, the Hasidim are clustering together in little groups. At first I don't understand what's going on. Then I see young men carrying trays with wine and cake. They bring a tray to each group. Someone in each group says *Kiddush* over the wine, and everyone else says, "Amen!" Then someone makes a blessing over the cake, and everyone has wine and cake. Rather than wait for someone to invite me into their group, I quietly slip out the door.

It's a little after 11:00 AM. The rain has stopped and a bit of cold winter sun is peeping out. The sidewalks of Ramot Polin are filled with men and boys walking home from *shul*.

Back at Efraim and Leah's, Wendy and Leah are talking in the living room. Wendy says that Leah told her about her women's group where each woman chooses special Psalms to read to bring about healing in the world. Leah has her own set of Psalms, which the two of them read together.

Leah offers me some cake that she has baked. On *Shabbos* morning, you can't really have a meal until the men return from *shul* and all the blessings are said, so it is customary to eat cake. Leah says that Efraim told her he would be back around 2:00, so we can eat then. I thank Leah for the cake, take a piece, and make a blessing. I'm hungry so I have two pieces.

Wendy and I take Yehoshua for a walk so Leah can have a little precious time to herself. The three of us must make quite a sight wandering around Ramot Polin, with me in my black ski jacket and *kippah*, Wendy in her pink ski jacket and black soft hat for covering her hair, and Yehoshua in his winter jacket, excited, wandering in all directions at once. Every once in a while he'll stop at something that catches his eye, like a leaf floating in a puddle of water. He'll bend over and look at the leaf, and then look up at us with great delight. Sometimes as we're walking he'll grab Wendy's hand and hold on tight as he lurches this way and that. The great gift he's giving us is to share his world of being totally in the present, seeing everything with excitement and surprise.

After we return, get our coats off and hung up, Wendy sits on the couch. Yehoshua wanders over and without any hesitation sits on her lap. Wendy's eyes widen in surprise and she looks a little uncomfortable. Then she adjusts her position and gently puts her arms around him.

Leah walks in and laughs and claps. "This is *very* unusual!" she says. "Yehoshua almost never sits on anyone's lap but mine."

Wendy has never had kids of her own. Building her relationships with Noe and Adam—getting to the point of comfortably sharing love—has taken time, and has been a learning curve for everyone.

I smile at Wendy. "He must feel something about how you feel about him," I say. Wendy nods and closes her eyes and tightens her arms around him just a little.

Leah tells us about Down Syndrome kids in Haredi communities, where there is an unusually high incidence of Down Syndrome. Part of it is that they don't terminate pregnancies. And part of it is that women often have children well into the older limits of their child-bearing years. The social safety net here has nothing to do with government agencies; it's all about families supporting each other. In Yehoshua's case, his birth family was unable to take care of him. Leah was in charge of the *mikveh,* the ritual bath where religious women go each month to immerse themselves in accordance with Jewish law. Many women confided in her. When she learned about Yehoshua, Leah, now a grandmother with 30 grandchildren, decided that she wanted to accept the *mitzvah* of raising this child.

The Torah describes 613 kinds of mitzvahs that a Jew can do. Some of them, like giving money to the poor, visiting the sick, praying, or keeping *Shabbos,* have limits, set times, or boundaries. Other mitzvahs have no boundaries, just as God has no boundaries. Leah spends most of her days caring for Yehoshua, and there is no end in sight. Tirelessly and joyfully performing this *mitzvah* with no boundaries, Leah is in a continual state of serving God.

While we're waiting for Efraim, I study some more from the S'fat Emet on Hanukah. Wendy and Leah talk. Wendy teaches Leah women's songs from women rabbis and teachers in Jewish Renewal. Then they read Leah's Psalms. Wendy reads them out loud in English, while Leah reads them in Hebrew.

Women's spirituality, it seems, also has no boundaries; maybe divisions between the spiritual right and spiritual left, between Jerusalem and California, which seem so impenetrable to men, can be more easily transcended by women. I get the image of Wendy finding women of wisdom across the spiritual spectrum and making the connections.

There's a knock at the door. It's already 2:45. Leah opens the door, and Dovid walks in. Dovid has a long black coat, but unlike Efraim, is wearing a fedora rather than a *strimel.* We all wish each other "Good *Shabbos.*" Dovid nods politely to each of the women, and they nod back. I get up and give him a hug.

Dovid and his family are also here because of the House of Love and Prayer. When he first came to the House as a 19 year old, the attraction was immediate and overwhelming. He soon moved in and was a complete holy beggar along with the rest of us. One of his early memories of the House is of me at age 24 teaching a class. What really struck him, he said, was the way I was teaching. I wasn't telling people what I knew or thought. I was asking them to tell me and each other what *they* knew or thought. The message to him was—the wisdom of Torah is in each of us.

When Dovid, then David, did what Efraim and so many others did, leaving the House in search of a place to learn, he wound up, not in a Hasidic community, but in a Litvak (Lithuanian Orthodox) *yeshiva* in New York.

Hasidic yeshivas emphasize the relationship between the *rebbe* and the student, on serving God with joy, on learning Torah by learning from your *rebbe*. Litvak yeshivas emphasize acquiring the tools of intellectual inquiry, being curious and skeptical, asking questions, and not accepting something, even if it comes from a revered teacher, until you really understand it.

Dovid is now a respected rabbi who teaches classes and leads kollels, adult study groups. When I was at the House, my image was, the Hasidim are filled with love and joy and God intoxication, and the Litvaks are dour and serious and judgmental. Dovid, with his joyful smile, his open heart, and his great humility, has totally blown away that stereotype.

He spots the book next to me. "What are you learning?" he asks.

"S'fat Emet on Hanukah," I say.

"Tell me something new you've learned this *Shabbos*," he says.

Looking at this distinguished Litvak rabbi with his long black coat and long gray beard sitting in front me, I instinctively feel a little intimidated. But Dovid's smile is disarming. I tell him about Hanukah as *hanu kah,* camping in the spiritual reality within the material one, and the S'fat Emet's commentary on this.

"So what does that mean to you?" he asks. I answer by talking about Hanukah as the miracle by which we are finding the reality of the divine sparks hidden in the illusion of the material world, and that when we kindle the lights we are really liberating those sparks, and that by doing so, we can restore the world to wholeness.

"Okay," he says, "so what does that mean personally to you in the way you are living your life?"

343

I pause and think about this. "Good question," I say. After reflecting a bit, I talk about my experience of this trip, represented by my image of traveling from Palo Alto, California, capital of the land of stuff, to Jerusalem, capital of the land of soul.

Dovid leans forward and makes eye contact with me. "And how is all this relevant for the choices that you made today, and for the ones that you'll make tomorrow and the day after?"

"Another good question," I say. I try to think about my ordinary day-to-day life, about waking up early in the morning to work on my book, about the hours I spend on e-mail and the phone organizing the HR Forums, about my relationships with Wendy and Noe and Adam, about the various health issues of my aging body. How would holding the awareness of *hanu kah* change my actions?

Suddenly I realize something. Now it's my turn to lean forward and smile.

"What?" says Dovid.

"You were just showing me your teaching style," I say. "This must be the way you teach Torah to your students!"

Dovid laughs. "You're right," he says. "And you know something?"

"What?" I say.

"I first learned to teach this way from you, 35 years ago." I look at him and nod, then close my eyes.

At 3:30 Efraim rushes in, breathless. He apologizes, explaining that the Rav extended the Torah study longer than usual.

As Leah and Wendy hurriedly set food on the table, Efraim invites Dovid to join us for our meal. Dovid politely declines, reminding us that tonight is the House of Love and Prayer reunion at Joe and Shoshana Michaels', organized in honor of my and Wendy's visit, and that we'll all be seeing each other again soon. I give Dovid a hug and we wish each other "Good *Shabbos.*"

While we're eating, Efraim says he has something very special to tell us.

Earlier today, *Shabbos* morning, at the high point of the morning service, with hundreds of Hasidim in attendance, the Rav was standing on the *bimah* as he always did, reading from the Torah. A few Hasidim were on the *bimah* with him. Efraim was sitting toward the back of the room. In between *aliyot* (sections of the reading), for no apparent reason, the Rav interrupted the ceremony and suddenly turned to the Hasidim standing around him. "Where's Simcha?" he asked. The Hasidim looked at each other, not knowing what to make of this. "Where's Simcha?" the Rav repeated.

Everything stopped while the Hasidim searched through the crowd. They found Efraim, and brought him up to the *bimah*. When he got there, standing with the Rav at the Torah in front of the hundreds of Hasidim, the Rav put his arm around him and asked him about his guests from the States. Efraim hadn't told the Rav about having guests.

"Your friend," the Rav said, "is he from the House of Love and Prayer?" Efraim never talked to him about the House.

"I'd like to see him," the Rav said. "Can you bring him to see me after *Shabbos?*"

As we sit there listening to Efraim's story, we're all blown away. People travel from all over the world to see the Rav, and usually have to make an appointment weeks or even months in advance.

"How did he know about me, or that Wendy and I are in Israel?" I say.

Efraim smiles and shrugs.

"Why does he want to see me?"

Efraim has no idea. Wendy is looking at me, beaming as if I had just been summoned by the Nobel Prize committee. Leah closes her eyes, smiles and holds her hands together. *"Barukh HaShem!"* she says. "This is such a *mehaya*, such a blessing for life and such an honor! You have no idea."

"The House of Love and Prayer reunion is at Joe and Shoshana's at 8:00 tonight, right?" I say to Leah. She nods. "Can we go to the Rav after *Shabbos* and get back on time?" I ask Efraim.

Efraim promises me, with great certainty, that time will not be a problem.

345

34

Feast of the Queen

Jerusalem, Israel – Saturday Night, December 2003

We get to Joe and Shoshana's over an hour late.

Efraim, who must be picking up on my mood, glances over at me with a smile as I'm parking the car. "Don't worry. It'll be okay," he says. "Maybe people take the time on their watches very seriously in California; I don't know, I don't remember so much. But, you know, time is different here."

Earlier this evening we were standing in the entrance hall of the Rav's apartment. It occupies the second floor of a four-storey building in Mea Shearim and has its own elevator stop. His wife the Rabbanit, a small, thin woman in her 60s with a big smile, apologized and said that the Rav was sleeping because he was so busy with visitors that he hadn't slept in three days. She asked if we could return again tomorrow evening. She'll call Efraim tomorrow to let us know a good time, and he'll call me at the Moshav. Efraim asked her if it would be okay for me to bring Wendy. She smiled at him mischievously. That's wonderful, she said, but then you have to bring Leah too. He laughed, and promised he would.

Joe and Shoshana live in a large house situated on a large lot on a hillside with a panoramic view of the lights of Jerusalem below and the stars above. They're hosting this get together as a *Melava Malka,* which literally means Feast of the Queen. It is a traditional Saturday night celebration for saying goodbye to *Shabbos,* the Queen. We walk up to the high front door, kiss the *mezuzah,* and knock. We can hear sounds of people inside. No one answers so we walk in.

People are scurrying about, talking to each other. I see Joe, a big bear of a man in his *strimel* and black silk robe. A doctor, rabbi, and professor, well into his seventies, he has the drive, energy and enthusiasm of someone many years younger. He recognizes me and we greet each other with a hug. As with my other friends in Jerusalem from the good old days – on one level, we're very different now and everything has changed; and on another level, nothing has changed. Shoshana spots us. Her face lights up and she comes over. She looks a little like the Rabbanit, small and thin and frail, but her high-pitched voice is as musical as ever, and her smile is as sweet.

Joe and I walk through the house. It's large, with many rooms. Shoshana is an artist and her paintings hang on the walls, filled with images of radiant luminosity, magical circles, rainbows, nature, children, light breaking into this world from Beyond. Joe tells me about the institute that he and Shoshana have started. They have programs which offer medical professionals, clergy, and lay people opportunities to study healing from both a medical and a spiritual perspective. This house serves as the institute headquarters as well as their home.

People are swarming around a big table set up in one of the rooms. Not quite knowing what to do with myself, I sit down at one end of the table. Moishe Yitzchak with his camera sits down at the other end. Uri Simcha, Efraim and Leah's oldest son, has brought his digital video camera. The last time I saw him, I was 25 years old and he was three. Now he's a competent and kind religious man in his late 30s, who will be video recording this celebration.

After everyone is sitting I ask Joe and Shoshana what they would like to see happen tonight. Shoshana smiles at all of us and says how beautiful it is that life has brought us together again. Joe says that he was thinking we could all give each other blessings.

I then talk about my desire for us to share stories and memories, and that I would like, with everyone's permission, to record these. I look around to try to read peoples' expressions. Mostly I see blank stares. There's a long silence. Then Elana leans forward and speaks. "What will our stories and memories be used for?"

Aryae: I feel like what *HaShem* most wants me to do at this point in my life is to tell the story, the way I experienced it, of Shlomo and all of us and the House of Love and Prayer. So about eight years ago I started writing this book. My dream is, with God's help, to share this story with millions of people all over the world.

It's been really hard for me to do this. Wendy can tell you. [laughs] My *yetzer ha'ra* [bad inclination, inner opponent], which is at least as creative as my writing ability, keeps telling me it will never happen. But I've promised a lot of people, including myself, that with God's help it will.

So Elana, what I'm really hoping for is that, by sharing your stories and memories, you'll help me keep my promise.

Aryae, Wendy, and Elana Schachter. Photo by Moshe Yitzchak Kussoy.

Wendy: I would like to put in a plug for those of us who never met Shlomo but were very influenced by him. We would like to know what our roots are. We would be grateful to all of you to tell us about the beginning, because we're so influenced now. You all made a big difference for us.

Aryae: Okay, so who's got a story?

Efraim: When we were first coming to see Shlomo, we were with Ian . . .

Leah: Ian Grand.

Efraim: Ian Grand. He introduced us to Shlomo. It was in '65 or something. He heard that Shlomo was coming to Berkeley and San Francisco, and he said, "You gotta come see my friend." He said, "He's a rabbi and a folksinger." So I thought to myself, that he's a rabbi is not so interesting to me, but that he's a folksinger sounds interesting.

So I went to meet him, and after that it was incredible. Because Shlomo—first of all, there's something about the melody. You know, when you open with the melody, it just gets into your heart. The melody is one of the deepest things that there is in the world, if not the deepest. [strumming his guitar] A melody can transform all time. It's out of time; it's connecting you to the roots of your soul.

349

So anyway, we were back there, and Shlomo was singing these melodies. If there would have been just the melodies . . . You know, there's a lot of nice melodies—*Barukh HaShem*, there are no melodies like these—but there are nice melodies. But the words . . . the words and the words and the words.

What was Shlomo telling us in those days? Mostly, there were stories. He knew us; he knew who he was talking to. It wasn't the time to get into long, complicated Torah teachings and everything. So we're hearing the stories and we're thinking, *What's going on here? Who are we? Where are we? What are we supposed to be doing with our lives?*

So after a couple of years Leah and I decided it was time to leave San Francisco. We were in New Jersey staying at my parents' house . . .

Leah: We were on our way to Israel.

Efraim: In the mean time, Shlomo was in New York. We spent Pesah at Shlomo's house—Shlomo's mother's house. That was the first time I really saw Pesah. The way that Shlomo's mother set up the house was incredible. [To Leah] She put these boards, remember, in the sink? And she was doing everything, running around, getting everything ready. We thought Pesah was just to eat *matzah!* [laughter] And there weren't that many people. Shlomo's father had already passed away.

Leah: He had *just* passed away; it was the first Pesah he wasn't there.

Efraim: We were at a concert, I don't know if anybody else was there. We were at the concert where his father passed away.

Leah: Donna Maimes was there.

Efraim: He was giving a concert in San Diego, and we were there, singing with Shlomo, and he invited everybody up onto the stage, anybody who wanted to.

The person in charge of the concert came up to Shlomo while he was right in the middle of the concert and whispered in his ear, "Your father has passed away." It was really a mistake, *al pi halakha* [according to Jewish law] to tell

350

him right in the middle of the concert; but we didn't really know *halakha* so well.

Shlomo told us afterwards that he went on automatic pilot. He went completely blank, and he kept going, and he did the whole concert 'til the end, and then he . . .

Elana: But Donna said when they were leaving, he squeezed four of her fingers in her hand so hard.

Leah: And he wrote a song.

Elana: Which one?

Aryae: U'Makah HaShem.

Elana: How does that go again?

Efraim: [Hands Aryae the guitar.]

Aryae: I heard Donna tell the story of her version of the concert. We had a kind of a *Shloshim* [traditional 30 day memorial] at my place in '94, and Donna was there, and Jill was there. Donna told the story and said it was on the plane that he composed this song. She considers it his greatest song. [I play and sing the song. Everyone gradually joins in. A slow, simple melody in a minor key.]

> *U'makah, makah*
> *Makah HaShem*
> *Dima, dima*
> *Me'al kol panim.**

So we were in the middle of the story of how you got to the House.

Efraim: We were back in New Jersey, and there was a Shlomo concert in Brooklyn College. We went to the concert, and it was outside, I think. After the concert Shlomo came over to us, and he said to us, "Aryae just got this great house; it's *mammash* an *incredible* house! You gotta go back there and join him!"

---

* Isaiah 25:8. In translation, "Wipe, wipe / God will wipe / tears, tears /from every face."

Aryae: He had never seen the house! [laughter]

Leah: He said a very strong thing. He said, "If you try to go to Israel now, it's not the time." He said, "If you go now, they'll just knock you off. If you go back to the House, maybe after a year . . ."

And it turned out just a year, even though we didn't time it or anything. We went back to San Francisco during the Omer [the period of counting 49 days after Pesah], and we left during the Omer of the next year.

Joseph: It was awesome, because Shlomo only came out maybe once out of three or four Shabboses. So Efraim and Aryae were really carrying the whole energy of the place for three out of four Shabboses, with huge crowds of people who were incredibly turned on by the spirit of *Shabbos.* It was very awesome.

Shoshana: It was so peaceful!

Joseph: It was hard for us to imagine how you could do *Shabbos* without Shlomo, but you people did *Shabbos* without Shlomo. It was awesome; it was a Shlomo *Shabbos.*

Efraim: Well we didn't do *Shabbos* without Shlomo, we did *Shabbos* with Shlomo; he just wasn't there. [laughter]

Joseph: There were always food miracles at the House of Love and Prayer. It seems like on Friday night there would be multiple hundreds of people . . .

Moshe Yitzchak: At least, at least.

Joseph: We'd be davening *Erev Shabbos* [Friday night], people hadn't eaten since lunch, and we'd be davening until what, one, two in the morning? How much food was there for these few hundred people? There was what, maybe a couple of boxes of *matzah* and a couple of jars of *gefilte* fish? [Various comments from the group about the food.] This was the first year, and there was . . . Unbelievable! Everybody seemed satisfied. I don't think anybody ever complained that they didn't have enough to eat.

Elana: I remember going down to the farmers market on Friday and collecting produce from the people there—that they didn't think would make it through the weekend [laughs]—and bringing home cases of, I don't know . . . And Lois would turn it all into *Shabbos* food.

One of my strongest images is Lois making *hallah,* in one of those pots like that, sleeves rolled up to her armpits . . . [gestures to show rolling the dough—laughter] Hundreds of people. Hundreds of people.

I remember one *Shabbos* . . . Remember Hibiscus? There was this guy named Hibiscus, who was like . . . Let's just say he was eccentric. [laughter] He used to dress in lace tablecloths. [laughter] He was the creator of the Cockettes. It was the gay Rockettes dance troop. [laughter] One Friday night he brought his whole *hevra,* his whole dance troop. And they had gone to the flower market, like we went to the vegetable market, and they got all the roses that wouldn't make it through the weekend. They came with this truckload of roses. And I remember they scattered rose petals over the whole floor of the House of Love and Prayer. As we were dancing, the aroma of roses was just overwhelming. So amazing; all night, it was just like—roses!

Elana Schachter. Photo by Moshe Yitzchak Kussoy.

353

The way it all started for me was, I was going to college at a little school in Claremont, California, and I became a hippie. [laughs] And this friend of mine says, "Come, we're going to see the Singing Rabbi." It just so happened that this was the same friend that turned me onto LSD, so I figured, I can trust his judgment! [laughter]

By the end of the evening, Shlomo had everybody singing and dancing and crying and hanging on to each other and sweating together and just . . . You know—you all know what he could do to an audience, right?

I wanted to see him again, so I set up a concert for him in Claremont. It was May Day 1968. After the concert he said, "I just started this house in San Francisco called the House of Love and Prayer, and everybody's invited to come for *Shabbos*."

That summer I was hiking in Yosemite, and I was hitch-hiking back to Los Angeles, and I got a ride, and they said, "We'll take you as far as San Francisco." When we got to San Francisco they said, "Where should we drop you?" I whipped out Shlomo's card, and it said "House of Love and Prayer, Arguello Boulevard," so I said, "How about here?" And they dropped me off.

As I got out of the car, everybody was piling into the VW bus, and they said, "Come on, come on! Get in, get in!" And I said, "Where are you going?" And they said, "We're going to the *mikveh!*" And I said, "The what?" [laughter] And they said, "Never mind, just get in." [laughter] It was Friday afternoon, and we went to the *mikveh*. And that was it, I'm still there! [laughter]

So that's how I got there. And I walked in . . . I didn't even make it in the door before I felt welcome! And since I haven't left, I guess I wasn't missed!

Judi: The first time I came to the House was Hanukah, when Efraim spoke at the *Hobonim* [a non-religious Zionist youth group] meeting. [laughter] And I decided . . . He said, "We have this House where we keep *Shabbos*, and everyone's invited."

So I felt that I had to like, dress the part, and I put on my hippie clothes because I was like, really very conservative. And I remember tying a scarf around my hair, and trying to look very hippie-ish and cool, because I really wasn't very

354

cool. [laughter], and going in there and just being completely, like, overwhelmed.

I remember having a lot of questions, and nothing really made sense to me. I had recently lost my brother, and I also lost my grandfather, and I felt my family — at that point — was disintegrating. We had been a very close family, and all of a sudden, it started disintegrating because of these two tragedies. And I felt very strongly that I was Jewish, but I didn't understand why. And I knew that I was an atheist, because I had always been told that I was an atheist. I never really thought about it.

And I just remember like, I was at a Shlomo concert and he was talking about, you know, the six million and the concentration camps, and he was still saying *"Od Avinu Hai!"* [The name of one of Shlomo's songs: Our Father still Lives. God still Lives.] We're still here. *Od Avinu Hai.* And it made such a connection with me. I suddenly realized that I'm here, and I'm Jewish, because our Father in Heaven is still here. And it was, it was . . . when I think about it, it was such a mind boggling realization to me. Everything in life just became different and clear and real.

And Aryae, you were such a part of this. I mean, it was really in you're *z'khus* [merit]. I can't thank you enough; because it was really you who showed me that, and brought me to that realization.

I still remember when you went to my parents' house. [laughs] Because I was trying to keep kosher on *Shabbos* and my parents weren't allowing me to; and you and Shlomo, and the little Volkswagen and me [laughter], we all went to my parents' house. And there was this whole big argument, because I wanted to keep kosher, and my parents wouldn't let me. And my father said, "He's not a real rabbi!" [laughter] And it was a big tear scene.

And shortly afterwards, I think a few months later, I was at Beis Yaakov! [An Orthodox girl's high school in Denver for girls from religious families.] And I remember like, they accepted me, which was a miracle within itself.

I remember when a whole bunch of people from the House came to visit me at Beis Yaakov [laughter]. It was a real scene! I was in my . . . not only were there uniforms, but they were striped green. They were like hospital green [laughing] with puffy sleeves and a pleated skirt. And I was like, you know, if I was trying to be hip before, I was exactly

355

the opposite now. I was in the class, and the rabbi comes in, and he says, "Judi, there are some . . . ah, some . . . [laughter] people . . . to see you." And I came out there, and there was a whole group of people from the House, and they were like, "Judi, I love you!" [lots of laughter and comments] I remember the scene so well. And I remember the principal watching this, like you know — this is absolutely amazing.

Anyway, okay, that was like one scene from Beis Yaakov. But one thing that really . . . after Reb Shlomo passed away [sighs], I went to the funeral. I felt, although I had no *kesher* [connection] with him all those years, I felt a tremendous sense of gratitude for what he had given me, and I wanted to show that. And then, I was at the next Beis Yaakov reunion, which we have every year. The principal took me aside and he said, "Do you remember that singing rabbi? Did you know that he passed away?"

I said, "Well yes, of course, I was at his funeral."

And he did a double take. And he said, "You went to his funeral?"

And I said, "Well Rabbi Schwab, you always taught us the importance of *hakaras ha'tov* [recognizing goodness], and I think that, for a person who gave me so much, I should have done much more; the least I could have done was go to his funeral." And then he said something that totally, totally, totally amazed me.

He said, "You know, I didn't want to take you into our high school. I had a big argument with Rabbi Lipner [the rabbi in San Francisco who recommended her]. And I said, 'I will not take her, she's a hippie!'" [laughter]

And Rav Shlomo got on the phone, and he said — he lied — he said, "She's not a hippie; I can promise you she's not a hippie! Please take her to your school. And if you don't take her, her blood's gonna be on your head. That's how you're gonna save her."

And he was so strong with him that he took me into his school. And he said, "Under no circumstances is she ever to know that I spoke to you." Shlomo said that to the principal. And it dawned on me afterward what a tremendous thing he did; because he didn't want to hold me back. He wanted me to be able to go into the community and become who I am, and integrate myself as part of the community, and not to pull me back where I always had to feel . . . Well I owe it to him for doing this for me; and I mean, it was such a tremendous, tremendous *mitzvah*. I can't . . . [sighs] Well you know, I think I've said enough.

When I look at myself and my family, Aryae, I just really think, *thank you*.

Aryae: Thank *you* Judi!

Judi: Because I wouldn't be here today, and I wouldn't have what I have if it wasn't for you.

Moshe Yitzchak: Judi, you ought to write that in a story.

Judi: Some things you can't write.

Shulamis: Memories . . . Growing up in Berkeley was really transitional. The summer of, what I think was '68, was the summer that I met all of you.

You guys came to my high school. From the beginning of the year to the end, that school went through a total transformation, you know, kind of a microcosm of what was going on in the world. In the beginning of the year, I was telling Aryae the other day, all the teachers were dressed like teachers with, you know, shirts and ties. By the end of the year, there were no shirts, no ties [laughter], their hair was down to their shoulders. The kids had all "turned-on" the teachers. They were smoking dope down on the playing field. There was no furniture left in the classrooms, no desks, just a big rug, with a teapot in the middle [lots of laughter]. I'd show up with my *Shabbos*-keeping friends, jumping up and down, singing. I feel very grateful, really. All of you were so much a part of that, my finishing growing up.

I was literally on the first plane out of high school, to Israel. I even finished high school early so I could leave sooner.

It was the winter of '72. It was cold; it was freezing. I didn't know. It was such a shock to find out that it was *cold* in Israel, and also inside my apartment. I don't think I crawled out of my down sleeping bag all winter! [laughter] I did because I was going to *ulpan*.

I think my role model of what a Jewish family was, were you [reaches her hand toward Efraim and Leah]. I wanted that; I wanted that for myself. I was miserable when I first came to Israel, but I was too ashamed to admit it. You were living in Migdal at the time. I used to come for *Shabbos*.

I had to decide what I was going to do, and Leah turned to me that spring and said, "Shulamis, I just can't see you leaving the land." [To Leah] And I wanted to leave, but after you said that I just felt like I couldn't. So I didn't. I stayed. So, I'm still here.

Shulamis Green. Photo by Moshe Yitzchak Kussoy.

I feel very grateful. [To me] We had a wonderful day the other day sharing, sharing things that are important in my life. Thanks.

Aryae: You gave me the great gift, for the first time in my life, bringing me to the *Kotel* (Wall).

Shulamis: I really felt very honored.

Aryae: I didn't really know what the *Kotel* was until I was there.

Shulamis: I never had a real idea about what it was, either. I still don't.

I learned *Yerushalaym* [Jerusalem] by walking to the *Kotel* three times a day from wherever I was. I felt always like a bird, you know, finding the spot. And I really felt then each time like I was coming home. So [to me] I hope you find your spot. [long silence]

My boys are both into Shlomo's music. They both play the guitar. They actually wanted to come tonight, but they're each, you know, doing their thing. But they feel close.

Aryae: I hope I have a chance to meet them.

Shulamis: [smiling] I hope you do.

Shoshana: We've experiencing here again the extraordinary energy of the House of Love and Prayer. Everybody wrote their unique form of soul-understanding and service. You know? It was like creating an awesome crown, a sacred crown for the King, when people get together with so much connectedness to something very holy and very beautiful. And we all experienced it so totally differently, but the core, the essence, the beauty, the strength, the *kavod* [honor], the *kedushah* [holiness], the awesomeness, you know, it was feeling *HaShem's* presence. When we were with Shlomo, we could feel *HaShem's* presence.

And we have no concept of what's behind the scene. Sometimes maybe we will know. But *HaShem* was so pleased with us because He could use us to bring down His blessings to the world. You know the 60s was an extraordinary time. The whole world desperately needed it, that awakening. The 60s, 70s, 80s. And the hippies were very brave; they could feel that it was so necessary that there should be a change away from the horrendous materialism. And they went in the absolute opposite direction, barefoot, disheveled, doing crazy things. People were, you know, bewildered, and parents were desperate.

It settled down in a very beautiful way in Israel. All those wonderful flower children found their way to a good life, creating beautiful families, and doing *teshuvah* [returning] in very, very holy ways. We've been so privileged to be part of this great phenomenon.

Dovid: I have trouble speaking. [To me] I told you this before we got together. I start crying, so if I stop in the middle, you'll know why.

359

Elana: We have plenty of tissue.

Dovid: I'll try to stay away from the emotional stuff, so I can keep going. . . . Lois, I just want to say thank you; you should live until 120.

Several people: Amen, amen!

Dovid: [To Lois] I'm sure that on the Moshav you're doing the kind of things that you were doing in the House. You should be blessed with *nahas* [pleasure] from your children.

When I came to the House, it was a very tumultuous time in the world at large, and . . . [long silence] the experience of coming to the House was very, very meaningful.

[To me] You had a profound effect. I didn't meet Shlomo for months until after I had come to the House. My *hinukh* [education], my initial starting with all this, was from you, and Dovid Din, and all the people that were there at the time. The House was a *neshama* [soul], a very, very special *neshama*. And it had many special aspects to it—a lot crazy aspects to it—but there was a presence of the *Shekhinah* [Divine Presence] there that was . . . you could cut it with a knife sometimes.

I mentioned to Aryae that I had also been on a spiritual search that took me into many avenues. All of them were very, very short-lived, because for me, there was no substance to it. The House was a place that was so full of substance. [People are sitting with their eyes closed, nodding.]

The ringleader of the substance was Aryae. [laughter]

But it came from everybody. The House was a group of people that all were trying to bring out their best. The best is too weak a word. There was something special. It's the *Shoresh HaShekhinah* [the root of the *Shekhinah*], the *Shekhinah* that was in each of us, was being brought out in different ways, and being tapped into in different ways, at a time when it was unheard of. There was no *Shekhinah* in the world. It was lost, at least in that part of the world. And here were people all coming together, and the effect of all of them together was just tremendous.

I remember sometimes when somebody would go to *Eretz Yisroel* [the land of Israel], you know, go to the airport, and we'd see them off. [laughter] It was unbelievable!

Elana: [laughing] With the guitars!

Dovid: "May your going be in peace . . ." [To me] Was that your song?

Aryae: [laughs] Yeah, yeah.

Dovid: It was such an occasion when somebody was going to *Eretz Yisroel*. It was the togetherness. There were times when, you know, it needed vessels to hold it. There were times when sort of a gate would open up, and you would see this togetherness, and light, and the specialness that was nowhere else in the world to be had. And I think it was from everybody opening up their specialness. And the mass effect of this was awesome.

So that was the House of Love and Prayer that I came to. I just felt this, this specialness. So that's what brought me back and grew on me. It became a part of me, and I'm eternally grateful.

I love you Aryae.

Aryae: I love you too man.

Dovid: I'm so grateful that we had this opportunity. I'm so glad you came to *Eretz Yisroel*.

Elana: Yeah! [laughter]

Dovid and Aryae embracing. Photo by Moshe Yitzchak Kussoy.

Dovid and I stand and hold each other. When we're done, Efraim passes me the guitar. I play and we sing my song that we would sing to people at the airport when they were going to Israel.

May your going be in peace,
May your going be in peace,
Messengers of peace,
Messengers of the Most High.

I'm feeling overwhelmed at the outpouring of love and gratitude.

I've always known about the amazing impact of the House on peoples' lives. What I didn't know is that they attribute so much of their choice, and of the direction their lives took, to me. It's almost more than I can handle.

Someone, maybe it's Elana, says, "Let's give blessings to Aryae and Wendy!" Everyone agrees. People start giving us all kinds of blessings. Shlomo taught us all how to bless each other, and everyone here is very good at it. The pace and the excitement build.

Abundance after abundance after abundance flows from people's hearts to Wendy and me. The blessings are like rivers of water rushing down a great mountain toward the sea, seeking and finding a direction of their own. The direction that's emerging is that, now that I've come to the Holy Land after so many years to reunite with my friends in such joy and love, and have brought Wendy with me, that this momentum will continue.

We are blessed that we no longer have to be separated from the Holy Land.

We are blessed that She should open Her gates for us.

We are blessed that *HaShem* should lead us to our place here, a beautiful home, loving community, abundant livelihood, fulfillment of all the dreams of our souls.

We are all blessed that we can reconnect to rekindle the fire of Shlomo's vision that first brought us together 30 years ago—of bringing the Great Shabbos, the great day of love and peace, to the world.

The excitement builds to such a pitch that the blessings morph into concrete ideas about how Wendy and I could actually get started with our move: good places to live, business opportunities, places to study. With a fast Internet connection, Internet phone service, and smart ways to pick up frequent flyer miles, I could run my business from here, and benefit from the same income I've been earning in the States.

I begin to picture all this happening. Maybe I've found my answer. Maybe I've really come to the end of my journey. Maybe it's time, after all these years, to finally arrive in Jerusalem.

I look over at Wendy. She looks startled, even a little panicked.

In the midst of all the commotion, I see Efraim hold up his hand. The room gradually quiets down and soon everyone is looking at him. He catches my eye and smiles. "I have a little *brakhah* [blessing] for you and Wendy," he says softly.

He speaks with a kind of authority—born of the passionate, humble and gentle simplicity of his life—that we all recognize.

"What does *HaShem* want you to do?" Efraim says. "I don't know. How can we know what *HaShem* wants?" He smiles and shrugs. "All I know is—what you're doing now is, you're traveling back and forth between California and Yerushalayim—and the Holy Sparks in both places, so many Holy Sparks, and where *HaShem* wants them to be . . . we have absolutely no idea. What do we know?

"So Aryae I want to bless you that on all your journeys, you'll bring the Holy Sparks with you, from California to Jerusalem, from Jerusalem to California, as *HaShem's* faithful messenger, for as long as *HaShem* is sending you."

He looks at both of us, Wendy and me. "And I want to bless both of you, and Leah and me too, and all of us, that it shouldn't take you

30 years to come back this time, and that we should have the joy of being together again soon."

Everyone in the room says, "Amen!"

I make eye contact with Wendy. I feel the knot that has been in my gut for a long time, finally relax and let go. Something important has just happened. We can both feel it.

After everyone else leaves, sometime around 3:00 AM, Wendy and I are exhausted, but we decide to stay to help Shoshana and Joe clean up. It's a lot to do and they're in their 70s, and for the first time, I've noticed that Joe is limping. At first they refuse our offer. Joe says that we're their honored guests. I say that we would like the honor of being able to stay with the hosts and to have some extra time together. They relent, so we stay and help.

There are two ways to drive back to the Moshav. We decide to avoid the northern route, Route 443, the winding two-lane road that twists its way through the West Bank. Instead we opt for southern route, Route 1, the four-lane freeway that connects Jerusalem to Tel Aviv. It's longer but safer. For most of the way back, we're the only car on the freeway. I'm straining my eyes in the darkness to make sure we don't veer off the road. There's something, a thought that I'm trying to put together, to put into words.

"Efraim's blessing . . ." I say. Wendy looks at me.

"When he gave me that blessing tonight, something happened. All those years, over 30 years, since I broke away from Shlomo and left the House . . . On one level, I've been doing good things, worthwhile things, right? I've had a good life, and I'm blessed with fulfilling work, a beautiful place to live, wonderful children, and good friends. And I married you!" I smile at her, and she smiles back. "But on another level, I haven't really been able to find my place again, to connect with what I'm here in this world to do, you know? But tonight I feel like Efraim's blessing just cleared that up for me. Does that sound weird?"

Wendy doesn't say anything. I see a pair of distant headlights, pinpoints in the dark, moving toward us.

"It's not about doing anything different. It's not like being on a journey to *get* somewhere. There's no *there* to get to!"

As the headlights come close, they turn into a large, noisy truck hauling a long trailer. The wind in its wake rocks us as it roars past. Then the night is once more dark and quiet.

"It's like I've been traveling a long time back and forth between worlds, between paradoxes and contradictions—the 5,000 year old world and the five billion year old one, the Land of Stuff and the Land of Soul, Shlomo the holy teacher and Shlomo the complex human being, Aryae the "Orthodox rabbi" and Aryae the Silicon Valley businessman.

"Efraim's blessing is, to *get it* that I already am *where* and *who* I'm supposed to be—and I have been the whole time!" I laugh. "It's amazing—it's so simple. And it's true for all of us, right? Both sides of these things—the light and darkness, the paradoxes—don't they all come from the same Source? They're the holy sparks, the gifts we've been sent. Our job in this lifetime is to gather them up and hold them, *all* of them, together. Our job is creating space in this world for wholeness. The blessing is, wher*ever* we're going, what*ever* we're doing, to bring the sparks, and the wholeness, with us!"

I look over at Wendy. "That doesn't sound weird," she says.

The next day at the Moshav, we sleep in as late as we can. When we finally get up, sometime in the late morning, the house is empty. Bernice has left us some coffee, juice and cold cereal for breakfast in the kitchen.

As I'm drinking my coffee and eating my cereal, I play one of the cassette tapes I recorded last night. I want to review what people said and think about how it fits together.

"Wendy!" I say. "I don't remember this."

"What?" she says.

"It's Efraim. He's talking about the last time he ever spoke to Shlomo. Do you remember that?"

"I don't think so," she says. "Let me hear."

It's a short segment, less than a minute. I play it for her. Efraim's voice is quiet. At one point he chokes up, and he has to stop and take a breath. Neither one of us says anything. Then I play it again.

35
The Rav

The West Bank, Israel – Sunday Night, December 2003

It's after 11:00 PM as we drive through the West Bank. We're the only car on Route 443. We're driving this way to save time. Wendy and I are still feeling sleep deprived from last night at Joe and Shoshana's.

The cell phone rings. It's Efraim. He wants to know where we are.

Less than an hour before, the Rabbinit called Efraim to tell him that the Rav had finally found an opening in his schedule, and that we should come right over. Now he tells me that he told her that we'd try to get there at 10:30!

"Efraim!" I say, "You called us at 10:20, while we were getting into bed! You told the Rabbanit we'd be there at 10:30?"

He sounds sheepish. He asks me to call him when we're close, so that he and Leah can walk down and meet us in the parking lot.

We pick them up and drive into Mea Shearim. Wendy and I sit in the front with Efraim and Leah in the back. The narrow streets are filled with cars, and men in long black coats rushing in all directions.

We walk up to the second floor of the Rav's building. We kiss the *mezuzah,* open the door and walk into the brightly lit reception room. I'm surprised to see so many people, including lots of young people, energetically bustling around. Although it's 11:30 at night, it feels like it's the middle of the day. Efraim knows some of the young people, the Rav's grandchildren. He speaks quietly with them, and they exchange smiles.

Wendy sees something that caught my attention last night. There is a museum style wooden stand. On top of it sits a remarkable, brightly colored ceramic sculpture of an island with a forest, a mountain in the middle, a tower near the shore, birds and animals, a stream and fountains, and people wandering in the forest.

"Look at this!" she says. "Can you see what it is?"

"What?" I say.

"It's the story of 'The Seven Beggars!'"

I look again. The island, the forest, the mountain, the fountain, the tower . . . Wendy's right. It all fits together and it all makes sense. "The Seven Beggars" is probably Reb Nachman's best known and best loved story. On one level it's a kind of magical fairy tale, but very few people understand its secret depths. The Breslover Hasidim believe that it contains the deepest kabbalistic mysteries of the fate of the world and the way we can bring about its redemption.

Wendy and I love the story so much that, when we were married last year, we placed it at the center of our wedding. A Jewish wedding has seven blessings for the bride and groom. After each blessing, we had one of our guests play one of the Seven Beggars, telling that beggar's story. Victor and Nadya flew in from Colorado to conduct the wedding. Reuven was one of the Beggars. Lynn was another. Reb Zalman, who was unable to travel to join us in person, kept his promise to be with us by recording a special rendition of one of the seven blessings. We played it at the wedding.

The Rabbanit walks into the reception room, smiling and joyful, looking very much like she did the night before. She gives Leah a hug. Leah introduces her to Wendy. The Rabbanit tells Wendy in Hebrew that she is so glad to see her. Leah translates. Wendy thanks the Rabbanit for inviting her.

The Rabbanit ushers us into a beautiful room, long and narrow, something like a formal dining room. In the center of the room is a long table of polished dark wood. At the far end of the table, bent over a large book and intently absorbed in it, sits the Rav. He is small and thin, with a long white beard and bright, sparkling eyes. The Rabbanit sits down at the opposite end of the long table, and invites Leah and Wendy to join her.

Efraim and I walk over to the other end, where the Rav is sitting. I wonder what he's reading so intently. Maybe it's the Zohar. Maybe he'll talk to us about deep kabbalistic mysteries. The Rav looks up at us with a big smile. He invites us to sit close to him, so we can see the book. He looks so delighted.

When I look at the book, I see large photographs of the earth as seen from space. The Rav is utterly captivated by these images. He reads one of the captions in English, asking Efraim for help with a word or two. He looks at me and explains, in broken English, that he is just learning English and needs help from people like Efraim. It is a wonderful language, he says, and he is very excited about learning it.

I glance at the women at the other end of the table, which seems very long. They are watching us. I wave a little wave at Wendy, who smiles. Leah is softly translating the Rav's words into Hebrew for the Rabbanit.

Suddenly, the Rav changes moods. He closes the book and starts speaking to us in a combination of Hebrew and English, because he wants to take advantage of this opportunity, he explains, nodding at Efraim, for a little English lesson. He tells us a story about a man who came to see him earlier today. This man came from your part of the world, he says laughing, gesturing at me. A couple of years ago he started a new company, based on a new technology. The combined assets of the company were worth over half a billion dollars. The man had a business partner, an old friend whom he trusted totally. The man wanted to make an extended trip to Israel as a kind of spiritual pilgrimage. So he signed some documents giving his partner and friend authority to run the company. While he was gone, his friend sold the company, keeping all the proceeds, and left the man with nothing.

At the other end of the table, the women lean toward each other as Leah translates, into Hebrew for the Rabbanit, and English for Wendy.

So after all these things happened, the man came to the Rav for help. As he's telling us this, the Rav suddenly laughs. I'm startled. "Why does he come to me?" the Rav says, lifting up his hands in a gesture of helplessness in the face of God's will. "What he wants is to get his money back! Does he think that I'll help him get rich again? What I deal with is a different kind of wealth!"

The Rabbanit looks straight at her husband and nods. Efraim smiles and closes his eyes. It takes me a few seconds to realize that the Rav isn't laughing at the suffering of this man; he's laughing at the predicament of the human condition. We all have props that make us feel secure—health, wealth, honor, prosperous economic times. But life can strip these away, any of them, in an instant. What do we do then? The six of us sit there silently, contemplating the lesson.

Efraim introduces me to the Rav, says that I'll play some songs for the him, and hands me the guitar. As Wendy and I had anticipated, I totally freeze, and my mind goes blank. So we have a plan. I look down the long table at her, and she silently mouths the first few words of a song. Then I strum the guitar and sing it. The words are from the Psalms; the melody is mine, composed at the House 33 years ago.

To my surprise, the Rav and the Rabbanit are both delighted, clapping their hands and laughing. The Rav asks if I can sing him more songs. I sing more of my songs, most of them from the Psalms, according to the play list that Wendy and I had put together. Each time the Rav and Rabbanit respond in a similar way. Their joy fills the room, and fills all of us. It feels like—inside the serious looking bodies huddled at both ends of this very serious looking table—we're all really children playing together.

Efraim plays a couple of songs also, his own compositions. Then he tells the Rav that he'd like to tell us all a story, which he says the Rav may recognize. I'm fascinated with the role reversal, of the student telling a story to the teacher.

So here's the story:

> Once there was a kingdom where the people could approach the king whenever they wanted, and ask the king for whatever they needed, and the king would give it to them. This went on for many years, but after a while, the king's family and his advisors grew concerned that if he kept this up, he could give away the whole kingdom. So they persuaded the king to make a new law. From now on, anyone in the kingdom could approach the king just once in his lifetime.
>
> One day a man came to see the king, and the king said, "What can I do for you?"
>
> The man said, "I would like the pleasure of singing for the king." So he pulled out his lute, plucked the strings, and sang the most beautiful song the king had ever heard.
>
> The king was delighted and said, "Now you must tell me what you would like; you can have anything in the kingdom."
>
> And the man said, "I would like the pleasure of playing for the king again tomorrow."
>
> The king said okay, and the man came again the next day, and played and sang a song that was even more beautiful. The king was very happy and said, "Since you can have anything in the kingdom, you must now tell me what you *really* want!" The man said what he wanted more than anything was to come again the next day.
>
> So he came again. This kept happening each day until finally the king said, "This has been wonderful, but I'm sorry to put you to so much trouble, going back and forth every

day. So I've had a special apartment built here in the palace, and I'd like you to accept my invitation to come here and live with me!"

The Rav laughs and slaps his hands on the table. The Rabbanit laughs and claps her hands. Efraim will tell me later that he heard this story 17 years ago from a Breslover Hasid, who had heard it from the Rav's son, who had heard it from the Rav. Efraim is now giving the Rav and Rabbanit the gift of the Rav's own story, many years later.

The Rabbanit looks at her watch and then at the clock on the wall. She says something softly to her husband. It's about the young couple about to get married who are waiting outside. They were supposed to see them at 11:30; it's now 12:30. The Rav nods and waives his hand, as if to waive away this intrusion. Then he asks Efraim if maybe we could do one last song. The Rabbanit says that she would like me to sing it. Efraim suggests "I'm Really Not Here."

I hold the guitar and tell the Rav a story. It's about Efraim's cousin Gavriel and his autistic niece Amy. After our road trip together from California to New Jersey in 1969, Gavriel visited Amy. This little girl spent all her time in her room, completely isolated from other people. She was in touch with the angels that no one could see but her. He sat in her room with her and wrote her a song. Amy learned the song and sang it to herself every day for the rest of her childhood. Gavriel taught it to me and it became a favorite at the House of Love and Prayer. Gavriel and his wife Sari and all their children later became Chabad Hasidim. As I'm telling the story, the Rav listens closely. Every once and a while he holds up his hand to ask me to pause, and translates for the Rabbanit. Before starting the song, I tell the Rav the words in English, and he translates. Then I sing:

> I'm really not here;
> I'm just a dream;
> The only one here is the King.
> I'm really not here;
> I'm just a dream;
> The only one here is the Queen.
>
> All you kings and queens,
> Find your dreams;
> All you kings and queens
> Find your dreams.

371

After I'm done, I see that both the Rav and Rabbanit have tears in their eyes. I can feel the tears in mine too. We all sit there in silence. It's a moment of pure magic, beyond words.

The Rav takes a pad and a pen, and starts writing down the words to the song. I say that he doesn't have to do that, that I can write them for him. He ignores me and keeps writing, looking like he's thoroughly enjoying it. Then he looks up at me and laughs. He says that I'm like the man in the story, and that soon I'll have to move in here with him and his family!

I look over at Efraim and in a flash I can see how everything fits together: this visit to the Rav, the guitar, the songs, the story. He's set this whole thing up! This is his gift to me.

It's time for us to go, so we all stand up. If this had been 1968 at the House of Love and Prayer in San Francisco, we would all be hugging each other, with our heads bowed so they're touching, and our arms around each others' backs, feeling each other breathe. Since it's 2003 in Mea Shearim in Jerusalem, we just stand there, smiling. But the level of closeness is the same.

When we get back to the car, Efraim says, "Let's go to the Wall!"

"What?" I say. "It's one in the morning!"

"That's okay," he says. "People go there all night long." The idea's just crazy enough that it appeals to all of us, so we agree. We have to do something with the amazing energy we received from the Rav and Rabbanit, so why not take it to the Wall?

Wendy and I sit in front and Efraim and Leah in back. The streets are deserted. It's a little scary to me to be driving through the Old City like this. I'm grateful that Efraim has been here so many times that he knows every cobblestone. Wendy giggles. "It's like we're on a double date!" she whispers.

We park in the lot above the Wall and walk down the stone steps, Efraim and I on the men's side, Leah and Wendy on the women's. The stone courtyard in front of the Wall looks vast and empty, stretched out under a clear night sky that is also empty with no moon, but carpeted with glistening stars. There are a few men in long black coats standing near the Wall, rocking back and forth, praying. Efraim walks up to the Wall, holds up his hands to touch it, and leans forward to press his head against it. I just stand there and look up at the Wall, at the sky, at the world, in total amazement. My cup is overflowing.

After we drop off Efraim and Leah at around three in the morning and start driving down the hill, I glance at the gas gauge.

"Oh my God!" I say.

"What?" Wendy says.

"We're getting close to empty."

We drive to the gas station at the corner of the main road near Ramot Polin. It's closed. There's no traffic. Everything is quiet. In Israel it's rare to find anything open at 3:00 AM. The only people awake at this hour are mystics like Efraim who are meditating in the forest or hunched over a lonely table somewhere studying the Zohar, and soldiers at checkpoints along the borders.

"What do we do?" says Wendy.

I don't know if we have enough gas to get back to the Moshav. Route 1, the freeway, is safer at night, but it's longer and there are no gas stations. Route 443 through the West Bank is shorter and has gas stations, but we don't know if any are open. And if we get stuck there alone at night without gas, we don't know what will happen.

I wonder about the Palestinians who live in the West Bank hills just ahead of us. Are any of them awake at this hour? What is it like for them to look down at night, to see the lights of my car on the Israeli road that winds through land where their homes had once stood?

We decide on Route 443. Wendy is terrified. I try to pretend I'm not. We get to a check-point with a roadblock, floodlights, a guardhouse and Israeli soldiers. I stop the car about 100 feet from the guardhouse and get out. "Maybe they can tell us if there's an open gas station," I say. I don't know how to approach them without looking like a possible terrorist.

A young soldier approaches slowly, with his automatic weapon pointed at me. I hold my hands in the air. I tell him in Hebrew that we're Americans, that our car is low on gas, and we're looking for a gas station.

Suddenly two guys rush toward me from the right. The soldier points his weapon at them. Then he recognizes them, smiles and lowers the weapon. They are two young men dressed like *yeshiva* students, in long black coats and black hats. They are both talking at once, very excited.

One tells me in halting English that he knows where there's an all night gas station just a few kilometers up the road. If we give him a ride, he'll show us.

I ask him why he's going this way in the middle of the night. He's here visiting his brother, he says, pointing to the other young man. Now he's going home.

I look at the soldier. "Is there really a gas station a few kilometers away?" I ask him.

"Yes, yes," he nods impatiently. He says I need to get back in the car and keep going. I look at the two young men, and at Wendy.

"Okay," I say to the one who wants a ride, "let's go." The two brothers say goodbye and the young man gets in the back of the car. The soldier waves us through.

The road is empty and dark as it winds through the rolling hills. The only lights anywhere are our headlight beams and the stars. In the rearview mirror I catch the image of the crescent moon rising behind us.

I ask the young man about himself. He teaches school at a religious settlement in the West Bank. This is a special school, for learning disabled kids from Orthodox families. People from all over the world send their kids here, he says. There are quite a few from Australia, and from South America.

The gas station is large with bright lights. We fill up. Wendy and I breathe a sigh of relief, and we continue on our way. I ask the young man where his exit is. His settlement is not far from the road, he says. We can just drop him off, and he can walk the rest of the way.

"How far is it from the highway?" I say.

He gives a little laugh. "Oh, about eight kilometers."

"Eight kilometers?" I say. "That's more than three miles; that's a long way! Isn't that dangerous to walk?"

"We can't let you walk here in the middle of the night!" Wendy says. "We'll drive you."

"No, thank you," he says. "That is not really very far." Why doesn't he want us to drive him? I wonder. Does he think it would be risky for us? Is he trying to protect us?

We insist that we want to drive him, so he finally agrees. We drive in silence for a while. Suddenly he says, "Stop! Stop please. We are here."

"I don't see an exit," I say, putting my foot on the brake. "Are you sure?"

"Yes, I am sure."

I pull over and stop. I still don't see an exit. I don't see anything. The young man steps out of the car, holding his leather overnight bag.

"*Todah rabbah,*" he says. "Thank you very much. *Shalom, shalom.*" Before Wendy and I know what's happening, he's slipped through the bushes along the side of the road, and is gone. We can only stare out into the darkness in amazement.

A few days later, at the Moshav, as I'm walking over to Lois's house to visit her, my cell phone rings. It's Efraim.

"I want to tell you something," he says.

"What?"

It's about the Rabbanit. She is a true *rebbe* in her own right, with hundreds of women in the classes she teaches. Earlier this week at a class with over two hundred women, the Rabbanit, without mentioning names, said there was a Breslover couple who had visited the Rav and herself. They had brought a guitar, and their friend from America and his wife. The friend sang songs for her and her husband, and brought them great joy.

I take a deep breath and take this in. Then something occurs to me. "If this was a class with hundreds of women, and the Rabbanit didn't mention any names, how did you find out?"

Efraim laughs. "We all know each other here. I'm the only Breslover Hasid with a guitar!"

36
Legacy

The Buddhists say that the purpose of a conscious life is to prepare for the moment of death. "Death" is not only the death of the body; it is also liberation from the wheel of *karma* and the suffering caused by our attachments and desires.

In our tradition the metaphor for liberation is the journey, starting with the Exodus from Egypt. The Passover *Haggada* says, "God didn't only liberate our ancestors; He also liberated us!" The holy Ba'al Shem Tov 250 years ago said that our task is to re-live this journey *everyday*. The 6th Lubavitcher Rebbe 54 years ago, when he sent Shlomo and Zalman out of New York, wanted them to teach young Jews to re-live this journey every *moment*. Shlomo said that when God taps us on the shoulder, we have to be ready to go *now*.

We Jews have so many stories and teachings about journeys and dying. Sitting at a long table with a group of Haredi families at the home of Dovid and his wife Tzipora, Wendy and I are listening to a rabbi in his 70s in a long black coat, speaking softly in Hebrew:

> Our Rabbis ask, "How much pleasure is awaiting us in the World to Come?"
>
> Think back over your day. What has given you the most pleasure? Was it the taste of some delicious food, the sight of a magnificent tree or clouds blowing across the sky? Was it the sound of a bird singing, or of beautiful music, or the sight of a smile on the face of another person? Put this pleasure in your cup.
>
> Now think back over your entire past year, of all the pleasures you have experienced, the pleasures of days and nights, the pleasures of the seasons, of winter and summer, of spring and fall, the pleasures of the weekdays and the pleasures of *Shabbos,* the pleasures of the holidays, of learning and praying, the pleasures of being with your wife or

husband, the pleasures of being with your parents and children. There are so many, with such abundance and variety, that this is almost impossible to imagine. Add these pleasures to your cup.

Whenever someone in the religious world finishes learning a section of the Torah, including the Mishnah and the Talmud, it is a cause for celebration and rejoicing. Religious people celebrate with a *siyum*, a special festive meal celebrating the completion.

Dovid and Tzipora's youngest child, their nine year old son Naftali, has just finished learning the sixth and final book of the Mishnah, which is called *Tohorot* (literally, Purities). It is considered the most difficult book in the Mishnah, and for a nine year old to master it is extraordinary indeed, so this *siyum* is an occasion of special joy. Dovid and Tzipora have honored Wendy and me by inviting us.

Their condo, not far from Efraim and Leah's, is filled with people, all from the ultra-Orthodox world except for Wendy and me. Several tables have been placed together and covered with tablecloths to create a single long table. Dovid is at one end, with Naftali sitting near him. Most of the men and boys are sitting on one side of the table, with most of the women and girls on the other. Some of the women and girls are standing, going back and forth to the kitchen and coming back with plates, glasses, utensils, platters of food, bottles of wine and seltzer and soda.

The old rabbi who's speaking, who lives down the hall, is head of a local *yeshiva*. He sits and moves with simple, quiet dignity, and everyone treats him with great respect.

When the time came for Naftali to speak and give over his teaching from *Tohorot*, the room became silent. He spoke quickly, without pausing or stumbling. On one level I didn't hear emotion in his voice. He was a kid reciting for the admiring adults. On another level, I could hear his passion for learning, as his words, sentences, ideas, connections, conclusions, came tumbling out with great energy. Women caught each other's eyes and smiled; men nodded thoughtfully; the old rabbi leaned forward and listened intently.

The old rabbi's teaching is also from *Tohorot*. He continues:

Now think back over your whole life, and imagine if you could remember every pleasure that you have ever experienced. Add these to your cup. Now think about the rest of your life in the future, for the remainder of the days that

HaShem has allotted you in this world, and of all the pleasures you are yet to discover. Add these to your cup.

As he talks, he breaks out into a smile, becomes more and more animated, and rocks back and forth. Everyone in the room is mesmerized. Every once in a while I translate for Wendy, leaning over to whisper a quick summary into her ear.

> Now think about every person alive in this world today. Imagine if you could *feel* all the pleasures in each of their lives. Billions and billions of pleasures. Gather these all together and add them to your cup.

> Now think about every single person who has ever been alive since *HaShem* created Adam and Eve, and of all of our ancestors from the time of our father Abraham until today. Imagine all the pleasures in *their* lives and add these to your cup. Now think about our children, and their children's children, and every child who will be born into the world until Messiah comes at the end of time. Imagine all the pleasures in *their* lives. Add these to your cup.

> Can you imagine if we could put this cup to our lips, and drink and taste all these pleasures? What would that be like? *Can you imagine?*

> Our Rabbis say that if we could do this, it would be only $1/60^{th}$ part of $1/60^{th}$ part of the pleasure that is awaiting us in the *courtyard*, not the palace mind you but the *courtyard*, of the World to Come!

The rabbi leans back in his chair and laughs. Someone starts a song and others join in. The singing is very spirited and goes on and on for a long time, followed eventually by the blessing after the meal. The guests are animated but the old rabbi suddenly looks tired and says he needs to go back to his apartment. Someone gets up to help him out of his chair.

As the old rabbi bids us *"Shalom"* and leaves, I notice that Naftali has been watching him intently. Clearly this is a most special and important moment, not only for this boy and his family, but also for the life of the community. This is his legacy, and theirs. This is how the Torah, and with it the soul of the Jewish people and the redemption of the world, gets passed on from one generation to the next.

People talk to each other and a few start getting up. Dovid bangs on the table to get their attention. "Before everyone gets up, there's

379

one more thing I want to say." People sit back down. Naftali, sitting next to him, is distracted, making faces at one of the older kids. Dovid puts his hand on Naftali's shoulder. "I want you to hear this too," he says to him gently.

"I just want to thank my friend Aryae from California and his wife Wendy for being here at this time of joy. Many years ago in San Francisco, Aryae was my first teacher. At a time when I didn't know what it was to be a Jew, and didn't have any vessels yet for Torah, it was Aryae who first opened the door for me.

"Naftali, I want you to know that, if I hadn't met this man 35 years ago, you wouldn't have studied *Tohorot*. Aryae, I want you to know that, if it hadn't been for you, none of us would be here together like this today."

Later, after everyone else has left, Dovid and I hold each other. We're both crying.

Friday

It was in the early spring of 1965 when I was a young college student and first stood at King David's Tomb. I was all alone, unprepared for what was about to happen. The intensity of the mystery into which I was plunged was a whirlwind that carried me all the way to Haight Street where, for a brief time, the finger of God was poking through the fabric of the universe. It carried me all the way to the college campus where I first met Rabbi Shlomo Carlebach.

Now, on a short, chilly day in December, on the eighth and last day of Hanukah, I'm back, 38 years later. I've returned, this time with my wife and my best friend.

I ask Efraim to stand at the entrance of King David's Tomb, where I take his picture. He obliges. Then he asks Wendy and me to stand in the same spot, and he takes ours.

We go inside. I feel myself shaking a little, remembering what it was like 38 years ago. Efraim and I go the men's side, and Wendy goes to the women's.

Inside King David's Tomb. Photo by Aryae Coopersmith.

King David's coffin is like I remember it, a massive presence in front of us, light in the midst of darkness, trimmed in gold and surrounded by gold, very close but just out of reach.

Then I start to realize that the room I'm standing in is a little different from the room in my memory. *Where are the crowns,* I think, *the three magnificent jeweled crowns that were on the coffin?* I don't see them anywhere. And the room in my memory is darker, more mysterious, with echoes that reverberated further.

But when I close my eyes, I know this is the same place. This is where it all began for me. Efraim walks over to the iron fence on the left side of the coffin and pulls out his little book of Reb Nachman's *Tikkun Klali.* His lips move silently as he recites King David's Psalms. I reach in my pocket and take out my copy, the one he's given me. But instead of opening it, I just close my eyes and rock back and forth, davening silently. Shlomo was a direct descendent of King David on his father's side. Maybe that's where he got the gift of music; maybe it was his legacy from King David. Maybe what happened when I was here 38 years ago was that King David sent me on a journey because he wanted me to meet his great-great grandson, so he could pass it on to my generation and to me.

When I open my eyes, I see that Efraim is finished davening and is standing in his spot, waiting patiently. When he sees that I'm done, he looks over at me and smiles. We leave the room and meet Wendy, who's waiting for us in the entrance hallway.

We get in the car and drive toward Har Menuhot (Mountain of Comforts), the cemetery in Jerusalem where Shlomo is buried, Wendy and I in the front seat and Efraim in the back. I didn't know if I could visit Shlomo's grave because I'm a *kohen*, and *kohenim* are not allowed to defile themselves by going to cemeteries. Efraim however has pointed out two loopholes. The first is that I'll be there to pay homage to a Torah scholar; the second is that there is a path that is far enough from the grave-sites so that I won't be violating the prohibition.

The Jerusalem traffic is in its normal frenzy, with everyone honking at each other. Efraim directs me. As we're driving on a busy four-lane street where traffic is moving fast, he suddenly says, "Here, here!" and points to a street to the left, just ahead of us, that winds up the hill. I scoot into the left lane and start making the turn. Suddenly, out of nowhere, there's a bus coming fast from the opposite direction, also turning, barreling right at us. It's one of those times where everything shifts to slow motion. The bus looks like a monster about to crush us. I have the incongruous thought — *Here we are, speeding to get to the graveyard!* I cut hard to the left and floor the accelerator. We miss the bus by inches.

The scene switches back to normal speed. *"Barukh HaShem* (Praise God) — we made it!" Wendy cries out. Leah uses this expression all the time, but this is the first time I've heard Wendy use it. Efraim laughs. Then we all laugh, like kids running away from a scene where we just broke all the rules, realizing we won't get caught. Wendy looks back at Efraim. It feels like something between them has shifted, like some of the reserve has melted. Life is not a given; it's a gift. Every second we're here, it's only through God's grace and God's will, a miracle and a blessing.

Wendy and Efraim and I walk up a main walkway at Har Menuhot. It climbs along a ridge, surrounded on both sides by thousands of grave-sites in neat rows. What is most unusual for this part of the world is that there are trees, evergreens, everywhere. The cold winter sunlight shines through the foliage in radiant translucent greens. Beyond the cemetery, surrounding it in all directions and enfolding it, are the hills of Jerusalem. I recognize, sitting on a distant hilltop, Mount Scopus, site of the original campus of the Hebrew University, opened in 1925, the same year that Shlomo was born.

Efraim stops near Shlomo's grave-site. He and Wendy walk over to it. As a *kohen* I can only stand and watch. The grave is like a large stone box, of the dimensions to hold a casket, that sits almost chest high on the ground. It is surrounded by trees, a couple of which are close. On one end, sitting on four tubular metal pillars, is a glass case, which I assume holds holy books. Efraim positions himself on that end, the one with the glass case. Wendy positions herself on the other. Across the middle, directly facing me, as if to connect Wendy and Efraim, is a stone slab on which are engraved the words:

*Rabbi Shlomo Carlebach ZTL**
Mamash A. Gevalt The Sweetest of the Sweet

Wendy touches the stones and bows her head. Efraim leans forward and rests his head on his forearm, which is on the vertical stone slab under the glass case. I look at the two of them there for a moment, then close my eyes.

I can hear one of Shlomo's melodies, then another, then another. I keep my eyes closed and sway back and forth, davening silently. The angels are singing Shlomo's songs. I'm singing with them. I can hear Efraim's voice again, speaking as I recorded him at the House of Love and Prayer Reunion a few nights ago. I can see us all at the table at Joe and Shoshana's, listening. And I can see the angels surrounding all of us, also listening to Efraim's words:

You know, anybody can say whatever they want. This is my own story, what I heard from Shlomo, 'cause it was the last time that he ever talked to me.

He said, "You know, when I was in *yeshiva,* I was the most *shomer eynaim* [guarding the eyes from looking at forbidden things; for men, this means not looking at women] of anybody in the *yeshiva.* I was guarding my eyes more than anybody."

He also told me, "Where did I get my melodies from?" He said, "My songs came from that; other *bokhorim* [young men] at the *yeshiva,* they could be up late at night, late Friday night, and then they would all go to sleep."

He said, "I couldn't sleep Friday night. I would be there, and after everybody would be sleeping, I would be sitting up with the *Gemorah* [Talmud]. It would be singing. The *Gemorah* started singing to me. I heard these melodies late, late, late at night. I would hear them in my head, in my heart."

So he said, "I was the most *shomer eynaim,* I was guarding my eyes more than anybody else. If I heard that somebody in the *yeshiva* was looking where he was not supposed to be looking for a *yeshiva bokher,* I wouldn't even talk to him."

---

* May the memory of a *tzaddik* be for a blessing.

He said, "But I heard the cry of a generation. I heard the cry of these young people." He looked at me—you know Shlomo—we have no idea . . . He looked at me with a look of, I don't know . . . "I just did what I felt like I had to do. Maybe I was right; maybe I was wrong."

He said to me [Efraim's voice choking], he said, "Don't forget to stick up for me in the next life."

RABBI SHLOMO CARLEBACH ZTL
MAMASH A GEVALT THE SWEETEST OF THE SWEET

Efraim at Reb Shlomo's gravesite. Photo by Aryae Coopersmith.

When they finally walk away from the grave site and return to the main walkway, I can see the tears in both Efraim's and Wendy's eyes. We just stand there in silence. The feelings are beyond what we can say to each other in words. The journey that King David started me on 38 years ago has brought me back here, full circle.

Wendy and I drive Efraim home, and go in with him to say goodbye to Leah. We spend this one last moment together, feeling the glow of each others' presence. It's been 33 years since Efraim and Leah and I last saw each other, and no one knows when the next time will be.

It's Friday afternoon now, and they both have to rush to get ready for *Shabbos*. One of their children, together with a half-dozen of their grandchildren, will be here soon. Wendy and I have to get back to the Moshav for our last *Shabbos* in Israel.

Lod International Airport, Israel – 5:30 AM, Sunday Morning, December 2003

Wendy and I are on the shuttle bus from the car rental drop-off point to the airport terminal. It's still dark out. The shuttle is full. Our flight isn't until 8:30, but security here is very tight and it takes a long time to get through. Our fellow passengers are a mixture of secular and religious people, all of us sitting in silence, as though not yet ready step into the day's cold cacophony of international travel, as though we all need to linger one last moment in the darkness of the Holy Land's warm embrace. A middle-aged secular man in jeans and a leather jacket glances at his watch and shuffles through his papers. A religious woman in a long dark coat and wig whispers something to her two young daughters.

The silence is broken by the jarring sound of a cell phone. It's mine. Startled, I pull it out of my pocket. It's Efraim.

"Where are you?" I say, scanning the faces on the bus to see who's looking at me.

"I'm at the *Kotel*," he says matter-of-factly. I close my eyes and picture what it was like when the four of us were there together at night.

"Ah, it must be beautiful," I say. I wait, but he doesn't say anything. I think about the way he spends his nights. Four hours meditating in the forest, followed by a hike to the Wall to *daven* with his fellow Breslover Hasidim as soon as the sun rises. I try to picture him standing there, waiting for them. "What did you call for?"

"I'm trying to remember that *niggun*, that melody that you sang."

"Which one?"

"The one that you sang when you came over with Judi."

The shuttle bus stops in front of the terminal. People get up, pull their luggage off the rack, and push their way out.

"Wait a second," I say, "we're just getting our stuff off of this bus." Wendy pulls her bag off of the rack and I grab mine. The driver helps Wendy get hers off the bus. With my cell phone in one hand and my large bag in the other, I smile at the driver signaling, "No thanks, I don't need help." Standing on the curb in front of the terminal, the silence is broken. Crowds of people are shoving and rushing in all directions, calling out to each other, trying to figure out where to go.

I find a spot to stand still for a moment. Wendy stands next to me. "Efraim," I say, "do you mean the Modzhitz *niggun* we used to sing at your house in Forrest Knolls to welcome *Shabbos?*"

"Rhizhin," he says, laughing.

"You don't remember it?"

"I'm not so sure," he says. "I want to remember it. Can we sing it a little bit?" I look at Wendy. She's standing next to her bag, looking a little cold, but patient. Rushing passengers are swirling all around us. I look up at the sky and see the first signs of light in the east.

"Okay," I say. I close my eyes and start to sing. It's hard to sing together on the cell phones, but somehow we do it. I can see us back then, 37 years ago, standing on his porch in Forrest Knolls, singing this melody as the Friday afternoon sun sank into the redwood forest. It seemed like the forest was singing with us. Surrounding us and the forest, I can hear the Hasidim of Eastern Europe from hundreds of years ago, and surrounding them I can hear the angels.

The melody is our legacy. *The facts reach to the mind,* Shlomo said, *the story reaches to the heart, but the melody reaches all the way to the soul.* As long as we can keep the melody close, as long as we can hear it and feel it and sing it, the journey continues.

Aryae Coopersmith and Wendy Berk at King David's Tomb.

Appendix:
Shlomo on Teaching Zohar

Even though I could not find an appropriate place for this anecdote within the text, I felt it was too interesting to lose. So I have included it here for those of you might be interested in Shlomo's attitude to teaching Zohar to the uninitiated.

Rabbi Gavriel Dror: So I brought Shlomo into my philosophy class at Santa Rosa Junior College. It was full, really packed with students, mostly 18 or 19 years old. I hadn't talked to him about what he was going to teach. And I said, "Shlomo, this is the book we're learning."

He looked at it, and his eyes nearly popped out of his head [laughs]. He said, "You're teaching the *Zohar HaKodesh* [Holy Zohar] *in public?*" [Traditionally Kabbalah was taught only privately, between student and teacher, and only when the teacher determined that the student, through years of preparation, was ready.]

So he turns around, puts his back to the class and says to me, "Gavriel, before I do this, I wanna tell you one thing. When I start to teach, *I want you to stop thinking.* Don't think about anything I say. Just let it go in. Maybe in five, 10, 15, 20 years, we'll become friends. Then it will be okay. Otherwise, there's nothing to teach you."

So I said, "Okay, no problem!"

So he started to teach. Afterward some of the students told me that they thought he was pulling their leg. He started out by teaching, for the first five minutes, how *God did not create this world.* He went through this and that; he went through the whole thing . . . until you finally felt something was happening to what he was saying, that you were really just listening and not thinking about it.

Then he took a deep breath and he said, "But there is a world God created. *This world, You created.*"

Then he said [whispers], *"Now let's go to the world God created."* Amazing.

389

Glossary

Bar-mitzvah – Heb., lit. "son of the commandment"; a boy of 13 who is now obligated to keep the *mitzvot*.

Beis HaMikdash –Heb., lit. "house of the holy"; the holy temple in Jerusalem.

Bentch – Yid., "benediction"; saying grace after a meal.

Bimah – Heb., a raised platform in the synagogue.

Daven/davenen – Yid., "pray," "prayer" or "praying"; a more colloquial way to speak of *tefillah* (prayer), and yet *davenen* is also more than merely formal prayer, or prayer as a formality; it is living the liturgical life in truth. The word itself is possibly derived from the Latin *divinum*, 'the divine,' as in doing divine work.

Eretz Yisrael – Heb., lit. "holy land"; Israel.

Eruv – Heb., lit. "mixture"; an enclosure around a house or a community which allows Jews to carry object on *Shabbat* without violating the law.

Farbrengen – Yid., "time spent together"; a session of Hasidic fellowship, at times presided over by a *mashpiyya* or, occasionally, a *rebbe,* during which Hasidim gather for the purpose of telling stories, singing, drinking, and learning the teachings of the rebbes.

Frum – Yid., "devout"; wholly committed to the Orthodox life.

Gan Eden – Heb., "garden of delight"; the Garden of Eden, Paradise.

Gemorah – Ara., "learned by tradition"; the commentary and discussion around the Mishnah; the Talmud.

Gevalt! – Yid., an expression of shock or amazement.

Halakhah /halakhot – Heb., lit. "way to walk" or "the process"; Jewish law.

Ha'motzi – Heb., the blessing over the bread.

Hanukiah/hanukiot – Heb., "candelabra," "candelabras"; a Hanukah menorah.

Haredi – Heb., lit. "one who trembles"; ultra-Orthodox.

HaShem – Heb., lit. "the name"; substitute for the unutterable divine name, *Y-H-V-H;* God.

Hasid – Heb., "one who is pious"; a member of the Hasidic movement; a person who has a Hasidic *rebbe.*

Hasidim – Heb., "pious ones"; followers of the religious movement founded by the Ba'al Shem Tov in the 17th century.

Hasidut – Heb., "piety"; Hasidism, the teachings of the Hasidim.

Hasidishe – Yid., Hasidic.

Havdalah – Heb., lit. "separation"; the ceremony we use to transition between the holy space of *Shabbos* and the ordinary space of the rest of our lives.

Hevra – Heb., fellowship.

Humash – Heb., fifth; a book-bound edition of the Torah, as opposed to a scroll.

Huppah – Heb., wedding canopy.

Kappote – Yid./Latin, a long-frock coat worn by Hasidim, or a long-sleeved gown or kaftan fastened by a sash (*gartel*) worn by Hasidim on *Shabbat* and festivals.

Kashrut – Heb., fit-ness; the laws that define what is ritually fit and prepared, as opposed to *treif* (unfit).

Kiddush – Heb., sanctification; the prayer of sanctification recited over wine on the *Shabbat* and festivals.

Kippah – Heb., a skull-cap or yarmulke.

Kohen – Heb., priest; of the priestly caste of Judaism.

Kotel – Heb., the western wall of the holy Temple in Jerusalem.

Lashon ha'ra – Heb., lit. "language of evil"; a body of Jewish law which prohibits injuring people or destroying their reputations by making derogatory statements about them.

Mammash – Yid., "really so"; the feeling that something is immediately and palpably evident.

Mehitza – Heb., partition or division; a partition used to separate men and women in a synagogue.

Mikveh – Heb., gathering of water; ritual immersion pool for purification; ritual bath.

Minhah – Heb., gift; the afternoon prayer service.

Minyan – Heb., lit. "number"; quorum of 10; the minimum number of 10 Jews required for communal prayer.

mitzvah/mitzvot – Heb., divine commandment/s; commandment or God-connection in the Jewish tradition, popularly equated with a good deed.

Nebbukh – Yid., alas!; poor, pitiful; an expression of sympathy or alarm.

Niggun/niggunim – Heb., melody; a Hasidic melody, often wordless, which Abraham Joshua Heschel once described as "a tune in search of its own unattainable end."

Oy vey! – Yid., lit. "oh woe!"; an exclamation of sympathy, dismay, or exasperation.

Payos – Heb., side locks; the hair in front of the ears extending to beneath the cheekbone, on a level with the nose; side locks worn in various ways by some in the Orthodox Jewish community, especially Hasidim, respecting the biblical injunction not to round the *pe'at* (sides, edges) of your head (Lev. 19:27).

Rabbanit – Heb., title used in the traditional Jewish world for the wife of a rabbi.

Rav – Heb., rabbi, lit. "master"; a city's chief rabbi and authority on legal matters; or sometimes used in the Orthodox community to refer to their own rabbi.

Reb – Yid., a title of respect and friendly admiration.

Rebbe – Yid., rabbi; the spiritual leader of a Hasidic community.

Shabbos/Shabbat – Heb., rest, cessation; the seventh and holiest day of the week, the day on which God rested from the work of creation.

Seder – Heb., lit. "order"; the ritual meal held on *Pesah* (Passover).

Sefer – Heb., book; a Hebrew text.

Shaliah tzibur – Heb., the representative or emissary of the community before God, leading the davening.

Shekhinah – Heb., dwelling, presence; the divine in-dwelling, the divine feminine; the Presence of God in creation.

Shema – Heb., "hear"; the statement that says, "Hear O Yisrael, Y-H-V-H is our God, Y-H-V-H is One."

Shomer – Heb., "guardian"; according to Jewish law, a legal guardian.

Shomer eynaim – Heb., "guarding the eyes"; guarding one's eyes from looking at forbidden things; for men, this means not looking at women.

shtender – Yid., a large lectern or prayer stand upon which a prayer book may be set.

Shul – Yid., house of worship, synagogue.

Siddur – Heb., "order"; a Jewish prayer book.

Strimel – Yid., festive fur hat worn on *Shabbat* by most rebbes and some Hasidim.

Smikhah – Heb., ordination; a rabbinic ordination.

Sukkah – Heb., booth; a temporary hut constructed for the holiday of Sukkot.

Tallis, tallisim – Heb., a Jewish prayer shawl.

Tefillin – Heb., small leather boxes attached to the head and arm for prayer containing scrolls with Exod. 13:1–10, 13:11–16, Deut. 6:4–9, 11:13–21.

Tzaddik – Heb., righteous person; a term for a saintly, righteous person, a charismatic leader, and particularly for a Hasidic leader or teacher, a *rebbe*.

Tzitzit – Heb., fringes; the ritual threads hanging from the *tallis* to signify the 613 *mitzvot* and to remind one to observe them.

Yeshiva – Heb., an advanced academy for studying Torah, especially for the training of rabbis.

Yeshiva bokher – Heb., a *yeshiva* student.

About the Author

Aryae Coopersmith was co-founder of Rabbi Shlomo Carlebach's House of Love and Prayer in San Francisco in 1968. The "House" became a milestone in the history of 20th century American Judaism, and a well known part of the legend of 1960s San Francisco.

Together with his wife Wendy Berk, Aryae teaches and leads Torah Circles, an approach to studying sacred texts where people at all stages in their spiritual journeys can learn from each other and build sacred community. In 2010 he was recognized for his lifetime contribution to Jewish spiritual life by Rabbi Zalman Shalomi Schachter, founder of the Jewish Renewal movement, who gave him a special ordination as a Spiritual Teacher.*

In his professional life Aryae is Founder and CEO of the HR Forums, a community of human resource leaders with a home base in Silicon Valley, with the mission of growing the capability of their profession to advance the success and well being of all stakeholders. Aryae founded the HR Forums in 1992 together with Tom Peters, co-author of *In Search of Excellence*. During the "dot.com" era in the 1990s, Aryae was an on-line columnist for the San Jose Mercury News with his column, "The Future of Work."

Aryae has a B.A. in English Literature and Creative Writing from California State University, San Francisco, and an M.A. in Humanistic Psychology from California State University, Sonoma.

Aryae and Wendy live near the coastal town of Half Moon Bay, south of San Francisco, where he is a leader of CoastWriters, a writers' community that supports authors in getting their work out to the public.

---

* *Moreinu Ha'gabai L'tzarkhei Tzibour shel Emunah.*

7902557R0

Made in the USA
Charleston, SC
20 April 2011